State Papers and Correspondence
bearing upon the purchase of the
Territory of Louisiana

© Ross & Perry, Inc. 2001 All rights reserved.

No claim to U.S. government work contained throughout this book.

Protected under the Berne Convention. Published 2001

Printed in The United States of America
Ross & Perry, Inc. Publishers
717 Second St., N.E., Suite 200
Washington, D.C. 20002
Telephone (202) 675-8300
Facsimile (202) 675-8400
info@RossPerry.com

SAN 253-8555

Government Reprints Press Edition 2001

Government Reprints Press is an Imprint of Ross & Perry, Inc.

Library of Congress Control Number: 2001095042
http://www.GPOreprints.com

ISBN 1-931641-70-6

∞ The paper used in this publication meets the requirements for permanence established by the American National Standard for Information Sciences "Permanence of Paper for Printed Library Materials" (ANSI Z39.48-1984).

All rights reserved. No copyrighted part of this publication may be reproduced, stored in a retrieval system, or transmitted, in any form or by any means, electronic, photocopying, recording, or otherwise, without the prior written permission of the publisher.

State Papers and Correspondence bearing upon the Purchase of the Territory of Louisiana

HOUSE CONCURRENT RESOLUTION.

By Mr. GAINES.

Resolved by the House of Representatives (the Senate concurring), That there be published and bound 6,000 copies of the State papers and all correspondence bearing upon the purchase of the territory of Louisiana by the United States, including the treaty of purchase, 4,000 for the use of the House of Representatives and 2,000 for the use of the Senate.

Passed the House May 10, 1902.
Concurred in by the Senate May 13, 1902.

STATE PAPERS AND CORRESPONDENCE BEARING UPON THE PURCHASE OF THE TERRITORY OF LOUISIANA.

Mr. King to the Secretary of State.

LONDON, *March 29, 1801.*

DEAR SIR: In confirmation of the rumors of the day, Carnot's answer to Bailleul, published during the exile of the former, states the project which has been discussed in the Directory, to obtain from Spain a cession of Louisiana and the Floridas. A reference to that performance, copies of which I at the time sent to the Department of State, will show the manner in which it was expected to obtain the consent of Spain, as well as afford a clue to the views of France in seeking this establishment. What was then meditated, has, in all probability, since been executed. The cession of Tuscany to the Infant, Duke of Parma, by the treaty between France and Austria, forms a more compact and valuable compensation to this branch of the House of Spain than was formerly thought of, and adds very great credit to the opinion which, at this time, prevails both at Paris and London, that Spain has in return actually ceded Louisiana and the Floridas to France. There is reason to know that it is the opinion of certain influential persons in France, that nature has marked a line of separation between the people of the United States living upon the two sides of the range of mountains which divides their territory. Without discussing the considerations which are suggested in support of this opinion, or the false consequences, as I wish to believe them, deduced from it, I am apprehensive that this cession is intended to have, and may actually produce, effects injurious to the Union and consequent happiness of the people of the United States. Louisiana and the Floridas may be given to the French emigrants, as England once thought of giving them to the American tories; or, they may constitute the reward of some of the armies which can be spared at the end of the war.

I learn that General Collot, who was a few years ago in America, and a traveler in the western country, and who, for some time, has been in disgrace and confinement in France, has been lately set at liberty; and that he, with a considerable number of disaffected and exiled Englishmen, Scotchmen, and Irishmen, is soon to proceed from France to the United States. Whether their voyage has any relation to the cession of Louisiana is a matter of mere conjecture; but having heard of it in connection with that project I think proper to mention it to you.

What effect a plain and judicious representation upon this subject, made to the French Government by a minister of talents and entitled to confidence, would be likely to have, is quite beyond any means of judging which I possess; but on this account, as well as others of importance, it is a subject of regret that we have not such a character at Paris at this time.

With perfect respect and esteem, I have the honor to be, dear sir, your obedient and faithful servant,

RUFUS KING.

[Extract.]

Mr. King to the Secretary of State.

LONDON, *June 1, 1801.*

On this occasion, among other topics of conversation, His Lordship (Hawkesbury) introduced the subject of Louisiana. He had, from different quarters, received information of its cession to France, and very unreservedly expressed the reluctance with which they should be led to acquiesce in a measure that might be followed by the most important consequences. The acquisition might enable France to extend her influence and perhaps her dominion up the Mississippi; and through the Lakes even to Canada. This would be realizing the plan, to prevent the accomplishment of which, the seven years' war took place; besides, the vicinity of the Floridas to the West Indies, and the facility with which the trade of the latter might be interrupted, and the islands even invaded should the transfer be made, were strong reason why England must be unwilling that the territory should pass under the dominion of France. As I could not mistake his Lordship's object in speaking to me on the subject, I had no difficulty or reserve in expressing my private sentiments respecting it; taking for my text the observation of Montesquieu, "That it is happy for trading Powers that God has permitted Turks and Spaniards to be in the world, since of all nations they are the most proper to possess a great empire with insignificance." The purport of what I said was, that we are contented that the Floridas remain in the hands of Spain, but should not be willing to see them transferred except to ourselves.

With perfect respect and esteem, I have the honor to be, sir, your obedient and faithful servant,

RUFUS KING.

[Extract.]

Mr. Madison, Secretary of State, to Charles Pinckney.

DEPARTMENT OF STATE,
Washington, June 9, 1801.

On different occasions, since the commencement of the French Revolution, opinions and reports have prevailed that some part of the Spanish possessions, including New Orleans and the mouth of the Mississippi, had been or was to be transferred to France. Of late, information has been received through several channels, making it probable that some arrangement for that purpose has been concerted. Neither the extent of the cession, however, nor the consideration on which it is made, is yet reduced to certainty and precision. The whole subject will deserve and engage your early and vigilant inquiries, and may require a very delicate and circumspect management. What the motives of Spain in this transaction may be, is not so obvious. The policy of France in it, so far, at least, as relates to the United States, can not be mistaken. While she remained on the footing of confidence and affection with the United States, which originated during our Revolution and was strengthened during the early stages of her own, it may be presumed that she adhered to the policy which, in the treaty of 1778, renounced the acquisition of continental territory in North America, and was more disposed to shun the collisions threatened by possessions in that quarter, coterminous with ours, than to pursue objects to which the commanding position at the mouth of the Mississippi might be made subservient. Circumstances are not now the same. Although the two countries are again brought together by stipulations of amity and commerce, the confidence and cordiality which formerly subsisted have had a deep wound from the occurrences of late years.

Jealousies probably still remain, that the Atlantic States have a partiality for Great Britain, which may, in future, throw their weight into the scale of that rival. It is more than possible, also, that, under the influence of those jealousies, and of the alarms which have at times prevailed, of a projected operation for wresting the mouth of the Mississippi into the hands of Great Britain, she may have concluded a preoccupancy of it by herself to be a necessary safeguard against an event from which that nation would derive the double advantage of strengthening her hold on the United States, and of adding to her commerce a monopoly of the immense and fertile region communicating with the sea through a single outlet. This view of the subject, which suggests the difficulty which may be found in diverting France from the object, points, at the same time, to the means that may most tend to induce a voluntary relinquishment of it. She must infer, from our conduct and our communications, that the Atlantic States are not disposed to enter, nor are in danger of being drawn, into partialities toward Great Britain unjust or injurious to France; that our political and commercial interests afford a sufficient guaranty against such a state of things; that without the cooperation of the United States, Great Britain is not likely to acquire any part of the Spanish possessions on the Mississippi; and that the United States never have favored nor, so long as they are guided by the clearest policy, ever can favor, such a project. She must be led to see again, and with a desire to shun, the danger of collisions between the two Republics from the contact of their territories; and from the conflicts in their regulations of a commerce involving the peculiarities which distinguish that of the Mississippi. Such are the general observations which the President has thought it proper should be communicated to you, that, knowing the light in which the subject is viewed by him, you may be less in danger of presenting it in any other. It is not expected that you will have occasion to make any positive use of them in relation to the councils of the French Republic, the Minister to which will be charged with that task. In relation to the Spanish Government, although the chief difficulty is not supposed to lie there, the President wishes you to cultivate a favorable disposition by every proper demonstration of the preference given by the United States to the neighborhood of that of every other nation. This may be the more important, as it is not improbable that her councils also may have been affected by rumors of proceedings in this country, connected with schemes of Great Britain for getting possession of New Orleans.

[Extract.]

James Madison, Secretary of State, to Robert R. Livingston, Minister to France.

DEPARTMENT OF STATE, *September 28, 1801.*

You have been already informed of the intention of the President that your departure from France should be hastened, and that you would be furnished with a passage in the Boston frigate, which, after landing you in Bordeaux, is to proceed to the Mediterranean.

From different sources information has been received that, by some transaction concluded or contemplated between France and Spain, the mouth of the Mississippi, with certain portions of adjacent territory, is to pass from the hands of the latter to the former nation. Such a change of our neighbors in that quarter is of too momentous concern not to have engaged the most serious attention of the Executive. It was accordingly made one of the subjects of instruction to Mr. Charles Pinckney, our Minister Plenipotentiary to the Court of Spain. You will find an extract of the passage hereto annexed,

No. 1. A paragraph connected with the same subject, in a letter to Mr. King, is also extracted and annexed, No. 2. In these extracts you will see the ideas entertained by the Executive, and the general considerations which, it is presumed, will have most tendency to is d-suade the parties from adhering to their object. As soon as you shall have prepared the way by the necessary inquiries at Paris, it will be proper for you to break the subject to the French Government, and to make the use of these considerations most likely to give them their full weight. You will probably find it advantageous to press, in a particular manner, the anxiety of the United States to maintain harmony and confidence with the French Republic, the danger to which these will be exposed by collisions, more or less inseparable from a neighborhood under such circumstances, and the security which France ought to feel that it can not be the interest of this country to favor any voluntary or compulsive transfer of the possessions in question from Spain to France.

Among other topics to be employed on the occasion, you may, perhaps, find it eligible to remark on the frequent recurrence of war between France and Great Britain, the danger to which the Western settlements of the United States would be subject, of being embroiled by military expeditions between Canada and Louisiana, the inquietudes which would be excited in the Southern States, whose numerous slaves have been taught to regard the French as the patrons of their cause, and the tendency of a French neighborhood, on this and other accounts, to inspire jealousies and apprehensions which may turn the thoughts of our citizens toward a closer connection with her rival, and possibly produce a crisis in which a very valuable part of her dominions would be exposed to the joint operation of a naval and territorial power. Suggestions of these kinds must be managed with much delicacy, or rather the expediency of hazarding them at all, as well as the manner of doing it, must be left to your own information and discretion.

Should it be found that the cession from Spain to France has irrevocably taken place, or certainly will take place, sound policy will require in that state of things, that nothing be said or done which will unnecessarily irritate our future neighbors, or check the liberality which they may be disposed to exercise in relation to the trade and navigation through the mouth of the Mississippi; everything being equally avoided at the same time, which may compromit the rights of the United States beyond those stipulated in the treaty between them and Spain. It will be proper, on the contrary, to patronize the interests of our Western fellow-citizens by cherishing in France every just and liberal disposition toward their commerce. In the next place, it will deserve to be tried whether France can not be induced to make over to the United States the Floridas, if included in the cession to her from Spain, or at least West Florida, through which several of our rivers (particularly the important river Mobile) empty themselves into the sea. Such a proof on the part of France, of good will toward the United States, would contribute to reconcile the latter to an arrangement in itself much disrelished by them and to strengthen the returning friendship between the two countries; and by affording a fund for indemnifying and soothing our fellow-citizens who have suffered from her wrongs, would, in that view also, be a measure founded not less in an enlarged policy than in solid justice. The great importance of West Florida to the United States recommends to your patriotism the prudent use of every fair consideration which may favor the attainment of the object.

These ideas suppose that the cession to the United States is to be obtained from the single will of France. But it may happen that the Floridas are so far suspended, on unfinished negotiations between her and Spain, as to admit or require the concurrence of both in gratifying the wishes of the United States. In this state of things, France may yield to the considerations suggested with less of concession and reluctance; and as Spain, too, must feel an interest in the good will of the United States, and is responsible, in justice, for very considerable depredations on their commerce, there may be the greater possibility of her joining in the measure.

Should the Floridas neither have been ceded to France, nor be an acquisition contemplated by her, still it will be material, considering her intimate and influential relations to Spain, to dispose her to favor experiments on the part of the United States, for obtaining from Spain the cession in view. The interest which the latter has in cultivating our friendly dispositions, and the obligation she is under to satisfy our claims for spoliations, for doing which no other mode may be so convenient to her, are motives to which an appeal may be made with no inconsiderable force. Mr. Pinckney is accordingly to avail himself of the most auspicious occasions for sounding and exciting the dispositions of the Spanish Government on this subject; and your efforts at Paris can not be too attentively combined with his at Madrid, as well on the last supposition that Spain alone is to make the cession, as on the former, that France is to have a direct share in the transaction. Mr. Pinckney's instructions will relate to each alternative, and you will be sensible of the advantages of such a correspondence between you as will give the proper concert to your operations.

Mr. King to the Secretary of State.

LONDON, *November 20, 1801.*

SIR: If the annexed copy of the treaty between France and Spain, respecting the establishment of the Prince of Parma in Tuscany, be genuine, of which I have no reason to doubt, you will perceive the value which these Powers seem to have placed upon Louisiana; the cession whereof to France is confirmed by the seventh article of this treaty.

I am in hopes that I shall be able to obtain and send you a copy of the treaty ceding Louisiana to France: this would enable us to determine whether it includes New Orleans and the Floridas.

There is, doubtless, an understanding between England and France in respect to the expedition now nearly ready to proceed to Saint Domingo, and I think I am not mistaken in the belief, whatever may be the intentions of France in respect to the occupation of Louisiana, that no part of the forces now collecting and which are going to Saint Domingo, will be employed for this purpose.

It is not a little extraordinary that during the whole negotiation between France and England not a word was mentioned on either side respecting Louisiana, though this Government was not ignorant of the views of France in this quarter.

With perfect respect and esteem, I have the honor to be, sir, your obedient and faithful servant,

RUFUS KING.

[Extract.]

Mr. Livingston to the Secretary of State.

PARIS, *December 10, 1801.*

I found, from a variety of sources here, and some I think I can depend on, the business of Louisiana has been concluded, and it was understood it had been given in exchange for the Spanish port of St. Domingo, to be restored to its old master. Several circumstances concurred to induce me to believe this report was not void of truth. I therefore took the earliest opportunity to touch upon that subject with the Minister, and to hint at the reason of policy (as it respected the French Government as well as ourselves) that made the object interesting to us. He seemed at first inclined to waive the subject; but when he found I pressed more closely he admitted that it had been a subject of conversation, but nothing had been concluded or even resolved on, in that affair. I left him with a hint that perhaps both France and Spain might find a mutual interest in ceding the Floridas to the United States.

[Extract.]

Mr. Livingston to the Secretary of State.

PARIS, *December 12, 1801.*

In addition to what I wrote yesterday, I have only to mention that I am more and more confirmed, notwithstanding what I there say of the Minister's assurance, that Louisiana is a favorite object, and that they will be unwilling to part with it on the condition I mentioned. Speaking of the means of paying their debts to one of their Ministers, yesterday, I hinted at this. His answer was, "None but spendthrifts satisfy their debts by selling their lands;" adding, however, after a short pause, "but it is not ours to give."

[Extract.]

Mr. Livingston to Mr. King, Minister to England.

PARIS, *December 30, 1801.*

Among the objects that would most naturally engage my attention on my arrival was the state of the negotiation between France and Spain regarding Louisiana; with a view, if it had not been concluded on, to throw obstacles in the way, so far as it could be advantageously done; or, if it had been effected, to make some such arrangements as would lessen the inconveniences which might result from it to our Western territory. I have, however, reason to think the whole business had been settled before my arrival. I took occasion, on my first private audience of the Minister of Exterior Relations, to press him directly upon the subject, taking the common reports as a foundation for my inquiry. He explicitly denied that anything had been concluded, but admitted that it had been a subject of conversation. I know, however, from a variety of channels, that it is not a mere matter of conversation, but that the exchange has actually been agreed upon; that the armament destined, in the first instance, for Hispaniola, is to proceed to Louisiana, provided Toussaint makes no opposition. General Collot, whom you may have seen in America, was originally intended for Governor of the province, but he is at present out of favor. I think it probable the Minister will justify his concealment to me, by its not having been definitely closed with Spain, as this, though determined between the two Governments, may form an article in the general treaty. His absence (being at Lyons) prevents my coming to something more explicit with him. That Spain has made this cession (which contravenes all her former maxims of policy) can not be doubted, but she is no longer a free agent.

I wish to know from you in what light this is seen by England. It will certainly, in its consequences, be extremely dangerous to her, as it will give an almost unbounded power to her rival.

It puts Spain in a perpetual state of pupilage, since she must always tremble for the safety of her colonies in case of rupture. To avoid this evil, she must grant every commercial and political advantage to France. Her manufactures will find their way, through this channel, into every part of the Spanish territory, to the exclusion of those of

Britain. Our Western territory may be rendered so dependent upon them as to promote their political views, while the interest they have always nurtured with the Indians, and the national character of the peasantry of Canada, may render the possessions of Britain very precarious, to say nothing of the danger which must threaten her islands in case a respectable establishment should be made by France in Louisiana, which will not fail to be the case, as the territory is uncommonly fine, and produces sugar and every article now cultivated in the islands.

I suggest these hints, that they, with many others which may occur to you, may be made use of with the British Ministry to induce them to throw all the obstacles in their power in the way of a final settlement of this business, if it is not already too late. You know, however, the importance of not appearing yourself or permitting me to appear much opposed to it, if you find the thing concluded, since it might be made use of to embroil us with France, and Britain will have sufficient address to endeavor to keep up a mutual jealousy, if possible, between us.

[Extract.]

Mr. Livingston to the Secretary of State.

PARIS, *December 31, 1801.*

The business of Louisiana is very disagreeable to Spain, as far as I can learn. If it should be equally so to Britain, perhaps it may meet with some obstacles. It is a very favorite measure here. Marbois told me yesterday it was considered important to have an outlet for their turbulent spirits; yet would not explicitly acknowledge that the business had been concluded.

[Extract.]

Mr. Livingston to the Secretary of State.

PARIS, *January 13, 1802.*

My former letters left you little doubt on the subject of the cession of Louisiana. By the inclosed copy of the late treaty between France, and Spain you will find that it is a transaction of pretty long standing.

The absence of the Minister prevents my applying to him for the former treaty, which he will hardly know how to give me after absolutely denying that any had been formed on the subject. By the secrecy and duplicity practiced relative to this object, it is clear to me that they apprehend some opposition on the part of America to their plans. I have, however, upon all occasions, declared that, as long as France conforms to the existing treaty between us and Spain, the

Government of the United States does not consider herself as having any interest in opposing the exchange. The evil our country has suffered by their rupture with France is not to be calculated. We have become an object of jealousy both to the Government and people.

The reluctance we have shown to a renewal of the Treaty of 1778 has created many suspicions. Among other absurd ones, they believe seriously that we have an eye to a conquest of their islands. The business of Louisiana also originated in that; and they say expressly that they could have no pretense, so far as related to the Floridas, to make this exchange, had the treaty been renewed, since by the sixth article they were expressly prohibited from touching the Floridas. I own I have always considered this article and the guaranty of our independence as more important to us than the guaranty of the islands was to France; and the sacrifices we have made of an immense claim to get rid of it at a dead loss. We must calculate upon every effort from every maritime Power in Europe to diminish our commerce. France has already excluded us from her African colonies. Her premiums will exclude our oil; and her heavy duties upon tobacco in foreign bottoms will prevent our carrying that article for ourselves. She refuses to naturalize our ships, so that a large capital in that article will sink in our hands. The American Government have it in their power to counteract these measures; but they must do it instantly and decidedly, so as to show that measures of hostility to her commerce will not produce the effect contemplated by the nations of Europe. Let the United States impose a duty upon special articles, of her own produce, exported in foreign bottoms, equivalent to the difference of duty paid in Europe on such articles when imported in American or national vessels. This will secure to us the carriage of our own articles; first, because we can carry cheaper; and, second, because this duty being paid in advance imposes a greater burden than one that is paid out of the sale of the produce.

[Extract.]

Mr. King to the Secretary of State.

LONDON, *January 15, 1802.*

SIR: I have before mentioned to you that the cession of Louisiana (of which it seems to me we can have no doubt, notwithstanding what may be said to amuse us) was not only a topic of inquiry or discussion in the negotiation of the preliminaries: and for the same reason that it was not heard of on that occasion, Lord Hawkesbury has recently informed me that it had not been and would not be, mentioned at Amiens. It is impossible for me to suspect collusion in this affair, and my persuasion, after most careful attention, is, that England abstains from mixing herself in it, precisely from those considerations which have led her to acquiesce in others of great importance to the balance of Europe, as well as her own repose, and upon which she has been altogether silent.

RUFUS KING.

[Extract.]

Mr. King to the Secretary of State.

LONDON, *February 5, 1802.*

SIR: I have seen a letter, dated Paris, February 26, which says, it is definitively settled to send a colony to Louisiana and Florida. General Bernadotte is to have the direction and command of it: preparations are making for the first expedition, whose departure will perhaps depend upon the accounts expected from St. Domingo. It is asserted that the Indian nations, adjoining to Florida, have agents, now here, for the purpose of making treaties with this country to unite themselves with the troops and settlers that may be sent hence. The establishment of this colony is a darling object, and will be pursued with ardor and upon a great scale, unless affairs of St. Domingo shall, for the moment, derange the plan. Louisiana, Guiana, and the desert islands of Tristan de Cunha, are each spoken of as places to which the rebellious and untractable negroes and people of color may be sent from St. Domingo and the other French colonies.

With perfect respect and esteem, I have the honor to be, sir, your obedient and faithful servant,

RUFUS KING.

[Extract.]

Mr. Livingston to the Secretary of State.

PARIS, *February 26, 1802.*

On the subject of Louisiana, I have nothing new. The establishment is disapproved by every statesman here as one that will occasion a great waste of men and money, excite enmities with us, and produce no possible advantage to the nation. But it is a scheme to which the First Consul is extremely attached; and it must, of course, be supported. You will find, by the enclosed note, that I have pressed an explanation on the subject, but I have received no answer. I have it, however, through a friend, from the First Consul, that it is by no means their intention to obstruct the navigation of the Mississippi, or violate our Treaty with Spain. General Bernadotte is understood to be designed for the command, and to have asked 10,000 troops.

Mr. Livingston to the Minister of Exterior Relations.

PARIS, *February 20, 1802.*

The undersigned, Minister Plenipotentiary of the United States, has seen, with some concern, the reserve of the French Government, with respect to the cession they have received from Spain of Louisiana.

He had hoped that they would have found a propriety in making such frank and open communications to him as would have enabled him to satisfy the Government of the United States that neither their boundary, nor the navigation of the Mississippi, secured by their treaties with Spain, would be, in any way, affected by the measure. It would also have been very satisfactory to him to have taken such arrangements with the Minister of Exterior Relations as would have had a tendency to dissipate the alarms the people of the Western territory of the United States will not fail to feel on the arrival of a large body of French troops in their vicinity; alarms which will probably be increased by the exertions of those Powers that are interested in keeping the two Republics from cementing their connection. The policy of the former Government of France led it to avoid all ground of controversy with the United States, not only by declining to possess any territory in their neighborhood, but by stipulating never to hold any. The undersigned does not, by this reference to the Treaty of 1778, mean to reclaim any rights under it, since, by the convention of Paris, 30th September, 1800, it is understood to be revoked; but merely to lead the French Government to reflect how far a regard to the same policy might render it conducive to the mutual interests of both nations to cover, by a natural barrier, their possessions in America, as France has invariably sought to do in Europe.

The undersigned prays the Minister of Exterior Relations (if the request is not inconsistent with the views of the Government) to inform him whether East and West Florida, or either of them, are included in the treaty made between France and Spain; and to afford him such assurances, with respect to the limits of their territory and the navigation of the Mississippi, heretofore agreed on between Spain and the United States, as may prove satisfactory to the latter.

If the territories of East and West Florida should be included within the limits of the cession obtained by France, the undersigned desires to be informed how far it would be practicable to make such arrangements between their respective Governments as would, at the same time, aid the financial operations of France, and remove, by a strong natural boundary, all future causes of discontent between her and the United States. The undersigned embraces this opportunity of renewing to the Minister of Exterior Relations his, etc.

[Extract.]

Mr. King to the Secretary of State.

LONDON, *February 27, 1802.*

SIR: From all I can gather upon the subject we may consider the cession of Louisiana and the Floridas as an affair decided. Without doubt, you are fully aware of its various and extensive consequences. Has it occurred to you that the French Government will probably send thither a large body of people from France, and that it may add to them all the refractory and discontented blacks and persons of color of their West India colonies?

With perfect respect and esteem, etc.,

RUFUS KING.

Mr. Livingston to the Secretary of State.

PARIS, *March 15, 1802.*

SIR: After closing my packet, I received the note of which the within is a copy. It amounts to nothing, but must serve to keep me quite a few days longer, till they see what turn the business takes at Amiens, which becomes more and more doubtful. The bad news from St. Domingo also renders it necessary to keep us in suspense. I have already expressed my fear that American property in the island will not be very safe; and the passage in Leclerc's letter relative to the powder and arms may serve as an apology.

I am, sir, etc., R. R. L.

PARIS, *March 13, year 10.*

SIR: I have received the different notes which you have done me the honor to address to me, relating to the debts, and to the American captures; and I have made them the subject of a report to the First Consul. As soon as his decision shall be made, I shall hasten to inform you of the result.

Do you doubt, sir, that the questions which concern the United States, the determination of which may affect their relations with France, will be examined with equal interest and attention?

Accept, sir, the assurances of my high consideration.

CH. MAU. TALLEYRAND.

President Jefferson to Mr. Livingston.

WASHINGTON, *April 18, 1802.*

The cession of Louisiana and the Floridas by Spain to France, works most sorely on the United States. On this subject the Secretary of

State has written to you fully, yet I cannot forbear recurring to it personally, so deep is the impression it makes on my mind. It completely reverses all the political relations of the United States, and will form a new epoch in our political course. Of all nations of any consideration, France is the one which, hitherto, has offered the fewest points on which we could have any conflict of right, and the most points of a communion of interests. From these causes, we have ever looked to her as our *natural friend*, as one with which we never could have an occasion of difference. Her growth, therefore, we viewed as our own, her misfortunes ours. There is on the globe one single spot, the possessor of which is our natural and habitual enemy. It is New Orleans, through which the produce of three-eighths of our territory must pass to market, and from its fertility it will ere long yield more than half of our whole produce, and contain more than half of our inhabitants. France, placing herself in that door, assumes to us the attitude of defiance. Spain might have retained it quietly for years. Her pacific dispositions, her feeble state, would induce her to increase our facilities there, so that her possession of the place would be hardly felt by us, and it would not, perhaps, be very long before some circumstance might arise, which might make the cession of it to us the price of something of more worth to her. Not so can it ever be in the hands of France: the impetuosity of her temper, the energy and restlessness of her character, placed in a point of eternal friction with us, and our character, which, though quiet and loving peace and the pursuit of wealth, is high-minded, despising wealth in competition with insult or injury, enterprising and energetic as any nation on earth; these circumstances render it impossible that France and the United States can continue long friends, when they meet in so irritable a position. They, as well as we, must be blind if they do not see this; and we must be very improvident if we do not begin to make arrangements on that hypothesis. The day that France takes possession of New Orleans, fixes the sentence which is to restrain her forever within her low-water mark. It seals the union of two nations, who, in conjunction, can maintain exclusive possession of the ocean. From that moment, we must marry ourselves to the British fleet and nation. We must turn all our attention to a maritime force, for which our resources place us on very high ground; and having formed and connected together a power which may render reinforcement of her settlements here impossible to France, make the first cannon which shall be fired in Europe the signal for the tearing up any settlement she may have made, and for holding the two continents of America in sequestration for the common purposes of the United British and American nations. This is not a state of things we seek or desire. It is one which this measure, if adopted by France, forces on us as necessarily, as any other cause, by the laws of nature, brings on its necessary effect. It is not from a fear of France that we deprecate this measure proposed by her. For however greater her force is than ours, compared in the abstract, it is nothing in comparison of ours, when to be exerted on our soil. But it is from a sincere love of peace, and a firm persuasion, that bound to France by the interests and the strong sympathies still existing in the minds of our citizens, and holding relative positions which insure their continuance, we are secure of a long course of peace. Whereas, the change of friends, which will be rendered necessary if France changes that position, embarks us necessarily as a belligerent power in the first war of Europe. In that case, France will have held possession of New Orleans during the interval of a peace, long or short, at the end of which it will be wrested from her. Will this short-lived possession have been an equivalent to her for the transfer of such a weight into the scale of her enemy? Will not the amalgamation of a young, thriving nation, continue to that enemy the health and force which are at present so evidently on the decline? And will a few years' possession of New Orleans add equally to the strength of France? She may say she needs Louisiana for the supply of her West Indies. She does not need it in time of peace, and in war she could not depend on them, because they would be so easily intercepted. I should suppose that all these considerations might, in some proper form, be brought into view of the Government of France. Though stated by us, it ought not to give offence; because we do not bring them forward as a menace, but as consequences not controllable by us, but inevitable from the course of things. We mention them, not as things which we desire by any means, but as things we deprecate; and we beseech a friend to look forward and to prevent them for our common interest.

If France considers Louisiana, however, as indispensable for her views, she might perhaps be willing to look about for arrangements which might reconcile it to our interests. If anything could do this, it would be the ceding to us the island of New Orleans and the Floridas. This would certainly, in a great degree, remove the causes of jarring and irritation between us, and perhaps for such a length of time, as might produce other means of making the measure permanently conciliatory to our interests and friendships. It would, at any rate, relieve us from the necessity of taking immediate measures for countervailing such an operation by arrangements in another quarter. But still we should consider New Orleans and the Floridas as no equivalent for the risk of a quarrel with France, produced by her vicinage.

I have no doubt you have urged these considerations, on every proper occasion, with the government where you are. They are such as must have effect, if you can find means of producing thorough reflection on them by that government. The idea here is, that the troops sent to St. Domingo, were to proceed to Louisiana after finishing their work in that island. If this were the arrangement, it will give you time to return again and again to the charge. For the conquest of St. Domingo will not be a short work. It will take considerable time, and wear down a great number of soldiers. Every eye in the United States is now fixed on the affairs of Louisiana. Perhaps nothing since the revolutionary war, has produced more uneasy sensations through the body of the nation. Notwithstanding temporary bickerings have taken place with France, she has still a strong hold on the affections of our citizens generally. I have thought it not amiss, by way of supplement to the letters of the Secretary of State, to write you this private one, to impress you with the importance we affix to this transaction. I pray you to cherish Dupont. He has the best disposition for the continuance of friendship between the two nations, and perhaps you may be able to make a good use of him.

President Jefferson to M. Dupont de Nemours.

WASHINGTON, *April 25, 1802.*

DEAR SIR,—The week being now closed, during which you had given me a hope of seeing you here, I think it safe to enclose you my letters for Paris, lest they should fail of the benefit of so desirable a conveyance. They are addressed to Kosciugha, Madame de Corney, Mrs. Short, and Chancellor Livingston. You will perceive the unlimited confidence I repose in your good faith, and in your cordial dispositions to serve both countries, when you observe that I leave the letters for Chancellor Livingston open for your perusal. The first page respects a cypher, as do the loose sheets folded with the letter. These are interesting to him and myself only, and therefore are not for your perusal. It is the second, third, and fourth pages which I wish you to read to possess yourself of completely, and then seal the letter with wafers stuck under the flying seal, that it may be seen by nobody else if any accident should happen to you. I wish you to be possessed of the subject, because you may be able to impress on the government of France the inevitable consequences of their taking possession of Louisiana; and though, as I here mention, the cession of New Orleans and the Floridas to us would be a palliation, yet I believe it would be no more, and that this measure will cost France, and perhaps not very long hence, a war which will annihilate her on the ocean, and place that element under the despotism of two nations, which I am not reconciled to the more because my own would be one of them. Add to this the exclusive appropriation of both continents of America as a consequence. I wish the present order of things to continue, and with a view to this I value highly a state of friendship between France and us. You know too well how sincere I have ever been in these dispositions to doubt them. You know, too, how much I value peace, and how unwillingly I should see any event take place which would render war a necessary resource; and that all our movements should change their character and object. I am thus open with you, because I trust that you will have it in your power to impress on that government considerations, in the scale against which the possession of Louisiana is nothing. In Europe, nothing but Europe is seen, or supposed to have any right in the affairs of nations; but this little event, of France's possessing herself of Louisiana, which is thrown in as nothing, as a mere makeweight in the general settlement of accounts,—this speck which now appears as an almost invisible point in the horizon, is the embryo of a tornado which will burst on the countries on both sides of the Atlantic, and involve in its effects their highest destinies. That it may yet be avoided is my sincere prayer; and if you can be the means of informing the wisdom of Bonaparte of all its consequences, you have deserved well of both countries. Peace and abstinence from European interferences are our objects, and so will continue while the present order of things in America remain uninterrupted. There is another service you can render. I am told that Talleyrand is personally hostile to us. This, I suppose, has been occasioned by the X Y Z history. But he should consider that that was the artifice of a party, willing to sacrifice him to the consolidation of their power. This nation has done him justice by dismissing them; that those in power are precisely those who disbelieved that story, and saw in it nothing but an attempt to deceive our country; that we entertain towards him personally the most friendly dispositions; that as to the government of France, we know too little of the state of things there to understand what it is, and have no inclination to meddle in their settlement. Whatever government they establish, we wish to be well with it. One more request,—that you deliver the letter to Chancellor Livingston with your own hands, and, moreover, that you charge Madam Dupont, if any accident happen to you, that she deliver the letter with her own hands. If it passes only through her's and your's, I shall have perfect confidence in its safety. Present her my most sincere respects, and accept yourself assurances of my constant affection, and my prayers, that a genial sky and propitious gales may place you, after a pleasant voyage, in the midst of your friends.

[Extract.]

James Madison, Secretary of State, to R. R. Livingston, Minister to France.

DEPARTMENT OF STATE, *March 16, 1802.*

The subject of your letter to Mr. King, of the 30th of December, is regarded by the President as not less delicate than you have supposed.

Considering the particular views which Great Britain may mingle with ours, and the danger that a confidential resort to her may be abused, for the purpose of sowing jealousies in France, and thereby thwart our object, you and Mr. King will both be sensible that too much circumspection cannot be employed.

[Extract.]

Mr. Livingston to the Secretary of State.

PARIS, *March 24, 1802.*

On the business of Louisiana, they have, as yet, not thought it proper to give me any explanations, though I have omitted no opportunity to press the subject in conversation, and ultimately, by the note sent you on the 25th of February, (a duplicate of which was forwarded on the 28th), with a copy of another note enforcing the above, to which I have, as yet, received no answer.

The fact is, they believe us to be certainly hostile to this measure, and they mean to take possession of it as early as possible, and with as little notice to us as they can.

They are made to believe this is one of the most fertile and important countries in the world; that they have a much greater interest with the Indians than any other people; that New Orleans must command the trade of our whole Western country; and, of course, that they will have a leading interest in its politics. It is a darling object with the First Consul, who sees in it a mean to gratify his friends, and to dispose of his armies. There is a man here, who calls himself a Frenchman, by the name of Francis Tatergem, who pretends to have great interest with the Creek nations. He has been advanced to the rank of General of Division. He persuades them that the Indians are extremely attached to France, and hate the Americans; that they can raise 20,000 warriors; that the country is a paradise, etc. I believe him to be a mere adventurer; but he is listened to, and was first taken up by the old Directors.

I can not help thinking that it would be advisable for the present Congress to take measures for establishing the Natchez, or some other port, and giving it such advantages as would bring our vessels to it without touching at Orleans. On this subject, however, you will form a better judgment than I can. I have but one hope left as to defeating this cession: it consists in alarming Spain and England. The Spanish Minister is now absent; but I have not failed to show, in the strongest light, to the Minister of Britain, the danger that will result to them from the extension of the French possessions into Mexico, and the probable loss of Canada, if they are suffered to possess it.

I have requested Mr. King to press this subject, also as opportunity offers. I enclose a copy of my last letter to him. If the treaty does not close soon, I think it would be advisable for us to meet at Amiens, and have accordingly proposed it to him.

I believe, such is the state of things here and such the desire for peace, that Britain may force them to relinquish Louisiana; particularly as the people here are far from desiring the establishment of any foreign colony which they consider as a weak point and drain for the population and wealth.

[Extract.]

Mr. Livingston to Mr. King, Minister at London.

PARIS, *March 10, 1802.*

If Louisiana goes into the hands of France without any explanations on the part of her Government to us, (and this I have not yet been able to bring it to, though I have pointedly pressed it, both verbally and by note,) on the subject either of her boundary or the navigation of the Mississippi, it is impossible to see the extent of the power she will have in and over America. As part of the territory of Spain, Louisiana has no precise boundary; so that it is easy to foresee the fate of Mexico, especially when it is considered that General Bernadotte, who is marked for this expedition, has demanded, it is said, a large body of men. Britain will judge how far she is able to contend with France, enriched by the treasures of Spain. The boundary between Canada and Louisiana is alike unsettled. The dispositions of a great part of the natives of that country are friendly to France; her influence over the Indian tribes has always been, and will again be, much greater than that of the British, both from the disposition and manners of her people, and from the whole body of carriers in the Indian trade being native Canadians, and much the greater part of them mongrel French. It is impossible to say what their influence may be upon our Western country, in case of a controversy with Great Britain, particularly if they keep the keys of it by possessing the mouth of the Mississippi or invite their aid in the plunder of Mexico. That the possession of that country, aided by the power of France in Europe, will draw after it that of all the islands, is easily foreseen. I mention these circumstances to you (though I know they could hardly escape you) as hints that you may use with advantage to introduce this business at Amiens. You well know how to give them additional weight. Nor is the right of Britain to interfere unfounded. By the sixth article of the treaty with us of 1778, they absolutely renounce all right to take, under any circumstances, any part of the country possessed then or before by Great Britain on that continent. Though we have relinquished all advantages deducible from that treaty, yet, so far as other nations were interested in it, at the close of the last war, they have a right to enforce it. And surely it was a very important guaranty to Britain of her colonies; and it might, for aught we know, have had great influence upon the terms of the then peace.

[Extract.]

James Madison, Secretary of State, to Mr. Pinckney.

DEPARTMENT OF STATE, *March 30, 1802.*

We are anxious to hear from you on the several subjects with which you have been charged; particularly on that of Louisiana. By a treaty entered into between Spain and France, in March, 1801, and lately published in the Paris newspapers, it appears that in an antecedent treaty the cession of that country had been stipulated by Spain. Still it is possible that the cession may have been since annulled; and that such was, or was to be the case, has been stated in verbal accounts from Madrid. At Paris Mr. Livingston has been given to understand, by the French Government, that the cession has never been more than a subject of conversation between the two Governments. No information, however, has been received from him subsequent to the publication of the Treaty of March, 1801, which must have led to some more decisive explanations.

The copies herewith enclosed of a memorial of sundry inhabitants living on waters running from the United States through Florida into the Gulf of Mexico, and of a letter from the late Mr. Hunter, representative in Congress of the Mississippi Territory, will present to your attention a subject of some importance at this time, and of very great importance in a future view. The Treaty with Spain having, as these documents observe, omitted to provide for the use of the Mobile, Chatahoochee, and other rivers running from our territory through that of Spain, by the citizens of the United States, in like manner with the use of the Mississippi, it will be proper to make early efforts to supply the defect. Should a cession, indeed, including the Spanish territory eastward of the Mississippi, have finally taken place, it can answer no purpose to seek from the Spanish Government this supplemental arrangement. On a contrary supposition you will avail yourself of the most favorable moment and manner of calling its attention to the object. In support of our claim you will be able to use the arguments which enforced that to the navigation of the Mississippi. If it should be observed that a greater proportion of these rivers than of the Mississippi run through the exclusive territory of Spain, it may be a set-off that the upper parts of the rivers run, exclusively, through the territory of the United States, and do not merely divide it, like the Mississippi, from that of Spain.

But neither the one nor the other circumstance can essentially affect our natural rights. Should the Spanish Government be favorably disposed, it will be proper for you to pave the way for a formal convention on the subject, endeavoring to obtain, in the meantime, such regulations from its authority, and such instructions to its officers, as will answer the purposes of our citizens. Among other hardships, of which they now complain, and for which a regulation is particularly wanted, one I understand, is, that the article, cotton, which is acquiring rapid importance in that quarter, must, after it has been conveyed to Mobile, be shipped to New Orleans and pay a duty of about twelve and one-half per cent. before it can be exported.

[Extract.]

Mr. Livingston to the Secretary of State.

PARIS, *April 24, 1802.*

The business most interesting to us, that of Louisiana, still remains in the state it was. The Minister will give no answer to any inquiries I make on that subject. He will not say what their boundaries are, what are their intentions, and when they are to take possession. And what appears very extraordinary to me, is, that by a letter I have just received from Mr. Pinckney, I find that he still supposes that the Floridas are not included in the cession: and he writes me that he has made a proposition to purchase them, which lies before the Minister, with whom he is to have a conference on the subject. You may, however, be fully assured that the Floridas are given to France; that they are at this moment fitting out an armament from here to take possession. This will be commanded by General Bernadotte. The number of troops designed for this object is between five and seven thousand. They will shortly sail for New Orleans, unless the state of affairs in St. Domingo should change their destination. You may act upon this information with absolute certainty, since I have no doubt of the channel through which I have received it. It would be wise immediately to take measures to enable the Natchez to rival Orleans. I have suggested the means: and I hope they will not be neglected by the Congress now sitting. That you may judge of the light in which this country is viewed by some here, I send you the extract of a paper that now lies before the Minister. If Congress makes the Natchez a free port, and if the state of affairs in St. Domingo should employ the troops designed for Louisiana, time will still be left for gold to operate here. But it must be plentifully and liberally bestowed, not barely in the assumption of debts, but in active capital, afforded in supplies, to aid their armaments in the islands. Give me your instructions as to the utmost amount, if, as you will be better able to judge than I can, the affairs of St. Domingo are likely to be protracted.

[Extract.]

James Madison, Secretary of State, to Robert R. Livingston.

DEPARTMENT OF STATE,
Washington, May 1, 1802.

The conduct of the French Government, in paying so little attention to its obligations under the treaty; in neglecting its debts to our citizens; in giving no answer to your complaints and expostulations, which you say is the case with those of other foreign Ministers also; and particularly in its reserve as to Louisiana, which tacitly contradicts the language first held to you by the Minister of Foreign Relations—gives tokens as little auspicious to the true interests of France herself, as to the rights and just objects of the United States.

The cession of Louisiana to France becomes daily more and more a source of painful apprehensions. Notwithstanding the Treaty of March, 1801, and notwithstanding the general belief in France on the subject, and the accounts from St. Domingo that part of the armament sent to that island was eventually destined for Louisiana, a hope was still drawn, from your early conversations with M. Talleyrand, that the French Government did not mean to pursue the object. Since the receipt of your last communication, no hope remains, but, from the accumulating difficulties of going through with the undertaking, and from the conviction you may be able to impress, that it must have an instant and powerful effect in changing the relations between France and the United States. The change is obvious: and the more it can be developed in candid and friendly appeals to the reflections of the French Government, the more it will urge it to revise and abandon the project. A mere *neighborhood* could not be friendly to the harmony which both countries have so much an interest in cherishing; but if a possession of the mouth of the Mississippi is to be added to other causes of discord, the worst events are to be apprehended. You will consequently spare no efforts, that will consist with prudence and dignity, to lead the councils of France to proper views of this subject, and to an abandonment of her present purpose. You will also pursue, by prudent means, the inquiry into the extent of the cession—particularly whether it includes the Floridas as well as New Orleans—and endeavor to ascertain the price at which these, if included in the cession, would be yielded to the United States. I cannot, in the present state of things, be more particular on this head than to observe that, in every view, it would be a most precious acquisition, and that, as far as the terms could be satisfied by charging on the acquisition itself the restitution and other debts to American citizens, great liberality would doubtless be indulged by this Government. The President wishes you to devote every attention to this object, and to be frequent and particular in your communications relating to it.

[Extract.]

James Madison, Secretary of State, to Rufus King, Minister to England.

DEPARTMENT OF STATE, *May 1, 1802.*

We are fully aware of the tendency of the reported cession of Louisiana to plant in our neighborhood troubles of different kinds, and to prepare the way for very serious events. It has accordingly been a primary object with the President to obviate such an event.

Mr. King to the Secretary of State.

LONDON, *May 7, 1802.*

SIR: Among the few great principles of national policy worthy of fixing the attention of our statesmen, I am willing to hope there is not one concerning which there is greater unanimity, in opinion, than in that which enjoins upon us all to do our utmost in every way, and upon all occasions, to maintain and perpetuate the union of our country.

With this persuasion, though the subject may not be thought to be included among the duties of my mission, I have not been able to remain inattentive or indifferent to the cession of Louisiana and the Floridas to France, because I have viewed it as a measure calculated and possibly intended to weaken and divide us. I have already communicated to you what passed between me and the Minister of this country in relation to this cession, during the negotiation of peace; but as these communications were merely verbal, and as it appeared to me to be of some importance that they should be distinctly and formally confirmed, as well as that we should be ascertained of the sentiments of this Government in respect to this cession, I prepared and sent to Lord Hawkesbury a confidential letter upon the subject, a copy whereof, together with a copy of his answer, is annexed. I will only add that I have reason to be satisfied that the cession of Louisiana and the Floridas is considered by all the late Ministry, as well as all other men of influence in this country, as a measure of the greatest consequence, and which must have an unavoidable influence upon the duration of peace.

With perfect respect and esteem, I have the honor to be, sir, your obedient and faithful servant,

RUFUS KING.

Mr. King to Lord Hawkesbury.

LONDON, *April 21, 1802.*

MY LORD: By the Treaty of Alliance concluded at Paris, in 1778, between the United States of America and France, the latter renounced forever the possession of every part of the continent of America lying to the east of the course of the river Mississippi. This renunciation, confirming that which had been previously made in the treaty of 1763, between Great Britain and France, authorized the expectation that France, content with her widely spread dominions, would abstain from seeking an extension of them in this part of the American continent; an expectation that appeared the more reasonable, inasmuch as the motives to such extension could not be satisfactorily reconciled with a just regard to the rights and security of those Powers between which this portion of America is divided, and by which the same is at present possessed.

Contrary, nevertheless, to expectations which have been entertained on this subject, if credit be due to uniform and uncontradicted reports, the Government of France has prevailed upon His Catholic Majesty to cede to France both the provinces of Louisiana and the Floridas, and having thus acquired a station at the mouth, and on the sides of the Mississippi, may be inclined to interfere with and interrupt the open navigation of the same.

By the Treaty of Peace concluded at Paris, in 1783, between the United States of America and Great Britain, it is mutually stipulated that "the navigation of the river Mississippi, from its source to the ocean, shall forever remain free and open to the subjects of Great Britain and the citizens of the United States." Without enlarging upon the great and peculiar importance of this navigation to the United States, a large and increasing proportion of whose people can conveniently communicate with each other, and with foreign countries, by no other route, I take the liberty, through your Lordship, to request that the British Government will, in confidence, explain itself upon this subject, and especially that it will explicitly declare whether any communication has been received by it from the Government of France or Spain respecting the said cession; or whether His Britannic Majesty has, in any manner, acquiesced in or sanctioned the same, so as to impair or affect the stipulation above referred to concerning the free navigation of the Mississippi. In a word, I entreat your Lordship to open yourself on this occasion with that freedom which, in matters of weighty concern, is due from one friendly nation to another, and which, in the present instance, will have the effect to do away all those misconceptions that may otherwise prevail in respect to the privity of Great Britain to the cession in question.

With the highest consideration, I have the honor to be,

RUFUS KING.

Lord Hawkesbury to Mr. King.

DOWNING STREET, *May 7, 1802.*

SIR: I have the honor to acknowledge receipt of your letter of the 21st ultimo.

It is impossible that so important an event as the cession of Louisiana by Spain to France should be regarded by the King in any other light than as highly interesting to His Majesty, and to the United States; and should render it more necessary than ever that there should subsist between the two Governments that spirit of confidence which is become so essential to the security of their respective territories and possessions.

With regard to the free navigation of the Mississippi, I conceive that it is perfectly clear, according to the law of nations, that, in the event of the district of Louisiana being ceded to France, that country would come into possession of it subject to all the engagements which appertained to it at the time of cession; and that the French Government could, consequently, allege no colorable pretext for excluding His Majesty's subjects, or the citizens of the United States, from the navigation of the river Mississippi.

With regard to the second question in your letter, I can have no difficulty in informing you that no communication whatever has been received by His Majesty from the Government of France or Spain, relative to any convention or treaty for the cession of Louisiana or the Floridas; and I can, at the same time, most truly assure you that His Majesty has not in any manner, directly or indirectly, acquiesced in or sanctioned this cession.

In making this communication to you, for the information of the Government of the United States, I think it right to acquaint you that His Majesty will be anxious to learn their sentiments on every part of this subject, and the line of policy which they will be inclined to adopt in the event of this arrangement being carried into effect.

I have the honor to be, with great respect, sir, your most obedient, humble servant,

HAWKESBURY.

James Madison, Secretary of State, to Charles Pinckney, Minister of Spain.

DEPARTMENT OF STATE, *May 11, 1802.*

We are still without a line from you since your arrival at Madrid, and feel an increasing solicitude to hear from you on the subject of Louisiana. The latest information from Paris has confirmed the fact that it was ceded by a treaty prior to that of March, 1801; and, notwithstanding the virtual denial of the cession in the early conversations between Mr. Livingston and the Minister of Foreign Relations, a refusal of any explanations at present seems to admit that the cession has taken place. Still there are chances of obtaining a reversal of the transaction. The repugnance of the United States to it is, and will be, pressed in a manner that can not be without some effect: it is known that most of the French statesmen best informed on the subject, disapproved of it; the pecuniary difficulties of the French Government must, also, be felt as a check; whilst the prospect of a protracted and expensive war in St. Domingo; must form a very powerful obstacle to the execution of the project. The councils of England appear to have been torpid on this occasion. Whether it proceeded from an unwillingness to risk a fresh altercation with France, or from a hope that such a neighborhood between France and the United States would lead to collisions which might be turned to her advantage, is more than I can decide. The latter consideration might justly have great weight with her; but as her eyes may be more readily turned to the immediate and certain purposes to be answered to her rival, it is to be presumed that the policy of England will contribute to thwart the acquisition. What the intentions of Spain may be, we wait to learn from you. Verbal information from inofficial sources, has led us to infer that she disowns the instrument of cession, and will rigorously oppose it. Should the cession actually fail from this, or any other cause, and Spain retain New Orleans and the Floridas, I repeat to you the wish of the President, that every effort and address be employed to obtain the arrangement by which the territory on the east side of the Mississippi, including New Orleans, may be ceded to the United States, and the Mississippi made a common boundary, with a common use of its navigation for them and Spain. The inducements to be held out to Spain were intimated in your original instructions on this point. I am charged by the President now to add, that you may not only receive and transmit a proposition of guaranty of her territory beyond the Mississippi, as a condition of her ceding to the United States the territory, including New Orleans, on this side, but, in case it may be necessary, may make the proposition yourself, in the forms required by our constitution. You will infer from this enlargement of your authority, how much importance is attached to the object in question, as securing a precious acquisition to the United States, as well as a natural and quiet boundary with Spain; and will derive from this consideration additional motives to discharge, with a prudent zeal, the task committed to you.

[Extract.]

Mr. Livingston to the Secretary of State.

PARIS, *May 20, 1802.*

The same conduct was held (by the Minister of Exterior Relations) with respect to Louisiana. He would not acknowledge that the Government had yet formed any specific plan with respect to it, or that any troops were going out; but assured me, in general terms, that nothing should be done that should give us any ground of complaint; on the contrary, their vicinity would promote our friendship.

I will not trouble you with the answers that obviously presented to this reasoning. It terminated, however, as all my conversations on the subject have done, in nothing.

I shall wait a few days in hopes of hearing from you, after having received a copy of my first note, when I shall act agreeably to your instructions, or, if you afford me none, send in a second, in which I shall press for a communication of the treaty with Spain, which, however, I am in hopes you may receive through Mr. Pinckney.

I believe that, for the present, the armament designed for Louisiana will be sent to Hispaniola, about which, I find, that much anxiety is entertained here.

Mr. Livingston to the Secretary of State.

PARIS, *May 28, 1802.*

SIR: Since my last I have acquired information which I can depend on, relative to the intentions of this Government with respect to Louisiana. Bernadotte is, as I told you, to command: Collot second in command. Adet is to be prefect: but the expedition is delayed till about September, on account (as Talleyrand expressed himself to Bernadotte) of some difficulty which he did not explain; but which, I have no doubt, has arisen from the different apprehensions of France and Spain relative to the meaning of the term Lousiana, which has been understood by France to include the Floridas, but probably by Spain to have been confined to the strict meaning of the term. This explains why I could never get an answer to my questions relative to the extent of the cessions; and upon which the French Government had probably no doubt till we started it. Believing, if this conjecture as to the cause of delay of the expedition was right, that no time should be lost in throwing obstructions in the way of its conclusion, I wrote the note of which the inclosed is a copy, with the double purpose of alarming Spain, and furnishing with arguments, arising from the good faith they owed us, against giving their cession the construction France would wish. I consider this as the more important, because I believe that every negotiation for this object will be carried on here. I shall, however, give the earliest and fullest information I can on this subject to Mr. Pinckney, who will enforce at Madrid the arguments I may use here to excite the alarm of the Court of Spain.

I wait impatiently some further instructions from you; those I have in some sort prohibiting such measures as may show any dissatisfaction on the subject, of which, however, I doubt the policy. The subject is so interesting as to induce us to risk something to defeat it.

If I do not hear from you soon I shall present a pointed memorial to this Government stating fully and candidly our objections to their taking possession of the Floridas, and demanding security for the rights we had originally, and by treaty with Spain.

I am, sir, etc.,
R. R. L.

Mr. Livingston, Minister Plenipotentiary of the United States, to His Excellency Chevalier d'Azara, Ambassador of His Catholic Majesty.

PARIS, *May 28, 1802.*

SIR: The powerful interests that our respective Governments have, that the sincerest friendship and harmony should subsist between their territories in America, naturally leads to mutual confidence between their Ministers, and a full exposition of their sentiments upon subjects which may have a tendency to interrupt that union. I think it my duty, therefore, to open myself to you with freedom on one which is very important as it regards the good faith which, I trust, both your Government and mine will consider as the first of obligations, as it respects the great territorial interests of both Spain and the United States; and I flatter myself, sir, that with these objects in view, I shall meet with equal frankness and confidence on your part. It is generally understood that Spain has made a cession of Louisiana to France; and it might have been expected, considering the situation of this territory, and the friendly connection between both countries and the United States, that a communication would have been made of this treaty to their Government. Passing over this circumstance, probably owing rather to inattention than to a want of confidence, I proceed to make some observations on the treaty now in force between the Court of Madrid and the United States, and to inquire how far Spain has provided for the stipulations contained in that treaty, and secured thereby to the United States. The boundary between our respective Governments having been established, it is not to be doubted that the cession has confined itself to the same limits. But, sir, by the fourth article of that treaty, it is agreed that the midchannel of the Mississippi, where it divides the territories of Spain from those of the United States, shall be the boundary, and that the navigation of this river shall be confined to the subjects of Spain and the citizens of the United States, unless it shall be extended to others by special convention. I am solicitous to know, sir, in what manner the rights of the citizens of the United States in this river are preserved by the terms of the cession.

Where the river runs wholly within the territory of Spain, the

United States have, by the treaty, a qualified right of navigation of which they can not be divested. They have also the assurance of Spain that no other nation shall share this right unless by convention; by which I understand that Spain binds herself not to grant this right without some previous agreement on the subject with the United States: and this is rendered more evident from the words of the article not being confined to the river below the thirty-first degree of north latitude, but extending to the whole of the Mississippi, as well above as below: whereas, half the river above that boundary belonging to the United States, it could not have been intended that either of the contracting parties should have a right to grant, without the consent of the other, a right that was held in common. The word convention must, therefore, be intended to mean a convention between Spain and the United States; nor can any cession of the territory carry with it a right to admit other Powers to a participation of the advantages of the navigation of the Mississippi, unless by convention previously entered into between His Catholic Majesty and the United States. It is to be presumed that, in the cession which Spain has made, the Floridas are not included, because of the evident interest that she has in retaining them as security for her territories in South America, if unfortunate events should hereafter produce a rupture between France and Spain. In this case, the Floridas, by lying in the rear of the French colonies, would serve as an effectual check as well to them as to those turbulent spirits in the adjoining States who might, in spite of the efforts of their Government, incline to associate in the enterprises of France. Upon this subject, sir, however, I pray to have more explicit information, because you will observe that, by the existing treaty between our respective nations, there are special stipulations mutually agreed upon, and which the United States have a right to expect some security for, in any cession that Spain may make of that country.

By the fifth article it is agreed that Spain will restrain by force all hostilities on the part of the Indian nations living within their boundary, either on the citizens of the United States, or the Indians within their territory, &c. You will easily see, sir, that as this is a national obligation, it may be doubtful whether it will pass with the territory, and yet is of such a nature as to entitle the United States to look for its performance from the good faith of Spain, who can not, without the consent of the United States, place herself in a situation to render it of no effect. By the twenty-second article of the same treaty, Spain stipulates to permit the citizens of the United States to deposit their goods at New Orleans, and to export from thence free of duty; or, in case of withdrawing this permission, to assign them an establishment for this purpose on another part of the banks of the Mississippi. I take the liberty to ask, sir, (if the Floridas are included in the cession to France,) what stipulations the cession contains insuring to the

United States this important privilege, which they considered themselves entitled to by the best of all guaranties, the good faith of His Catholic Majesty? You will easily see, sir, that if a naked cession has been made to France, without attention to these articles, how much reason the United States will have to complain of the measure: and I trust, sir, that you will see the propriety of their forming one of the parties to any treaty in which their rights may be so materially affected. I know, sir, that observations might, and I doubt not will be made officially to your Court by the Minister of the United States at Madrid; but, in the meantime, sir, as it is my intention to address myself upon this subject to the Government of France, I wish to receive from you every information which might throw light upon the subject, and the rather as knowing the confidence that His Catholic Majesty reposed in your talents and patriotism; and seeing, at the same time, that in everything that related to this object our respective nations had a joint interest. I have believed that you will receive with pleasure this unofficial note as a mark of my confidence, and afford me your aid in giving efficacy to a treaty which has served as a basis of friendship between our respective nations.

R. R. L.

[Extract.]
Mr. Livingston to the Secretary of State.

PARIS, *June 8, 1802.*

Enclosed is the answer of the Spanish Ambassador to my letter, a copy of which was forwarded on the 28th ult. It accords with the conclusions I drew from the delay of the expedition, and the conduct of the Minister of Exterior Relations. I have had a conversation with Collot and Adet, separately. I find that, though they both consider their going in official characters to Louisiana as settled, yet that they have neither seen the treaty, nor know precisely the boundary of the territory acquired. Pensacola and Mobile, they say, are expressly given: as to the rest, or whether it includes West Florida, they can not say. That France intended that it should, I have no doubt; and I still think it probable that she will make it yield to her intentions: for in Europe she does what she will, and it will require firmness and exertion to prevent her doing so in America.

The Chevalier d'Azara, Ambassador of His Catholic Majesty, near the French Republic, to Mr. Livingston, Minister Plenipotentiary of the United States.

PARIS, *June 2, 1802.*

SIR: I pray you to excuse my not having been able to see you when you were so good as to call at my dwelling; the ill state of my health for the last ten days has deprived me of that honor.

I return you thanks for the frankness disclosed in your unofficial note of the 28th May; and, in adopting the same friendship and equal frankness, I have the honor to inform you that the affair concerning which you have addressed me, not having passed through my hands, I am unable to give you all the information which you have desired. It appears certain, however, that a treaty ceding Louisiana has been concluded; but I am of opinion that the Floridas are not comprised in the cession.

As the Minister of the United States at Madrid will be required, (agreeably to what you have had the goodness to inform me), to demand explanation of my Court concerning the treaty in question, your Government will receive, through him, all the information which may be proper. Nevertheless, I will write to my Court, and will not fail to communicate all that I may learn, for the purpose, as far as depends on me, of removing your doubts and dispelling your inquietude.

J. NICOLAY D'AZARA.

[Extract.]

James Madison, Secretary of State, to Rufus King, Minister to England.

DEPARTMENT OF STATE, *July 23, 1802*,

The subject of your letter of May 7th, namely, your correspondence with Lord Hawkesbury on the cession of Louisiana and the Floridas to France will receive from the President all the consideration which its great importance demands; and as soon as an answer can be founded on the result of his reflections no time will be lost in transmitting it.

[Extract.]

James Madison, Secretary of State, to C. Pinckney, Minister to Spain.

DEPARTMENT OF STATE, *July 26, 1802.*

The information from Paris renders it certain that the cession of Louisiana to France has actually been concluded, and that the cession comprehends the two Floridas. In this state of the business, it seems unnecessary to decide on the price which Spain might be led to expect for a cession of the Floridas, including New Orleans, to the United States; and the more so, as it would be of use for us previously to know the value she places on the guaranty proposed in my letter to you of the 25th of September last. For the present, the cession wished by the United States must be an object of negotiation with the French Government. It will, notwithstanding, continue to be proper for you to cultivate the good dispositions of Spain in relation to it, both as they may not be entirely disregarded by France, and as, in the turn of events, Spain may possibly be extricated from her engagements to France, and again have the disposal of the territories in question.

[Extract.]

Mr. Livingston to the Secretary of State.

PARIS, *July 30, 1802.*

I have received your dispatches and the President's by M. Dupont de Nemours. I shall reply more particularly to them at the next opportunity, as I am now very much engaged in preparing a lengthy memoir on the subject of the mutual interests of France and the United States, relative to Louisiana, by which I hope to convince them that, both in a commercial and a political view, the posession of it would be disadvantageous to France. In my last, I hinted to you my suspicions that France and Spain did not understand each other on the subject of Louisiana, and communicated to you my letters to the Spanish Ambassador, calculated to sound this business, and interpose some difficulty to its execution. His answer confirmed my opinion. I have since received, verbally, his explicit assurance that the Floridas are not included in the cession; and I have been applied to, by one of the Ministers here, to know what we understand, in America, by Louisiana. You can easily conceive my answer. I have just received a letter from Mr. Graham, in which he communicates the Spanish Minister's answer to Mr. Pinckney's application upon the same subject, in these words: "If the King should think proper to cede Louisiana, he will take care that the interest of the United States shall not be affected by it." It appears also, by the fifth article of the Treaty of Madrid, March 21st, 1801, that the cession had been made of Louisiana generally. The French, you know, have always extended it to South Carolina and all the country on the Ohio. Since the possession of the Floridas by Britain, and the Treaty of 1763, I think there can be no doubt as to the precise meaning of the term.

I find a certain degree of *raideur* in the Spanish Ambassador, on that subject, which it will be our interest to cherish at the Court of Spain unless we should have a prospect of purchasing the Floridas. In the present state of things, until the point is settled, I think it probable the expedition to Louisiana will be postponed. In the meantime, all that can be done here will be to endeavor to obtain a cession of New Orleans, either by purchase, or by offering to make it a port of entry to France, on such terms as shall promise advantages to her commerce, and give her hopes of introducing her manufactures and wines into our western country. An arrangement of this sort, if they listen to it, would certainly be beneficial to both countries and only hurtful to

Britain. If to this we could add a stipulation that she shall never possess the Floridas, but, on the contrary, in case of a rupture with Spain, and a conquest of them, cede them to us, our affairs in that quarter would stand as well as I would wish; and the colonies that France might attempt to establish on the west side of the Mississippi would be too feeble to injure us.

I find them very anxious to have the ports of Pensacola and St. Augustine, as they dread our having command of the Gulf. I confess this appears to me no very important object; and if they would be content with these, and give us West Florida and New Orleans, even at a large price, we should not hesitate. I am sorry that you have not communicated to me what are precisely the utmost limits of the sum I may venture to offer in cash, or in our own demands. As the Minister has been absent some time, and has but just returned, I can not state precisely to you what we may hope on this subject; but be persuaded that I am fully impressed with the importance of the subject, and that nothing will be left undone which I can do to effectuate your wishes. I saw him last night, and was very cordially received. His health is so much amended by the waters, that I hope he will be able to go through business more speedily than he has done.

[Extract.]

Mr. Livingston to the Secretary of State.

PARIS, *August 10, 1802.*

Our own affairs have advanced but little, since the whole attention of those in power are turned to objects nearer home. I have had several conferences on the subject of Louisiana, but can get nothing more from them than I have already communicated. I have thought it best, by conversation and by writing, to pave the way, prior to any direct application, till I know better to what object to point. For this purpose, I have written the enclosed essay, which I have had translated, and struck off twenty copies; I have just got them finished; I have placed some of them in such hands as I think will best serve our purposes. Talleyrand has promised me to give it an attentive perusal; after which, when I find how it works, I will come forward with some proposition. I am very much, however, at a loss, as to what terms you would consider it as allowable to offer, if they can be brought to a sale of the Floridas, either with or without New Orleans: which last place will be of little consequence, if we possess the Floridas, because a much better passage may be formed on the east side of the river. I may, perhaps, carry my estimate of them too high; but when I consider, first, the expense it will save us in guards and garrisons, the risk of war, the value of duties, and what may be raised by the sale of lands, I should think them a cheap purchase. I trust, however, that you will give me some directions on this head, and not leave the responsibility of offering too much or too little, entirely at my door. I speak, in all this business, as if the affair of the Floridas was arranged with Spain; which, I believe, is not yet the case. But I took occasion to touch on the subject three days ago, with the Spanish Ambassador, with whom I was dining, and think he appeared to have somewhat relaxed on that ground, but would say nothing decisive; nor were the time and place proper to press him.

Memoir, referred to in the preceding dispatch.

Whether it will be advantageous to France to take possession of Louisiana?

This question presents itself in two points of view:

First, as it affects the commerce and manufactures of France.

Second, as it affects her positive or relative strength.

Colonies are never cherished for themselves, but on account of the influence they may have upon the general prosperity of the nation. And as one man at home, contributes more to this than two at a distance, no wise nation colonizes but when it has a superfluous population, or when it has a superfluous capital that can not otherwise be rendered productive.

The population of France, though very considerable, has by no means attained the point which renders it necessary to colonize. The soil, climate, and local situation, give it advantages as a commercial and more particularly as a manufacturing, nation, over every other part of Europe. The ingenuity, taste, and industry of the inhabitants have placed them in the highest rank; but these advantages are very much restricted by the want of a sufficient capital to bring them into operation. A rival nation, inferior in all the circumstances I have mentioned, by the single effect of a large capital, has attained a superiority both in commerce and manufactures which, in return, those circumstances enable it to maintain by continually adding to that national wealth. Capital increases manufactures by the introduction of machines, by the regular payment of workmen, by reducing the interest of money, and, above all, by forcing new markets. The wealthy mechanic alone can afford those expensive and slow operations which, in many cases, give perfection to a fabric. And the rich merchant, alone, can afford to make long voyages, from which he has slow returns; or give such extensive credits as will tempt those of foreign countries to purchase his commodities in preference to such as are offered by nations who expect more speedy payment. Such is the want of capital in France, that no manufacturer has any quantity of goods on hand to answer an immediate demand; and, of course, no foreign merchant can rely upon the certainty of obtaining such an assortment of goods from the French consignee of his cargo, as will answer his purpose, without either detaining his vessel, or being compelled to take a considerable proportion in articles of very inferior value, picked up from different manufactories; so that if frauds are committed, no one can be charged with them; a circumstance that renders character of little importance to the French mechanic.

To this cause is owing that when a foreign ship, particularly one from a distant nation, disposes of her cargo in France, she has orders to take wines and brandies in return, because these are the only articles that the owner can depend upon having, in time, of the quantity he orders. On the contrary, any species of goods is obtained in England at an hour's warning from a single manufacturer, whose character is at stake if they should not prove equal to the sample. This circumstance will always induce a foreign merchant to prefer dealing for goods of the same nature with a British, rather than with a French factor: and accordingly we find cargoes sold in France, and the money remitted to England to purchase articles that France might furnish, were her manufacturers sufficiently rich to supply them, at a short notice, without compelling the buyer to seek them at different deposits. This evil can only be remedied by an increase of capital in the hands of manufacturers. To show how this capital might be obtained, would lead me too far out of my present subject. But it must be obviously diminished either where a navy is raised at the expense of the manufacturer, or where the capital of the nation is employed in distant countries. The operation of capital in opening new markets is obvious; for nothing is more evident than that merchants of foreign countries, not possessing large capitals, are content to be agents of those who can furnish them goods upon credit. And it is by this means that Britain has found no loss of market in America, in consequence of their having become independent; their immense capital having created a moneyed dependence which has supplied, in a commercial point of view, that which they before derived from the supremacy of her Government. The increase of American capital is now freeing her, in some sort, from that dependence, and enabling her to extend her commercial operations, and even to afford a capital to other nations, who shall know how to estimate the value of the market she affords to the manufactures and luxuries of Europe. It will readily be admitted that transmarine colonies add nothing to the strength of a nation. They are, on the contrary, weak points, that are guarded at great expense of men and money; more particularly where they are placed in warm and unhealthy climates. The simple question, then, is—Has France such a superfluity of capital or people as will justify the establishment of new colonies?

Those that France already possesses in the West Indies and at Cayenne are more than sufficient to supply all the demands of France, and indeed, the demands of all Europe, were they fully cultivated, for those commodities that constitute their staples. But how are they to be cultivated? Experience has proved that the inhabitants of warm climates are never led by their necessities to labor. Force alone can supply those taskmasters (cold and hunger) which nature has placed under northern skies. Hence the necessity of slaves in rendering the West Indies productive. These are only to be procured at a very considerable expense. The Spanish port of St. Domingo was almost uncultivated for want of slaves. It is now in the hands of France; and to render it productive, an immense capital in slaves, in buildings, and in improvements of uncultivated lands, will be necessary. Great capital will also be required to supply the losses that the French part of the island has sustained, to say nothing of the other islands. From whence is this capital to be drawn? Persons that settle in remote and unhealthy climates seldom possess much. It must, then, be drawn either from France, or some other country that possesses superfluous capital. If drawn from France, it must, to a certain degree, injure the manufactures of France at home. It may, however, where the territory is so extremely productive as the French islands are, where the lands are already in a state of cultivation, and the capital advanced will produce an *immediate* interest, be found advantageous, in a national point of view, to encourage the application of French capital to this object. But while the interest of money is high in France, while the interior of the Republic affords a variety of profitable speculations to the capitalist, and while few persons are found possessed of superfluous wealth, it will be difficult to induce many to vest their capital in a distant country, subject to risk from the dishonesty of their agents, and those others which recent transactions will teach them to dread. Foreign capital was once drawn from the United Provinces. The state, however, of the Batavian colonies, and the losses sustained by the war, preclude all hope that much of this will now be applied to ameliorate the French islands. The United States possess an extensive capital in money, and in products necessary for the reestablishment of the islands. Money will not be lent, in large quantities, upon the credit of the planters; but with proper encouragement, there is little doubt that products for which money must otherwise be paid, might be obtained. And the mercantile speculations of the United States will embrace the French islands, when the private and public credit of France shall be reestablished, and experience shall have taught her the futility of attempting to raise a revenue upon foreign commerce, while in fact she is throwing it upon her own citizens.

In St. Domingo 20 per cent is paid on articles introduced by foreigners. This is, indeed, collected from the foreigners; and owing to the mismanagement and frauds which generally prevail in custom-houses at a distance, is a source of very considerable vexation to the trader. But the money is paid by the planter: for it is always added to the price, and even an interest or profit charged upon the duty itself, and a compensation for all the vexations the merchant suffers. What, then, is the effect of this operation but to deduct, at least, one-quarter from the money which the planter has with difficulty drawn from France or elsewhere, and so far to impede the reestablishment of the capital that can alone render the island ultimately productive to France? I say ultimately, for it will be idle to expect that they should compensate the actual expenses of the French Government till years have elapsed. Nay, I will venture to say, that, unless the ports of St. Domingo are thrown open to all vessels bringing necessaries, unless the inhabitants are permitted to buy cheap and to sell dear, by encouraging a competition among buyers and sellers, unless every species of vexation is removed, and every possible assurance given that foreign capitals entrusted to the islands will be perfectly safe, ages will elapse before St. Domingo will cease to drain the wealth and strength of France without offering an equivalent return. It is obvious, then, that if France possessed no other transmarine property than her islands in the West Indies, she would find room to place all the capital she can now, or probably will be able to spare in a long course of years. But, if, in connection with this, we look to her immense territory in the Brazils, to its productions, and the capital it will require to give it the value it is susceptible of; if we add to this the establishments it may be necessary to make in the East Indies in order to enable the French ports to possess all that variety of commodities which invite exchanges and give activity to commerce; we shall find a century, at least, will elapse before France needs such new establishments. But as she, like every other country, possesses a limited capital, the sole object of inquiry should be, where can this capital be best placed? At home? In the islands? At Cayenne? In the East Indies? Or in Louisiana? For it is obvious, that whatever is placed in one is taken from the other. It is equally obvious that the national expense must be increased by the increase of its establishments, and the points of attack and defense be multiplied in the same proportion in case of war.

Many able statesmen have doubted whether, to a country situated as France, any colonies were of use; but it is not my design to enter into those theories. France possesses colonies. She has urged her citizens to remove themselves, and invest their property therein, and she is bound in good faith to retain and protect them. But she is not bound to create new colonies, to multiply her points of defense, and to waste a capital which she needs both at home and abroad. In what view would the possession of Louisiana be useful to France? First, like every other warm climate, it must be cultivated by slaves. The capital employed in purchasing these slaves, or the slaves themselves, would be carried to the islands, if a new market was not open for them. The competition will enhance the price to the planters in the islands, and so far obstruct their speedy reestablishment. When the slaves arrive in Louisiana, they must be employed in the unproductive labor of clearing the immense forests with which that country is covered; a labor ill calculated for slaves, since it requires long habit in the use of the ax, and a strength and activity seldom found in slaves. At all events, they must be maintained, clothed, and fed for years before any profit will result from their labor: how long, may be determined, in some sort, from this fact. When new lands are put out to lease in the Northern or Middle States of America the usual terms are ten years free of rent, and, after that, twelve bushels of wheat per hundred acres forever. It is obvious, then, that the first ten years are considered as years of expense, during which the landlord asks nothing; but, in the Southern States, land can not even be put out on these terms, because there the white inhabitants place a higher value upon their labor, and the clearing lands by slaves involves too great an expense for any man who is not absolute owner of the soil. Who, then, will cultivate Louisiana with slaves? Who among the French citizens will vest a large capital in so precarious a property, with the hope of a distant return? There are, also, circumstances in the situation of Louisiana which render it more difficult.

Louisiana is bounded by an immense wilderness. Slaves, employed in the clearing of forests, will form acquaintances with the natives; and they will, upon every occasion, escape from labor to the indolence of a savage life. It may be asked, why does this not happen in the Southern States of America? First, because none are so far south as to be free from the rigors of winter, which make it difficult for the inhabitants of a warm climate to endure a savage life; and, next, because the Southern States are, in a great measure, surrounded by the sea, and by the mountains which only know a white population, and intercept the communication of the slaves with the waste forests in their rear. But supposing all these difficulties surmounted, what advantage would result to France, in a commercial point of view, from the establishment of this colony; so far as its productions are similar to those of their islands, nothing would be gained, because the islands, well cultivated, are equal to every demand of France, and, indeed, of Europe. The introduction of those from Louisiana would only reduce the price, without adding to the value; and France would find herself compelled, in order to prevent the ruin of those who had vested their capital in the colonies, to imitate the Dutch, who destroy their spices and teas when they find that the quantity debases the value. Commodities not raised in the islands, and which might be found in Louisiana, are only wood, and, perhaps, rice; but it is certain that these productions, when attended with the expense of procuring them in a warm and unhealthy climate, will not compensate the expense, or, at least, furnish the same profit to labor that might be obtained, were it employed as in the islands, in raising more valuable commodities; a proof of which will be found in the United States. It is not from Georgia or South Carolina that the West India islands are supplied with wood, but principally from the Northern States, though wood lands are much scarcer and more valuable with them than to the Southward. The reason is, that the furnishing, lumber, the preparing it for the market, the mills necessary for that purpose, all require the labor of free hands content to work for a small profit.

Though it may seem paradoxical, I will venture to say that it is not the interest of France to supply herself with wood, even if she could do it from Louisiana: and that, for two reasons. The lumber supplied to her islands by the Northern States is paid for in molasses, and a small quantity of taffia. The first costs nothing to the planter, being an otherwise useless product of his sugar; and the second a trifling expense in the distillation. If these were not consumed in America, the molasses would absolutely be thrown away, (as it was when the United States were British colonies,) because the commerce of France offers no other market for it. The islands may then be truly said to have their lumber from the United States for nothing. If, on the contrary, an establishment was made in Louisiana for the purpose of furnishing lumber, all the expense of such an establishment to the nation, together with all the labor employed in cutting the wood, preparing and sending it to market, would be actual loss to the nation, even supposing the woodcutter content to be paid in molasses and rum, because his labor produces nothing to the nation. But it is certain that Louisiana would afford no market for either molasses or rum. The consumption of those is found only in the Northern States of America: the Southern prefer spirits made from grain, apples, and peaches, to that distilled from molasses. The planters, then, supposing their supply of lumber to be exclusively furnished by a French colony in Louisiana, would be compelled to pay for it in money, or in some article of real value. If it was not exclusively furnished, it would not be furnished at all; because the woodcutter in a southern climate could never work so cheap as to compete with the hardy sons of the North. It may be thought that the molasses would find a market in the Northern States, even if not given in return for lumber: but this is not the fact. The only inducement with them to take it is that they get it in return for another commodity for which they have little other market. Let the islands refuse to take the wood of the Northern States, and they will instantly substitute spirits distilled from grains and apples, for that drawn from molasses: (because, in this case, the price of rum must necessarily rise,) and all commerce between the islands will stop, except for articles of provision, in return for which they will only take money, or what will produce money at a foreign market. The second reason why France should not, were it even in her power, seek her supply of lumber from a colony in Louisiana, is, that, in case of a war, supposing Britain to maintain her naval superiority, those supplies would be rendered extremely precarious. Nor would the want of them be easily supplied from the United States; for having, during peace, given up that branch of commerce, (and the persons employed in it having turned their attention to other objects, and the mills created for sawing the lumber having gone to decay,) it would not be easily reestablished on the breaking out of a war; the calamities of which would by this means fall doubly hard upon the islands.

In a commercial point of view, then, it is obvious that the colonization of Louisiana would be injurious to France; because it would divert a capital that might be more usefully employed in her other colonies; because that capital would be unproductive for many years; and because, when it became productive to the individual, it would add nothing to the mass of national wealth, but merely lower the price of commodities supplied by the West Indies, and lessen the profits of labor. It may, however, be supposed that the possession of Louisiana would afford an additional market to French manufactures, and so far compensate the nation for the expense of the establishment. This question is worthy of examination: and the supply or consumption of French fabrics must have a reference either to the free population, or to that of the slaves. If the free population is to be supplied by emigration from France, it will consist of that class of people who could not only maintain themselves in France, but add something to its wealth by their labor; for France is not overstocked with inhabitants; and, of course, none can emigrate without leaving a void somewhere or some useful labor unperformed. The actual emigrant, then, takes something from the general stock of productive labor in the parent State. He also carries with him a part of the capital, (for he can not go empty-handed,) and he must remain, as I have stated, ten years before he renders his new establishment more than sufficient to support himself. In the meantime, he must live with the utmost economy; for having nothing to give in exchange, he can furnish little from the parent country; and, indeed, the nature of a Southern climate exacts very few of those articles which are necessaries in Europe. There can be no question, then, that, so far as relates to the actual emigrant, the few articles he will require from French looms will not compensate the nation for the loss of his labor: nay, that he will consume so much less in America than he would have done in France, that, besides his labor, the manufacturer that supplied in both countries will be an actual loser by his removal. Black population will contribute still less to aid the manufactures of France, because their consumption is extremely small in the article of clothing. Even in South Carolina it does not amount to more than forty francs a year for each black. In Louisiana, as the winter is less severe, it will be proportionably less. It will consist of cotton, much of it made at home, and much more of it obtained from the United States by an illicit commerce. But if even the whole were brought from France, after deducting the value of the raw material which France must purchase, the whole profit of the French manufacturer and merchant would not exceed thirty livres a head for each slave.

Now, every slave sent to Louisiana will cost the nation one thousand francs; and as this capital should produce at least ten per cent. employed in any species of commerce or manufacture, the whole difference between one hundred francs, the product in France, and thirty francs, drawn from the advantage of clothing him, will be an actual loss to France, for the first ten years, at least, in which they can, (as I have before proved,) at the utmost, do no more than support themselves. As numbers will die in the seasoning, and many will elope, the actual loss to France on every slave imported and employed in Louisiana will be 160 francs per annum. But if the profit resulting from the labor of the same slave, who might have been carried to one of the islands, instead of Louisiana, is added to the account, (and certain it is that all carried to Louisiana are taken from the islands,) it will be found that the actual loss to the nation, in the mis-employment of his labor, will amount to upwards of 600 francs a year, so that the first loss to the nation, on the introduction of one thousand slaves into Louisiana, beyond the first cost of the slaves, will be six hundred thousand francs. It is true, that if peace continues, and the colony, contrary to every reasonable expectation, should flourish, the wealthy planters would consume more French fabrics, but the consumption of the slaves will always be trifling, and their labor absolutely unprofitable; because, as I have before observed, being employed in raising articles that can be better raised in quantities equal to the demand in the islands, and for which the market is limited, they will only, by adding to the quantity, lower the price of those commodities which it is the interest of France, who possesses such productive islands, to keep up. I know an idea prevails that the commodities of France can, by means of the Mississippi, find their way into the western part of the United States. Nothing could give birth to this idea but the most perfect ignorance of the navigation of that river; and of the wants of the inhabitants.

It is certain that the wines of France are ill calculated for so warm a climate as they must pass through to arrive in the Western States, and worse suited to the palates or purses of the inhabitants; both of which are better adapted to their own liquors, cider, beer, whisky, and peach brandy; the last of which, with age, is superior to the best brandy of France. Instead, then, of receiving these articles from France, through Louisiana, they will more probably supply the colony with them. Glass, or earthenware, as they have all the materials on hand, they make for themselves, in all the back countries of America. The consumption of china is exceedingly small, and, were it greater, the French china is too dear to enter into competition with that of the East Indies. Bulky articles in iron are also made among themselves; and the hardware of England has such an acknowledged superiority over that of France, that none of the latter could be vended, were the market open to both. The only articles, then, that could be possibly introduced, would be silks, cambrics, and other light articles of luxury. These, however, will never pass by the way of the Mississippi. The dangerous navigation of the Gulf, the slow and expensive passage up the river against the current, the large capital of the American and British merchants at Philadelphia, and the great improvements that are daily making in the inland canals and roads, will always carry these by land to the Ohio and other rivers, from which they can be transported to every other settlement on cheap and easy terms. It is a well-known fact that dry goods have been carried from Philadelphia to New Orleans by this route, in preference to going thither directly by water. It is chimerical, therefore, to expect to vend the commodities of France, through that channel, when even England, with all her enterprise, her right to the navigation of the Mississippi, and the prejudice of Americans in favor of her fabrics, has never ventured to send her commodities by that channel, well knowing that through Baltimore and Philadelphia they will find an easier entrance.

But should France wish to introduce more bulky articles by this channel, and habituate the inhabitants of the Western States to her wines and to her fabrics, it can only be done by putting New Orleans into their hands, stipulating, at the same time, that it shall ever remain a free port of entry to French ships and French fabrics, subject to no greater duties than those paid by American ships. This will, at once, interest the American merchants settled in New Orleans, in their commerce, turn their capital from England to France, and give the latter all the advantages of the island, without the expense of maintaining it; and the money acquired by the activity of America from the Spanish Government would center in France, because England, not having the same facilities, and paying higher duties, could not supply them upon the same terms. Should France, on the other hand, determine to keep the island, a great part of the commercial capital now in Orleans (which is principally American and British) will, in that case, be moved to such other place as the United States shall fix upon, and this being naturally placed in a state of rivalry to New Orleans, and freed from the vexations that never fail to attend a military Government at a distance from the eye of the sovereign, will, notwithstanding any disadvantage in point of situation, draw after it the commerce that now centers there. The limits settled between Spain and the United States, and lately between the latter and Britain, preclude the inhabitants of Louisiana from any share of the fur trade, which, indeed, never could have been considerable, as the southern furs are of little value; the few deer skins they receive are an object of no moment in a commercial view, as will be found from a view of the exports of New Orleans, even now that the United States Mississippi territory transports through that channel.

In these reflections I have not taken into account the hardships, expenses, and loss of lives, that result from the establishment of new colonies in a marshy country and warm climate, the inroads of savages, the insurrection of slaves, the insubordination of troops, and the abuses of officers when far removed from the superintending eye of the Sovereign; any or all of which may defeat the object, and ruin the establishment. There is, however, one consideration, and that a very important one, that ought to have some weight. Many who carry their families and their capital into Louisiana, finding that land is equally cheap on the American side of the line, will, sometimes from a preference for their form of government, sometimes from caprice, sometimes from pique, or to get rid of the oppression of a military government, (for such that of Louisiana must necessarily be,) remove to the territory of the United States, even in time of peace. In case of a war between France and Spain, this desire will be general; because, supposing Britain to maintain her naval superiority, (which I have upon a former occasion shown that she will, unless the commercial system of France shall be much more liberal than it now is,) the mouth of the Mississippi will be blocked up and the planters of the French Colony be reduced to the utmost distress, while those of the United States will acquire advantages from the war. In this case, a great proportion of the capital that France shall place in Louisiana will be transferred to the United States, where farms ready cleared may be purchased at half the price at which a French planter can clear his, owing to the dexterity of American woodsmen, who have been educated to the use of the ax, and acquired that strength in the muscles of the arm, which is unattainable by men who have been brought up to other employments. Past experience has evinced the truth of these observations. Louisiana, though settled near a century, has flourished neither in the hands of Spain nor of France; and, at this moment, at least half the trade of Orleans is carried on upon the capital of citizens of the United States, under the faith of their treaty with Spain. When France shall establish a rival colony there, this will be removed to such other place on the Mississippi as it shall be the policy of the United States to encourage.

If, in a commercial view, the settlement of Louisiana shall not be advantageous to France, but, on the contrary, really injurious, by diverting her capital from more important objects; in a political one, it will be found still more inconsistent with her interests. To France, considered either as a maritime or a commercial nation, the United States are of the last importance. On the first subject, I have, upon a former occasion, expressed my sentiments fully. On the latter, there can be no doubt that an agricultural nation, whose industry enables them to purchase with the product of their raw materials the luxuries and fabrics of Europe, and whose habits and pursuits prevent them from manufacturing for themselves, must offer an important market to the inhabitants of the Old World. In this view the trade of the United States is considered as extremely valuable to Britain. But France, when her manufactures shall attain the perfection of which they are susceptible, and her trade be placed upon the proper foundation, presents a much greater variety of subjects for the support of this commerce than Britain. From the last, America receives only the product of her looms and her forges. From the first, she will not only take these, but aid her agriculture by the purchase of her wines, her oils, and her brandies; while, on the other hand, France affords a better market than Britain to many of the products of the United States. These circumstances, and the relative position of France, which precludes all idea of danger or rivalship, either by sea or by land, between her and the United States, has made them view her as a natural ally, and consider the measure of her power as an additional pledge for the safety of their commerce and their future tranquillity. They have done homage to the wisdom of those statesmen who, at the end of a successful war, conceived it more advantageous to France to insure the lasting friendship of the United States, than to acquire a territory which might excite their jealousy, and throw them back into the hands of the nation from whom they had but just aided to liberate them.

I am aware of the delicacy of touching upon the political evils that may result to France and to the United States from the former possessing itself of New Orleans and the Floridas, lest, on the one hand, I should leave unsaid what truth requires to be spoken, and, on the other, give umbrage by freedom which haughty spirits may construe into menace. Feeling myself, however, a citizen of one of these States, and warmly attached to the other, I trust that those into whose hands this shall be placed, will duly appreciate my motives in endeavoring to remove all ground of controversy between nations formed to aid each other; and, while they believe me sufficiently acquainted with the resources of my own country, not to dread the power of any European nation, they will think me equally incapable of so ridiculous an idea as that of menacing a Government before whose power united Europe has bowed. I have observed that France and the United States are so happily placed with respect to each other, as to have no point of collision. They can mutually aid, without having the smallest temptation to injure, each other. And as there is no nation at present on the globe whose consumption offers such encouragement to foreign manufactures as that of the United States; as this consumption is rapidly increasing; as they have the means of establishing a navy whenever their situation shall render it necessary, how strong, how powerful, should the inducement be that compels France to lose these advantages, and convert a natural and warm ally into a jealous and suspicious neighbor, and, perhaps, in the progress of events, into an open enemy!

Experience has evinced that no two nations can border upon each other, without having the spirit of rivalry excited; and if this is true with respect to neighboring nations, it will be found to apply more forcibly to the Colony, of a great and powerful nation placed at a distance from home, and a Sovereign adjoining such nation. The reason is obvious. Where two nations join each other, everything passes under the eye of the Sovereign; and differences may be accommodated as soon as they arise; but when the Governor of a Colony, relying for protection from home, is guilty of an act of hostility, the wound festers before the physician can be called in. The offended Sovereign, will presume that the officer will meet with support, the greater as his nation is more powerful; will endeavor to anticipate the hostilities it dreads; it will recriminate; and the nations will be plunged into a war before explanations can take place. If there is a situation in the world that would lead to these melancholy consequences, it would be that of France in possession of New Orleans. It blocks up the great outlet to a great number of the American States, and to a very extensive and growing population. On this island a military government will be established. The commander and his troops, justly elated with the glory of their nation, will look down upon surrounding people. Commerce will be despised, and those who practice it be subjected to the despotism of men who will seek a compensation for their privations in being sent to a distant country and unhealthy climate, in the acquisition of wealth. The Colony itself affords no legitimate sources for this, but those which arise gradually from commerce and agriculture, equally ill suited to the military character. No vigilance on the part of the parent country can control the oppressions that will be practiced by men at such a distance; nor will the ardent spirits of the new settlers in States that border on the Mississippi, in many cases, be sufficiently controlled, (even by their own Government,) to prevent their endeavors to avenge themselves, rather than to wait the tardy justice that they may hope for from diplomatic representations. The resentments of the people will be sharpened against each other; the ties of friendship will be broken, and the Government of the United States, which always partakes of the feelings of the people, will find itself unavoidably placed in such a situation as to change its connexion, and to guard against the supposed hostility of its old ally, by forming cautionary connexions with Britain, who will court their alliance and stimulate their resentments against France; because by this connexion she will hope to retain the commerce of America, which she almost exclusively possesses, give security to her Colonies, and, in case of war, facilitate her attempts to conquer the French islands; and, above all, prevent that commercial and maritime union between France and the United States, on which alone France can hope to engraft a naval superiority. It may be asked why these jealousies, that I appear so greatly to apprehend with respect to France, do not prevail with respect to Britain in possession of Canada.

First, because Britain has, very prudently, separated her territory by a natural boundry, which keeps the inhabitants of the respective nations from coming into contact. While she held posts on the south side of the lakes, the United States viewed her with jealousy, and there is no sort of doubt that hostilities and national hatred would have been the consequences of her retaining them, when the American population in their neighborhood had increased; symptoms of which had frequently been exhibited before they were relinquished. Second, because the natural export of the United States being by their own rivers, there is no communication of any moment between them and Canada; but, thirdly, because Upper Canada is principally settled by emigrants from the United States, who, in case of a rupture, would probably join them if the spirit of the American Government did not prohibit an extension of their limits.

And, after all, what advantages, political or commercial, can France obtain by the possession of New Orleans and the east side of the Mississippi, that can compensate for the losses she will sustain in both respects, by placing herself in a state of rivalry with the United States? The Floridas are a narrow slip of very barren lands, absolutely indefensible in case of a rupture, and which will require more than they are worth in guards, garrisons, and Indian subsidies; and however valuable New Orleans may be to the United States, it will be of little value to France, when the foreign capital shall be withdrawn from it, or a rival city established by the United States. I find, upon the most careful inquiry, that one-third of the mercantile houses now employed in New Orleans belongs to the citizens of the United States. No sooner shall a military government be established there, than these houses, with all the capital that gives activity to the commerce of New Orleans, will be removed either to such other place as the United States shall receive agreeably to the terms of their treaty with Spain, or to the Natchez, to which any vessel that may enter at New Orleans can be received. Large vessels have already gone from France and unloaded their cargoes there without any difficulty. As the market is always the better the further you advance, there is little doubt that this will become a rival city to that of New Orleans; and when the American capital shall be withdrawn from the latter, when the Government of the United States shall declare it a port free of duties, New Orleans will become of little consequence as a commercial city, and only remain a useless expense to France, and a source of endless jealousies between them and the United States.

The cession of Louisiana is, however, very important to France if she avails herself of it in the only way that sound policy would dictate. I speak of Louisiana proper; in which I do not include the Floridas, presuming that they make no part of the cession. Since, by this cession, she may acquire a right to navigate the Mississippi, and a free trade; and if she knows how to avail herself of this circumstance, by a perfect understanding with the United States, she will find a vent through it for a vast variety of her commodities when she has given the people of the Western States the habit of consuming them, in preference to those they receive from Britain. This can only be done by affording them cheaper. She can only afford them cheaper by interesting the American merchant in their sale, and having the use of his capital, and by engaging the Government of the United States to give them a preference. These objects can only be attained by a cession of New Orleans to the United States, with a reservation of a right of entry, at all times, free of any other duties than such as are exacted from the vessels of the United States; together with a right to navigate the Mississippi. This will give her ships an advantage over those of every other nation, will retain and increase the capital of New Orleans, from which her supplies for her islands will be purchased on the easiest terms, will carry the fabrics of France into all the Western territory, which the United States will have no interest in checking, as all rivalry between the two nations would then be removed. France will then command the respect, without exciting the fear of the two nations whose friendship is most important to her commerce, and to the preservation of her islands; and all this without the expense of establishments that would drain the National Treasury, and divert the national capital from its proper objects; while, on the other hand, should France retain New Orleans, and endeavor to colonize Louisiana, she will render herself an object of jealousy to Spain, the United States and Britain, who will not only discourage her commerce, but compel her to make expensive establishments for the security of her rights.

In reasoning upon this subject, I have confined myself to such observations as obviously presented themselves, without seeking any of those subtleties which might serve to mislead the judgment. I have candidly exposed the plainest facts, in the simplest language. If ever they are opposed, it will be by a contrary course. Eloquence and sophistry may reply to and may obscure them; but time and experience will evince their truth.

[Extract.]

Mr. Livingston to the Secretary of State.

PARIS, *August 16, 1802.*

I informed you in my last letter that I found some relaxation on the subject of the Floridas in my last conversation with the Spanish Minister. I have reason to think that within these few days they have come to a settlement with France on that subject. What it is I can not precisely say; but I presume it is whatever France wishes it to be. I find all the old French maps mark the river Perdido as the boundary between Florida and Louisiana. It is possible that this may have been insisted upon. If so, the remainder was hardly worth the keeping. Whatever it is, the project of taking possession has resumed a certain degree of activity. General Victor is appointed. He is to have under him a General of Division, two Generals of Brigade, and three thousand men only. No more than two millions of francs are allowed to this service; so that they must starve or find resources in the country. Saturday the General was all day with the Minister of Marine, arranging the inferior appointments to be submitted to the First Consul. I have been pressing, for some time past, with everybody that I thought could have any influence in this business. And, as I have been happy enough to convince most of them, I do not absolutely despair, though I am much discouraged from this last arrangement. The same silence is observed by the Minister. I can get him to tell me nothing. I shall see him this morning again, and if I can not induce him to speak on the subject more plainly than he has done, I will put in a note insisting on our claims under the Spanish Treaty, and demanding an explicit recognition of them. On this I believe there will be little difficulty, as they have always agreed that the cession must be subject to the restrictions under which Spain held the territory. There are obvious symptoms of ill humor between this country and Britain, and I think it will not be long before they assume a serious aspect. Good may arise out of this evil, if it should happen.

Mr. Livingston to the Secretary of State.

PARIS, *August 19, 1802*

SIR: I write in haste, in hopes that this may overtake Mr. Lyle, and correct an error in my last. Notwithstanding the appointment of General Victor, and several other officers for Louisiana, among others a comptroller of the forests, no prefect is yet appointed. Nor is the difference relative to the Floridas settled. Spain insists that they are not ceded; and I have certain information that two days ago the Minister of Marine wrote to the Minister of Foreign Affairs that without the Floridas there could be no Louisiana. Nothing shall be neglected on my part to keep up this difference; for, while it lasts, there will, I believe, be no expedition; and time and change may work in our favor.

I am, sir, etc.,

R. R. L.

Mr. Livingston to the Secretary of State.

PARIS, *September 1, 1808 (?)*.

SIR: I yesterday made several propositions to the Minister on the subject of Louisiana. He told me frankly, that every offer was premature; that the French Government had determined to take possession first; so that you must consider the business as absolutely determined on. The armament is what I have already mentioned, and will be ready in about six weeks. I have every reason to believe the Floridas are not included. They will, for the present, at least, remain in the hands of Spain. There never was a Government in which less could be done by negotiation than here. There is no people, no Legislature, no counsellors. One man is everything. He seldom asks advice, and never hears it unasked. His Ministers are mere clerks; and his Legislature and counsellors parade officers. Though the sense of every reflecting man about him is against this wild expedition, no one dares to tell him so. Were it not for the uneasiness it excites at home, it would give me none; for I am persuaded that the whole will end in a relinquishment of the country, and transfer of the capital to the United States. Their islands call for much more than France can ever furnish. The extreme hauteur of this Government to all around them will not suffer peace to be of long continuance. The French Minister at Lisbon, it is said, is coming home without taking leave. England is very sour; the debts due the Northern Powers unpaid, as well as ours, though their justice is admitted. Helvetia is still in arms; the little Cantons not acceding to the new form of Government.

I propose to make an excursion of about fifteen days into the Low Countries, as I find nothing pressing at this moment here that I can forward by my stay.

I am, sir, etc.,

R. R. L.

President Jefferson to Mr. Livingston.

WASHINGTON, *October 10, 1802*.

DEAR SIR,—The departure of Madame Brugnard for France furnishes me a safe conveyance of a letter, which I cannot avoid embracing, although I have nothing particular for the subject of it. It is well, however, to be able to inform you, generally, through a safe channel, that we stand completely corrected of the error, that either the government or the nation of France has any remains of friendship for us. The portion of that country which forms an exception, though respectable in weight, is weak in numbers. On the contrary, it appears evident, that an unfriendly spirit prevails in the most important individuals of the government, towards us. In this state of things, we shall so take our distance between the two rival nations, as, remaining disengaged till necessity compels us, we may haul finally to the enemy of that which shall make it necessary. We see all the disadvantageous consequences of taking a side, and shall be forced into it only by a more disagreeable alternative; in which event, we must countervail the disadvantages by measures which will give us splendor and power, but not as much happiness as our present system. We wish, therefore, to remain well with France. But we see that no consequences, however ruinous to them, can secure us with certainty against the extravagance of her present rulers. I think, therefore, that while we do nothing which the first nation on earth would deem crouching, we had better give to all our communications with them a very mild, complaisant, and even friendly complexion, but always independent. Ask no favors, leave small and irritating things to be conducted by the individuals interested in them, interfere ourselves but in the greatest cases, and then not push them to irritation. No matter at present existing between them and us is important enough to risk a breach of peace; peace being indeed the most important of all things for us, except the preserving an erect and independent attitude. Although I know your own judgment leads you to pursue this line identically, yet I thought it just to strengthen it by the concurrence of my own. * * *

[Extract.]

James Madison, Secretary of State, to Robert R. Livingston, Minister to France.

DEPARTMENT OF STATE, *October 15, 1802.*

The suspense which has taken place in relation to Louisiana and the Floridas is favorable to the efforts for diverting the French Government from its unwise project. Whether we regard the sentiments prevailing in this country on the subject, or the striking tendencies of the project itself, no pains ought to be spared for putting an end to it. If the occasion can be so improved as to obtain for the United States, on convenient terms, New Orleans and Florida, the happiest of issues will be given to one of the most perplexing of occurrences. I postpone more particular remarks on this subject until the President shall know the impressions on the French Councils, resulting from the views of it to which you will be led by the despatches, of which Mr. Dupont was the bearer.

President's Message.

GENTLEMEN OF THE HOUSE OF REPRESENTATIVES:

I now transmit a report from the Secretary o State, with the information requested in your resolution of the 17th instant.

In making this communication I deem it proper to observe that I was led by the regard due to the rights and interests of the United States, and to the just sensibility of the portion of our fellow-citizens more immediately affected by the irregular proceeding at New Orleans, to lose not a moment in causing every step to be taken which the occasion claimed from me; being equally aware of the obligation to maintain, in all cases, the rights of the nation, and to employ, for that purpose, those just and honorable means which belong to the character of the United States.

TH. JEFFERSON.

DECEMBER 22, 1802.

Report of the Secretary of State to the President.

DEPARTMENT OF STATE, *December 21, 1802.*

The Secretary of State, to whom the resolution of the House of Representatives of the United States of the 17th instant was referred by the President, has the honor to enclose to him the letters and communications annexed, from the Governor of the Mississippi Territory, the Governor of Kentucky, and from William E. Hulings, formerly appointed Vice-Consul of the United States at New Orleans. In addition to this information on the subject of the resolution, it is stated, from other sources, that, on the 29th of October, American vessels from sea remained under the prohibition to land their cargoes; and that the American produce carried down the Mississippi could be landed only on paying a duty of 6 per cent; with an intimation that this was a temporary permission. Whether, in these violations of treaty, the officer of Spain at New Orleans has proceeded with or without orders from his Government, can not as yet be decided by direct and positive testimony; but it ought not to be omitted in the statement here made, that other circumstances concur with the good faith and friendship otherwise observed by His Catholic Majesty, in favoring a belief that no such orders have been given.

JAMES MADISON.

Mr. Hulings's Statement.

NEW ORLEANS, *October 18, 1802.*

SIR: I have the honor to enclose you an extract from a decree this day published by the Intendant of the Province of Louisiana, by which you will see that the Americans are no longer permitted to deposit their merchandise in this city. No information of any other place being appropriated for an American deposit is yet given; nor have we any reason to hope that the Government has such place in view. The season for the cotton from the Natchez, and other produce from the settlements higher up to come down, approaches. The difficulties and risks of property that will fall on the citizens of the United States, if deprived of their deposit, are incalculable; their boats being so frail, and so subject to be sunk by storms, that they can not be converted into floating stores, to wait the arrival of sea vessels to carry away their cargoes.

The port is also this day shut against foreign commerce, which can only be carried on by Spanish subjects, in Spanish bottoms.

I am, sir, with greatest respect,

WM. E. HULINGS.

Hon. JAMES MADISON, *Secretary of State.*

[Extract.]

Proclamation of Juan Ventura Morales, Intendant at New Orleans.

As long as it was necessary to tolerate the commerce of neutrals which is now abolished, it would have been prejudicial to the province had the Intendant, in compliance with his duty, prevented the deposit in this city, of the property of the Americans, granted to them by the twenty-second article of the Treaty of Friendship, Limits, and Navigation, of the 27th of October, 1795, during the limited term of three years.

With the publication of the ratification of the Treaty of Amiens and the reestablishment of the communication between the English and Spanish subjects, that inconvenience has ceased. Considering that the twenty-second article of the said treaty takes from me the power of continuing the toleration which necessity required; since, after the fulfillment of the said term, this Ministry can no longer consent to it without an express order of the King; therefore, and without prejudice to the exportation of what has been admitted in proper time, I order, that from this date, the privilege which the Americans had of importing and depositing their merchandise and effects in this capital, shall be interdicted: and, that the foregoing may be publicly known, and that nobody may allege ignorance, I order it to be published in the usual places, copies to be posted up in the public *sitioes;* and that the necessary notice be given of it to the officers of finance, the administrator of rents, and otherwise, as may be necessary.

The present being given under my hand, and countersigned by the underwritten notary of finance *pro tempore*, in the office of Intendancy of New Orleans, October 16, 1802.

JUAN VENTURA MORALES.

By order of the Intendant:
PEDRO PEDESCLAUX.

Governor Claiborne to the Secretary of State.

NEAR NATCHEZ, *October 18, 1802.*

SIR: I have the honor to enclose you a letter which I last evening received from Mr. William E. Hulings, together with a translation of an extract from a publication made by Juan Ventura Morales, Intendant of the Province of Louisiana, etc., dated October 16, 1802. These dispatches announce that the port of New Orleans is shut against foreign commerce, and also the American deposit.

Not understanding from the Intendant's proclamation whether or not another place on the banks of the Mississippi had been assigned by His Catholic Majesty, (in conformity with our treaty with Spain,) for "an equivalent establishment," I have, by letter, (a copy of which is inclosed), requested information upon this point, from the Governor-General of the Province of Louisiana: when his answer is received it shall be forwarded to you.

The late act of the Spanish Government at New Orleans has excited considerable agitation at Natchez and its vicinity. It has inflicted a severe wound on the agricultural and commercial interests of this Territory, and will prove no less injurious to all the Western country.

There being at present an interruption in the post between this Territory and Tennessee, and supposing it of importance that the Government should be early apprized of the late event at New Orleans, I have forwarded this letter by express to Nashville, where it will be deposited in the mail.

I am, sir, etc.,

WM. C. C. CLAIBORNE.

Hon. SECRETARY OF STATE, U. S.

Mr. Hulings to Governor Claiborne.

NEW ORLEANS, *October 18, 1802.*

SIR: I have to announce to you that this day the port is shut against foreign commerce, and not against foreign commerce only, but against the American deposit in this city. In the decree posted up in the public places, no mention is made of any other place appointed for a deposit. You will use this information as you may think proper.

I am, with great respect, etc.,

Wm. E. Hulings.

Wm. C. C. Claiborne,
 Governor Mississippi Territory.

Governor Claiborne to the Governor-General of Louisiana.

Natchez, *October 28, 1802.*

Sir: I was this day informed that, in a proclamation issued on the 16th instant by the Intendant of the Province of Louisiana, it was announced, "That the citizens of the United States should no longer be permitted to deposit their merchandises and effects in the port of New Orleans."

Information of an event so immediately interesting to the citizens of the United States led me to peruse attentively "the Treaty of Friendship, Limits, and Navigation between the United States of America and the King of Spain," and, upon adverting to the twenty-second article, I found it expressly declared that, "His Catholic Majesty will permit the citizens of the United States, for the space of three years from this time, to deposit their merchandises and effects in the port of New Orleans, and to export them from thence, without paying any other duty than a fair price for the hire of the stores; and His Majesty promises either to continue this permission, if he finds, during that time, that it is not prejudicial to the interests of Spain, or, if he should not agree to continue it, then he will assign to them, on another part of the banks of the Mississippi, an equivalent establishment." I have here quoted the words of the treaty, and find them too explicit to reqire comment, or to admit of a doubtful construction.

If, therefore, His Catholic Majesty has discontinued his permission to the citizens of the United States to deposit their merchandises and effects at the port of New Orleans, will your Excellency be good enough to inform me whether any, and what, other place on the banks of the Mississippi has been assigned (in conformity to the treaty) for "an equivalent establishment?" The subject of this inquiry is so interesting to the commerce of the United States and to the welfare of her citizens, that I must request your excellency to favor me with an early answer.

Accept assurances of my great respect and high consideration.

Wm. C. C. Claiborne.

His Excellency Manuel de Salvado,
 Governor-General of Louisiana.

The Governor of Kentucky to the President of the United States.

STATE OF KENTUCKY,
Frankfort, November 30, 1802.

SIR: Two days ago, I received the enclosed letters from Dr. James Speed, and Meeker & Co., from New Orleans, together with a copy of a proclamation issued by Juan Ventura Morales, Intendant of the Spanish Government of Louisiana, and which I do myself the honor to enclose for your information. The citizens of this State are very much alarmed and agitated, as this measure of the Spanish Government will, if not altered, at one blow, cut up the present and future prosperity of their best interests by the roots. To you, sir, they naturally turn their eyes, and on your attention to this important subject their best hopes are fixed. Permit me to request you will give me information on this business as soon as you can say, with certainty, what we may rely on; and let my solicitude on this occasion be my apology for this request.

With sentiments of respect, etc., JAMES GARRARD.

Read in Senate February 23, 1803, by Mr. White, of Delaware.

ADVERTISEMENT.

Under date of the 16th instant (December) the Intendant-General of these provinces tells me that the citizens of the United States of America can have no commerce with His Majesty's subjects—they only having the free navigation of the river for the exportation of the fruits and produce of their establishments to foreign countries, and the importation of what they may want from them. As such I charge you, so far as respects you, to be zealous and vigilant, with particular care, that the inhabitants neither purchase nor sell anything to the shipping, flat-bottomed boats, barges, or any other smaller vessels that may go along the river, destined for the American possessions, or proceeding from them, that they shall be informed of it, for their due compliance of the same.

CARLOS DE GRANDPREE.
BATON ROUGE, *December 22, 1802.*

The foregoing is a translation of the original, directed to me by his Lordship Carlos de Grandpree, Colonel of the Royal Armies, and Governor of Baton Rouge.

J. O. CONNER,
Cyndic of Fourth District.

BATON ROUGE, *December 27, 1802.*

Mr. Livingston to the President of the United States.

PARIS, *October 28, 1802.*

DEAR SIR: Nothing very important having occurred for some time past, I have not thought it necessary to trouble you, particularly as I concluded that you would, for a time, have quitted the seat of Government, and sought repose from the fatigues of politics.

While the union between France and Russia subsists, the discontents which almost every nation in Europe feels at the extreme loftiness of the first will be suppressed. But as fear and not affection occasions the suppression, they are ready to break out on the first favorable moment. Many think that moment not very distant. Great changes have taken place in the Administration: Wormzoff is known to be inclined to Britain; and I find that the change occasions considerable sensation here, not only among the foreign Ministers, but among those of France. One effect of it has been to send off Andriotte, who has hitherto been retained till Lord Whitworth arrived, even though formal notice had long since been given that he was to go in eight days. Britain is seriously dissatisfied; and, indeed, has some reason to complain; several of her vessels which put in here, (as is said by stress of weather,) having been detained, and Mr. Murray's representations treated with neglect.

The affairs of Helvetia have also excited great uneasiness in England, where all parties seem to concur in wishing to oppose some barriers to the power of France. The British republicans are disgusted with the changes which have taken place here; while the royalists dread the stability that the Government has assumed in the hands of the First Consul. The mercantile and manufacturing interests, who looked to peace for the renewal of the Treaty of Commerce, from which they derived such advantages, are sore at the severity with which their commerce is interdicted here. You will accordingly find, by the British papers, that both those of the majority and minority teem with abuse on France, and blow aloud the trumpet of discord.

By the Treaty of Madrid, you recollect that the reigning Duke of Parma and Placentia was to renounce them in favor of France; in consideration of which, his heir was to have the kingdom of Etruria. This he has constantly refused to do, and has lately died without making any renunciation. The Spanish Ambassador here has been called upon to complete the treaty. He replied that he had no powers. And General Bournonville has gone express to Spain to effect this object—the King of Etruria being now Duke of Parma. Whether he will prefer the Crown he now holds to his hereditary dominions I know not; but I think he must submit to what is dictated here, or risk the loss of both.

The Mississippi business, though all the officers are appointed, and the army under orders, has met with a check. The army under orders is obstructed for the moment. Events may possibly arise, of which we may avail ourselves.

I had, two days ago, a very interesting conversation with Joseph Bonaparte, having put into his hands a copy of the memoir on Louisiana, which I sent the Secretary of State. I took occasion to tell him that the interest he had taken in settling the differences between our respective countries had entitled him to our confidence, and that I should take the liberty to ask his advice in matters that were likely to disturb the harmony that subsisted between our respective Republics. He seemed pleased at the compliment, and told me that he would receive with pleasure any communication I could make; but as he would not wish to appear to interfere with the Minister, he begged my communication might be informal and unsigned—exactly what I wished, because I should act with less danger of committing myself, and of course with more freedom. He added, you must not, however, suppose my power to serve you greater than it actually is; my brother is his own counsellor; but we are good brothers, he hears me with pleasure, and as I have access to him at all times, I have an opportunity of turning his attention to a particular subject that might otherwise be passed over. I then asked him whether he had read my notes on Louisiana. He told me that he had, and that he had conversed upon the subject with the First Consul, who, he found, had read them with attention; that his brother had told him that he had nothing more at heart than to be upon the best terms with the United States. I expressed to him my apprehensions of the jealousies that would naturally be excited from their vicinity, and the impossibility of preventing abuses in a military government established at so great a distance from home.

Wishing to know with certainty whether the Floridas were included, (which, however, I had pretty well ascertained before,) I told him that the only cause of difference that might arise between us, being the debt and Louisiana, I conceived that both might be happily and easily removed by making an exchange with Spain, returning them Lousiana, retaining New Orleans, and giving the latter and the Floridas for our debt.

He asked me whether we should prefer the Floridas or Louisiana? I told him that there was no comparison in their value, but that we had no wish to extend our boundary across the Mississippi, or give color to the doubts that had been entertained of the moderation of our views; that all we sought was security, and not extension of territory. He replied, that he believed any new cession on the part of Spain would be extremely difficult; that Spain had parted with Trinidad and Louisiana with great reluctance. I have, however, reason to think that Bournonville is instructed to effect this object, not, however, with a view to my project, but with intention to procure for France some port in the Gulf, from which they think they may secure their own and annoy the British commerce; so that, if we should, contrary, to our hopes, make any bargain with them, I fear that East Florida will not be included. However, everything is yet in air; and I doubt much, considering the present state of things in Europe, whether Spain will make any exchange that will give France a command of the Gulf. Though this is a favorite object with France, she may not, in the present state of things in Europe, think it prudent to press too hard. It is time that she should acquire some character for moderation.

The First Consul is gone to Rouen, and is to be back by the 18th Brumaire. The British fear he means to examine the coast. The prospect of a rupture grows more serious. I can tell you, with certainty, that a remonstrance, in pretty strong terms, has been presented by her Minister, on the subject of the Consul's interference in the affairs of Helvetia. How it will be received I know not; but I think it would not have been made if it had not been the intention of Britain to seek a quarrel.

I refer you to the Secretary of State for information on our particular affairs.

Lafayette's situation demands the aid of our country. * * * He was ready to sacrifice everything for us, and we owe him something effectual, I must pray you to get Mr. Randolph, or some other leading member of Congress, to patronize him. Our gratitude will do us honor abroad, and not be unpopular at home.

I have the honor to be, etc.,

R. R. LIVINGSTON.

TH. JEFFERSON, Esq.,
    President of the United States.

[Extract.]

Robert R. Livingston, Minister to France, to James Madison, Secretary of State.

PARIS, *November 2, 1802.*

My letter to the President, sent by the way of England, will show you that the business of Louisiana has met with a check, though I fear it will soon be resumed; and that troops will go out this Autumn, as everything was arranged, and they were under marching orders. Florida is not, as I before told you, included in the cession. You will see in the President's letter my conversation with Joseph Bonaparte; this I shall have a convenient opportunity to renew, as he has promised to give me a shooting party at his country house in a few days. Time may afford circumstances of which we may avail ourselves. I therefore pray you to be explicit in your instructions, and in your replies to some questions that I have asked you relative to this subject in my former letters, since I am at present wholly unauthorized as to any offers that it would be proper to make; and we certainly do not expect to receive this country, or any interest in it, as a free gift.

Robert R. Livingston, Minister to France, to James Madison, Secretary of State.

PARIS, *November 11, 1802.*

France has cut the knot. The difficulty relative to Parma and Placentia, that stopped the expedition to Louisiana, has ended by their taking possession of the first, as you see by the enclosed paper. Orders are given for the immediate embarkation of troops (two demibrigades) for Louisiana; they will sail in about twenty days from Holland. The Government here will give no answer to my notes on the subject. They will say nothing on that of our limits, or of our right under the Spanish Treaty. Clarke has been presented to General Victor as a merchant from Louisiana. The General did not probably conceal his views, which are nothing short of taking exactly what they find convenient. When asked what they meant to do as to our right of *entrepôt*, he spoke of the treaty as waste paper; and the prefect did not know that we had such right, though it had been the subject of many conversations with the Minister, and of three different notes. The sum voted for this service is two millions and a half; as to the rest, they expect to compel the people to support the expenses of the Government, which will be very heavy, as the number of the officers, civil and military, with their suits, is great; and they are empowered to draw: so that the first act of the new Government will be the oppression of their people and our commerce. I believe you may add to this an early attempt to corrupt our people, and, if I may judge by the temper that the General will carry with him, an early attempt upon the Nachez, which they consider as the rival of New Orleans. If you look back to some of my letters on this subject, you will see my opinion of the necessity of strengthening ourselves by force and ships at home, and by alliance abroad. No prudence will, I fear, prevent hostilities ere long; and perhaps the sooner their plans develop themselves the better. In a letter to the President, sent by way of England, I mention a conversation with Joseph Bonaparte, from which I derive some small hopes; but they are of no avail now that the expedition is determined upon. I had yesterday written you a long letter upon the general state of our affairs, but, having no one to copy it, and being anxious to give you this intelligence as early as possible, I confine myself to this single object, lest I should miss the ship which is about to sail from Havre.

I am, dear sir, with the most respectful consideration, your most obedient servant,

R. R. LIVINGSTON.

JAMES MADISON, *Secretary of State.*

Robert R. Livingston, Minister to France, to James Madison, Secretary of State.

PARIS, *November 11, 1802.*

SIR: After writing mine of this date, I called on the Minister and insisted on some positive answer to my notes. He told me that he was expressly instructed by the First Consul to give me the most positive assurances that the treaties we had entered into with Spain or them, relative to Louisiana, should be strictly observed. When I expressed my surprise that their officers should not be informed on that head, though on the eve of departing, he assured me that they would be furnished with copies of the treaties, and directed to conform strictly to them. I asked why these assurances were not given to me in the usual form, by replying to my notes? He said that he hoped that there would be no difficulty on that head, when the Consul should arrive (he is now absent). I have stated this that you might, by comparing this conversation with the contents of the letter, and the information derived from Clarke's conversation with the General, draw your own inferences. I shall endeavor to-day to see J. Bonaparte, though he has all along assured me that it was the Consul's intention to cultivate our friendship, and by no means to do anything that would endanger it. It will, however, be well to be on our guard, and, above all, to re-enforce the Natchez, and to give it every possible commercial advantage. If we can put ourselves in the situation to prevent the danger of hostility, I think we may hope that the dissatisfaction of inhabitants, the disappointment of officers, and the drain of money which the establishment will occasion, will facilitate our views after a very short time.

I am, dear sir, with the most respectful consideration, your most obedient servant,

ROBERT R. LIVINGSTON.

Hon. JAMES MADISON,
Secretary of State.

P. S.—In my letter to the President, I informed him that General Bournonville had gone post to Spain, and that I had reason to think he had it in charge to obtain the Floridas. I know that he went with the greatest speed; accordingly, on his very first conference, he proposed to Spain to relinquish Parma and Placentia for the Floridas. * * * But Spain may be forced to give them, though she should not like the exchange. You see by this how much it is a favorite object with the First Consul, and judge from thence of our prospects.

What effect the news from St. Domingo may have I know not. The army there is reduced to 1,200 effectives. Other particulars you will have more correctly than we have here.

The Consul is still absent, but daily expected. Lord Whitworth is on his way from Calais, and will be here to-morrow.

Robert R. Livingston, Minister to France, to James Madison, Secretary of State.

PARIS, *November 14, 1802.*

In addition to my last, (duplicates enclosed,) I have obtained accurate information of the offer to Spain. It is either to sell them Parma for forty-eight millions of livres, or to exchange it for Florida. You see by this the value they put on Florida. I fear Spain will accede to their proposition. Lord Whitworth has arrived. The affairs of Switzerland are in a train to be settled as France thinks proper; the Diet being dissolved and deputies appointed to come to Paris. Sweden has made a peace with Tripoli, for which she pays one hundred and fifty thousand dollars. The Emperor is not yet satisfied with the indemnities, and there are many symptoms of change in the politics of Russia.

Mr. Madison, Secretary of State, to Charles Pinckney, Minister to Spain.

DEPARTMENT OF STATE, *November 27, 1802.*

A letter from a confidential citizen at New Orleans, a copy of which is enclosed, has just informed us that the Intendant, at that place, by a proclamation, from which an extract is also enclosed, had prohibited the deposit of American effects stipulated by the Treaty of 1795; and, as the letter is interpreted, that the river was also shut against the external commerce of the United States from that port. Whether it be the fact or not that this latter prohibition has also taken place, it is evident that the useful navigation of the Mississippi so essentially depends on a suitable depository for the articles of commerce, that a privation of the latter is equivalent to a privation of both.

This proceeding is so direct and palpable a violation of the Treaty of 1795, that, in candor, it is to be imputed rather to the Intendant solely than to instructions of his Government. The Spanish Minister takes pains to impress this belief, and it is favored by private accounts from New Orleans, mentioning that the Governor did not concur with the Intendant. But, from whatever source the measure may have proceeded, the President expects that the Spanish Government will neither lose a moment in countermanding it, nor hesitate to repair every damage which may result from it. You are aware of the sensibility of our Western citizens to such an occurrence. This sensibility is justified by the interest they have at stake. The Mississippi is to them everything. It is the Hudson, the Delaware, the Potomac, and all the navigable rivers of the Atlantic States, formed into one stream. The produce exported through that channel last year amounted to one million six hundred and twenty-two thousand six hundred and seventy-two dollars from the districts of Kentucky and Mississippi only, and will probably be fifty per cent. more this year, (from the whole Western country. Kentucky alone has exported, for the first half of this year, five hundred and ninety-one thousand four hundred and thirty-two dollars in value,) a great part of which is now, or shortly will be, afloat for New Orleans, and consequently exposed to the effects of this extraordinary exercise of power. Whilst you presume, therefore, in your representations to the Spanish Government that the conduct of its officer is no less contrary to its intentions than it is to its good faith, you will take care to express the strongest confidence that the breach of the treaty will be repaired in every way which justice and a regard for a friendly neighborhood may require.

I have communicated the information received from New Orleans to the Chevalier d'Yrujo, with a view to obtain his immediate interposition, as you will find by the enclosed copy of a letter to him. He readily undertakes to use it with all the effect he can give it by writing immediately on the subject to the local authority at New Orleans. I shall write at the same time to Mr. Hulings, who will enforce, as far as he may have an opportunity, the motives for recalling the unwarrantable prohibitions. It is to be hoped that the Intendant will be led to see the error which he has committed, and to correct it before a very great share of its mischief will have happened. Should he prove as obstinate as he has been ignorant or wicked, nothing can temper the irritation and indignation of the Western country, but a persuasion that the energy of their own Government will obtain from the justice of that of Spain the most ample redress.

It has long been manifest that, whilst the injuries to the United States, so frequently occurring from the colonial officers scattered over our hemisphere, and in our neighborhood, can only be repaired by a resort to their respective Sovereigns in Europe, that it will be impossible to guard against most serious inconveniences. The instance before us strikes with peculiar force, and presents an occasion on which you may advantageously suggest to the Spanish Government the expediency of placing in their Minister on the spot, an authority to control or correct the mischievous proceedings of their colonial officers towards our citizens; without which any one of fifteen or twenty individuals, not always among either the wisest or best of men, may, at any time, threaten the good understanding of the two countries. The distance between the United States and the old continent, and the mortifying delays of explanations and negotiations across the Atlantic on emergencies in our neighborhood, render such a provision indispensable, and it can not be long before all the Governments of Europe, having American colonies, must see the policy of making it.

Extract from the Message of the President of the United States to Congress.

DECEMBER 15, 1802.

The cession of the Spanish province of Louisiana to France, which took place in the course of the late war, will, if carried into effect, make a change in the aspect of our foreign relations, which will doubtless have just weight in any deliberations of the Legislature connected with that subject.

Robert R. Livingston, Minister to France, to James Madison, Secretary of State.

PARIS, *December 20, 1802.*

SIR: I have received your favor by Mde. Broniau, and had, as you will find, anticipated your wishes in finding another manual to the First Consul. The consequence of which is, that I have, at this moment, a very strong memorial under his eye, and some projects which appear to be well received. But the subject is too delicate to treat here; when a safe conveyance offers I shall write to you more at large. The Minister has changed his conduct much for the better, either because of our late difference, or because he suspects that I have another passage to the First Consul. France has not yet got Florida; but there is not much doubt that her negotiations on this subject will succeed, as Parma is a favorite object with Spain. Pray be explicit in the amount of what I may offer, and consider the value of the country—its importance to peace—the expensive establishment it will save, and its intrinsic worth, from the price of the land and actual revenue. I do not, however, mean that you should infer from this that my prospects of obtaining the object are great, because I find, as Mr. Talleyrand told me yesterday, the First Consul *entêté* with this project. But I have made so many converts, that I would wish, in case favorable circumstances should arise, to know how to act. If left to myself I may go beyond the mark. General politics you will collect from the papers I send. I have mentioned that the storm in England will blow over for the present; and the peace will not be lasting. The armament for Louisiana has not yet sailed; the civil officers are yet here, if I am rightly informed by the Minister from whom I had it yesterday.

The necessity of my sending this immediately prevents my adding anything but the assurance of the highest esteem.

I have the honor to be, sir, your most obedient and humble servant,

ROBERT R. LIVINGSTON.

P. S. December 23.—The armament has not yet sailed; Florida not ceded; more hesitation and doubt on the subject than I have yet observed. I have, in a private memoir under the Consul's eye, touched a string that has alarmed them. I can not now explain. The Minister knows nothing of this. Set on foot negotiation fixing our bound with Britain, but by no means conclude until you hear from me that all hope here is lost. It is an important card in my hands, and must, for the present, at least, be somewhat under my control. Do not absolutely despair, though you may have no great reason to hope should New Orleans be possessed by a small force.

This letter goes by the way of England by Mr. Murray, who has not allowed me time to give it you in any better dress. I must wait for some more direct conveyance to write fully to you.

James Madison, Secretary of State, to Robert R. Livingston, Minister to France.

DEPARTMENT OF STATE,
December 23, 1802.

SIR: In the latter end of last month we received information from New Orleans of the interdiction of the deposit there for our merchandise, stipulated by the treaty with Spain, without an equivalent establishment being assigned. A copy of the Intendant's proclamation to that effect is enclosed. Private accounts render it probable that the Governor of the province openly dissented from that act; but private letters, of so late a date as the 29th of October, inform us that it is still enforced. The Legislature of Kentucky have voted a memorial to Congress complaining of it, and they will, probably, be followed by other portions of the Western people. Should it not be revoked before the time for the descent of the boats in the Spring, both the injury and irritation proceeding from it will be greatly increased. The House of Representatives passed a resolution on the 17th of this month, calling for information upon this subject, a copy of which, if it should be printed early enough, will be enclosed. The result of their deliberations can not be anticipated; but I may hazard the remark that, whilst we have no clear foundation on which to impute this infraction to orders from the Spanish Government, it would be contrary to the duty, policy, and character of our own to resort for redress in the first instance to the use of force.

JANUARY 3, 1803.

The delay in the sailing of the British packet, by which this is forwarded, gives an opportunity of adding that, since the date of the above, a letter has been received from Governor Claiborne, of the Mississippi Territory, inclosing one from the Governor of Louisiana, which says that the suspension of the deposit by the Intendant was without orders from the Spanish Government, and that the measure did not accord with his judgment. He observes, also, that he had communicated the proceeding to the Governor of the Havana, who has some kind of superintendence over the authorities at New Orleans. This information strengthens the hope that the irregularity may be corrected before it can have wrought extensive injury to our Mississippi commerce. The occurrence has drawn forth the clearest indications, not only of the sensibility of the Western country with respect to the navigation of the Mississippi, but of the sympathy of their Atlantic fellow-citizens on the subject.

I have the honor to be, etc., JAMES MADISON.

ROBERT R. LIVINGSTON, Esq.

James Madison, Secretary of State, to Charles Pinckney, Minister to Spain.

DEPARTMENT OF STATE, *January 10, 1803.*

SIR: Since my letter of November 27th, on the subject of what had taken place at New Orleans, a letter has been received from the Governor of Louisiana to Governor Claiborne, in which it is stated that the measure of the Intendant was without instructions from his Government, and admitted that his own judgment did not concur with that of the Intendant. You will find, by the printed documents herewith transmitted, that the subject engaged the early and earnest attention of the House of Representatives; and that all the information relating to it possessed by the Executive prior to the receipt of that letter, was reported, in consequence of a call for it. The letter itself has been added to that report; but being confidentially communicated, it does not appear in print; a translation of it, however, is herewith enclosed. You will find, also, that the House has passed a resolution explicitly declaring that the stipulated rights of the United States on the Mississippi will be inviolably maintained. The disposition of many members was to give to the resolution a tone and complexion still stronger. To these proofs of the sensation which has been produced, it is to be added, that representations, expressing the peculiar sensibility of the Western country, are on the way from every quarter of it to the Government. There is, in fact, but one sentiment throughout the Union with respect to the duty of maintaining our rights of navigation and boundary. The only existing difference relates to the degree of patience which ought to be exercised during the appeal to friendly modes of redress.

In this state of things, it is to be presumed that the Spanish Government will accelerate, by every possible means, its interposition for that purpose; and the President charges you to urge the necessity of so doing with as much amicable decision as you can employ. We are not without hopes that the Intendant will yield to the demands which have been made on him: and to the advice which he will have received from the Spanish Minister here. But it will be expected from the justice and good faith of the Spanish Government, that its precise orders to that effect will be forwarded by the quickest conveyance possible. The President wishes, also, that the expedient suggested in the letter above referred to, for preventing similar occurrences and delays, may also be duly pressed on that Government.

I have the honor to be, etc., JAMES MADISON.
CHARLES PINCKNEY, Esq.

President Jefferson to Mr. Monroe.

WASHINGTON, *January 13, 1803.*

DEAR SIR,—I dropped you a line on the 10th, informing you of a nomination I had made of you to the Senate, and yesterday I enclosed you their approbation, not then having time to write. The agitation of the public mind on occasion of the late suspension of our right of deposit at New Orleans is extreme. In the western country it is natural, and grounded on honest motives. In the seaports it proceeds from a desire for war, which increases the mercantile lottery: in the federalists, generally, and especially those of Congress, the object is to force us into war if possible, in order to derange our finances, or if this cannot be done, to attach the western country to them, as their best friend, and thus get again into power. Remonstrances, memorials, &c., are now circulating through the whole of the western country, and signed by the body of the people. The measures we have been pursuing, being invisible, do not satisfy their minds. Something sensible, therefore, has become necessary; and indeed our object of purchasing New Orleans and the Floridas is a measure liable to assume so many shapes, that no instructions could be squared to fit them. It was essential then, to send a minister extraordinary, to be joined with the ordinary one, with discretionary powers; first, however, well impressed with all our views, and therefore qualified to meet and modify to these every form of proposition which could come from the other party. This could be done only in full and frequent oral communications. Having determined on this, there could not be two opinions among the republicans as to the person. You possessed the unlimited confidence of the administration and of the western people; and generally of the republicans everywhere; and were you to refuse to go, no other man can be found who does this. The measure has already silenced the federalists here. Congress will no longer be agitated by them; and the country will become calm fast as the information extends over it. All eyes, all hopes are now fixed on you; and were you to decline, the chagrin would be universal, and would shake under your feet the high ground on which you stand with the public. Indeed, I know nothing which would produce such a shock. For on the event of this mission depend the future destinies of this republic. If we cannot by a purchase of the country, insure to ourselves a course of perpetual peace and friendship with all nations, then as war cannot be distant, it behooves us immediately to be preparing for that course, without, however, hastening it; and it may be necessary (on your failure on the continent) to cross the channel. We shall get entangled in European politics, and figuring more, be much less happy and prosperous. This can only be prevented by a successful issue to your present mission. I am sensible after the measures you have taken for getting into a different line of business, that it will be a great sacrifice on your part, and presents from the season and other circumstances serious difficulties. But some men are born for the public. Nature by fitting them for the service of the human race on a broad scale, has stamped them with the evidences of her destination and their duty.

*　　　*　　　*　　　*　　　*　　　*　　　*　　　*

James Madison, Secretary of State, to Robert R. Livingston, Minister to France.

DEPARTMENT OF STATE, *January 18, 1803.*

SIR: My letters of December 23d and January 3d, communicated the information which had been received at those dates, relating to the violation, at New Orleans, of our treaty with Spain; together with what had then passed between the House of Representatives and the Executive on the subject. I now enclose a subsequent resolution of that branch of the Legislature. Such of the debates connected with it as took place with open doors will be seen in the newspapers; which it is expected will be forwarded by the Collector at New York by the present opportunity. In these debates, as well as in indications from the press, you will perceive, as you would readily suppose, that the cession of Louisiana to France has been associated as a ground of much solicitude with the affair at New Orleans. Such, indeed, has been the impulse given to the public mind by these events, that every branch of the Government has felt the obligation of taking the measures most likely, not only to re-establish our present rights, but to promote arrangements by which they may be enlarged, and more effectually secured. In deliberating on this subject, it has appeared to the President that the importance of the crisis called for the experiment of an extraordinary mission; carrying with it the weight attached to such a measure, as well as the advantage of a more thorough knowledge of the views of the Government, and the sensibility of the people than could be otherwise conveyed.

He has, accordingly, selected for this service, with the approbation of the Senate, Mr. Monroe, formerly our Minister Plenipotentiary at Paris, and lately Governor of the State of Virginia; who will be joined with yourself in commission extraordinary to treat with the French Republic; and with Mr. Pinckney in a like commission to treat, if necessary, with the Spanish Government. The President has been careful, on this occasion, to guard effectually against any possible misconstructions in relation to yourself, by expressing, in his Message to the Senate, his undiminished confidence in the ordinary representation of the United States, and by referring the advantages of the additional mission to considerations perfectly consistent therewith.

Mr. Monroe will be the bearer of the instructions under which you are jointly to negotiate. The object of them will be to procure a cession of New Orleans and the Floridas to the United States; and consequently the establishment of the Mississippi as the boundary between the United States and Louisiana. In order to draw the French Government into the measure, a sum of money will mark part of our propositions; to which will be added, such regulations of the commerce of that river, and of the others entering the Gulf of Mexico, as ought to be satisfactory to France. From a letter, received by the President from the respectable person alluded to in my last, it is inferred, with probability, that the French Government is not averse to treat on those grounds. And such a disposition must be strengthened by the circumstances of the present moment.

I have thought it proper to communicate thus much to you, without waiting for the departure of Mr. Monroe, who will not be able to sail for two weeks, or perhaps more. I need not suggest to you that, in disclosing this diplomatic arrangement to the French Government, and preparing the way for the object of it, the utmost care is to be used in repressing extravagant anticipations of the terms to be offered by the United States, particularly the sum of money to be thrown into the transaction. The ultimatum on this point will be settled before the departure of Mr. Monroe, and will be communicated by him. The sum hinted at in the letter to the President above referred to, is ——— livres. If less will not do, we are prepared to meet it; but it is hoped that less will do, and the prospect of accommodation will concur with other motives in postponing the expedition to Louisiana. For the present I barely remark, that a proposition made to Congress with closed doors is under consideration, which, if agreed to, will authorize the payment of about ten millions of livres, under arrangement of time and place that may be so convenient to the French Government as to invite a prompt as well as favorable decision of the case. The sum to which the proposition is limited, and which will probably not be effectually concealed, may, at the same time, assist in keeping down the pecuniary expectations of the French Cabinet.

I have the honor to be, etc.

JAMES MADISON.

(The following is one of the memoirs, or essays, referred to in the preceding letter from Mr. Livingston to the President, dated March 12, and in Mr. Madison's letter to Mr. Livingston of May 25, 1803.)

Thoughts on the relative situation of France, Britain, and America, as commercial and maritime nations.

The power of France having reached a height that leaves her nothing to wish or to fear from the continental sovereignties of Europe, she might be considered as invulnerable if she could either divide the empire of the sea, or place it in so many hands as to command, by her influence, or the advantages of her commerce, such a portion of it as would, with her own maritime exertion, reduce her rival to terms of equality.

It is certain that, for the last century, she has not been able to effect this; although she has generally had the aid of Spain, and sometimes that of Holland. Spain and Holland are diminishing in naval importance. Holland, by the shallowness of her harbors, which do not, without great difficulty, admit ships of the great size which are every day found more necessary in battle; by the ruin of her colonies; by the cession of the island of Ceylon; by the derangement of the affairs of her commercial companies; and, above all, by the great comparative advantages enjoyed by Britain in the East Indies: add to these circumstances the loss of seamen which she has sustained by the war, and the disaffection which has led many of them into foreign service, together with the accumulated debt of the nation, and it will appear that little aid can be expected from her in case of a maritime war. It must, at least, be doubtful, if she quits that system of neutrality so congenial to her own situation, whether she will take part with Britain or France. The neighborhood and force of France must, indeed, make her tremble for her possessions in Europe; but still she may find resources against them in the aid of the neighboring nations. But where is she to look for support against the power of Britain, who, in the very commencement of a war, will strip her of every foreign possession, and cut off all her resources?

Spain is much in the same situation; her wealth and credit depend upon her colonies. One of the most valuable of these (part of Hispaniola) has been ceded to France: and the possession of Trinidad, which the great capital of England will soon render very important, will afford her such a point of support, in America, as must render the situation of the remaining islands very precarious, and always keep Spain in pain for her colonies; this will lead her to seek for safety, as far as possible, in neutrality. But at all events, the maritime power of Spain must diminish by the circumstances I have mentioned, and by the illicit trade which the possession of the Mosquito shore, the bay of Honduras, and the island of Trinidad, will enable the British to carry on in spite of the vigilance of Spain—a vigilance, too, which will be, in some sort, relaxed from the apprehension of provoking a war by too much rigor.

The naval power of Britain has, on the other hand, acquired an immense accession, during the last war, by that maritime superiority which gave protection to her commerce in every part of the world; by her conquests in the East Indies; and by the cession of Trinidad. But, besides the extent of her colonies; she has, in her peculiar position, an advantage unattainable by France. The fuel for all the great cities of England and Scotland is coal. Not less than three thousand and six hundred ships enter the port of London yearly, charged with this article alone. This, together with similar exports to other cities, and the situation of the capitals of England and Ireland, is a great nursery for seamen, which France wants; and makes a coasting trade, which is more than four-fold of all the coasting trade of France taken together, and is not less than the whole colonial trade of Britain, including the East Indies. It also has this peculiar advantage, that, in time of war, all the seamen employed in this commerce may be engaged in the navy with very little inconvenience, only by permitting (which is not done in peace) the coal to be brought to London by inland navigation.

It becomes, then, a serious question with France, how she is to counterbalance the advantages enjoyed by her rival. Shall she establish foreign colonies?

Unless she has a naval force capable of protecting them, these colonies must soon change their masters; and the whole expense employed in their support redound to the benefit of her rival. But admit that they could be secured by land forces. How trifling will all the seamen afforded by the commerce of those colonies be, compared to the number produced by the colonies of Britain in the East and West Indies, America, Africa, and the Southern Ocean. But supposing them equal, still the seamen Britain derives from her coasting trade alone more than equal those drawn from all these sources.

Will France create a marine by becoming the carrier of other nations? This is impossible. Except Britain, there is no nation in Europe which can not navigate their ships as cheap as France. The materials for shipbuilding, and more especially naval stores and provisions, are dearer in France than in the Northern States, and labor is equally high.

Will she be her own carrier? If she will it must be by restrictions on the trade of other nations, who will certainly not submit to them without imposing similar restrictions on France. Suppose, for instance, she should say (as indeed she has said) that tobacco brought to France in foreign vessels shall pay an extra duty. How easy will it be for the country which grows tobacco to say that that article, exported in French ships, shall pay a similar duty? And what will be the end of this commercial warfare, but that every nation shall carry its own produce, and let their ships return home empty, if the partial duties are high? Thus, if France imposes a high duty on tobacco, and America a high duty on wines and other articles of France in foreign bottoms, the tobacco must be brought in French ships, and charged with a double expense of freight, because they can carry out no cargo to pay the expense and insurance of the ships on their outward-bound voyage. Of course, this expense must fall on the consumer of tobacco; and for what? Why, in order that ten French seamen may be employed rather than ten foreigners. A ship of three hundred tons must make, in order to clear herself, seventy thousand francs a year. The whole of this, with insurance out and home, must be charged on the tobacco imported, in the case I mention; whereas only the one-half would be paid if she could take out a cargo. Thus, then, the consumer of tobacco in France, pays, annually, to the maintenance of ten seamen, thirty-five thousand francs, or three thousand five hundred for every seaman; and this, too, without being of the smallest advantage to that class of people whose wages are not thereby at all increased. This is purchasing sailors at such a rate as I believe no nation in the world would ever long submit to. But should the same reasoning be applied to the manufactures and wines of France, and she, by attempting to be her own carrier, charge them with a double freight, it must necessarily follow that, with respect to every article which other nations can supply, she would soon lose the carriage by losing the sale; for if a foreign ship can carry out a cargo to Lisbon, and take back one from thence, charged with no extra duty, the wine and oil of Lisbon will be preferred, though of inferior quality, to those of France. Thus, whatever she gives to her seamen by discouraging a free trade, she takes from her agriculture and manufactures: and yet her agriculture and manufactures can alone form the basis of her commerce. In time of war, unless this operation can really create a naval power, sufficient to protect her commerce, (of which there is not the smallest prospect,) foreigners having been driven from her ports by this operation, she must cease to trade altogether. Thus the sources of her wealth will be cut off at the moment she most needs them.

What, then, is to be done? Is France to abandon her colonies as weak points in her system, which she can not maintain? Is she to suffer a tyranny to be established upon the ocean, which shall forever hold her in check? Is she to allow such an accumulation of wealth as will forever enable her rival to interfere in the affairs of the Continent and provoke new combinations against her? I answer these questions by returning to my first position.

She must place the empire of the sea in more hands, without attempting to grasp it alone. She must make it the interest of those who aid her in the attainment of a considerable portion of it to maintain her superiority. Spain and Holland are not to be neglected; though, as I have stated, they will, in the situation in which their colonies are now placed, incline to neutrality; and if otherwise, their aid would be insufficient during a war. The United States have physical advantages which, like those of Britain, must necessarily lead them to be a considerable maritime nation. The mass of their population lies upon the ocean, and upon large rivers that are navigable for sea vessels to the interior of the country, which is generally rough and hilly between the rivers. Hence it happens that there is little land carriage in America. If merchandises are to be transported from one State to another, it is by water; and that not solely by rivers or canals, but by descending one river, passing out into the ocean, and ascending another. This circumstance, together with the variance between the productions of the Southern and Northern States, which promotes much intercourse, must give to them a nursery of seamen in their coasting trade, equal to that which Britain enjoys in her coal trade: to which a growing coal trade, from mines found in the banks of the James river, and in other places, will be added, when wood diminishes, or when the policy of the country shall charge the importation of British coal with heavier duties. Our large cities consume, even now, very considerable quantities of this article. The advantage also that the United States enjoy in the cheapness of the articles for building, and, above all, for victualling their ships, more than counterbalances the high price given to their seamen. Their situation relative to the cod and whale fisheries also calls numbers to a maritime life.

The islands, to whomsoever they may belong, from the various incidents to which they are liable, and the difficulty of supplying them from Europe, must receive their provision and timber from the United States; and, if they choose, they can compel them to receive only in American bottoms. Were the Powers of Europe, therefore, to lay the severest restrictions on her commerce, the United States would still be a very important commercial nation.

But who is interested in preventing their rapid rise to the height to which their position and their destinies lead them? No nation upon earth; unless Britain should one day fear them more as rivals than she will value them as customers. While they confine themselves to the production of raw materials, they must prove the best market for such nations as can afford them manufactures, wine, oil, and fruit, in return. Weak, indeed, would that nation be who should treat them with neglect, or drive them, by ill-judged laws, from their harbors. Britain is so sensible of this, that she has never attempted to prevent, by partial duties, the American vessels from carrying their own produce to them, or their fabrics back in return. She well knows that every such measure would have a tendency to drive them from her harbors, to which she so much wishes to invite them, that she even grants them a right, by treaty, to enter all her ports in the East Indies.

While Britain refuses to naturalize American ships she never will be able to navigate (because she can not build, fit, or victual) her ships so cheap as those of America. It must follow, therefore, that the trade of Britain to and from the United States will be chiefly carried on by American ships; and, as her articles are very bulky, a great number will be employed. There exists, indeed, at this moment a circumstance which will give them considerable advantages, unless France should instantly step in and prevent its operation.

The advanced price of living in Britain, owing to the debt contracted by the war, has naturally raised the price of labor; while the peace, which gives more activity to her commerce, will make this operate upon seamen's wages, and thus give some check to her carrying trade. On the other hand, this diminution of the trade of the United States will throw at least twenty-five thousand seamen out of employ. These will, from their habits and manners, naturally pass into the service of Britain, and thus enable her to keep down wages and maintain her advantages.

It is obvious that it is much the interest of France to prevent this; and more particularly when it is considered that all these men are skillful mariners, and many of them experienced fishermen; who may transplant the whale fishery to Britain, and thus add a new source to her naval power. The efforts of France to establish a fishery will be of little avail against this; nor will it ever be found practicable to render this a flourishing branch of business, except by the aid of American fishermen; and even then by a charge upon a material useful in their manufactures more than equivalent to the value of the fishery.

I shall be asked how long it will take to make the United States a naval Power equal to Great Britain? I answer, that a country which possesses timber, naval stores, provisions, and men accustomed, by an active commerce, to a sea life; a country whose credit is unblemished, and who has no debt but what she can instantly discharge; is certainly so far equal as her numbers are equal to one who has no advantages over her in any of these circumstances, and is inferior in others. It will be allowed, too, that, according to every rational probability, their numbers will be equal to those of the British isles in twenty years, and their wealth not inferior. But it is by no means necessary to carry the navy of America to the extent of that of Britain, in order to render her a useful ally, or a respectable enemy. The trade of Britain with her islands, and the Indies, must approach the coast of America. Her privateers could, even without protection from a navy, destroy a great proportion of this. With a navy of thirty ships of the line, and a proportionate number of frigates, which need never be more than one week's sail from their own shores, such protection would be given to smaller vessels as would enable them to capture a great part of their trade, unless protected by large fleets. For this purpose one-half of the British navy must be kept at a vast expense, at a great distance from home, and in an unhealthy climate; while all the expenditures of the American navy would be made in their own ports. It will certainly admit of little doubt, that a nation who has no frontier to defend, who has six hundred thousand armed men at home, and who has no debts, need only will it to have a fleet of the size I mention. And it is very certain that such a fleet by acting always together, would compel any European nation greatly to weaken her naval force in her own seas. No convoy could be less than the whole of the American fleet; nor could a smaller force be left in the islands; so that thirty ships in America, would demand for convoys, out and in, and the stations in the islands, not less than ninety ships of equal force. What power could Britain oppose to this force, combined with an equal number of French ships, with the advantage of all the harbors of the United States? What refuge would she have against storms and accidental separation when on the coast of America? And how, under these disadvantages, would she maintain her superiority in Europe? I infer, from this reasoning, that it is the true interest of France to promote the commerce and maritime force of America; and, at the same time, to interest her in the extension of the commerce of France? I do not mean to say that this force will always operate directly in favor of France. This will depend upon a variety of political circumstances that can not be foreseen or controlled. The first interest of America will doubtless lead her to a state of neutrality. But such has always been the overbearing spirit of Britain at sea, that it is highly probable occurrences will arise, which may compel America, when she feels her strength, to enter into a war to preserve her commercial rights from violation. But should she maintain her neutrality, she will indirectly serve France if the plan I suggest is adopted:

1st. By carrying on her commerce for her during a war; 2d. By employing a great number of seamen who would otherwise go into the service of Britain; 3d. By seizing upon many branches of trade from which Britain derives her wealth, and which, when once diverted, may never return. But my plan embraces not only an extension of the American maritime force, but that of France, by an easy and natural operation, without imposing a burden upon, but in fact giving the highest encouragement to, her manufactures and agriculture. It consists in a treaty of commerce which shall put the trade and shipping of both countries on the most perfect equality. That is to say, the ships of France shall be admitted into the ports of America, paying a duty of six per cent. ad valorem only on all articles, and the same tonnage duty as the American ships pay. The American ships shall be admitted into all the ports of France and her colonies upon the same terms, provided that they should never carry to the colonies anything but the produce of their own country or of France; that the colonial products in American ships should be subject to every regulation as to their being landed in France, as they are in French ships. The first advantage of this treaty would be, if immediately entered into, the saving to America of twenty-five thousand seamen, who will, without this encouragement go into the British service; and thus increase not only her relative but her actual force: 2d. The sale of a number of her ships to France, which will now become a dead capital in her hands: 3d. The preserving to the United States their fisheries, which may be otherwise greatly affected by the removal of their seamen to Britain. In these objects France has a mutual advantage; and I will venture to say, that she never acts more inconsistently with her own interest, or more conformably with that of Britain, than when, under the idea of raising a fishery at home, while she has not seamen or shipping for her other branches of commerce, she endeavors to discourage the fisheries of America, which, from a variety of physical causes, can alone keep them from falling into the hands of the English. France should bear in mind, that, were her colonies as extensive as those of Britain; were her trade in Europe and America equal to hers; yet, from the reasons I have mentioned, arising from the geographical and physical situation of England and Ireland, she would not possess more than two-thirds of the number of seamen, these circumstances alone producing nearly as many as all the other trade of Britain. France can only increase her relative strength by diminishing that of her rival, and keeping her from drawing from other sources new means of power.

France may injure, and perhaps ruin, the whale fishery in America; but England only will profit by it. The first war will break up her establishments; and the Americans in her service will return with their wealth into their own country.

The interest that France will have in this treaty will be much more extensive: 1st, The raising up a new marine Power; 2d, Giving that Power such an interest in her prosperity, as must not only keep it from being inimical to, but, on the contrary, frequently connected with her in hostile operations; 3d, The transfer of ships to France; 4th, The increase of French seamen: for, as the wages of seamen are lower in France than in America, and must continue to be so, on account of the demand for men in a new country, while, on the other hand, ships, and the provisions for their outfit, are cheaper in America, French merchants, by fitting many of these vessels, and navigating them with French seamen, will be able to sail cheaper than the Americans themselves, and thus increase the number of their seamen. These seamen in case, of a war, will be drawn into the navy; while their places will be supplied, during the war, at somewhat more expense, by Americans, without injuring their commerce. In the cod fishery, France will derive clear and obvious advantages from the American ports for her outfits, &c.

But even these advantages will be inferior to that derived from the increase of the commerce of exchange, by that removal of restrictions; an operation which, I will venture to say, will at least double the whole commerce and number of seamen employed by France, and quadruple it with respect to her navigation with America. It should also be considered that this works doubly in favor of France, 1st, So far as it is a direct advantage to her maritime power; 2nd, So far as it subtracts from the navigation of England.

The benefits that will result to the manufactures of France from this operation are incalculable: 1st, The raw materials will be purchased on easy terms to the manufacturer; 2nd, The intercourse that this system will establish between the two nations will make their fabrics known, and render them fashionable in America; will draw off their custom from England, whose fabrics will continue to be charged with a heavy duty, unless, receding from her navigation act, she purchases an exemption.

Useful as this act may have been in its commencement, when the Dutch were the general carriers and rivals of Britain, and while the nations of Europe were ignorant of commercial principles, very enlightened statesmen now see many inconveniences in it to the general commerce of England; nor is there anything necessary to its entire overthrow, but for other nations to pass similar laws, so far as respect Britain, while their trade is put upon a liberal footing with regard to other nations. This, by promoting their own commerce of exchange, while that of Britain is restricted, will place her flag under such disadvantages, that her own merchants will seek a foreign bottom when they have an operation that requires a circuitous voyage. This must ultimately, in spite of all her prejudices, compel her to repeal this selfish law, after having some time suffered under it. But while the navigation act exists in Britain, it will, under the circumstances of the treaty I suggest, operate as a bounty on the navigation and fabrics of France; because it is obvious that the freight and charge on any specific article carried in a ship that may make a circuitous voyage, is much less than they would be if part of the voyage was made in ballast. Thus, a French ship carrying a cargo of wine to America, taking in a load of tobacco, and returning from thence to Bordeaux, could take the wine on a much smaller freight than if the duties imposed in America on the importation of wine in a French ship should be equivalent to the duties upon tobacco imported in an American ship into France; because, in that case, the French ship would go out empty for the tobacco, and the American ship empty for the wine; and the double freight and insurance must be charged on each of these articles. It should always be remembered, that whatever is saved in freight is a bounty upon agriculture and manufactures. But even this is a small advantage compared to that derived from the increase of adventures that will be occasioned by the very circumstance of freight for the whole outward and homeward voyage, and the consequent consumption of the commodities of the country that encourages it.

In this plan, Spain, (under some restrictions with regard to South America,) the Italian States, and any others who should incline to engage in it, should be associated; without, however, delaying the project between France and the United States, lest they should lose, and Britain acquire, at this critical moment, that great body of seamen, who will, by the peace, be thrown out of employment.

Were France to declare her determination to support this liberal system, such is her advantage in point of product and manufactures, that she could not fail to command the greatest foreign commerce of any nation in the world.

The wealth arising from this source would be unbounded. But while her great capital is in the center of the Republic, she never can have an extensive coasting trade; and she can only make up this deficiency, in a contest with Britain, by the increase of her wealth and credit; by nursing up new maritime nations; by which, if she adds little to her positive power, she adds much to her relative strength, in diminishing that of her rival.

To cite a single instance: America can build and victual her whaling vessels much cheaper than either France or England, and of course afford oil cheaper; but if France excludes American oil from her market, she throws such a discouragement upon this fishery as will compel the whalers to seek another place of residence. In this case, though a few may be invited to France, the great bulk of them will go to England: First, because of their language, religion, and habits; and next, because they know that a war will ruin their establishments in France, and thus it will encourage those of Britain. The very companies established in France, at great national expense, will receive their oil at sea from English fishermen. Thus fifteen thousand men will be thrown into the scale of Britain, to support one thousand in the vain attempt to establish a fishery in France. This, however, is a small part of the loss. By the encouragement which France might give to the fisheries of the United States, she could destroy those of Britain; and, as the French ships that brought oil, or the American that brought French goods, would not go or return empty, a greater market would be created for French wines, brandies, &c. Let the loss upon this be calculated. The additional expense upon the first price to the inhabitants of France, and the countries given, they will find that they purchase their oil at a ruinous rate.

Let the difference between fifteen thousand men, added to those employed in the British fishery, and eight thousand taken from them by the encouragement given to the American fishery by France, making together the loss or gain of twenty-three thousand to Britain, be put in the scale with the comparatively few fishermen France can make, and she will form a fair estimate of the attempt, considering her as a rival power to Britain.

Great as are the advantages proposed by this system to the commerce and navigation of France, they are small compared to those which she will derive from having opened a way to the establishment of free and liberal principles, that can not fail to give room for the exertion of those talents and that industry for which her citizens are distinguished. Every nation, except one, will eagerly embrace them; and their mutual interest will lead them to protect them against the power of any maritime despot. The advantage that the vessels of this association would have over all others, could not fail to produce such a revolution in the principles and practice of commerce and navigation as would be highly interesting to humanity, honorable to the nations who should first adopt the system, and not unworthy of the enlarged views of that distinguished statesman to whom Europe is already so much indebted, and who, alone, has sufficient power to carry it into effect.

[Extract.]

Mr. Madison, Secretary of State, to Mr. C. Pinckney, American Minister at Madrid.

DEPARTMENT OF STATE, *January 18, 1803.*

[After informing Mr. Pinckney, as well as Mr. Livingston, of the reasons which had induced the mission of Mr. Monroe, the letter proceeds as follows:]

The President has been careful, on this occasion, to guard effectually against any misconstruction in relation to yourself, by expressing, in his Message to the Senate, his undiminished confidence in the ordinary representation of the United States, and by referring the advantages of the additional mission to considerations perfectly consistent therewith.

Mr. Monroe will be the bearer of instructions under which you are to negotiate. The object of them will be, to procure a cession of New Orleans and the Floridas to the United States, and consequently, the establishment of the Mississippi as the boundary between the United States and Louisiana. In order to draw the French Government into the measure, a sum of money will make part of our propositions; to which will be added such regulations of the commerce of that river, and of the others entering the Gulf of Mexico, as ought to be satisfactory to France. From a letter received by the President from a respectable person, it is inferred, with probability, that the French Government is not averse to treat on those grounds; and such a disposition must be strengthened by circumstances of the present moment.

Though it is probable that this mission will be completed at Paris, if its objects are at all attainable, yet it was necessary to apprize you thus far of what is contemplated, both for your own satisfaction, and that you may be prepared to co-operate on the occasion, as circumstances may demand. Mr. Monroe will not be able to sail for two weeks.

Robert R. Livingston, Minister to France, to James Madison, Secretary of State.

PARIS, *January 24, 1803.*

SIR: I have just now heard of an opportunity from Havre. I am doubtful whether my letter will arrive in time for it. I therefore confine myself to inform you that General Bernadotte is named Minister to the United States, in the place of Otto, who will be employed here. General Bernadotte is brother-in-law to Joseph Bonaparte, is a very respectable man, and has the character of a decided republican. I have endeavored to impress upon him the necessity of making some arrangements relative to the debt previous to his departure, which he has much at heart. But neither he nor anybody else can influence the councils of the First Consul. You can hardly conceive anything more timid than all about him are; they dare not be known to have a sentiment of their own, or to have expressed one to anybody. But I must defer writing to you more at large on this subject, as well as a full communication of a very delicate step that I have hazarded, which promised success for some time, but from which I, at present, hope for no important result. The Minister informs me that the expedition to Louisiana will sail shortly. General Bernadotte will go in about three weeks. He will have full powers to settle everything. I asked the Minister, what confidence you can have in any new offer to treat, when the last treaty is unexecuted; and if he had not better send out General Bernadotte with a treaty in his hand, than only with powers that will be suspected; and how he can make arrangements upon the debts, which must depend upon the Legislature? He answers this by saying, they want information as to right of deposit, &c. As to the debt, I have no hope that they have any intention to pay it, or even to fund it. From the disposition which I know to be entertained by some that go out with Victor, I have no doubt that they will provoke an Indian war, by paying them nothing; and that, in their solicitude to acquire wealth, they will act over again the tyranny of St. Domingo. It will be necessary, therefore, to take the position that will best guard you against the effects of these evils. As to myself, I am left wholly without any precise instruction how to act, or what to offer. Enclosed are two memoirs lately sent in, with as little effect as those that have gone before them; though I have reason to think that the Minister wishes well to my project for Louisiana, but the First Consul is immovable. I confess to you I see very little use for a Minister here, where there is but one will; and that will governed by no object but personal security and personal ambition: were it left to my discretion, I should bring matters to some positive issue, or leave them, which would be the only means of bringing them to an issue.

I am, &c.,

ROBERT R. LIVINGSTON.

Hon. JAMES MADISON, &c.

Mr. Livingston to ——— ———.

No. 4.]   DECEMBER 24, 1802.[a]

SIR: I can not but feel the utmost anxiety to know whether my project, which you had the goodness to submit to the inspection of the First Consul, is likely to meet with his concurrence. Upon ordinary occasions I should consider the delay of a few weeks as of little moment; but there are circumstances which render every day important in what relates to the United States and France. In the twelve months that I have been here, I have not been so happy as to receive a conclusive answer to any one business that I have had to transact with the Minister. Congress are now in session; they will infer from every paper submitted to them by the President, that the French Government are disposed to show them but little attention. The obscurity that covers the designs of France in Louisiana (for not the least light can I, officially, obtain on the subject) will double their apprehensions; this, added to the clamors of ruined creditors, and the extreme severity with which some of their citizens have been treated

---

[a] It does not appear with certainty by what dispatch this memoir was communicated.

in St. Domingo, and the extraordinary decisions of the Council of Prizes, &c., will leave a fair field for the intrigues of the enemies of France, and even enlist the best patriots of America on their side. At this moment Britain comes forward and pays, with the most scrupulous attention, every demand, and proposes to settle her Southwestern line with the United States. In doing this, she is anxious to come down to a navigable part of the Mississippi, so as to communicate with Canada by that channel. It is obvious that she can have no interest in this, but such as looks to the future possession of the mouth of that river; a project that she would naturally form the moment she saw Louisiana pass into the hands of her rival. I am sorry to say it is one that she will find no difficulty in executing, unless prevented by the United States; for France is too far to protect a young Colony from an established one, and the numerous savages, provincial troops, and others, that Canada will afford. While the conduct of France speaks a language so painful to the feelings of the American Government, there is too much reason to believe that there will be little solicitude in so forming their limits as to cover her possessions. I am anxious, sir, to know our prospects. If they should be such as I flatter myself the mutual interests of France and the United States would lead to, I would wish to have it in my power to arrest in Mr. King's hands any conclusion on the subject of our Western bounds. In case my project should be honored with the approbation of the First Consul, it will be essential to the security of the possessions of France and the peace of that country, to remove the British boundary as high up the river as possible, so as to prevent any communication with Canada, by the rivers that fall on the one side into the lakes, and, on the other, into the Mississippi. If this business is obstructed only by the non-conclusion of the treaty with Spain for the Floridas, one may still go between us for New Orleans and the territory above the Arkansas river, with a condition annexed, in case the treaty with the Floridas should succeed agreeably to the wishes of France. Should the treaty with Spain fall through, every reason of policy should induce France, either to relinquish her designs on Louisiana altogether, or to cover her frontier by a cession to the United States; since, without a single port in the Gulf, it will be impossible to protect their Colony; and all the expense incurred by the attempt will ultimately redound to the advantage of Britain, who will not fail to attack them with advantage both by sea and land.

The treaty I propose might also form a basis for the immediate discharge of the debts due to our citizens; in the doing of which, advantageous arrangements may be made, and, at the same time, the funds of France be considerably raised: provided such secrecy is observed in the whole of this transaction as will prevent the debts being the object of speculation. I know, sir, a distinction has been taken between debts due from the former Government and that which now happily prevails in France. But, sir, if this distinction is just, it does not apply to the demands of the United States. They are specifically assumed by the new Government, when they made the object of the treaty, and an equivalent has already been paid the present Government by that of the United States; so that they stand upon a different ground from that of the debts of other nations having demands on France; and they not only have to plead their justice, and the circumstance under which they were contracted, but the pledged faith of the existing Government.

I can not, sir, but be solicitous to know that what I have hitherto taken the liberty to write to you has passed into no hands but those of the First Consul, or some other member of your own family, as I fear my communications out of the ordinary channel might be ill taken where I am solicitous to stand well.

I have the honor to be, sir, with the most profound consideration, your most obedient servant,

R. R. LIVINGSTON.

Report of committee to whom was referred a resolution providing for an additional appropriation of two millions of dollars for the purpose of intercourse with foreign nations.

JANUARY 12, 1803.

The object of this resolution is to enable the Executive to commence, with more effect, a negotiation with the French and Spanish Governments relative to the purchase from them of the island of New Orleans, and the provinces of East and West Florida. This object is deemed highly important and has received the attentive consideration of the committee. The free and unmolested navigation of the river Mississippi is a point to which the attention of the General Government has been directed, ever since the peace of 1783, by which our independence as a nation was finally acknowledged. The immense tract of country owned by the United States, which lies immediately on the Mississippi, or communicates with it by means of large navigable rivers rising within our boundaries, renders its free navigation an object, not only of inestimable advantage, but of the very first necessity. The Mississipi forms the western boundary of the United States, from its source to the thirty-first degree of north latitude, and empties itself into the Gulf of Mexico, about the twenty-ninth degree of north latitude. It furnishes the only outlet through which the produce of the Indiana Territory, the States of Ohio, Kentucky and Tennessee, and of the western parts of Pennsylvania and Virginia, and a portion of the Mississippi Territory, can be transported to a foreign market, or to ports of the Atlantic States. From the thirty-first degree of north latitude, which is the southern boundary of the United States, to the mouth of the river, the territory on each side has heretofore been in possession of the Spanish Government; the province of Louisiana lying to the West, and those of East Florida, with the island of New Orleans, to the East.

Although the United States have insisted on an uncontrollable right to pass up and down the river, from its source to the sea, yet this right, if admitted in its most ample latitude, will not secure to them the full advantages of navigation. The strength and rapidity of the current of the Mississippi are known to render ascent so extremely difficult, that few vessels of burden have attempted to go as far as our boundary. This circumstance obliges the citizens of the Western country to carry their produce down the river in boats, from which it is put on board ships capable of sustaining a sea voyage. It follows, therefore, that to enjoy the full benefits of navigation, some place should be fixed which sea vessels can approach without great inconvenience, where the American produce may be deposited until it is again shipped to be carried abroad. This great point was secured to us in the year 1795, by the Spanish Government, who agreed, in the Treaty of San Lorenzo el Real, that Americans should have the right of deposit at New Orleans. This right has been used from that time till a late period; but the conduct of the Intendant at that place shows how liable the advantageous navigation of the river is to interruption, and strongly points out the impolicy of relying on a foreign nation for benefits, which our citizens have a right to expect should be secured to them by their own Government. It is hoped that the port of New Orleans may again be opened before any very material injuries arise; but should this be the case, or if, as the treaty provides, a new place of deposit should be assigned, the late occurrence shows the uncertainty of its continuance. Experience proves that the caprice or the interested views of a single officer may perpetually subject us to the alternative of submitting to injury, or of resorting to war.

The late violation of our treaty with Spain necessarily leads to the inquiry, how far the Western country may be affected in other points, not connected with New Orleans? The Mississippi Territory extends from the confines of Georgia to the river Mississippi, and from the thirty-first to the thirty-fifth degree of north latitude. It is estimated to contain more than fifty millions of acres, and, from its numerous advantages, must one day or other possess an immense population. The variety, richness, and abundance of its productions, hold out to settlers the strongest inducements to resort thither, and the United States may safely calculate on drawing a considerable revenue from the sale of lands in this, as well as in other quarters of the Western country. The value of these, however, may be diminished or increased, and the sale impeded or advanced by the impression made on the public mind, by shutting the port of New Orleans, and by eventual measures which may be adopted to guard against similar injuries.

West Florida is bounded on the north by the Mississippi Territory, from which it is separated by no natural boundary; on the east by the river Apalachicola, which divides it from East Florida; on the west by the river Mississippi, and on the south by the Gulf of Mexico. The Mississippi Territory is intersected by many large and valuable rivers, which rise within its own boundaries, and meander through it in a general direction from north to south, but empty themselves into the Gulf of Mexico through the province of West Florida. In fact, with the exception of that part of the Territory which lies immediately on the Mississippi, the whole must depend on the Mobile and the Apalachicola, with their numerous branches, and on some other rivers of inferior note, for the means of sending its produce to market, and of returning to itself such foreign supplies as the necessities or convenience of its inhabitants may require. In these rivers, too, the eastern parts of the State of Tennessee are deeply interested, as some of the great branches of the Mobile approach very near to some of those branches of the Tennessee River, which lie above the great Muscle Shoals. Even if it should prove difficult to connect them, yet the land carriage will be shorter, and the route to the sea more direct than the river Tennessee furnishes. These rivers possess, likewise, an advantage which is denied to the Mississippi. As their sources are not in the mountains, and their course is through a level country, their currents are gentle, and the tide flows considerably above our boundary. This circumstance, together with the depth of water which many of them afford, render them accessible to sea vessels, and ships of two hundred tons burden may ascend for several hundred miles into the heart of the Mississippi Territory. These rivers, however, which run almost exclusively within our own limits, and which it would seem as if nature had intended for our own benefit, we must be indebted to others for the beneficial use of, so long as the province of West Florida shall continue in possession of a foreign nation. If the province of West Florida were itself an independent empire, it would be the interest of its Government to promote the freedom of trade, by laying open the mouths of the rivers to all nations; this having been the policy of those Powers who possess the mouths of the Rhine, the Danube, the Po, and the Tagus, with some others. But the system of colonization which has always heretofore prevailed, proves that the mother country is ever anxious to engross to itself the trade of its colonies, and affords us every reason to apprehend that Spain will not readily admit us to pass through her territory to carry on a trade either with each other or with foreign nations. This right we may insist on, and perhaps it may be conceded to us; but it is possible that it may be denied. At all events, it may prove the source of endless disagreement and perpetual hostility.

In this respect East Florida may not perhaps be so important, but its acquisition is nevertheless deemed desirable. From its junction with the State of Georgia, at the river St. Marys, it stretches nearly four hundred miles into the sea, forming a large peninsula, and has some very fine harbors. The southern point, Cape Florida, is not more than one hundred miles distant from the Havana, and the possession of it may be beneficial to us in relation to our trade with the West Indies. It would likewise make our whole territory compact, would add considerably to our seacoast, and by giving us the Gulf of Mexico for our southern boundary, would render us less liable to attack, in what is now deemed the most vulnerable part of the Union.

From the aforegoing view of facts, it must be seen that the possession of New Orleans and the Floridas will not only be required for the convenience of the United States, but will be demanded by their most imperious necessities. The Mississippi and its branches, with those other rivers above referred to, drain an extent of country, not less, perhaps, than one-half of our whole territory, containing at this time one-eighth of our population and progressing with a rapidity beyond the experience of any former time, or of any other nation. The Floridas and New Orleans command the only outlets to the sea, and our best interests require that we should get possession of them. This requisition, however, arises not from a disposition to increase our territory; for neither the Floridas nor New Orleans offer any other inducements than their mere geographical relation to the United States. But if we look forward to the free use of the Mississippi, the Mobile, the Apalachicola, and the other rivers of the West, by ourselves and our posterity, New Orleans and the Floridas must become a part of the United States, either by purchase or by conquest.

The great question, then, which presents itself is, shall we at this time lay the foundation for future peace by offering a fair and equivalent consideration; or shall we hereafter incur the hazards and the horrors of war? The Government of the United States is differently organized from any other in the world. Its object is the happiness of man; its policy and its interest, to pursue right by right means. War is the great scourge of the human race, and should never be resorted to but in cases of the most imperious necessity. A wise government will avoid it, when its views can be attained by peaceful measures. Princes fight for glory, and the blood and treasure of their subjects is the price they pay. In all nations the people bear the burden of war, and in the United States the people rule. Their Representatives are the guardians of their rights, and it is the duty of those Representatives to provide against any event which may, even at a distant day, involve the interest and the happiness of the nation. We may, indeed, have our rights restored to us by treaty, but there is a want of fortitude in applying temporary remedies to permanent evils; thereby imposing on our posterity a burden which we ourselves ought to bear. If the purchase can be made, we ought not to hesitate. If the attempt shall fail, we shall have discharged an important duty.

War may be the result, but the American nation, satisfied with our conduct, will be animated by one soul, and will unite all its energies in the contest. Foreign powers will be convinced that it is not a war of aggrandizement on our part, and will feel no unreasonable jealousies toward us. We shall have proved that our object was justice; it will be seen that our propositions were fair; and it will be acknowledged that our cause is honorable. Should alliances be necessary they may be advantageously formed. We shall have merited, and shall therefore possess, general confidence. Our measures will stand justified not only to ourselves and our country, but to the world.

In another point of view, perhaps, it would be preferable to make the purchase, as it is believed that a smaller sum would be required for this subject, than would necessarily be expended, if we should attempt to take possession by force; the expenses of a war being, indeed, almost incalculable. The Committee have no information before them, to ascertain the amount for which the purchase can be made, but it is hoped that, with the assistance of two millions of dollars in hand, this will not be unreasonable. A similar course was pursued for the purpose of settling our differences with the Regency of Algiers, by an appropriation of one million of dollars, prior to the commencement of the negotiation, and we have since experienced its beneficial effects.

Mr. Livingston to the Minister of Exterior Relations.

SIR: I have so often had occasion to mention to you the claims of American citizens upon the French Government, and, with so little effect, that I feel pain whenever I am compelled to touch upon that subject. But, sir, I never had reason to doubt, both from the tenor of your note, and conversations, that it would become a question whether these debts, just in themselves, and solemnly confirmed by a treaty, should become the subject of liquidation. The Board of Accounts accordingly proceeded to liquidate and give certificates for about one-quarter of the whole amount. Upon the debt so liquidated the American merchant was enabled to raise the small sums necessary for his support, till arrangements were made (which they never permitted themselves to doubt would be finally done) for their discharge. But, sir, even of this support they are now deprived; for though the board has proceeded to liquidate more of their claims, the gentleman at the head of the Department refuses to give the usual certificates;

under what pretense I am at loss to conceive. I am told he considers the treaty as applying to debts contracted during the present Government, when, in fact, no such debts existed at the time of the treaty, nor is there a word in the treaty which authorizes such construction; the whole treaty referring to matters that had passed, not only under the Government that had preceded the present, but under that which preceded the Revolution. Upon what other principle has the United States, with the strictest good faith, paid the debt contracted under Louis XVI, and those which the existing Government demanded under the late Convention for injuries sustained under the late Directors?

It is time, sir, that matters should be brought to some issue; that the citizens of the United States and their Government should know how far the treaty is binding upon France, and what construction ought to be given to it; for hitherto, it has only served as a means to surprise their good faith, and to involve both the Government and the people of the United States in fresh expenses.

I have the honor to renew to your excellency the assurances of my high consideration.

R. R. LIVINGSTON.

Robert R. Livingston, Minister Plenipotentiary of the United States of America, to the Minister of Exterior Relations.

PARIS, *January 10, 1803.*

SIR: I have just learned through a channel, which, though not official, is such as leaves me no doubt of its authenticity, that the Governor of New Orleans has denied the citizens of the United States a right of depot there, under the pretense that the provision for that purpose in the treaty has expired. You are not ignorant, sir, of the value that the Western inhabitants of the United States place upon that right, nor of the spirit with which they will defend it; a spirit to which the Government must yield, even if they could themselves be indifferent to the object. It is peculiarly unhappy, sir, that this circumstance should have happened at the very moment that France is about to possess that country; since, taken in connexion with the silence of the French Government, as to its intention, it will (I very much fear) give room to jealous and suspicious persons to suppose that the Court of Spain has, in this instance, acted in concurrence with that of France; though, sir, I do too much justice to the integrity of France to believe that she would approve of a breach of treaty and render their first entrance into our vicinity an act of hostility; yet it certainly is of a nature to call the immediate attention of France to the several matters which I had the honor to mention to you, the neglect of which has excited the liveliest sensation in the United States. I therefore avail myself of this opportunity and the permission you gave me to offer you the outline of a treaty that I presume will afford the most obvious benefits to France, and strengthen the connexion which every enlightened American wishes to subsist between her and the United States.

Presuming that the Floridas are in the hands of France, and unless they are Louisiana can never be worth her possessing, because it affords no ports for its own protection, I shall predicate what I have to offer upon that presumption.

France can have but three objects in the possession of Louisiana and Florida: the first is the command of the Gulf; second, the supply of her islands; third, an outlet for her people, if (which however appears to me a very distant expectation) her European population should be too great for her territory. The first of these will be effectually secured by the possession of West Florida, which includes the bay of St. Esprit and Pensacola, together with the town and harbor of St. Augustine. There are no other ports of the smallest importance east of the Mississippi. The second will be better effected by confining their establishment to some reasonable limits on the seacoast, or within a moderate distance from it, than by scattering their capital and inhabitants over an extensive territory, which will have a tendency to render them savage and independent, and compel France to keep up a very expensive establishment to protect them from the incursions of savages.

This country must either be settled by foreigners, or by emigrants from France. In the first case, no nation in Europe can retain them in a state of dependence, because they will, when settled some hundred miles from the sea, be absolutely inaccessible to their power. In the second, the emigration will be such a drain to the wealth and population of France as will inflict as deep a wound to her agriculture and manufactures as that felt by her on the revocation of the Edict of Nantes, or by Spain, on the expulsion of the Moors; and, after all, the day on which they will be independent will arrive whenever they shall have sufficient wealth and strength no longer to need her aid.

Having treated this subject more at large in a paper which you have had the goodness to read, I will not dwell upon it here, but propose what it appears to be the true policy of France to adopt, as affecting all her objects, and at the same time conciliating the affections of the United States, giving permanency to her establishments, which she can in no other way hope for. First, let France cede to the United States so much of Louisiana as lays above the mouth of the river Arkansas. By this, a barrier will be placed between the colony of France and Canada, from which she may otherwise be attacked with the greatest facility, and driven out before she can derive any aid from Europe. Let her retain the country lying on the west of the Mississippi and below the Arkansas River—a country capable of supporting fifteen millions of inhabitants. By this, she will place a barrier between the United States and Mexico, if (which I hope will never be the case) they should have the wild idea of carrying their arms into that country, and at the same time be at hand to protect the Spanish establishments against the ambitious views of any European Power. Let her possess East Florida as far as the river Perdido, with all the ports on the Gulf, and cede West Florida, New Orleans, and the territory on the west bank of the Mississippi, to the United States. This cession will be only valuable to the latter from its giving them the mouths of the river Mobile and other small rivers which penetrate their territory, and in calming their apprehensions relative to the Mississippi. The land ceded (if we except a narrow strip on the bank of the river) will, for the most part, consist of barren sands and sunken marshes; while that retained by France, on the west side of the Mississippi, includes the great bulk of the settlements and a rich and fertile country. It may be supposed that New Orleans is a place of some moment; it will be so to the United States, but not to France, because Fort Leon, on the opposite bank, affords a much more advantageous station; has equal advantages as a harbor; is higher, healthier, and more defensible; and, as the great bulk of the settlements must necessarily be on that side, the capital must be transplanted there, even if France continued in possession of New Orleans, which is a small town, built of wood, and upon which all the expenses that France should make in public buildings, &c., would ultimately be thrown away when the capital was removed.

The right of depot which the United States claim, and will never relinquish, must be the source of continual disputes and animosities between the two nations, and ultimately lead the United States to aid any foreign Power in the expulsion of France from that colony. Independent of this, as the present commercial capital of New Orleans is mostly American, it will be instantly removed to Natchez, to which the United States can give such advantages as to render New Orleans of little importance.

Upon any other plan, sir, it needs but little foresight to predict that the whole of this establishment must pass into the hands of Great Britain, who has, at the same time, the command of the sea, and a martial colony containing every means of attack. While the fleets block up the seaports, she can, without the smallest difficulty, attack New Orleans from Canada with fifteen or twenty thousand men, and a host of savages.

France, by grasping at a desert and insignificant town, and thereby throwing the weight of the United States into the scale of Britain, will render her mistress of the New World. By the possession of Louisiana and Trinidad, the colonies of Spain will lie at her mercy. By expelling France from Florida, and possessing the ports on the Gulf, she will command the islands. The East and the West Indies will pour their commodities into her ports; and the precious metals of Mexico, combined with the treasures of Hindostan, enable her to purchase nations whose aid she may require in confirming her power.

Though it would comport with the true policy, and the magnanimity of France, gratuitously to offer these terms to the United States, yet they are not unwilling to purchase them at a price suited to their value, and to their own circumstances; in the hope that France will at the same time satisfy her distressed citizens the debts which they have a right by so many titles to demand.

These short hints, I flatter myself, will serve to draw your attention to the subject; in which case I am satisfied that many other reasons for the adoption of this plan will suggest themselves to your reflection; reasons on which I do not, from a respect to your time, think it necessary to enlarge. I would only observe that Congress are now in session; that if no treaty is concluded before they rise, or if a Minister should go only with powers to treat, without being the bearer of anything conclusive, he will have to encounter unnumbered suspicions and jealousies, and when he opens the negotiation, he will have to contend with all the intrigues of the Court that is most interested in preventing the completion of objects so hostile to its views. Many things are ratified when a treaty is formed, that would be obstacles to the formation of one in a popular Government.

Accept, sir, the assurances of my high consideration,

R. R. LIVINGSTON.

James Madison, Secretary of State, to Rufus King, Minister to England.

DEPARTMENT OF STATE, *January 29, 1803.*

SIR: My letter of the 23d ult., with a postscript of the 3d of this month, communicated the information which had been received at those dates relating to the violation at New Orleans of our treaty with Spain, together with what had then passed between the House of Representatives and the Executive on the subject. I now enclose a subsequent resolution of that branch of the Legislature. Such of the debates connected with it as took place with open doors will be seen in the newspapers. In those debates, as well as in indications from the press, you will perceive, as you would readily suppose, that the cession of Louisiana to France has been associated as a ground of much solicitude with the affair at New Orleans. Such, indeed, has been the impulse given to the public mind by these events that every branch of the Government has felt the obligation of taking the measures most likely, not only to re-establish our present rights, but to promote arrangements by which they may be enlarged and more effectually secured. In deliberating on this subject, it has appeared to the President that the importance of the crisis called for the experiment of an extraordinary mission, carrying with it the weight attached to such a measure, as well as the advantage of a more thorough knowledge of the views of the Government and of the sensibility of the public, than could be otherwise conveyed. He has accordingly selected for this service, with the approbation of the Senate, Mr. Monroe, formerly our Minister Plenipotentiary at Paris, and lately Governor of Virginia, who will be joined with Mr. Livingston in a commission extraordinary to treat with the French Republic; and with Mr. Pinckney in a like commission to treat, if necessary, with the Spanish Government.

Mr. Monroe is expected here to-morrow, and he will probably sail shortly afterwards to New York.

These communications will enable you to meet the British Minister in conversation on the subject stated in your letter of May 7th, 1802. The United States are disposed to live in amity with their neighbors, whoever they may be, as long as their neighbors shall duly respect their rights; but it is equally their determination to maintain their rights against those who may not respect them; premising, where the occasion may require, the peaceable modes of obtaining satisfaction for wrongs, and endeavoring, by friendly arrangements and provident stipulations, to guard against the controversies most likely to occur.

Whatever may be the result of the present mission extraordinary, nothing certainly will be admitted into it not consistent with our prior engagements. The United States and Great Britain have agreed, each for itself, to the free and common navigation by the other of the river Mississippi—each being left, at the same time, to a separate adjustment with other nations of questions between them relative to the same subject. This being the necessary meaning of our treaties with Great Britain, and the course pursued under them, a difference of opinion seems to be precluded. Any such difference would be matter of real regret; for it is not only our purpose to maintain the best faith with that nation, but our desire to cherish a mutual confidence and cordiality, which events may render highly important to both nations.

Your successor has not yet been named, and it is now possible that the time you may have fixed for leaving England will arrive before any arrangements for the vacancy can have their effect. Should this be the case, the President, sensible of the inconvenience to which you might be subjected by an unexpected detention, thinks it would not be reasonable to claim it of you. It may be hoped that the endeavors to prevent an interval in the legation be successful; and as it can not be more than a very short one, no great evil can well happen from it.

I have the honor, &c.,

JAMES MADISON.

President Jefferson to M. Dupont.

WASHINGTON, *February 1, 1803.*

DEAR SIR,—I have to acknowledge the receipt of your favors of August the 16th and October the 4th. The latter I received with peculiar satisfaction; because, while it holds up terms which cannot be entirely yielded, it proposes such as a mutual spirit of accommodation and sacrifice of opinion may bring to some point of union. While we were preparing on this subject such modifications of the propositions of your letter of October the 4th, as we could assent to, an event happened which obliged us to adopt measures of urgency. The suspension of the right of deposit at New Orleans, ceded to us by treaty with Spain, threw our whole country into such a ferment as imminently threatened its peace. This, however, was believed to be the act of the Intendant, unauthorized by his government. But it showed the necessity of making effectual arrangements to secure the peace of the two countries against the indiscreet acts of subordinate agents. The urgency of the case, as well as the public spirit, therefore induced us to make a more solemn appeal to the justice and judgment of our neighbors, by sending a minister extraordinary to impress them with the necessity of some arrangement. Mr. Monroe has been selected. His good dispositions cannot be doubted. Multiplied conversations with him, and views of the subject taken in all the shapes in which it can present itself, have possessed him with our estimates of everything relating to it, with a minuteness which no written communication to Mr. Livingston could ever have attained. These will prepare them to meet and decide on every form of proposition which can occur, without awaiting new instructions from hence, which might draw to an indefinite length a discussion where circumstances imperiously obliged us to a prompt decision. For the occlusion of the Mississippi is a state of things in which we cannot exist. He goes, therefore, joined with Chancellor Livingston, to aid in the issue of a crisis the most important the United States have ever met since their independence, and which is to decide their future character and career. The confidence which the government of France reposes in you, will undoubtedly give great weight to your information. An equal confidence on our part, founded on your knowledge of the subject, your just views of it, your good dispositions toward this country, and my long experience of your personal faith and friendship, assures me that you will render between us all the good offices in your power. The interests of the two countries being absolutely the same as to this matter, your aid may be conscientiously given. It will often perhaps, be possible for you, having a freedom of communication, *omnibus horis*, which diplomatic gentlemen will be excluded from by forms, to smooth difficulties by representations and reasonings, which would be received with more suspicion from them. You will thereby render great good to both countries. For our circumstances are so imperious as to admit of no delay as to our course; and the use of the Mississippi so indispensable, that we cannot hesitate one moment to hazard our existence for its maintenance. If we fail in this effort to put it beyond the reach of accident, we see the destinies we have to run, and prepare at once for them. Not but that we shall still endeavor to go on in peace and friendship with our neighbors as long as we can, *if our rights of navigation and deposit are respected*, but as we foresee that the caprices of the local officers, and the abuse of those rights by our boatmen and navigators, which neither government can prevent, will keep up a state of irritation which cannot long be kept inactive, we should be criminally improvident not to take at once eventual measures for strengthening ourselves for the contest. It may be said, if this object be so all-important to us, why do we not offer such a sum as to insure its purchase? The answer is simple. We are an agricultural people, poor in money, and owing great debts. These will be falling due by installments for fifteen years to come, and require from us the practice of rigorous economy to accomplish their payment; and it is our principle to pay to a moment whatever we have engaged, and never to engage what we cannot, and mean not faithfully to pay. We have calculated our resources, and find the sum to be moderate which they would enable us to pay, and we know from late trials that little can be added to it by borrowing. The country, too, which we wish to purchase, except the portion already granted, and which must be confirmed to the private holders, is a barren sand, six hundred miles from east to west, and from thirty to forty and fifty miles from north to south, formed by deposition of the sands by the Gulf Stream in its circular course round the Mexican Gulf, and which being spent after performing a semicircle, has made from its last depositions the sand bank of East Florida. In West Florida, indeed, there are on the borders of the rivers some rich bottoms, formed by the mud brought from the upper country. These bottoms are all possessed by individuals. But the spaces between river and river are mere banks of sand; and in East Florida there are neither rivers, nor consequently any bottoms. We can not then make anything by a sale of the lands to individuals. So that it is peace alone which makes it an object with us, and which ought to make the cession of it desirable to France. Whatever power, other than ourselves, holds the country east of the Mississippi becomes our natural enemy. Will such a possession do France as much good, as such an enemy may do her harm? And how long would it be hers, were such an enemy, situated at its door, added to Great Britain? I confess, it appears to me as essential to France to keep at peace with us, as it is to us to keep at peace with her; and that, if this cannot be secured without some compromise as to the territory in question, it will be useful for both to make some sacrifices to effect the compromise.

You see, my good friend, with what frankness I communicate with you on this subject; that I hide nothing from you, and that I am endeavoring to turn our private friendship to the good of our respective countries. And can private friendship ever answer a nobler end than by keeping two nations at peace, who, if this new position which one of them is taking were rendered innocent, have more points of common interest, and fewer of collision, than any two on earth; who become natural friends, instead of natural enemies, which this change of position would make them. My letters of April the 25th, May the 5th, and this present one have been written, without any disguise, in this view; and while safe in your hands they can never do anything but good. But you and I are now at the time of life when our call to another state of being cannot be distant, and may be near. Besides, your government is in the habit of seizing papers without notice. These letters might thus get into hands, which, like the hornet which extracts poison from the same flower that yields honey to the bee, might make them the ground of blowing up a flame between our two countries, and make our friendship and confidence in each other effect exactly the reverse of what we are aiming at. Being yourself thoroughly possessed of every idea in them, let me ask from your friendship an immediate consignment of them to the flames. That alone can make all safe, and ourselves secure.

President Jefferson to Mr. Livingston.

WASHINGTON, *February 3, 1803.*

DEAR SIR,—My last to you was by Mr. Dupont. Since that I received yours of May 22d. Mr. Madison supposes you have written a subsequent one which has never come to hand. A late suspension by the Intendant of New Orleans of our right of deposit there, without which the right of navigation is impracticable, has thrown this country into such a flame of hostile disposition as can scarcely be described. The western country was peculiarly sensible to it as you may suppose. Our business was to take the most effectual pacific measures in our power to remove the suspension, and at the same time to persuade our countrymen that pacific measures would be the most effectual and the most speedily so. The opposition caught it as a plank in a shipwreck, hoping it would enable them to tack the Western people to them. They raised the cry of war, were intriguing in all quarters to exasperate the Western inhabitants to arm and go down on their own authority and possess themselves of New Orleans, and in the meantime were daily reiterating, in new shapes, inflammatory resolutions for the adoption of the House. As a remedy to all this we determined to name a minister extraordinary to go immediately to

Paris and Madrid to settle this matter. This measure being a visible one, and the person named peculiarly proper with the Western country, crushed at once and put an end to all further attempts on the Legislature. From that moment all has become quiet; and the more readily in the Western country, as the sudden alliance of these new federal friends had of itself already began to make them suspect the wisdom of their own course. The measure was moreover proposed from another cause. We must know at once whether we can acquire New Orleans or not. We are satisfied nothing else will secure us against a war at no distant period; and we cannot press this reason without beginning those arrangements which will be necessary if war is hereafter to result. For this purpose it was necessary that the negotiators should be fully possessed of every idea we have on the subject, so as to meet the propositions of the opposite party, in what ever form they may be offered; and give them a shape admissible by us without being obliged to await new instructions hence. With this view, we have joined Mr. Monroe with yourself at Paris, and to Mr. Pinckney at Madrid, although we believe it will be hardly necessary for him to go to this last place. Should we fail in this object of the mission, a further one will be superadded for the other side of the channel. On this subject you will be informed by the Secretary of State, and Mr. Monroe will be able also to inform you of all our views and purposes. By him I send another letter to Dupont, whose aid may be of the greatest service, as it will be divested of the shackles of form. The letter is left open for your perusal, after which I wish a wafer stuck in it before it be delivered. The official and the verbal communications to you by Mr. Monroe will be so full and minute, that I need not trouble you with an inofficial repetition of them. The future destinies of our country hang on the event of this negotiation, and I am sure they could not be placed in more able or more zealous hands. On our parts we shall be satisfied that what you do not effect, connot be effected. Accept therefore assurances of my sincere and constant affection and high respect.

R. R. Livingston to James Madison.

PARIS, *February 5, 1803.*

DEAR SIR: Not knowing where to direct the enclosed, I submit it to your care. The bearer of this to Nantz waits, so that I can write you nothing but that the Louisiana armament is still icebound. The Floridas are not yet ceded, owing, I believe, to some difficulty about Parma, and the solicitude of the Emperor of Russia to provide for the King of Sardinia. Spain is however prepared to make the cession, and I presume it will be done. I have precise answers from you to none of my inquiries, and am much at a loss how to act. I have much to say, but am not allowed to enlarge. You shall hear from me by the first safe conveyance.

I am, etc.,

R. R. LIVINGSTON.

Hon. JAMES MADISON,
  Secretary of State.

James Madison, Secretary of State, to Charles Pinckney and James Monroe.

DEPARTMENT OF STATE,
February 17, 1803.

SIR: You will be herewith furnished with a joint commission to treat with His Catholic Majesty, and with a letter of credence to him. For the object of the commission, and as a guide to your negotiations, I refer you to the instructions given in relation to the French Government. Whatever portion of the arrangements contemplated may be found to depend not on the French, but on the Spanish Government, is to be sought from the latter, on the like terms as if they had depended on the former.

The scale of value applied to the distinct territories in question will deserve particular attention; so will the provision for paying our citizens who have claims on Spain out of the sums stipulated as the price of her territorial possessions. Among these claims it will be important to include, not only those within the description contained in the convention signed by Mr. Pinckney in August last, but such as may be founded on unlawful acts committed within Spanish responsibility by other than Spanish subjects, and on acts committed by Spanish subjects, within the Spanish colonies, inconsistent with true equity, though not with the forms of law.

Your particular attention will also be due, in case a cession should not be attained, to an enlargement of our right of deposit at New Orleans, to the establishment of suitable deposits at the mouths of the rivers, passing from the United States through the Floridas, as well as to the free navigation of those rivers by citizens of the United States. Useful hints on these subjects may be found in the letter of which a copy is annexed from the Consul of the United States at New Orleans.

I refer for another object which will deserve your attention, to the letter from the Department of State of the 27th of November, to the Minister Plenipotentiary of the United States, which urges the necessity of some provision by the Governments of Europe having American Colonies, by which the irregular and injurious proceedings of colonial officers towards the United States may be more effectually controlled, or more expeditiously corrected, than by crossing the Atlantic with representations on such occasions. Such a provision is not more due to our just expectations than to the interests which those Governments have in maintaining the amicable relations which subsist with the United States. In the same letter, notice was given that the Spanish Government would be held responsible for whatever damages might be sustained by our citizens in consequence of the violation of the treaty by the Intendant at New Orleans. It will be proper to obtain from that Government a stipulation that will provide for such contingent damages. In case the convention, already on foot, should be open for such an article, it may be therein inserted. Should that opportunity not exist, it will be necessary to authorize, by a supplemental article, the Commissioners appointed under that convention to award the indemnifications.

I have the honor, &c., JAMES MADISON.

R. R. Livingston to the Secretary of State.

PARIS, *February 18, 1803.*

DEAR SIR: I have been honored by yours of the — November. I am pleased to find that you are satisfied with my applications to the Government on the subject of the debt; I am only sorry that those applications have hitherto been unsuccessful, and, as far as appears, will continue to be, unless some motive more efficacious than that of justice, or national faith or credit, is held out. To enter into the financial arrangements of people in power here would lead me into very delicate discussion, which would not tend to any advantage proportioned to the risk it might subject me to. I still think that if anything is done to satisfy our citizens, it must be by some advantageous offer on the part of our Government. You will find some of my ideas on that subject sketched in my former letters.

As you have intimated the propriety of opening some other channel of communication with the First Consul than through the Minister, this I have effectually done, so as to have got several unofficial communications under his eye, and to have learnt his sentiments thereon. I can have a personal conference with him when I choose, having made arrangements for the purpose; but I defer it for two reasons: First, I have never yet had any specific instructions from you how to act or what to offer. To meet him merely to talk of the justice of our claims, and of our rights on the Mississippi, would be only to say ungracious truths, and excite prejudices which may render a future conference more difficult; and, second, because it is one of the traits of his character when he has once fully avowed a sentiment not easily to change it. I have, therefore, thought it best to address myself officially to the Minister, and unofficially to the only man supposed to have any sort of influence over him. I have accordingly put into his hands some notes containing plain truth mixed with that species of personal attention which I know to be most pleasing. The delicate subject of these notes makes me unwilling to send them unless I can find time to put them in cipher, which I fear will not be the case by this conveyance; you will, however, have them in the first letter I write to the President, which will be by this or the next conveyance. I do not mention the channel I allude to, because I wish it only to be known to yourself and the President, and my last letter to him has sufficiently explained it. The only basis on which I think it possible to do anything here is to connect our claims with our offers to purchase the Floridas. Upon this subject my notes turn. I have first endeavored to show how little advantage France is likely to make from these colonies; the temptation they offer to Britain to attack them by sea and from Canada; the effect the conquest of them by Britain would have upon the islands; and the monopoly which that conquest would give to a rival Power of the trade of the West as well as of the East Indies. I have dwelt upon the importance of a friendly intercourse between them and us, both as it respects their commerce and the security of their islands; and I have proposed to them the relinquishment of New Orleans and West Florida, as far as the river Perdido, together with all the territory lying to the north of the Arkansas, under an idea that it was necessary to interpose us between them and Canada, as the only means of preventing an attack from that quarter.

I did not speak of East Florida because I found they consider the navigation of the Gulf as very important; for this I proposed an indefinite sum, not wishing to mention any till I should receive your instructions, that it should be a condition of this treaty that the American debt should be inscribed on their 5 per cent. stock. I knew it would be vain to render them our creditors by deducting this out of our payment, because actual money would alone have any effect in carrying the plan through; and even that must be managed with some circumspection, or no plan will succeed. These propositions, with certain accompaniments, were well received, and were some days under the First Consul's consideration; when it was thought a better bargain might be made on the spot; and I was told that General Bernadotte would have full power to treat on this subject in America on the basis on which I had placed it. My answer to this information you will find in the enclosed note. I am now lying on my oars in hopes of something explicit from you. I consider the object of immense importance; and this, perhaps, the favorable moment to press it, because the affairs of the islands are yet very doubtful, and the armament is still blocked up by the ice in Holland; though as we now have a thaw here I fear they will not be so much longer. My plan is much relished by the person through whom it was proposed. General Bernadotte sees the awkward situation in which he will be placed if he goes out while our demands remain unsatisfied. But nobody dares to offer an opinion when that of the First Consul has been expressed. And, at present, a very unexpected difficulty has arisen. I told you that Parma would be offered for the Floridas, and that General Bournonville was sent to negotiate the business. It was never doubted a moment here that it would be effected; this I learned from Talleyrand and the Spanish Ambassador. They intimated that the treaty would be signed the day the King returned from Barcelona; and their information accorded with that which Lord Whitworth had received. I learn now from the Spanish Ambassador that the thing has met with some difficulty, as he says, not because of any aversion in the Court to make the cession, but of some difference between the Prince of Peace and General Bournonville. I believe, however, that this is not the sole cause; but that Spain begins to see that, in receiving Parma, she will receive nothing; as it will be rendered subservient to another arrangement, as I hinted in my last. You will consider this rather as a conjecture than as anything I am perfectly founded in relating. The essential fact for us is that the Floridas are not yet ceded.

Mr. Dazara, yesterday, told me that he began to have his doubts whether they would be; but France is fully impressed with the nullity of her possession in Louisiana unless she has some port in the Gulf. Indeed, the Minister told me yesterday that there were no difficulties of any moment. I presume that she will, ultimately, find some way to cut the Gordian knot; and I can not but sincerely wish that you may have availed yourselves of the pretense Spain has given you to take possession. It will be best to treat with the subject in our hands; but, at all events, tell me what to do if they should go into the hands of France; and fix the sum you are willing to give in case they should listen anew to my proposition; for as to Bernadotte doing anything with you I have no great faith. I pray you again to give me some instructions, for I may be acting contrary to your intentions; and I should be very sorry to do anything that you may find it proper to disavow. I am not satisfied, from examining my instructions and commission, that I am empowered to do anything but the common routine of business. As I did not receive this till I was going off I had no opportunity of objecting to them. I find that I have no precise diplomatic character, not even an envoy ordinary or extraordinary, though it had been usual for the United States to grant this latter grade to gentlemen of less standing than myself. But this by the bye, which I should not have mentioned if I did not find that it is not quite so agreeable here, as Bernadotte is a man of high rank, and would have wished, like his brother Generals, to have gone out with a more elevated rank, but which they can not give while the United States only retain a Minister Plenipotentiary here. It is proper that I should say a few words on General Bernadotte; he is one of the old Jacobin party, and has been much looked up to by them; but being brother-in-law to Joseph Bonaparte, he is favorably connected; but has not ceased to be an object of some jealousy. And I believe you may consider his present mission as an honorable banishment. He proposes only to stay a few months in America. I have had many conversations with him. His dispositions are just such as I would wish with respect to us; but his temper is warm and fiery, and you will have to flatter his pride and that of his nation, if you would stand well with him.

In several conversations that I have had with Lord Whitworth I find that Britain is very averse to the projected exchange for the Floridas; and he thinks that, if effected, it will be taken up very warmly by the nation. Mr. King, however, in an answer this day received to some questions I have put on that subject, thinks differently. I find that the sentiments of the two nations, with respect to each other, have totally changed from what they were a year ago; they at present mortally hate each other; and nothing but the want of allies keeps Britain from breaking out. You will find in one of the Moniteurs I have sent you, a curious journal of Sebastiana, which has been evidently published to prepare this nation for some new operation in Egypt; it is extremely offensive to the British. I have a letter from Mr. Graham, who is far from being satisfied with the conduct of the Spanish court; who act like this in saying nothing on the subject of their treaty with France, and who have passed a law prohibiting any American vessel to enter their ports till they have performed a quarantine in some foreign port.

I mentioned to you my wish to be empowered to recognize the Italian Republic; to be accredited to the Consul, as has been done by most of those Powers who wish to please him; and as this is a compliment without expense, it might not be amiss to pay it, particularly as we shall have some commercial connection with the Italian States.

From the best accounts I can receive from Holland the armament will be detained there till about the last of March, so that you will not have them in New Orleans till June; a precious interval, of which you may think it prudent to avail yourselves.

I broke off here that I might have an explicit conversation with the Minister, founded upon the newspaper intelligence from our country; for I have had no other since the date of your letter of — November. I endeavored to impress him strongly with the idea of our determination never to suffer our rights on the Mississippi to be impeded; and of the little value that that country would be to them in the production of a revenue; of the almost certainty of war between them and the savages in case their stipends were withheld; the pain it must give the First Consul to be the means of the destruction of the white inhabitants, whom it would be impossible to defend; and upon the benefits that would result to the commerce and manufactures of France from a friendly connection with us. These seemed to make an impression upon him; and he promised to represent them strongly to the First Consul to-morrow; but added, that however my other plans might be received, I must consider the purchase of the country as out of the question; intimating that a sale was below their dignity; so that I fear my hopes, founded on their necessities, are frustrated.

I am, sir, with the most respectful consideration, your obedient, humble servant.

ROBERT R. LIVINGSTON.

Hon. JAMES MADISON, *Secretary of State.*

(The following, Nos. 2 and 3, are supposed to be the memoirs referred to in Mr. Livingston's despatch of the 18th February.)

No. 2.

To —— ——:

I am sensible, sir, that I have already taxed your patience in the memoirs that I have submitted to your attention; but, sir, (pardon the frankness with which I speak,) the critical moment is arrived which rivets the connection of the United States to France, or binds a young and growing people for ages hereafter to her mortal and inveterate enemy.

How highly I estimate the alliance of France, and how much I believe the happiness of both nations may be promoted by it, not only appears from the whole of my political conduct, but has been stated in an essay upon the relative maritime power of France and Britain, which, as I have learned, has been honored by the First Consul's attention.

The United States have at present but two possible causes of difference with France—the debt due to her citizens, and the possession of Louisiana. The first of these France is not only bound to pay by the laws of justice, but by the solemn stipulations of a treaty which has been observed with the utmost good faith by the United States, who have advanced large sums in consequence, without suffering themselves to doubt that it would meet with equal attention on the part of France. Give me leave to add, sir, that your signature was considered as a guarantee of that treaty by the people of the United States, who had long since learned to estimate the candor and integrity of your character.

My present object, sir, is to show, in a very few words, that Louisiana affords France not only the means of discharging their debt, and promoting the other object which I took the liberty to hint at before, but even of placing her colony of Louisiana in a better situation, should it be her wish to retain that colony, than she would do by listening to no compromise with the United States.

The object of France in forming this colony is to supply her islands; to afford an outlet for such of her population as she thinks she can spare from home. But not to scatter her people over an immense wilderness, where they will be lost for her and to the world; or to fill her territory with inhabitants that would withdraw their allegiance the moment they found themselves in a situation so to do; which will certainly be the case if these, or if any but the natives of France are permitted to settle it.

It is, then, the interest of France to limit her territory, and to render it as compact as possible, without placing it at such a distance from the sea as to put it totally out of her control. While with the remainder of the territory, she fulfills other important objects, and, above all, builds her future connection with the United States upon mutual interests, and that strict and solemn regard for treaties which can alone lull the apprehensions that her power excites, and to which, more than the force of her arms, Rome was indebted for the dominion of the world.

The produce of Louisiana must be conveyed by the Mississippi, and there are no ports for her marine to the west of Pensacola. If, therefore, France should possess Pensacola, and all the ports to the east of it, she will have the complete command of the Gulf. And if she possesses the free navigation of the Mississippi, and all Louisiana lying to the west of that river, and south of the river Arkansas, comprehending a tract nearly as large as the ancient Government of France, she will have more territory than will suffice to supply all the wants of her marine, and West India colonies, with such articles as that country can produce.

Louisiana, within these limits, can support a population of 15,000,000 of people. You will judge, sir, whether it would be possible for France to retain more than that number in subjection; or whether it would be good policy to extend her population beyond the number she can govern.

The settlers to the north of the river Arkansas would be too far from the sea to fear any force from France. A distant colony must be of moderate size, compactly settled, and not remote from the sea, or the parent State will soon lose all control over it. The interest of France, then, requires that her colony in Louisiana should not exceed the limits I mention, and the separation of this territory from that lying to the east of the river Perdido would afford an additional security to France for the possession of both, not only as it would break the connection of the colonies, but as their interest would be totally different, the last possessing little valuable land, (for both East and West Florida are barren tracts,) would be military posts and commercial entrepôts; from which the trade would be carried on to and from the Mississippi in small vessels; while that with France would, on account of her safe and commodious harbors, center in East Florida.

The inhabitants of this country would be deeply interested in a continuance of their connection with the mother country. While the interposition of West Florida, in the hands of the United States, would prevent any coercion on the part of the inhabitants of Louisiana, if they should at any time be disposed to revolt; east Florida, on the contrary, while loyal to France, would, by means of her navy, have a powerful control on the colony of Louisiana.

The example of England should have some weight. The Dutch possessed New York; England, for the sake of uniting her colonies, purchased it from Holland. Had it been left in the hands of the Dutch, that union, which has lost the whole to Britain, would have been prevented.

The Colonies of Louisiana and East Florida, within the limits proposed, being thus secured, the remainder of the Spanish cession is only valuable as it enables France to pursue other great objects, to wit: the payment of the debt in conformity to her treaty; and the conciliation of an ally which may on so many important occasions be useful to her; and the one of no less magnitude to which I have in my last the honor to allude.

The United States possess the east side of the Mississippi, from its source to the thirty-first degree of north latitude. It would be very interesting to them to acquire the possession of the remainder of the east bank of that river to its mouth, and that narrow strip of land which lies between the thirty-first degree of latitude and the sea, as far as the river Perdido; not on account of the value of the land, for, except a small quantity on the banks of the river, it is for the most part a sandy barren, or a sunken marsh; but because it would give them the mouths of those rivers which run through their territory, and afford an outlet to the sea.

To the cession of this country but one possible objection can be raised on the part of France; it may attach a value to New Orleans which it by no means merits. The fact is, that to France, who has the choice of fixing her capital on either side of the river, New Orleans has no circumstance to recommend it. It is placed on the naked bank; it has no port, basin, or quay, for shipping; has no fortification of any strength; and is incapable of being rendered a good military position; and the houses are only of wood, subject to continual accidents. The situation was fixed first by France on account of its being on the Florida side of the river where the settlements commenced; but as it was soon found that the lands of the west side of the river were much richer, the principal part of the population is now there. The bank opposite to New Orleans is higher and better calculated for a town: it already has a strong post in Fort Leon, the most commanding position in that country; and the harbor, or rather the road, is in all things equal to that of New Orleans. As a Government house and barracks, stores, &c., must be built either at New Orleans or at Fort Leon, there can be no doubt, even if France retains both, that the latter ought to have the preference, since a regular and handsome capital could be laid out there, and in a healthier and stronger situation than at New Orleans.

It is highly probable that, in this case, the superiority it would have in point of health, the advantages of the Government, and, above all, the free trade with France and her islands, would render it in three years more populous than New Orleans now is. The French merchants would sell their houses in the one to the Americans, and establish themselves in the other. Should France retain the whole of the Spanish cession on both sides of the river, she will find it absolutely necessary to remove her capital to the west side. The river for three months is impassable from the violence of the inundation, and the trees that it brings down with it. As the bulk of the colony is on the west wide of the river, it must necessarily draw its capital after it, or submit to be cut off from it during this period. A town will, therefore, rise at Fort Leon, where the richest establishments are already formed, which must increase with the population of the country.

The difficulty of removing the capital from New Orleans will increase as its buildings become more numerous, and its population greater. It is, therefore, in every event the true interest of France to commence the establishment of a capital on a regular plan on the west side of the river, where it must ultimately be, rather than expend money upon the old town of New Orleans, which they will find too much insulated for the capital of Louisiana.

Permit me, sir, to examine the subject in a point of view which I conceive is important not only to France and the United States, but to every maritime power. It can not be doubted that the peace between France and Britain has been too disadvantageous to the latter to be of long duration. Strong symptoms of an approaching rupture have already appeared; and the statesmen of both countries will begin to examine the points of attack and defense, and the acquisitions that afford the most permanent advantages. The Cape, Malta, and Egypt, have already awakened the cupidity of Great Britain. Should she extend her views across the Atlantic, (and what is to limit them?) the cession of Louisiana to France offers her the fairest pretense to invade that country, either from Canada or by the Atlantic.

She felt no reluctance in leaving them to Spain; but she will not quietly see them in the hands of France. She will strain every nerve to acquire them. By uniting them with Canada and Nova Scotia she encircles the United States; and, having the same manners, the same religion, the same language, and a number of partisans among the commercial inhabitants of the United States; having carefully removed every conflicting question, and even conciliated, by the liberality of her restitutions, those whom her conduct during the war had irritated; it will be difficult to say what will be the extent of her influence. But, independently of this circumstance, if Britain should unite Louisiana and West Florida to her other American possessions, no power in Europe will be able to oppose her force. The bay of St. Esprit will become another Gibraltar, from which she will ravage every island and continental possession of France, Spain, and Holland; she will monopolize the commodities of the West as she has already done those of the East Indies. Not a moment, sir, should be lost for placing a barrier between the settlements that France may wish to retain in Louisiana and Canada, by ceding to the United States the portion I have proposed above the Arkansas; and by the cession of New Orleans and West Florida, to take from them the first inducement to attack that country. France should exert all her resources and all her strength in the immediate fortification of Pensacola and the bay of St. Esprit; or, if she has not the means of doing it, she should leave them in the hands of Spain (if she can consent to leave her at peace) or to some other neutral nation. For I will venture to say that the acquisition of that country, by a nation who possesses Newfoundland, Nova Scotia, and Canada, with a powerful maritime force, will annihilate the external trade of every other nation in Europe; and that it would be the true interest even of Spain herself, rather to see her ports in Florida in the hands of the United States, who alone can defend them, than to keep them in her own, at the risk of having them wrested from her by Britain. Perhaps, in the present state of things, considering the superiority of the British navy at this moment, the great capital that it will require to reinstate the French islands, and her continental possessions in the East Indies and in America, the wisest measure would be, not only to make the cession I have asked, but to hypothecate the whole of East Florida for a term of years, for such part of the American debt as may remain unsatisfied.

But as this is a mere hasty, undigested idea, rather intended to turn your attention to this subject, than as a matter sufficiently matured to take the form of a proposition. I can not, sir, conclude this note, without turning your attention to the present feelings of the people of all parties in the United States with respect to France. The total silence of the French Government on the subject of their intention as to the navigation of the Mississippi, and their rights of *entrepôt* at New Orleans, secured to them by the most solemn treaty with Spain; the mystery with which all the arrangements of France for taking possession of that country are concealed from the Minister of the United States, notwithstanding his repeated notes to the Minister of Exterior Relations on the subject; have excited the most lively apprehensions of designs unfriendly to their commerce and their rights. The total neglect of every measure that leads to a security for their debt, notwithstanding the provisions of the treaty, and the ruin of numbers of their citizens by this; and the very extraordinary decisions which have, in several instances, taken place in the Council of Prizes, for which I have been able to receive not merely no redress but even no answer; contrasted with the good faith displayed by their own Government with respect to France, with the scrupulous attention that Great Britain has paid to repair, by the most liberal conduct, the abuses she has permitted herself to commit during the war, leads to a belief that France limits her rights by her power; and insensibly disposes them to alliances, both offensive and defensive, which it has heretofore been her policy to avoid. Can it possibly be the interest of France, sir, to drive the United States into these alliances, while she forms colonies, and retains islands in their neighborhood? Can she look with contempt upon an enterprising and hardy nation who possesses means of defense at home, and for a maritime force which will render her respectable abroad? The immense power of France has rendered her an object of jealousy to the Old World; while the inhabitants of the New felt no other sensations than those of admiration and respect.

In Europe, France only knows secret enemies and hollow friends. In America, she has grateful allies. Let her not, sir, for the bubble of the day, cast them off; but let her avail herself of the advantages she has acquired, to bind them to her. Should she, relying on her own strength, never need their aid, she still will find a consolation in reflecting that the sacrifices (if such they may be called) she makes, are sacrifices at the altar of justice and national faith. She will cheaply purchase the esteem of men and the favor of Heaven by the surrender of a distant wilderness, which can neither add to her wealth nor to her strength.

R. R. L.

No. 3.

JANUARY 7, 1802. (?)

To —— ——.

In a conversation which I yesterday had with General Bernadotte, I find that some idea is at present entertained by the First Consul of treating at Washington of the several matters I had the honor to mention to you. I should be extremely pleased at this arrangement, because I should see in it those advantages to my country which are always derived from carrying on a negotiation at home, where the views of the Government are clearly known, where they can avail themselves of every light and information, while the Minister with whom they treat is isolated, and must rely on his own resources and those he draws from suspicious channels. But, sir, there are circumstances which, in the present instance, appear to me to counterbalance those advantages, and which render it peculiarly the interest of France and the United States to come to a more immediate arrangement of several matters that interest them in this negotiation.

I can not conceal from you, sir, that both the Government and the people of the United States are at present in such a state of mind as to be filled with doubts and jealousies with respect to the views and dispositions of France. Many among her firmest friends are ruined by the inexecution of that article of the treaty which provides for the payment of their debts; many by hasty measures at Santo Domingo, and the disregard, in some instances, of the common principles of the law of nations in the decisions of the Council of Prizes. The silence of the French and Spanish Governments on the subject of their intentions relative to the navigation of the Mississippi and the right of *entrepôt* at New Orleans, has given just grounds of alarm. But, sir, a circumstance has just come to my knowledge, though not officially, yet in such a way as leaves me little room to doubt of its authenticity, which can not fail to drive the United States into some violent measure.

"On the 20th of October, the Governor of New Orleans issued a proclamation, in which, speaking of the Americans, he says they will not in future be permitted to make a deposit of their cargo in New Orleans, in conformity to the twenty-second article of their Treaty of 27th October, 1795, which has expired." I have examined the treaty: there is no pretense for this construction of it; and, as the right has been regularly exercised till now, it will be generally believed in the United States that this construction could only have been suggested by a wish on the part of France to get rid of the provisions of the treaty before she took possession. Now, sir, I will frankly confess to you that the United States will rather hazard their very existence than suffer the Mississippi to be shut against them. Of this you will easily be convinced when you learn that, when their numbers were but half of what they now are, and their means of defense infinitely less, their instructions to their Ministers that made the first treaty with Great Britain were, by no means to sign a treaty without securing the free navigation of that river. You will not, therefore, be surprised if this step of Spain should wind up the American people and Government to so high a pitch of resentment as shall lead them to a close and intimate connection with Britain, and perhaps to an immediate rupture with Spain.

If, under these circumstances, an Ambassador should arrive in America without being the bearer of a treaty which terminates their differences, and should propose to enter upon a treaty with the American Government, they will naturally ask, why has our Minister been able to effect nothing in fourteen months? Why have our debts remained unpaid? Why has he received no sort of satisfaction on any subject on which he has addressed himself to the Government? And why does France now, at this late day, prefer making a treaty in America to concluding one at home? While, at the same time, she is sending out large armies to the islands, and possessing herself of Louisiana and the Floridas? Is it not to paralyze those measures of security that common prudence would suggest to the United States? Is it not to stop the treaty which we are about to make relative to our Western boundary with Great Britain? Is it not to give France time to arrange her affairs in the islands, to strengthen her ports in America? Some months will elapse before the treaty is made, and many before it is ratified. What security have we that this treaty, when made, will meet the approbation of the First Consul, when time has made a change in circumstances? These, sir, and a thousand other doubts, will arise in the minds of the citizens of the United States, and they will be blown into certainties by the agents of Britain, who are to be found in all our commercial towns.

There is no doubt that the Government of the United States will receive with attention the French Ambassador; that they will listen to his propositions; and will treat with him with pleasure upon the basis I have mentioned. But they will not, on that account, cease to consider the conclusion as very distant, or relinquish any measure that they may deem it wise to pursue, in case no treaty was proposed. Treating under these circumstances, I fear there will be much less ground to hope a cordial and friendly intercourse than if the earliest moment was embraced, and the Ambassador of France was the bearer of a treaty already completed.

There are other considerations, sir, which I believe will have some weight with the First Consul, if suggested to him. The terms I have proposed as a basis of a treaty, are precisely those which would be most repugnant to the interests of Britain. By interposing the United States between Canada and the French establishments on the Mississippi, her views upon a communication with the sea by that channel are completely cut off. By giving France the ports on the Gulf of Mexico, the British islands are held in check. By interposing the establishments of France between the United States and Mexico, by the only practicable route, the jealousies of Spain, with respect to the United States, will be calmed, and she will have in France an ally at hand to protect her from the ambitious views of Britain. At present, Britain feels little uneasiness about the possessions of France in Louisiana, because, believing that they will operate to render the United States enemies of France, they count upon their aid in dispossessing them, and in reaping the fruits of their labor. It will be extremely difficult, if a negotiation is set on foot in the United States to conduct it with such secrecy as to escape the vigilance of Britain. In a popular Government, where she has many friends, it may not be difficult to prevent success. Nor will she hesitate to make important sacrifices to defeat this object.

There are other matters which, though less important, deserve consideration. France apprehends that the rebels in the islands are supplied with arms, &c., from the United States. I trust that apprehension has hitherto been unfounded. She may wish for laws pointed to this object. The party hostile to France, the person jealous and suspicious of her views in their present state of irritation, may consider her islands as the point in which she is most vulnerable; and, while they decline any active part in support of the revolters, they may be unwilling to see them reduced to submission. The British influence will have room to operate on this subject. Laws pass very slowly, and there are many means of obstructing their passage. But a treaty is, in the United States, the most solemn of all laws. Any provision that we agree upon here must be binding. If, then, a treaty is formed here, the Minister, instead of having a law to solicit, in the face of a thousand intrigues and jealousies, will carry the law out with him, and will have only to watch over its execution.

All these, and many other reasons, which I will spare you the trouble reading, suggest the propriety of finishing the treaty here, and that as speedily as possible. It is certain that more light can be acquired relative to that country at Paris, (if doubt should be entertained as to my assertions,) than any foreign Minister could obtain at Washington.

I speak, sir, perhaps with too much freedom on the views of your country and my own. But I speak with freedom, from a conviction of the integrity of my own intentions, and the absolute certainty that the measures I suggest are not less the interest of the one than of the other. As no chicanery, no crooked policy, will mingle itself in our treaty, one may be concluded in a week, if the Consul shall be pleased to name yourself or General Bernadotte, in whose candor and information I have great confidence. It would certainly be very grateful to him to be the bearer of a treaty which insures him the cordial and friendly reception in the United States that his mission and his merits entitle him to.

I am, sir, &c., ROBERT R. LIVINGSTON.

James Madison, Secretary of State, to Robert R. Livingston, Minister to France.

DEPARTMENT OF STATE, *February 23, 1803.*

SIR: Since my last, which was of the 18th of January, I have received your several letters of the 11th and 14th of November, 1802.

As you will receive this from the hands of Mr. Monroe, I refer to him for full information relative to our internal affairs generally, and, in particular, to the violation to our right of deposit at New Orleans, with the impressions and proceedings which have resulted from it.

In his hands also, are the commission and instructions in which he is joined with yourself, to treat with the French Government for an enlargement of our rights and our security in the southwestern neighborhood of the United States. These documents, with the communications and explanations which Mr. Monroe will be able to add, will put you in full possession of the subject.

The negotiation to be opened will bring the disposition and views of the French Government to a test. If it should meet the negotiation in a proper spirit, and with a just estimate of the real interests of France, not only a favorable issue may be expected, but it will be proper for you to avail yourself of the occasion, to insist on a prompt and complete fulfillment of the convention, so long delayed on that side, but which was so readily and so liberally executed on ours; and on a fair discharge of the pecuniary engagements of every description, to the citizens of the United States.

The occasion may be proper, also, for obtaining satisfaction to Captains Rodgers and Davidson for the outrages committed on them in St. Domingo. The death of General Le Clerc will have lessened the influence of his connection with the subject, in obstructing a just consideration of it.

A return to your representations on the subject of the French navigation laws, may be equally recommended by the occasion. Although the present session of Congress, like the last, will pass over without any countervailing regulations here, it can not be doubted that the discriminations made by France, with a view to exclude our shipping from a fair share in the freight of our own productions, will, and can be effectually counteracted by the United States, if not corrected by herself. Should a disposition appear to take up the whole subject of commerce between the two countries, with a view to conventional regulations on just principles, the President authorizes you to express a like disposition in the Government of the United States. But he prefers for the discussions, this place to Paris, for the double reason that the requisite commercial information could be more readily gained here than there, and that a French negotiator might here be more easily and fully impressed with the importance of our commerce to France, than could be done at Paris. Mr. Otto, it is presumed, would not be an unfavorable Minister for such a business; and may, if the French Government incline, bring with him the necessary authorities and instructions for entering upon it.

If, instead of these friendly sentiments and purposes, which may be improved into a solid and satisfactory adjustment of the mutual interests of the two nations, the French Government should betray a settled repugnance to just arrangements with the United States; and, above all, if it should manifest or betray a hostile spirit towards them, or be found to meditate projects inconsistent with their rights, and, consequently, leading to a rupture, not a moment is to be lost in forwarding the information, in order that the measures, both external and internal, adapted to such a state of things, may be seasonably taken.

I have the honor, &c.,   JAMES MADISON.

R. R. LIVINGSTON, Esq., &c.

Mr. Madison to Mr. Monroe.

WASHINGTON, *March 1, 1803.*

DEAR SIR,—Since you left us we have no further intelligence from New Orleans, except a letter dated January 20th from the Vice Consular agent there, from which it appears that the letters to the Governor and Intendant from the Spanish Minister here had arrived about the 13th, and had not, on the 20th, produced the desired change in the state of things. The delay, however, does not seem to have been viewed by the Consul as any proof that the Intendant would not conform to the interposition. The idea continued that he had taken his measures without orders from his Government. There are letters (according to that from the Consul) for the Marquis Yrujo now on the way by land. These will probably shew whether the Intendant will yield or not. The despatch vessel which carried the Marquis's letters is not yet returned. The detention of her beyond the allotted time is favorably interpreted by him, on the presumption that she waits for a satisfactory answer, which the pride of the Intendant postpones as long as possible.

The newspapers will have informed you of the turn given to the proceedings of Congress on the subject of New Orleans, &c. The propositions of Mr. Ross in the Senate, which drove at war thro' a delegation of unconstitutional power to the Executive, were discussed very elaborately, and *with open doors*. The adversaries of them triumphed in the debate, and threw them out by 15 votes against 11. On the motion of Mr. Breckenridge, measures of expenseless or cheap preparation, in the style of those which attended Mr. Jay's mission to G. Britain, have been agreed on in the Senate. It is uncertain whether even these will pass the House of Representatives. If they should, as is, perhaps, not improper, they will not be understood as indicating views that ought to excite suspicions or unfriendly sensations in either of the Governments to which your Mission is addressed. The truth is, that justice and peace prevail not only in the public councils, but in the body of the community; and will continue to do so as long as the conduct of other nations will permit. But France and Spain cannot be too deeply impressed with the necessity of revising their relations to us thro' the Mississippi, if they wish to enjoy our friendship, or preclude a state of things which will be more formidable than any that either of those powers has yet experienced. Some adjustments, such as those which you have to propose, have become indispensable. The whole of what we wish is not too much to secure permanent harmony between the parties. Something much better than has hitherto been enjoyed by the States is essential to any tolerable degree of it, even for the present. * * *

[Extract.]

Mr. Madison, Secretary of State, to James Monroe.

DEPARTMENT OF STATE, *March 2, 1803.*

SIR: You will herewith receive two commissions with the correspondent instructions, in which you are associated as Minister Plenipotentiary and Extraordinary to the French Republic and to His Catholic Majesty; together with the respective letters of credence to those Governments.

Your mission to Madrid will depend on the event of that to Paris, and on the information there to be acquired. Should the entire cession in view be obtained from the French Republic, as the assignees of Spain, it will not be necessary to resort to the Spanish Government. Should the whole or any part of the cession be found to depend, not on the French, but on the Spanish Government, you will proceed to join Mr. Pinckney in the requisite negotiations with the latter. Although the United States are deeply interested in the complete success of your mission, the Floridas, or even either of them, without the island of New Orleans, on proportionate terms, will be a valuable acquisition.

I have the honor to be, &c.,

JAMES MADISON.

JAMES MONROE, Esq., &c.

Mr. Livingston to Mr. Madison.

PARIS, *March 3, 1803.*

DEAR SIR: You will receive, with this, duplicates of two letters which contain a general statement of our affairs here. This is merely to inform you that I have received your letter of the 18th of January, in which you notify me of Mr. Monroe's appointment. I shall do everything in my power to pave the way for him; and sincerely wish his mission may be attended with the desired effect. It will, however, cut off one resource on which I greatly relied; because I had established a confidence which it will take Mr. Monroe some time to inspire. Enclosed is a letter addressed to the First Consul himself, and sent him before I heard of Mr. Monroe's appointment. The Minister told me yesterday that I should have an answer to it in a few days. What that answer will be I know not: but I have been indefatigable in my applications to everybody who will probably be consulted on this subject. When I arrived here I found Louisiana a very favorite object. Some books were published representing it as a paradise. I think I have greatly aided in dispelling this mania; and, had the Floridas been granted, and the necessary powers given me, I believe that something might have been effected; because at this moment there is not a man about the Court but inclines to our ideas upon the subject. The Floridas are still in the hands of Spain. I have explained the cause in my last: and not knowing how far we might succeed in our negotiations, or what sacrifices you would make, I have thought it best to use every exertion with the Spanish Ambassador and the British Minister to obstruct that negotiation.

The person of whom you speak may be able to give you information as to the expedition; because he had passed as an important inhabitant of the island, and the General, &c., relied upon his aid in their money-making plans. I am much surprised, however, that he should talk of the designs of this Court, the price, &c.; because these he must have derived from his imagination only; as he had no means of seeing anybody here that could give him the least information on those subjects. I mention this that the President may not place any sort of reliance upon what he receives through that channel, except as it respects General Victor personally; who, I will venture to say, knows himself less about what passes here than you do: and even this information he must receive with some grains of allowance, as the gentleman has a pretty warm imagination, and is liable to be deceived.

The armament is still icebound in Holland.

I am, sir, &c.,

ROBERT R. LIVINGSTON.

Hon. JAMES MADISON,
Secretary of State.

Mr. Livingston to Citizen Bonaparte, First Consul of France and President of the Italian Republic.

PARIS, *February 27, 1803.*

CITIZEN FIRST CONSUL AND PRESIDENT: Though I am satisfied that my notes to the Minister of Exterior Relations have been truly represented to you, yet as, in the immense variety of important objects that occupy your time and attention, they may have escaped your memory, I can not justify myself to my Government without making every effort to bring them under your view; since I consider the object of them as too closely connected with that harmony which can not be indifferent to two countries whose physical and political relations enable them to be mutually serviceable to each other. And I find that it has not been unusual, upon great occasions, for the Ministers of foreign Powers to address themselves directly to you. This I prefer to do by letter, rather than by personal conference; as well because I consider it as more saving of your time, as because I feared that my imperfect knowledge of the French language would have prevented me from expressing myself with the clearness I might wish.

I pass over, citizen First Consul, a variety of circumstances of minor importance, and, which, without being useful to France, serve to distress the commerce and the mercantile citizens of the United States, which have, at different times, been represented to the Minister for Foreign Affairs, and others of your Ministers, without having hitherto met with the attention they merited. I presume, when a negotiation shall be set on foot for the arrangements on great points, smaller ones will meet with little difficulty.

The claims of the American citizens against the Government of France, are so well founded that no administration that ever prevailed in France has refused to recognize them; and even after the debts of the citizens of France were reduced by the law of 24th Frimaire, year 6, the Government declared that those due to foreigners were not comprised in the regulation; for this obvious reason, doubtless, that they were not to be benefited by the revolution, and that those only would be justly charged with the expenses to whom the advantages were to result; and they accordingly reported, that a large sum should be applied to the discharge of the demands of foreigners; who were only deprived of the benefit of the report by the change that was afterwards effected in the constitution. In this report France pursued the example of good faith set by the United States of America, who, in the fiscal arrangements, which necessity compelled them to adopt, respected the rights of foreigners, and paid their contracts, with the most scrupulous exactitude, in specie, while their own citizens were compelled to acquiesce in those arrangements which the general interest of their country (in whose prosperity they were benefited) rendered necessary.

If, sir, the validity of claims could be tested either by the advantages received by the debtor, or the loss sustained by the creditor, none can stand upon stronger ground than those of American citizens against France. They are chiefly founded upon contracts, for articles of the first necessity, furnished when they were most needed, and when the want of them would have plunged France in the utmost distress. They were furnished, too, at the greatest risk to the proprietor, and to so little comparative advantage to the furnisher, that those who either from political motives, or from juster combination, carried similar commodities to Britain or neutral ports, have been enriched, while those whose enthusiasm in the cause of France led them to seek her harbors will, if strictly paid their capital and interest, be barely snatched from ruin. It was this predilection, too, in favor of France, that furnished Britain with a pretense to commit those depredations on our commerce, by which it so materially suffered, but which, indeed, ever attentive to the preservation of her interests in the United States, she is, of late, very amply compensating by full payment of principal, interest, and damages, for any illegal capture made during the war; while compensation for those which fell under that description in France have, in a great measure, been given up by the late convention; and that due for the remaining few, which ought to have been satisfied by that treaty, have been eluded by some very extraordinary decisions of the Council of Prizes, or by that delay which all the claims of American citizens have hitherto met with.

But, citizen First Consul, it is not now necessary to state the justice of American claims: this has been solemnly recognized by a treaty which expressly stipulates for their payment, and distinguishes the claims of American citizens from those of every other nation. This treaty had been carried into effect in the United States, the Government of which, not allowing themselves to doubt the good faith of France, paid into the hands of the agent of France, and upon his application, a very considerable sum of money, even before it could be strictly claimed under the treaty, and at the moment when her own citizens were entitled to a considerable balance to France; listening, in this transaction, only to those sentiments of good will which influence the conduct of the present Government of the United States toward France, and to her wish to aid her military operations.

There may be cases, citizen First Consul, in which the necessities of a nation may compel her to leave the obligations of a treaty unfulfilled; but, after the flattering picture which is daily exhibited of the prosperity of France, I trust that no such necessity exists here; but, were it otherwise, I am persuaded that you will think that the nation who pleads her necessities for the breach of her treaties can not, with honor, avail herself of advantages to be drawn from those treaties.

France would never have permitted her Minister to claim a payment under the treaty, if she had not determined also, on her part, to pay all that was due from her in virtue of it.

Your signature, citizen First Consul, the attention you manifested to remove ambiguities, by the form under which you were pleased to ratify it, gave a peculiar weight to the treaty, because they show that it was naturally examined by you, and not passed over in the hurry of other business. But, sir, the receiving money under it is such a consummation of the act, as would make it criminal in me to doubt your ultimate intention to fulfill it.

If, sir, justice, if good faith, and those considerations of magnanimity which influence great nations, urge the immediate fulfillment of the treaty, the wisdom of the provision which stipulates for the discharge of the debt is evinced by its being more consistent even with the pecuniary interest of France to make the fullest payment under it, than it would have been to have canceled the debt by the treaty. How early, and how happily soever the war may terminate in the islands, it will take many years before this capital is restored, and the waste of war repaired.

During the whole of this period considerable supplies must be obtained from the United States. Let them stand at the moderate sum of twenty millions annually. This must be paid either in specie shipped from France, or by credits obtained in the United States. The interest of money, as applied to any improvement in agriculture or manufactures in France, is at least worth eight per cent.; the loss upon the French coin shipped to the United States, is not less than two and one-half per cent., the risk or insurance two and one-half, the time the money must be unemployed before it is shipped in its transit and in America, will average about six months; which makes, at the rate of eight per cent. interest, four per cent.: these different sums make the loss upon the shipment of money to America not less than nine per cent. This, upon twenty millions, is one million eight hundred thousand, whereas, the American debt, principal and interest, computing it at twenty millions, if funded, would only require one million to discharge the interest; and in case this debt was funded, it would be unnecessary to ship any money: for, in that case, the credit of France would be so firmly established, that money might be obtained in any part of America for Government bills, at the current rate of exchange, which is generally in favor of the commercial nations of Europe, but would, in no event, amount to more than three per cent.; upon which, supposing the bills were drawn at sixty days, France would receive an actual profit to more than this amount in the use of money in America, many months before it became payable in France.

But this consideration, citizen First Consul, is trifling when compared to the advantage France would derive from keeping her money at home, where it is so much needed to invigorate her commerce and manufactures, and from the facilities that payments made here to American merchants would afford, in the extension of their commerce with France; notwithstanding the loss that the American creditor would sustain by receiving stock instead of money, after so many years of delay, yet, accommodating themselves to the circumstances of the nation, they would readily acquiesce in accepting that species of payment, if none more advantageous can be conveniently offered by the Government. Nor can I, citizen First Consul, see but one possible objection to placing the American debt upon the five per cent stock; the trifling interest can certainly be no consideration, unless the Government should apprehend a depression of the stock by the quantity of American debt that their necessities may induce them to throw into the market. But, sir, this may be easily guarded against, if some plan should be adopted, which, having a reference to Louisiana, may render the United States debtor to France for a greater amount than what is due to their citizens; in which case, I am prepared to enter into stipulations for such provisions as will prevent any possible depression of the French funds. Or if, citizen First Consul, you should not think it proper to treat upon the affairs of Louisiana, as having any reference to this object, still it will be easy (by compelling the American creditors to subscribe, in the name of some trustee that shall be appointed by their minister,) to prevent any sale of the stock they hold, under a limited price, or within a limited time.

The next object that has awakened the sensibilities of the United States is, the change that is about to take place in the situation of Louisiana, heightened, as they are, by the silence which the Governments of France and Spain have observed, and still observe, with respect to their treaty, and the rights that the United States claim, and have long exercised, at New Orleans. I have pressed the Minister to some pointed declaration on the subject of our right of depot at New Orleans, on the limits as settled with Spain, and on the navigation of the Mississippi; for though it necessarily follows that those rights can not be injured by a change of jurisdiction, yet it would have been highly satisfactory to the United States to have received some such assurances upon these subjects as would have shown that the treaty between them and Spain was clearly understood, and served to overawe such of the officers of Government, as, emboldened by their distance from the Sovereign, might act from their own impressions. A recent event, citizen First Consul, has demonstrated the extreme sensibility of the United States on this subject. The Intendant of New Orleans having thought it proper to withdraw the right of depot, secured to the citizens of the United States by the Treaty of Madrid, a spirit of resentment has been manifested from one end of the Union to the other, and nothing but the interposition of the Spanish Minister, the disavowal of the act by the Governor of New Orleans, and the extreme solicitude of the American Government to avoid everything which might have a tendency to interrupt the harmony which at present so happily subsists between the United States and every Power in Europe, could have prevented an immediate recurrence to arms; nor am I now without apprehension that, if nothing is done to calm their anxiety before the season for bringing down the produce of the country occurs, the Government will be compelled to follow the impulse of the people. Under these circumstances, citizen First Consul, it can not appear improper, prizing, as I do, the connexion between our respective countries, to press for some such explicit and early declaration on the subject of our rights as will serve to calm the anxiety of the United States. Should the agents of France, who are to take possession of the Colony, continue the regulations in the face of the treaty which they may find established by the Spanish Intendant, a fatal blow will be struck at the future peace and harmony of both countries. That I may not intrude too far upon your patience, I will merely take the liberty to transport such loose hints as you may possibly think might be improved into some arrangements, alike useful to France and the United States, should you deem it proper to appoint some person to treat with me on this subject. But, in the meantime, as the moments are precious, and the United States will suffer extremely in their commerce, if the officers of France, who are directed to take possession, should not be explicitly instructed to respect the right of navigation and depot claimed by the United States, I must earnestly solicit some treaty; explanatory of the terms on which France has received the cession of Louisiana from Spain, and recognizing the rights of the United States. Should you, citizen First Consul, voluntarily add, as an expression of your good will, provisionally, in case the cession of the Floridas should be completed, a grant to the United States of the free passage through the rivers Mobile and Pensacola, together with a right of depot at their mouths, you would, while you were serving the commerce of France, confer an obligation on the United States that would greatly tend to strengthen the bands of friendship between the allied nations. For though the commerce of these rivers is, at present, very insignificant, yet, at some future period, when the country settles, it may become more important; and, in the meantime, the cession would derive considerable value from the evidence it would afford to the United States of your friendly disposition.

That France will never derive any advantage from the colonization of New Orleans and the Floridas, is fairly to be presumed, from their having been possessed, for more than a century past, by three different nations. While the other colonies of these nations were increasing rapidly, these have always remained weak and languid and an expensive burden to the possessor. Even at this moment, with all the advantages that New Orleans has derived from foreign capital, and an accession of inhabitants from the United States, which has brought its free population to about 7,000 souls, the whole of the inhabitants east of the Mississippi does not more than double that number; and those, too, are, for the most part, poor and miserable; and there are physical reasons that must forever render them inadequate to their own support, in the hands of any European nation. They are, however, important to the United States, because they contain the mouths of some of their rivers, which must make them the source of continual disputes. The interest that the United States attach, citizen First Consul, to your friendship, and the alliance of France, is the principal cause of their anxiety to procure your consent to their accession of that country, and of the sacrifices that they are willing to make to attain it. They consider it as the only possible ground of collision between nations whom so many other interests unite. I can not, then, citizen First Consul, but express my doubt of any advantage to be derived to France from the retaining of that country in its whole extent; and I think I could show that her true interest would lead her to make such cessions out of them to the United States as would at once afford supplies to her islands, without draining the money of France, and rivet the friendship of the United States, by removing all ground of jealousy relative to a country of little value in itself, and which will be perpetually exposed to the attacks of her natural enemy, as well from Canada as by sea.

Should this idea not be so fortunate as to meet your approbation, there are still a variety of views in which, by a partial cession, permanent commercial advantages may be acquired; but it would be to intrude too much upon your time to detail them here, deeming them more proper subjects for discussion, if you should think it proper to render them the objects of a treaty.

Permit me, citizen First Consul, before I conclude, to mention a circumstance which embraces the interest both of France and the United States, and of humanity. The savages on the east side of the Mississippi are numerous and brave; considerable sums of money are annually expended by Spain in purchasing their friendship. Should these supplies be withheld, through neglect or misapplication, a universal massacre of all the planters will ensue. Their detached situation renders it impossible to protect them. I am the more emboldened in making this observation, from the interest the United States have in turning your attention to this object, since, should this melancholy event take place, malignity, or those whose negligence or infidelity may have occasioned it, will not fail to impute it to the intrigues of the United States.

I pray you, citizen First Consul, to pardon the length of this letter, which you will have the goodness to attribute to my extreme anxiety to remove all causes of dispute between France and the country I represent, and to my conviction that some early and effectual arrangements are necessary to prevent those that already exist from growing to an alarming height. No evil can possibly arise from empowering the Minister, or such other person as you shall please, to treat with me on the subject of New Orleans; since even the appointment itself will have a conciliatory appearance, and you, citizen First Consul, will govern the negotiation, in which, I trust, nothing will be proposed on my part, that will not be equally beneficial to both France and the United States.

I have the honor, citizen First Consul, to remain, with the most profound respect and the highest consideration, your most obedient, humble servant,

ROBERT R. LIVINGSTON.

The Secretary of State to Messrs. Livingston and Monroe.

DEPARTMENT OF STATE, *March 2, 1803.*

GENTLEMEN: You will herewith receive a commission and letters of credence, one of you as Minister Plenipotentiary, the other as Minister Extraordinary and Plenipotentiary, to treat with the Government of the French Republic on the subject of the Mississippi, and the territories eastward thereof, and without the limits of the United States. The object in view is to procure, by just and satisfactory arrangements, a cession to the United States of New Orleans, and of West and East Florida, or as much thereof as the actual proprietor can be prevailed on to part with.

The French Republic is understood to have become the proprietor, by a cession from Spain, in the year ———, of New Orleans, as part of Louisiana, if not of the Floridas also. If the Floridas should not have been then included in the cession, it is not improbable that they will have been since added to it.

It is foreseen that you may have considerable difficulty in overcoming the repugnance and the prejudices of the French Government against a transfer to the United States of so important a part of the acquisition. The apparent solicitude and exertions, amidst many embarrassing circumstances, to carry into effect the cession made to the French Republic; the reserve so long used on this subject by the French Government, in its communications with the Minister of the United States at Paris, and the declaration finally made by the French Minister of Foreign Relations, that it was meant to take possession before any overtures from the United States would be discussed, show the importance which is attached to the territories in question. On the other hand, as the United States have the strongest motives of interest, and of a pacific policy, to seek by just means the establishment of the Mississippi, down to its mouth, as their boundary, so there are considerations which urge on France a concurrence in so natural and so convenient an arrangement.

Notwithstanding the circumstances which have been thought to indicate, in the French Government, designs of unjust encroachment, and even direct hostility, on the United States, it is scarcely possible to reconcile a policy of that sort with any motives which can be presumed to sway either the Government or the nation. To say nothing of the assurances given both by the French Minister at Paris, and by the Spanish Minister at Madrid, that the cession by Spain to France was understood to carry with it all the conditions stipulated by the former to the United States, the manifest tendency of hostile measures against the United States to connect their councils and their colossal growth with the great and formidable rival of France, can neither escape her discernment, nor be disregarded by her prudence, and might alone be expected to produce very different views in the Government.

On the supposition that the French Government does not mean to force or to court war with the United States, but, on the contrary, that it sees the interest which France has in cultivating their neutrality and amity, the dangers to so desirable a relation between the two countries which lurk under a neighborhood modified as is that of Spain at present, must have great weight in recommending the change which you will have to propose. These dangers have been always sufficiently evident; and have, moreover, been repeatedly suggested by collisions between the stipulated rights or reasonable expectations of the United States and the Spanish jurisdiction at New Orleans. But they have been brought more strikingly into view by the late proceeding of the Intendant at that place. The sensibility and unanimity in our nation, which have appeared on this occasion, must convince France that friendship and peace with us must be precarious until the Mississippi shall be made the boundary between the United States and Louisiana; and consequently render the present moment favorable to the object with which you are charged.

The time chosen for the experiment is pointed out also by other important considerations. The instability of the peace of Europe, the attitude taken by Great Britain, the languishing state of the French finances, and the absolute necessity of either abandoning the West India islands, or of sending thither large armaments at great expense, all contribute at the present crisis to prepare in the French Government a disposition to listen to an arrangement which will at once dry up one source of foreign controversy, and furnish some aid in struggling with internal embarrassments. It is to be added, that the overtures committed to you coincide in great measure with the ideas of the person through whom the letter of the President of April 30, 1802, was conveyed to Mr. Livingston, and who is presumed to have gained some insight into the present sentiments of the French Cabinet.

Among the considerations which have led the French Government into the project of regaining from Spain the province of Louisiana, and which you may find it necessary to meet in your discussions, the following suggest themselves as highly probable:

First. A jealousy of the Atlantic States, as leaning to a coalition with Great Britain not consistent with neutrality and amity toward France, and a belief that, by holding the key to the commerce of the Mississippi, she will be able to command the interests and attachments of the western portion of the United States, and thereby either control the Atlantic portion also, or, if that can not be done, to seduce the former into a separate Government and a close alliance with herself.

In each of these particulars the calculation is founded in error.

It is not true that the Atlantic States lean toward any connexion with Great Britain inconsistent with their amicable relations to France. Their dispositions and their interests equally prescribe to them amity and impartiality to both of those nations. If a departure from this simple and salutary line of policy should take place, the causes of it will be found in the unjust or unfriendly conduct experienced from one or other of them. In general, it may be remarked, that there are many points on which the interests and views of the United States and of Great Britain may not be thought to coincide, as can be discovered in relation to France. If less harmony and confidence should, therefore, prevail between France and the United States than may be maintained between Great Britain and the United States, the difference will lie, not in the want of motives, drawn from the mutual advantage of the two nations, but in the want of favorable dispositions in the Government of one or other of them. That the blame, in this respect, will not justly fall on the Government of the United States, is sufficiently demonstrated by the mission, and the objects with which you are now charged.

The French Government is not less mistaken, if it supposes that the Western part of the United States can be withdrawn from their present union with the Atlantic part into a separate Government, closely allied with France.

Our Western fellow-citizens are bound to the Union, not only by the ties of kindred and affection, which for a long time will derive strength from the stream of emigration peopling that region, but by two considerations which flow from clear and essential interests.

One of these considerations is, the passage through the Atlantic ports of the foreign merchandise consumed by the Western inhabitants, and the payment thence made to a treasury, in which they would lose their participation by erecting a separate Government. The bulky productions of the Western country may continue to pass down the Mississippi; but the difficulties of the ascending navigation of that river, however free it may be made, will cause the imports for consumption to pass through the Atlantic States. This is the course through which they are now received; nor will the impost to which they will be subject change the course, even if the passage up the Mississippi should be duty free. It will not equal the difference in the freight through the latter channels. It is true that mechanical and other improvements in the navigation of the Mississippi may lessen the labor and expense of ascending the stream; but it is not the least probable, that savings of this sort will keep pace with the improvements in canals and roads, by which the present course of impost will be favored. Let it be added, that the loss of the contributions thus made to a foreign treasury would be accompanied with the necessity of providing, by less convenient revenues, for the expense of a separate Government, and of the defensive precautions required by the change of situation.

The other of these considerations results from the insecurity to which the trade from the Mississippi would be exposed by such a revolution in the western part of the United States. A connection of the Western people, as a separate State, with France, implies a connexion between the Atlantic States and Great Britain. It is found, from long experience, that France and Great Britain are nearly half their time at war. The case would be the same with their allies. During nearly one-half the time, therefore, the trade of the Western country from the Mississippi would have no protection but that of France, and would suffer all the interruptions which nations having the command of the sea could inflict on it.

It will be the more impossible for France to draw the Western country under her influence, by conciliatory regulations of the trade through the Mississippi; because regulations which would be regarded by her as liberal, and claiming returns of gratitude, would be viewed on the other side as falling short of justice. If this should not be at first the case, it soon would be so. The Western people believe, as do their Atlantic brethren, that they have a natural and indefeasible right to trade freely through the Mississippi. They are conscious of their power to enforce this right against any nation whatever. With these ideas in their minds, it is evident that France will not be able to excite either a sense of favor, or of fear, that would establish an ascendency over them. On the contrary, it is more than probable, that the different views of their respective rights would quickly lead to disappointments and disgusts on both sides, and thence to collisions and controversies fatal to the harmony of the two nations. To guard against these consequences is a primary motive with the United States in wishing the arrangement proposed. As France has equal reasons to guard against them, she ought to feel an equal motive to concur in the arrangement.

Secondly. The advancement of the commerce of France, by an establishment on the Mississippi, has, doubtless, great weight with the Government in espousing this project.

The commerce through the Mississippi will consist, first, of that of the United States; second, of that of the adjacent territories to be acquired by France.

The first is now, and must for ages continue, the principal commerce. As far as the faculties of France will enable her to share in it, the article to be proposed to her, on the part of the United States, on that subject, promises every advantage she can desire. It is a fair calculation that, under the proposed arrangement, her commercial opportunities would be extended rather than diminished; inasmuch as our present right of deposit gives her the same competitors as she would then have, and the effect of the more rapid settlement of the Western country, consequent on that arrangement, would proportionally augment the mass of commerce to be shared by her.

The other portion of commerce, with the exception of the island of New Orleans, and the contiguous ports of West Florida, depends on the territory westward of the Mississippi. With respect to this portion, it will be little affected by the cession desired by the United States. The footing proposed for her commerce, on the shore to be ceded, gives it every advantage she could reasonably wish, during a period within which she will be able to provide every requisite establishment on the right shore, which, according to the best information, possesses the same facilities for such establishments as are found on the island of New Orleans itself. These circumstances essentially distinguish the situation of the French commerce in the Mississippi, after a cession of New Orleans to the United States, from the situation of the commerce of the United States, without such a cession; their right of deposit being so much more circumscribed, and their territory on the Mississippi not reaching low enough for a commercial establishment on the shore, within their present limits.

There remain to be considered the commerce of the ports in the Floridas. With respect to this branch the advantages which will be secured to France by the proposed arrangement ought to be satisfactory. She will here also derive a greater share from the increase which will be given, by a more rapid settlement of a fertile territory, to the exports and imports through those ports, than she would obtain from any restrictive use she could make of those ports as her own property. But this is not all. The United States have a just claim to the use of the rivers which pass from their territories through the Floridas. They found their claim on like principles with those which supported their claim to the use of the Mississippi. If the length of these rivers be not in the same proportion with that of the Mississippi, the difference is balanced by the circumstance that both banks, in the former case, belong to the United States.

With a view to permanent harmony between the two nations, a cession of the Floridas is particularly to be desired, as obviating serious controversies that might otherwise grow even out of the regulations, however liberal in the opinion of France, which she may establish at the mouths of those rivers. One of the rivers, the Mobile, is said to be at present navigable for four hundred miles above the thirty-first degree of north latitude, and the navigation may no doubt be opened still further. On all of them, the country within the boundary of the United States, though otherwise between that and the sea, is fertile. Settlements on it are beginning; and the people have already called on the Government to procure the proper outlets to foreign markets. The President, accordingly, gave, some time ago, the proper instructions to the Minister of the United States at Madrid. In fact, our free communication with the sea through those channels is so natural, so reasonable, and so essential, that, eventually, it must take place: and in prudence, therefore, ought to be amicably and effectually adjusted without delay.

Third. A further object with France may be, to form a colonial establishment having a convenient relation to her West India islands, and forming an independent source of supplies for them.

This object ought to weigh but little against the cession we wish to obtain, for two reasons: first, because the country which the cession will leave in her hands on the right side of the Mississippi is capable of employing more than all the faculties she can spare for such an object, and of yielding all the supplies which she could expect or wish from such an establishment: second, because in times of general peace she will be sure of receiving whatever supplies her islands may want, from the United States, and even through the Mississippi, if more convenient to her; because in time of peace with the United States, though of war with Great Britain, the same sources will be open to her, whilst her own would be interrupted; and because in case of a war with the United States, which is not likely to happen without a concurrent war with Great Britain, (the only case in which she could need a distinct fund of supplies,) the entire command of the sea, and of the trade through the Mississippi, would be against her, and would cut off the source in question. She would consequently never need the aid of her new colony, but when she could make little or no use of it.

There may be other objects with France in the projected acquisition; but they are probably such as would be either satisfied by a reservation to herself of the country on the right side of the Mississippi, or are of too subordinate a character to prevail against the plan of adjustment we have in view, in case other difficulties in the way of it can be overcome. The principles and outlines of this plan are as follows, viz:

ARTICLE 1. France cedes to the United States forever the territory east of the river Mississippi, comprehending the two Floridas, the island of New Orleans, and the islands lying to the north and east of that channel of the said river, which is commonly called the South Pass, together with all such other islands as appertain to either West or East Florida; France reserving to herself all her territory on the west side of the Mississippi.

ART. 2. The boundary between the territory ceded and reserved by France, shall be a continuation of that already defined above the thirty-first degree of north latitude, viz: the middle of the channel or bed of the river through the said South Pass to the sea. The navigation of the river Mississippi in its whole breadth from its source to the ocean, and in all its passages to and from the same shall be equally free and common of the United States and of the French Republic.

ART. 3. The vessels and citizens of the French Republic may exercise commerce to and at such places on their respective shores below the said thirty-first degree of north latitude as may be allowed for that use by the parties to their respective citizens and vessels. And it is agreed that no other nation shall be allowed to exercise commerce to or at the same or any other place on either shore, below the said thirty-first degree of latitude. For the term of ten years, to be computed from the exchange of ratifications hereof, the citizens, vessels, and merchandises of the United States, and of France, shall be subject to no other duties on their respective shores, below the said thirty-first degree of latitude, than are imposed on their own citizens, vessels, and merchandises. No duty whatever shall, after the expiration of ten years, be laid on articles the growth or manufacture of the United States, or of the ceded territory, exported through the Mississippi in French vessels; so long as such articles so exported in vessels of the United States shall be exempt from duty: nor shall French vessels exporting such articles ever afterwards be subject to pay a higher duty than vessels of the United States.

ART. 4. The citizens of France may, for the term of ten years, deposit their effects at New Orleans, and at such other places on the ceded shore of the Mississippi, as are allowed for the commerce of the United States, without paying any other duty than a fair price for the hire of stores.

ART. 5. In ports of commerce of West and East Florida, France shall never be on a worse footing than the most favored nation; and for the term of ten years her vessels and merchandise shall be subject therein to no higher duties than are paid by those of the United States. Articles of the growth or manufacture of the United States, and of the ceded territory, exported in French vessels from any port in West or East Florida, shall be exempt from duty as long as vessels of the United States shall enjoy this exemption.

ART. 6. The United States, in consideration of the cession of territory made by this treaty, shall pay to France —— millions of livres tournois, in the manner following, viz: They shall pay —— millions of livres tournois immediately on the exchange of the ratifications hereof; they shall assume, in such order of priority as the Government of the United States may approve, the payment of claims which have been or may be acknowledged by the French Republic to be due to American citizens, or so much thereof as, with the payment to be made on the exchange of ratifications, will not exceed the sum of ———; and in case a balance should remain due after such payment and assumption, the same shall be paid at the end of one year from the final liquidation of the claim hereby assumed, which shall be payable in three equal annual payments, the first of which is to take place one year after the exchange of ratifications, or they shall bear interest, at the rate of 6 per cent. per annum, from the dates of such intended payments, until they shall be discharged. All the above-mentioned payments shall be made at the Treasury of the United States, and at the rate of one dollar and ten cents for every six livres tournois.

ART. 7. To incorporate the inhabitants of the hereby ceded territory with the citizens of the United States on an equal footing, being a provision which can not now be made, it is to be expected, from the character and policy of the United States, that such incorporation will take place without unnecessary delay. In the meantime they shall be secure in their persons and property, and in the free enjoyment of their religion.

OBSERVATIONS ON THE PLAN.

1st. As the cession to be made by France in this case must rest on the cession made to her by Spain, it might be proper that Spain should be a party to the transaction. The objections, however, to delay, require that nothing more be asked on our part than either an exhibition and recital of the treaty between France and Spain, or an engagement on the part of France, that the accession of Spain will be given. Nor will it be advisable to insist even on this much, if attended with difficulty or delay, unless there be ground to suppose that Spain will contest the validity of the transaction.

2d. The plan takes for granted, also, that the Treaty of 1795, between the United States and Spain, is to lose none of its force in behalf of the former, by any transactions whatever between the latter and France. No change, it is evident, will be, or can be admitted to be produced in that treaty, or in the arrangements carried into effect under it, further than it may be superceded by stipulations between the United States and France, who will stand in the place of Spain. It will not be amiss to insist on an express recognition of this by France as an effectual bar against pretexts of any sort, not compatible with the stipulations of Spain.

3d. The first of the articles proposed, in defining the cession, refers to the south pass of the Mississippi, and to the islands north and east of that channel. As this is the most navigable of the several channels, as well as the most direct course to the sea, it is expected that it will not be objected to. It is of the greater importance to make it the boundary, because several islands will be thereby acquired, one of which is said to command this channel, and to be already fortified. The article expressly includes also the islands appertaining to the Floridas. To this there can be no objection. The islands within six leagues of the shore are the subject of a British proclamation in the year 1763, subsequent to the cession of the Floridas to Great Britain by France, which is not known to have ever been called in question by either France or Spain.

The second article requires no particular observations.

Article three is one whose import may be expected to undergo the severest scrutiny. The modification to be desired is that which, whilst it provides for the interests of the United States, will be acceptable to France, and will give no just ground of complaint and the least of discontent to Great Britain.

The present form of the article ought, and probably will be, satisfactory to France: first, because it secures to her all the commercial advantages in the river which she can well desire; secondly, because it leaves her free to contest the mere navigation of the river by Great Britain, without the consent of France.

The article, also, in its present form, violates no right of Great Britain, nor can she reasonably expect of the United States that they will contend, beyond their obligation, for her interest, at the expense of their own. As far as Great Britain can claim the use of the river under her treaties with us, or by virtue of contiguous territory, the silence of the article on that subject leaves the claim unaffected. As far again as she is entitled under the treaty of 1794, to the use of our bank of the Mississippi above the thirty-first degree of north latitude, her title will be equally entire. The article stipulates against her only in its exclusion of her commerce from the bank to be ceded below our present limits. To this she can not of right object. First, because, the territory not belonging to the United States at the date of our treaty with her, is not included in its stipulations. Secondly, because the privileges to be enjoyed by France are for a consideration which Great Britain has not given and can not give. Thirdly, because the exclusion in this case being a condition on which the territory will be ceded and accepted, the right to communicate the privilege to Great Britain will never have been vested in the United States. But although these reasons fully justify the article in its relation to Great Britain, it will be advisable, before it be proposed, to feel the pulse of the French Government with respect to a stipulation, that each of the parties may, without the consent of the other, admit whomsoever it pleases to navigate the river and trade with their respective shores, on the same terms as in other parts of France and the United States, and as far as the disposition of that Government will concur, to vary the proposition accordingly. It is not probable that this concurrence will be given, but the trial to obtain it will not only manifest a friendly regard to the wishes of Great Britain, and, if successful, furnish a future price for privileges within her grant, but is a just attention to the interests of our Western fellow-citizens, whose commerce will not otherwise be on an equal footing with that of the Atlantic States.

Should France not only refuse any such change in the article, but insist on a recognition of her right to exclude all nations other than the United States from navigating the Mississippi, it may be observed to her that a positive stipulation to that effect might subject us to the charge of intermeddling with and prejudging questions merely existing between her and Great Britain; that the silence of the article is sufficient; that, as Great Britain never asserted a claim on this subject against Spain, it is not to be presumed that she will assert it against France, on her taking the place of Spain; that, if the claim should be asserted, the treaties between the United States and Great Britain will have no connexion with it, the United States having, in those treaties, given their separate consent only to the use of the river by Great Britain, leaving her to seek whatever other consent may be necessary.

If, notwithstanding such expostulations as these, France shall inflexibly insist on an express recognition to the above effect, it will be better to acquiesce in it, than to lose the opportunity of fixing an arrangement in other respects satisfactory; taking care to put the recognition into a form not inconsistent with our treaties with Great Britain, or with an explanatory article that may not improbably be desired by her.

In truth, it must be admitted, that France, holding one bank, may exclude from the use of the river any nation not more connected with it by territory than Great Britain is understood to be. As a river where both its banks are owned by one nation belongs exclusively to that nation, it is clear that, when the territory on one side is owned by one nation, and on the other side by another nation, the river belongs equally to both, in exclusion of all others. There are two modes by which an equal right may be exercised; the one by a negative in each on the use of the river by any other nation, except the joint proprietor: the other by allowing each to grant the use of the river to other nations, with the consent of the joint proprietor. The latter mode would be preferable to the United States. But if it be found absolutely inadmissible to France, the former must, in point of expediency, since it may in point of right, be admitted by the United States. Great Britain will have less reason to be dissatisfied on this account, as she has never asserted against Spain a right of entering and navigating the Mississippi, nor has either she or the United States ever founded on the treaties between them a claim to the interposition of the other party in any respect, although the river has been constantly shut against Great Britain from the year 1783 to the present moment, and was not opened to the United States until 1795, the year of their treaty with Spain.

It is possible, also, that France may refuse to the United States the same commercial use of her shores, as she will require for herself on those ceded to the United States. In this case, it will be better to relinquish a reciprocity than to frustrate the negotiation. If the United States held in their own right the shore to be ceded to them, the commercial use of it allowed to France would render a reciprocal use of her shore by the United States an indispensable condition. But as France may, if she chooses, reserve to herself the commercial use of the ceded shore as a condition of the cession, the claim of the United States to the like use of her shore would not be supported by the principle of reciprocity, and may, therefore, without violating that principle, be waived in the transaction.

The article limits to ten years the equality of French citizens, vessels, and merchandises, with those of the United States: should a longer period be insisted on, it may be yielded. The limitation may even be struck out, if made essential by France; but a limitation in this case is so desirable, that it is to be particularly pressed, and the shorter the period the better.

Art. 4. The right of deposit, provided for in this article, will accommodate the commerce of France to and from her own side of the river, until an emporium shall be established on that side, which it is well known will admit of a convenient one. The right is limited to ten years, because such an establishment may within that period be formed by her; should a longer period be required, it may be allowed, especially as the use of such a deposit would probably fall within the general regulations of our commerce there. At the same time, as it will be better that it should rest on our own regulations than on a stipulation, it will be proper to insert a limitation of time, if France can be induced to acquiesce in it.

Art. 5. This article makes a reasonable provision for the commerce of France in the ports of West and East Florida. If the limitation to ten years of its being on the same footing with that of the United States should form an insuperable objection, the term may be enlarged; but it is much to be wished that the privilege may not in this case be made perpetual.

Art. 6. The pecuniary consideration to be offered for the territories in question is stated in the sixth article: you will of course favor the United States as much as possible, both in the amount and modifications of the payments. There is some reason to believe that the gross sum expressed in the article has occurred to the French Government, and is as much as will be finally insisted on: it is possible that less may be accepted, and the negotiation ought to be adapted to that supposition. Should a greater sum be made an ultimatum on the part of France, the President has made up his mind to go as far as fifty millions of livres tournois, rather than lose the main object. Every struggle, however, is to be made against such an augmentation of the price, that will consist with ultimate acquiescence in it.

The payment to be made immediately on the exchange of ratifications is left blank; because it can not be foreseen either what the gross sum or the assumed debts will be, or how far a reduction of the gross sum may be influenced by the anticipated payments provided for by the act of Congress herewith communicated, and by the authorization of the President and Secretary of the Treasury indorsed thereon. This provision has been made with a view to enable you to take advantage of the urgency of the French Government for money, which may be such as to overcome their repugnance to part with what we want, and to induce them to part with it on lower terms, in case a payment can be made before the exchange of ratifications. The letter from the Secretary of the Treasury to the Secretary of State, of which a copy is herewith inclosed, will explain the manner in which this advance of the ten millions of livres, or so much thereof as may be necessary, will be raised most conveniently for the United States. It only remains here to point out the condition or event on which the advance may be made. It will be essential that the convention be ratified by the French Government before any such advance be made; and it may be further required, in addition to the stipulation to transfer possession of the ceded territory as soon as possible, that the orders for the purpose, from the competent source, may be actually and immediately put into your hands. It will be proper, also, to provide for the payment of the advances, in the event of a refusal of the United States to ratify the convention.

It is apprehended that the French Government will feel no repugnance to our designating the classes of claims and debts, which, embracing more equitable considerations than the rest, we may believe entitled to a priority of payment. It is probable, therefore, that the clause of the sixth article, referring it to our discretion, may be safely insisted upon. We think the following classification such as ought to be adopted by ourselves:

First. Claims under the fourth article of the Convention of September, 1800;

Secondly. Forced contracts or sales imposed upon our citizens by French authorities; and,

Thirdly. Voluntary contracts which have been suffered to remain unfulfilled by them.

Where our citizens have become creditors of the French Government in consequence of agencies or appointments derived from it, the

United States are under no particular obligation to patronize their claims, and, therefore, no sacrifice of any sort, in their behalf, ought to be made in the arrangement. As far as this class of claimants can be embraced without embarrassing the negotiation, or influencing in any respect the demands or expectations of the French Government, it will not be improper to admit them into the provision. It is not probable, however, that such a deduction, from the sum ultimately to be received by the French Government, will be permitted, without some equivalent accommodation to its interests, at the expense of the United States.

The claim of Mr. Beaumarchais, and several other French individuals, on our Government, founded upon antiquated or irrelevant grounds, although they may be attempted to be included in this negotiation, have no connexion with it. The American Government is distinguished for its just regard to the rights of foreigners, and does not require those of individuals to become subjects of treaty in order to be admitted. Besides, their discussion involves a variety of minute topics, with which you may fairly declare yourselves to be unacquainted. Should it appear, however, in the course of the negotiation, that so much stress is laid on this point, that, without some accommodation, your success will be endangered, it will be allowed to bind the United States for the payment of one million of livres tournois to the representatives of Beaumarchais, heretofore deducted from his accounts against them; the French Government declaring the same never to have been advanced to him on account of the United States.

Article 7 is suggested by the respect due to the rights of the people inhabiting the ceded territory, and by the delay which may be found in constituting them a regular and integral portion of the Union. A full respect for their rights might require their consent to the act of cession; and if the French Government should be disposed to concur in any proper mode of obtaining it, the provision would be honorable to both nations. There is no doubt that the inhabitants would readily agree to the proposed transfer of their allegiance.

It is hoped that the idea of a guaranty of the country reserved to France may not be brought into the negotiation. Should France propose such a stipulation, it will be expedient to evade it, if possible, as more likely to be a source of disagreeable questions between the parties, concerning the actual *casus foederis*, than of real advantage to France. It is not in the least probable that Louisiana, in the hands of that nation, will be attacked by any other, whilst it is in the relations to United States on which the guaranty would be founded; whereas, nothing is more probable than some difference of opinion as to the circumstances and the degree of danger necessary to put the stipulations in force. There will be less reason in the demand of such an article, as the United States would set little value on a guaranty of any part of this territory; and, consequently, there would be no just reciprocity in it. Should France, notwithstanding these considerations, make a guaranty an essential point, it will be better to accede to it than to abandon the object of the negotiation; mitigating the evil as much as possible, by requiring, for the *casus foederis*, a great and manifest danger threatened to the territory guaranteed, and by substituting for an indefinite succor, or even a definite succor, in military force, a fixed sum of money payable at the Treasury of the United States. It is difficult to name the proper sum which is in no posture of the business to be exceeded, but it can scarcely be presumed that more than about —— dollars, to be paid annually during the existence of the danger, will be insisted on. Should it be unavoidable to stipulate troops in place of money, it will be prudent to settle the details with as much precision as possible, that there may be no room for controversy, either with France or with her enemy, on the fulfillment of the stipulation.

The instructions, thus far given, suppose that France may be willing to cede to the United States the whole of the island of New Orleans, and both the Floridas. As she may be inclined to dispose of a part or parts, and of such only, it is proper for you to know that the Floridas, together, are estimated at one-fourth the value of the whole island of New Orleans, and East Florida at one-half that of West Florida. In case of a partial cession, it is expected that the regulations of every other kind, so far as they are onerous to the United States, will be more favorably modified.

Should France refuse to cede the whole of the island, as large a portion as she can be prevailed on to part with may be accepted; should no considerable portion of it be attainable, it will still be of vast importance to get a jurisdiction over space enough for a large commercial town, and its appurtenances, on the back of the river, and as little remote from the mouth of the river as may be. A right to choose the place would be better than a designation of it in the treaty. Should it be impossible to procure a complete jurisdiction over any convenient spot whatever, it will only remain to explain and improve the present right of deposit, by adding thereto the express privilege of holding real estate for commercial purposes, of providing hospitals, of having consuls residing there, and other agents who may be authorized to authenticate and deliver all documents requisite for vessels belonging to, and engaged in, the trade of the United States, to and from the place of deposit. The United States can not remain satisfied, nor the Western people be kept patient, under the restrictions which the existing treaty with Spain authorizes.

Should a cession of the Floridas not be attainable, your attention will also be due to the establishment of suitable deposits at the mouth of the rivers passing from the United States through the Floridas, as well as of the free navigation of those rivers by citizens of the United States. What has been above suggested in relation to the Mississippi, and the deposit on its banks, is applicable to the other rivers; and additional hints relative to them all may be derived from the letter, of which a copy is enclosed, from the Consul at New Orleans

It has been long manifest that, whilst the injuries to the United States, so frequently occurring from the colonial officers scattered over our hemisphere and in our neighborhood, can only be repaired by a resort to their respective Governments in Europe, it will be impossible to guard against the most serious inconveniences. The late events at New Orleans strongly manifest the necessity of placing a power somewhere nearer to us capable of correcting and controlling the mischievous proceedings of such officers toward our citizens; without which, a few individuals, not always among the wisest or best of men, may at any time threaten the good understanding of the two nations. The distance between the United States and the old continent, and the mortifying delays of explanations and negotiations across the Atlantic on emergencies in our neighborhood, render such a provision indispensable; and it can not be long before all the Governments of Europe, having American Colonies, must see the necessity of making it. This object, will likewise claim your special attention.

It only remains to suggest, that, considering the possibility of some intermediate violences between citizens of the United States and the French or Spaniards, in consequence of the interruption of our right of deposit, and the probability that considerable damages will have been occasioned by that measure to citizens of the United States, it will be proper that indemnification in the latter case be provided for, and that in the former it shall not be taken on either sides as a ground or pretext for hostilities.

These instructions, though as full as they could be conveniently made, will necessarily leave much to your discretion. For the proper exercise of it, the President relies on your information, your judgment, and your fidelity to the interests of your country.

JAMES MADISON.

Mr. Monroe to Mr. Jefferson.

NEW YORK *March 7. 1803.*

DEAR SIR,—I rec^d. yours of the 25. ulto. with one to M^r. Cepeda this morning, when I also rec^d. my instructions from the department of State, with all the other documents connected with my mission to France & Sp^n. The ship, Richmond, of ab^t. 400 tons burden, whose cabbin I have taken, cleared at the custom house on Saturday, my baggage was put on board, in expectation of sailing yesterday as M^r. Madison informed me my instructions ought to arrive by 8 in the morning; but it being Sunday, they were delayed till to-day. We are now detained by a snowstorm and contrary wind, but I shall sail as soon as it clears up, & the wind shifts.

The resolutions of M^r. Ross proved that the federal party will stick at nothing to embarrass the adm^n., and recover its lost power. They nevertheless produce a great effect on the publick mind and I presume more especially in the western country. The unanimity in the publick councils respecting our right to the free navigation of the river, and its importance to every part of the U States, the dissatisfaction at the interference of Sp^n. which will not be appeased while the power of a similar one exists, are calculated to inspire the hope of a result which may put us at ease forever on those points. If the negotiation secures all the objects sought, or a deposit with the sovereignty over it, the federalists will be overwhelmed completely: the union of the western with the Eastern people will be consolidated, republican principles confirmed, and a fair prospect of peace and happiness presented to our country. But if the negotiation compromises short of that, and leaves the management of our great concerns in that river, which comprise everything appertaining to the western parts of the U States, in the hands of a foreign power, may we not expect that the publick will be disappointed and disapprove of the result. So far as I can judge, I think much would be hazarded by any adjustment which did not put us in complete security for the future. It is doubtful whether an adjustment short of that would be approved in any part of the union; I am thoroughly persuaded it would not to the westward. If they were discontented, there would grow up an union of councils and measures between them and the Eastern people which might lead to other measures & be perverted to bad purposes. The Eastern towns, which govern the country wish war for the sake of privateering: the western would not dislike it especially if they were withheld from a just right, or the enjoyment of a privilege necessary to their welfare, the pursuit of which by force would create a vast expenditure of money among them. Their confidence is now reposed in the adm^n. from the best of motives,—a knowledge that it is sincerely friendly to their interests: it is strengthened by a distrust of these new *friends;* but an inquietude has been created by the late event, an inquiry has taken place which has shown that every part of the union especially the Eastern, is deeply interested in opening the river; that the attempt to occlude it on a former occasion was a base perhaps a corrupt intrigue of a few; their hopes and expectations have been raised, and it is probable they expect from the mission by a peaceful course everything which their enemies promised by war. The consequences of a disappointment are not easily calculated. If it restored the federal party to power and involved us in war, the result might be fatal. It therefore highly merits consideration whether we should not take that ground as the ultimatum in the negotiation which must in every possible event preserve the confidence & affection of the western people. While we stand well with them we shall prosper. We shall be most apt to avoid war, taking ten years ensuing together; and if we are driven by necessity into it, it is much better that it be under the auspices of a republican than a monarchial adm^n. These ideas are expressed in haste for y^r. consideration for I have not time to give them method or form. I shall most certainly labor to obtain the best terms possible, but it is for you to say, what are the least favorable we must accept. You will have time to weigh the subject & feel the publick pulse on it before anything conclusive may be done. I hope the French gov^t. will have wisdom enough to see that we will never suffer France or any other power to tamper with our interior; if that is not the object there can be no reason for declining an accommodation to the whole of our demands. * * *

[Extract.]

James Madison, Secretary of State, to Charles Pinckney, Minister to Spain.

DEPARTMENT OF STATE, *March 8, 1803.*

SIR: My last letter was of January 18. Yours since received are of the 6th and 28th of November.

Our latest authentic information from New Orleans is of January 20. At that date the edict of the Intendant against our right of deposit had not been revoked, although the letters to him and the Governor from the Spanish Minister here had been previously received. And it appears that the first outrage had been followed by orders of the most rigid tenor against every hospitable intercourse between our citizens navigating the river and the Spanish inhabitants.

This continuation of the obstruction to our trade, and the approach of the season for carrying down the Mississippi the exports of the Western country, have had the natural effect of increasing the Western irritation, and imboldening the advocates for immediate redress by arms. Among the papers enclosed, you will find the propositions moved in the Senate by Mr. Ross, of Pennsylvania. They were debated at considerable length, and with much ardor, and, on the question, had 11 votes in their favor against 14. The resolutions moved by Mr. Breckinridge, and which have passed into a law, will, with the law itself, be also found among the enclosed papers.

These proceedings ought more and more to convince the Spanish Government that it must not only maintain good faith with the United States, but must add, to this pledge of peace, some provident and effectual arrangement, as heretofore urged, for controlling or correcting the wrongs of Spanish officers in America, without the necessity of crossing the Atlantic for the purpose. The same proceeding, will show, at the same time, that, with proper dispositions and arrangements on the part of Spain, she may reckon with confidence on harmony and friendship with this country. Notwithstanding the deep stroke made at our rights and our interests, and the opportunity given for self-redress, in a summary manner, a love of peace, a respect for the just usages of nations, and a reliance on the voluntary justice of the Spanish Government, have given a preference to remonstrance, as the first appeal on the occasion, and to negotiation as a source of adequate provisions for perpetuating the good understanding between the two nations; the measures taken on the proposition of Mr. Breckinridge being merely those of ordinary precaution, and precisely similar to those which accompanied the mission of Mr. Jay to Great Britian in 1794. Should the deposit, however, not be restored in time for the arrival of the Spring craft, a new crisis will occur, which it is presumed that the Spanish Government will have been stimulated to prevent, by the very heavy claims of indemnification to which it would be otherwise fairly subjected. The Marquis de Casa Yrujo does not yet despair of receiving from New Orleans favorable answers to his letters; but the remedy seems now to be no more reasonably expected from Madrid. If the attention of the Spanish Government should not have been sufficiently quickened by the first notice of the proceeding, from its own officers, we hope that the energy of your interpositions will have overcome its tardy habits, and have produced an instant despatch of the necessary orders.

Mr. Monroe was to sail from New York to Havre de Grace yesterday. He carries with him the instructions in which you are joined with him, as well as those which include Mr. Livingston.

The convention signed with Spain in August, though laid before the Senate at an early day, had no question taken on it till the close of the session. It was then postponed till the next session, which is to commence in November. More than a majority, but less than two-thirds, which the Constitution requires, would have acquiesced in the instrument in its present form; trusting to the success of further negotiations for supplying its defects, particularly the omission of the claims founded on French irregularities. But it is understood that it would have been a mere acquiescence; no doubt being entertained that Spain is bound to satisfy the omitted as well as the included claims. In explaining, therefore, the course taken by the Senate, which mingles respect for the Spanish Government with a cautious regard to our own rights, you will avail yourself of the opportunity of pressing the reasonableness and the sound policy of remodeling the convention in such a manner as to do full justice. I need not repeat the observations heretofore made on the Spanish responsibility for the conduct of French citizens within Spanish jurisdiction; but it may be of use to refer you to the enclosed copy of a royal order, issued by the Spanish Government, in 1799, which will enable you to remind them of their own view of the subject at that time. In this document it is expressly declared that the French consular jurisdiction was not admitted, and that French Consuls, in Spanish ports, were in the same condition as those of every other nation. After such a declaration against the authority of French Consuls the Spanish Government would be chargeable with no less disrespect to the French Republic than to itself, in saying that Spain was not left at liberty to prevent an exercise of the usurped authority; and, if at liberty, she is indisputably answerable for the consequences of not preventing it.

With sentiments, &c.,

JAMES MADISON.

CHARLES PINCKNEY, Esq.

R. R. Livingston to James Madison, Secretary of State.

PARIS, *March 11, 1803.*

DEAR SIR: I have a few days since written to you, transmitting a letter addressed to the First Consul: for though I had numerous notes and observations under his eye, in an informal way, yet I have reason to fear that what I wrote to the Minister, particularly on the subject of the debt, had not reached him; besides that, I believed that he could not pass over a more direct address to him personally. I found, upon conversing with some of the Ministers here, that they considered my direct address as improper, and likely to offend the Minister, if not the Consul. But our situation was such as to require something decisive; and as I daily found the dispositions of M. Talleyrand were friendly to our views, I promised the Minister to write, and offered to submit my letter to him before I sent it. He was pleased with this mark of confidence, and promised not only to deliver it, but to support my application. When I showed him the letter, he seemed to think that all relating to the debt was hopeless. I, however, could not abandon this important object, but immediately upon sending it, took care to have that part of it supported by Consul Le Brun, who has the principal direction of the affairs of finances, with whom I am upon a very friendly footing, and between whom and my friend Marbois, there is a family connexion, strengthened by the marriage of their children. I have the pleasure to enclose you an answer to that letter; you will find in it such strong and such satisfactory assurances on the subject of the debt, as I think gives us the firmest prospects of its speedy payment. I have thought it necessary to communicate this to the Americans here, in order to prevent their parting with their claims at an insignificant price. I have, also, as I know that this account would reach

America by private conveyances, before you could communicate it, thought it proper to mention it generally to one of my friends, with directions to speak of it publicly, in order to prevent the creditors from suffering by the speculations of those who were in the secret.

I told you that M. Talleyrand had assured me that no sale would be heard of. You will find a passage in the note which was doubtless intended to convey that idea in very strong terms. As I know it to be the fixed determinatian of this Government to treat only in America, I have nothing more to do on this subject than to endeavor to get the right of depot left upon the footing it was till your negotiations are concluded. This I shall endeavor to effect. If, upon the arrival of Mr. Monroe, he can suggest anything better, I shall heartily concur with him. In treating with General Bernadotte, you will have every possible advantage. The nearer he views the object, the less he will value it. His dispositions are as friendly as possible to our Government and country; and his ideas relative to our connexion, and the little importance of Louisiana, exactly such as I would wish. My conversations with him on that subject were frequent and interesting; as well with Mr. Adet, who is much in his confidence, and who thinks exactly as I do. The great object that he will be instructed to keep in view will be, I think, from what I learn here, to keep the British out of the river, and to secure as much as possible of the carrying trade to France. Dupont de Nemours has shown me a plan that he gave to Consul Le Brun, of which I send you a copy. I have endeavored to convince those who may be consulted of its impracticability. The reasons are too obvious to make it necessary for me to state them to you. I have hinted at making the island of New Orleans an independent State, under the Government of Spain, France, and the United States, with a right of depot to each, subject to a duty on imports of one and a half per cent. in lieu of storage, wharfage, &c., suggesting the advantage that France would derive from being the only manufacturing nation of the three. The advantages of this to our carrying trade (while it left our revenue untouched) are obvious. And in such a treaty, arrangements might be made extremely advantageous to the Western people. The new nation must always feel its dependence upon us, and, of course, respect our rights. I should not have thought it worth while to mention this, had it not been that I gave an unsigned and informal sketch of it to Joseph Bonaparte: it may possibly be given to General Bernadotte. If, as I begin to believe, they do not get the Floridas, they will put the less value on New Orleans.

Things every day look more towards a rupture between this country and Britain; and though the politicians think otherwise, I believe a war not very distant. The stocks here have been sixty-five: they are now sixty-one. This, however, is an artificial operation; money being employed by the Government to keep them up. Their real price would be about fifty-seven.

I am, dear sir, with the highest consideration, your most obedient humble servant,

ROBERT R. LIVINGSTON.

JAMES MADISON, *Secretary of State.*

Mr. Talleyrand to Mr. Livingston.

PARIS, *Ventose, an 11, (February 19), 1803.*

SIR: The First Consul, in placing in my hands the memoir which you have presented to him, has ordered me to assure you that he has taken into serious consideration the objects you have had in view, and the various demands which you have presented.

He has, at the same time, caused a report to be made on all the subjects which may arise in consequence of these demands, and on the clauses of the convention between France and the United States, to which you refer. It is the intention of the First Consul (and he has charged me to make it known to you) that this convention shall be executed, in every particular, with scrupulous exactness.

The reflections contained in your memoir, in relation to the difficulties which, on the part of France, may attend its execution, do not apply, with the least foundation, either to the dispositions of the Government of the French Republic, or to the state of her finances. The First Consul is persuaded that the impressions by which you have on this point been misled, have been occasioned by your friendly solicitude; but these impressions are not supported by facts. No embarrassment exists in the finances of France. The French Government has the means, as well as the inclination, to be just; and if it should be placed in a position in which the discharge of its obligations would be attended with difficulties, it will know how to surmount those obstacles, and satisfy every claim that can be justly demanded.

As to the American debts, of which you have given an estimate, in the memoir addressed to the First Consul, I ought to apprize you that it is entirely new to us that they can be raised, by any valuation whatever, to the sum of twenty millions. The First Consul charges me to request of you an exact, full, certain, and verified statement of these debts. The perfect confidence with which you have inspired him will not permit him to doubt that in the examination of the particulars, which will form this statement, you will exercise your accustomed acuteness of mind and frankness of character. You may rest assured, sir, that, upon being furnished with such a statement, every claim will be promptly and fully discharged.

As to the second question in your memoir, which relates to Louisiana, the First Consul would have preferred its having been the subject of a separate note. Affairs so different in their nature ought to be kept as much as possible apart, and should certainly not be united. It is entirely opposed to the maxims of Government, adopted by the Republic, to mingle important and delicate political relations with calculations of account and mere pecuniary interests.

The First Consul, always appreciating the motives which have induced you to insist on an explanation of the new relations which ought to exist between the two Republics, has charged me to inform you, that, aware of the solicitude, perhaps premature, but, in reality, natural and plausible, which the United States have manifested in this discussion, has come to the determination to send immediately to the United States a Minister Plenipotentiary, who will communicate on every point the information necessary to a final decision.

Under these circumstances, as well as in all others presenting topics for discussion between the two Governments, the First Consul desires that you shall give, on the subject of his dispositions towards the United States, the most positive and formal assurances, that attachment for your Republic, and esteem and personal consideration for its present Chief Magistrate, are national sentiments which, as a Frenchman, and as the chief of a people, the ancient and uniform friend of the American nation, he loves to profess, and of which he will always be under the pleasing obligation to furnish unequivocal proofs.

While I felicitate myself upon being, at this time, the medium by which these sentiments of the First Consul are expressed, allow me, sir, to renew the assurance of my high consideration.

CH. MAU. TALLEYRAND.

His Excellency R. R. LIVINGSTON,
    Minister plenipotentiary, &c.

Extract of a note from Mr. Dupont de Nemours to the Consul Le Brun.

"I see many ways of terminating this contest, and I desire that, whatever it may be, while favoring our commerce, it may exclude as much as possible the commerce of the five States of the West which are most interested in this question. The first, and most simple, appears to be this: to declare New Orleans a free port for the two nations, France and Spain, whose commerce shall enter and depart through the delta of the Mississippi; and that the United States shall only enter from above, and depart by the same embouchure of the river. The navigation remaining free to the three nations throughout its whole course, on the express condition that the United States shall exempt from every species of duty French or Spanish merchandise entering their territory by the Mississippi or Ohio.

"In this manner we shall have conquered, for the benefit of our manufactures, our silks, ironmongery, and glass of every description, and for the consumption of our wines, vinegar, oil, and dried fruits, all the commerce of the five States of the West, as well as of the new States, which, in this country, multiply so rapidly.

"The products of the English manufactories not being admitted, except by land, and then burdened with a duty of twelve or fifteen per cent., will, in reality, be excluded from competition with those of France. Thus will our enemies be struck in the part most susceptible of injury, while the good will of our friends will be advantageously confirmed. This will give us the assurance that the interior of America, from the Allegheny on the one side, to the elevated mountains beyond the Lakes on the other, will only be populated and supplied by means of the manufacturing industry, the agricultural prosperity, and the commercial riches of France."

[Extract.]

Robert R. Livingston to the President of the United States.

PARIS, *March 12, 1803.*

DEAR SIR: I have delayed replying to your friendly letter by Madame Brougniart, in the hope of having something important to communicate; but, in the meantime, have been so full in my letter to the Secretary of State, that I have left myself little to say on the subject of my public affairs. I can only tell you, generally, that we have been gaining ground here for some time past; and although some propositions which I had an opportunity to make to Joseph Bonaparte to be submitted to the Consul's inspection were not agreed to, yet the matter and the manner left a favorable impression, and I meant to renew the subject on the same grounds.

My letter to the First Consul, which you will find couched in pretty strong terms, and such as are not usual here, and, so far as it related to the claims, repugnant to the Minister's sentiments, has been attended with happy effects, as you will find by the answer transmitted herewith to the Secretary of State. I think it impossible, after this, for him to go back; and I have accordingly given information to the American creditors of the state of their affairs, that they may not be speculated upon.

With respect to a negotiation for Louisiana, I think nothing will be effected here. I have done everything I can, through the Spanish Ambassador, to obstruct the bargain for the Floridas, and I have great hope that it will not be soon concluded. The Ambassador tells me that the Consul often complains to him of the delay that business meets with: and, while Spain keeps the Floridas, Louisiana will be considered here as an object of little moment, as they are absolutely without ports in the Gulf, and so far facilitate your negotiations with General Bernadotte. I have had many interesting conversations with him, and have nothing to complain of. Remember, however, neither to wound his pride nor that of his nation; both being extremely irritable.

Mr. Madison has never told me whether he has received two little essays, calculated, the one to raise our importance in the views of this Government as a naval Power; and the other to disgust them with Louisiana, preparatory to our future negotiations. They were both read with considerable attention by the First Consul, having had them translated for that purpose.

I broke off this part of my letter to attend Madame Bonaparte's drawing-room, where a circumstance happened of sufficient importance to merit your attention. * * * After the First Consul had gone the circuit of one room, he turned to me, and made some of the common inquiries usual on those occasions. He afterwards returned, and entered into a further conversation. When he quitted me, he passed most of the other Ministers merely with a bow, went up to Lord Whitworth, and, after the first civilities, said: "I find, my Lord, your nation wants war again." L. W. "No, sir, we are very desirous of peace." First Consul. "You have just finished a war of fifteen years." L. W. "It is true, sir, and that was fifteen years too long." Consul. "But you want another war of fifteen years." L. W. "Pardon, me, sir, we are very desirous of peace." Consul. "I must either have Malta or war." L. W. "I am not prepared, sir, to speak on that subject; and I can only assure you, citizen First Consul, that we wish for peace."

The prefect of the palace, at this time, came up to the Consul, and informed him that there were ladies in the next room, and asked him to go in. He made no reply, but, bowing hastily to the company, retired immediately to his cabinet, without entering the other room. Lord Whitworth came up to me, and repeated the conversation as I now give it to you. I asked Lord Whitworth whether there were any pending negotiations relative to Malta. He told me that there were; that the conduct of France having convinced them that they still had views upon Egypt, and the guaranties to which they were entitled, with respect to Malta, not having been executed, they thought they could not surrender it with safety. But what brought on the business to-day was, a message from the King of Great Britain to the Parliament on the 1st, which has just been received here, speaking with distrust of the armaments in the French ports, and, in fact, preparing them for war.

This you will have sooner by the way of England than this letter. It is, then, highly probable that a new rupture will take place, since it is hardly possible that the First Consul would commit himself so publicly, unless his determination had been taken. I am fearful that this may again throw some impediment in the way of our claims, which I believed in so prosperous a train. In other views it may serve us, and I shall give all my attention to avail myself of circumstances as they arise; in which I hope shortly to receive the assistance of Mr. Monroe.

I must pray you, sir, to furnish Mr. Madison with such an extract from this letter as ought to be on his file of correspondence with me; since the fear of losing the opportunity, and the necessity of the greater activity at this interesting moment, will deprive me of the pleasure of writing further to him by this conveyance.

I am, &c.,

ROBERT R. LIVINGSTON.

Mr. King to the Secretary of State.

LONDON, *March 17, 1803.*

SIR: War seems more and more probable; indeed, it appears to me inevitable. Holland will be involved, and Spain and Portugal must obey the commands of France. The day after the King's message to Parliament was communicated to the French Government, Bonaparte delivered to Lord Whitworth a paper (a copy of which I have seen) stating:

1. That the expedition preparing in the Dutch ports was, as all the world knew, destined for America; but, in consequence of the message, that it had been recalled and would not proceed.

2. That if the armament announced in the message be not satisfactorily explained, or, if it take place, France would march twenty thousand men into Holland.

3. That the forces debarked in the ports of Holland would be reenforced and assembled on the coast of Flanders.

4. That the French army will be immediately put on a war establishment.

5. That camps would be formed on the coast between Dunkirk and Boulogne.

6. That an army would enter Switzerland.

7. That an army would march into Italy, and occupy Tarento. And,

8. That England must not expect, under the cover of an armament, to avoid the execution of the Treaty of Amiens.

The greatest activity continues to prevail in the military and naval departments. It is understood that the squadrons in the West and East Indies, and in the Mediterranean, will not immediately require reenforcement, and that a respectable fleet will soon appear in the Channel and on the coast of Ireland. The regular army on foot in Great Britain (exclusive of the force in Ireland, Egypt, Malta, Gibraltar, and the Colonies,) consists of twenty-seven thousand infantry, and twelve thousand cavalry; and will be reenforced immediately by thirty-seven thousand of the militia, which have been called out.

I do not hear of Mr. Monroe's arrival, though I learn from Mr. Livingston that he is daily expected in France. Mr. Merry is preparing to embark for the United States, and is pressed by his Government to be ready to leave England in the first week of April.

With perfect respect and esteem, I have the honor to be, sir, your obedient and humble servant.

RUFUS KING.

Mr. Livingston to Mr. Madison.

PARIS, *March 18, 1803.*

SIR: I sent despatches a few days ago to Havre, in expectation of their going by a vessel which left that place for Philadelphia, but they arrived too late. Duplicates were sent to go by a vessel bound for New York. You will, therefore, I fear, have originals and duplicates by the same vessel. This compels me to send triplicates by this conveyance. You will see that, on the subject of New Orleans, the answer to my letter is very unsatisfactory. I, at first, intended to let the matter rest till Mr. Monroe arrived; but, on reflection, I dreaded the consequences of delay, if France should take possession, and continue the policy of Spain; and, as the moment was critical, and the time of Mr. Monroe's arrival uncertain, I sent in the enclosed note, and am doing all that I can to get a speedy and favorable answer.

On the subject of the debts, I have already met with a great deal of trouble in procuring the necessary information, and this is not to be wondered at. I hope to get through with it, strengthened as I am by the First Consul's engagement.

I can not but wish, sir, that my fellow-citizens should not be led to believe, from Mr. Monroe's appointment, that I had been negligent of their interests, or too delicate on any of the great points intrusted to my care. I trust that a communication of my notes to some of them would show that I had gone as far as it was possible for me to go, and perhaps further than my instructions would justify.

We are here all in a bustle, not knowing whether we are to have war or peace. In England, they expect war certainly. Here they are very anxious to avoid it; and I, who have hitherto believed that a rupture would happen, begin, from some circumstances I heard last night at Consul Le Brun's, to believe the storm will pass over. But this is by no means certain; because it is possible that England will rise in her terms as France recedes. Peace will, in no event, last long. I frankly confess, that, though I believe a war would be extremely dangerous for Great Britian, yet I think her ruin inevitable if France continues ten years at peace.

MARCH 19.

Nothing decisive, as yet, on the subject of war or peace. The idea of peace seems to gain ground; and, in fact, war is so much dreaded by all the neighbors of France that they will make every effort to maintain peace, lest they should be drawn into the vortex. I shall call this morning on the Minister in order to enforce upon him the subject of my note.

I have the honor to be, &c., ROBT. R. LIVINGSTON.

Mr. Livingston, Minister Plenipotentiary of the United States of America, to His Excellency the Minister for Exterior Relations of the French Republic.

PARIS, *March 16, 1803.*

SIR: I have received, with great sensibility, your note containing the First Consul's reply to that which I had the honor to present to him on the subject of the American claims. The sentiments are such as would naturally be entertained by an enlightened statesman, who, after advancing his country to the highest pinnacle of military glory and national prospects, had determined to give permanency to that prosperity, by establishing it upon the firm basis of religion, good faith, justice, and national credit. On this subject, sir, I have no doubts; and I am satisfied that, when the claims are brought forward, they will, as you have the goodness to declare, be promptly and fully satisfied. But, sir, as this will form the subject of a future note, I shall beg leave to proceed to the consideration of a question in the highest degree interesting to the harmony of France and the United States, and which, I am sorry to say, is of a nature too pressing to admit of any delay.

The First Consul has done me the honor, through you, to inform me that he proposes to send a Minister to the United States, to acquire such information as he may deem necessary previous to his taking any measures relative to the situation in which the acquisition of Louisiana will place France with respect to the United States. If, sir, the question related to the formation of a new treaty, I should find no objection to this measure. On the contrary, I should readily acquiesce in it, as that which would be best calculated to render the treaty mutually advantageous. But, sir, it is not a new treaty for which we now press, (though one mutually advantageous might be made,) but the recognition of an old one, by which the United States have acquired rights, that no change in the circumstances of the country obliges them to relinquish, and which they never will relinquish but with their political existence. By their treaty with Spain, their right to the navigation of the Mississippi is recognized, and a right of depot granted, with a provision, on the part of the King of Spain, to revoke this right, if, within three years, he found it prejudicial to his interests; in which case, he is to assign another equivalent establishment. The King of Spain has never revoked that right; but, after having made the experiment of its effects upon his interests for three years, he has continued it. The United States have, by this continuance, acquired a permanent and irrevocable right to a depot at New Orleans; nor can that right now be called in question, either by Spain or by any other nation to whom she may transfer her title. Even the assignment of another equivalent establishment can not, at this day, be forced upon the United States without their consent. The time allowed to Spain has passed, and she has preferred to have the depot at New Orleans to placing it elsewhere; and I will venture to say, that, in so doing, she has acted wisely, for New Orleans derives its whole value from its being the market for American produce, and their principal port of entry; and, if this consideration was important to Spain, it is infinitely more so to France, the produce of whose agriculture and manufactures will then find a ready exchange for the raw materials of the United States. Under these circumstances, at the very moment that Spain is about to relinquish the possession of that country to France, she violates her treaty without any apparent interest, and leaves the country with a stain upon her character.

In what situation, sir, are we now placed? An armament is on the point of sailing for New Orleans; the port has been shut by the order of Spain; the French commandant will find it shut. Will he think himself authorized to open it? If not, it must remain shut till the Envoy of France shall have arrived in America, and made the necessary inquiries, and transmitted the result of those inquiries to the First Consul. In the meanwhile, all the produce of five States is left to rot upon their hands. There is only one season in which the navigation of the Mississippi is practicable. This season must necessarily pass before the Envoy of France can arrive and make his report. Is it supposable, sir, that the people of the United States will tranquilly wait the progress of negotiations when the ruin of themselves and their families will be attendant on the delay? Be assured, sir, that, even were it possible that the Government of the United States could be insensible to their sufferings, they would find it as easy to prevent the Mississippi from rolling its waters into the ocean, as to control the impulse of the people to do themselves justice. If, sir, in pursuance of the treaties that France has made with the Porte, she had established valuable *comptoirs* upon the Black Sea, and, subsequent to this, the Dardenelles were ceded to the Emperor, would France suffer him to shut up the passage, and ruin their merchants, till a new treaty had been negotiated for an object that she already possessed? Sir, I would venture to say, that, were a fleet to shut up the mouths of the Chesapeake, Delaware, and Hudson, it would create less sensation in the United States than the denial of the right of depot at New Orleans has done. The people of the Western country were emigrants from the different States, in which they have left connexions deeply interested in their prosperity. This circumstance, combining with the just sense of national independence and national dignity, makes them extremely sensible to the injustice they have suffered. Nor is it without the utmost difficulty that they have been restrained from breaking out into acts of immediate hostility against Spain, by the prudent measures of Government, and by the hope that the mission of a Minister, who will bring with him a conviction of their feelings on this subject, will procure them the most immediate and express recognition of their rights by France, in whose justice and good faith they hope to find a resource against the breach of faith by the officers of Spain.

I can not but flatter myself, sir, that the answer which the First Consul has been pleased to honor me with, has a reference only to such new treaties as it may be for the mutual interest of both countries early to negotiate. But that relative to the rights the United States already possess, in virtue of existing treaties with Spain, he is ready to afford me those explicit and formal assurances which are necessary to calm the emotions which have been so unwisely excited in the United States. I can never bring myself to believe, sir, that the First Consul will, by deferring for a moment the recognition of a right that admits of no discussion, break all those ties which bind the United States to France, obliterate the sense of past obligations, change every political relation that it has been, and still is, the earnest wish of the United States to preserve, and force them to connect their interests with those of a rival Power; and this, too, for an object of no real moment in itself. Louisiana is, and ever must be, from physical causes, a miserable country in the hands of a European Power. Nor can any principal of sound policy dictate to France (even if bound by no treaty) a change in the circumstances of New Orleans, that should exclude the citizens of the United States from that right of depot to which alone it must be indebted for its prosperity. I feel a pleasure in declaring, sir, that the people and Government of the United States will receive the highest satisfaction from the assurances that the First Consul has empowered you to make to me of his attachment to them; and will reflect with pleasure on his having called to mind, that, amidst the changes that both nations have undergone, they have been mutually forward in tendering their alliance to each other. Nor will it be less flattering to the President to have acquired, as a magistrate and as a man, the esteem of a chief who has merited and obtained that of the world. But these occurrences add to my pain when I reflect on occurrences that may lay the foundation for future enmities; and I trust, sir, that they will serve as an apology for anything that may appear harsh in this note. For, if ever there was a moment in which it becomes a Minister to speak with freedom, it is when he feels that the dearest interests of his country are at stake, and has reason to hope that a knowledge of the truth may prevent the breach of relations between nations that esteem and respect each other, and the calamities that humanity may feel in such breach.

I pray your Excellency to receive my thanks for the interesting manner in which you have made the communications of the First Consul, and my assurances of the highest consideration.

ROBERT R. LIVINGSTON.

Mr. Livingston to the Secretary of State.

PARIS, *March 24, 1803.*

DEAR SIR: The question of war yet remains undetermined. My letters from Mr. King of the 18th leave me to believe, as well as my persuasion of the present system of politics in England, that war will come soon. Here there is an earnest and sincere desire to avoid it, as well in the Government as the people. I enclosed, in my last, a note to the Minister. Some days after, I called on him. He told me that an answer was prepared, and that everything should be arranged; and I have no doubt the answer contained all those assurances which I have been so long soliciting. Unfortunately, despatches arrived at that moment from Mr. Pichon, informing them that the appointment of Mr. Monroe had tranquilized everything. Conceiving, then, that they might safely await his arrival, they determined to see whether the storm would not blow over; in which case, they will treat to more advantage. They accordingly substituted, for the first note, which, as the Minister told me, arranged everything, the inclosed No. 1, which contains nothing. To this I put in the note No. 2, which I suppose will produce no effect if the war does not happen. Last night I received another note, No. 3, complaining of our supplying the blacks at St. Domingo; to this I returned the answer No. 4.

I have had a great deal of conversation with General Bernadotte, and communicated my two notes to him. I gave them to him to show to the gentlemen I have mentioned, and endeavored to convince him that he was personally interested; that the specific declarations I require should be given before he goes out, which will be in a few days. Upon the whole, I think everything is prepared for Mr. Monroe. I can not but hope that something may be effected, though I fear Dupont de Nemours has given them, with the best intentions, ideas that we shall find it hard to eradicate, and impossible to yield to.

Florida is not yet ceded, nor, as I hope, very likely to be so. The armament in Holland, designed for Louisiana, is stopped for the present, in consequence of the state of things here.

I am, dear sir, with the highest consideration, your most obedient, humble servant,

ROBERT R. LIVINGSTON.

Hon. JAMES MADISON,
    Secretary of State.

Mr. Talleyrand to Mr. Livingston.

PARIS, *March 21, 1803.*

SIR: I see with pleasure, by the last letters from the French legation in the United States, that the excitement which had been raised on the subject of Louisiana has been allayed by the wisdom of your Government, and the just confidence which it inspires, to that state of tranquillity which is alone proper for discussion, and which, in the existing relations between the two nations, can not fail to lead to suitable explanations on difficulties arising from contingent circumstances, and draw still closer the bands by which they are mutually united. I ought to acknowledge, sir, that, in the publicity recently given to the proceedings respecting Louisiana, it is difficult to recognize the ancient sentiments of attachment and confidence with which France has always been desirous to inspire the people of the United States, and by which, from the first moment of their existence as an independent and sovereign nation, she has been induced to consider her concerns with the United States as among the most important of her political relations.

On what account, then, either political or commercial, can the American nation view the proximity of France with so unfriendly an eye? Has the French Republic ever evinced a desire to arrest the prosperity of the United States, assume an influence to which she had no right, weaken her means of safety or annoyance, or place an obstacle in the way of their expanding commerce? Your Government, sir, ought to be persuaded that the First Consul entertains for the American nation the same affection with which France has been at all times animated; and that, among the advantages which he expects to derive from the possession of Louisiana, he estimates the additional means which will be at his command, to convince the Government and people of the United States of his uniformly liberal and friendly sentiments.

I ought, sir, at the present time, to confine myself to this declaration, which alone should be sufficient to quiet the apprehensions expressed in your last letters. The subject itself does not rest on that accurate and extensive information which alone could authorize a more detailed explanation. In announcing to me, moreover, the speedy departure of Mr. Monroe, who has been appointed a Minister Extraordinary to discuss this matter, you give me reason to conclude that your Government desires that this Minister should be received and heard; because every point susceptible of contradiction should be completely and definitely discussed. In the meantime, the First Consul charges me to assure your Government, that, although he does not think that his new position in relation to Louisiana ought to be the subject of just inquietude, or can occasion the least injury to the United States, he will yet receive with the greatest pleasure the Minister Extraordinary whom the President is about to send, and that he hopes his mission will terminate in a way to give mutual satisfaction to both nations.

At the same time, sir, I avail myself of this occasion to renew the assurance of my high consideration.

CH. MAU. TALLEYRAND.

No. 2.

R. R. Livingston to the Minister of Exterior Relations.

PARIS, *20 Ventose, an 11* (*March 11, 1803*).[a]

SIR: I acknowledge that I feel some mortification in finding that the note with which you honor me yesterday contains nothing more decisive upon the interesting subject that I have submitted to your consideration; and still more, that you should think the sensibility that the inhabitants of the United States have manifested upon the change in the situation of Louisiana repugnant to the sentiments of friendship which the former conduct of France ought to inspire.

I should be deficient, sir, in that frankness which has always formed the basis of my communications with you, if I should conceal that the vicinity of a nation whose political situation puts it out of her power to injure the United States, was less alarming than that of an active, powerful, and enterprising people, whom a variety of circumstances might lead, in the common course of events, to painful discussions; and you will, sir, readily admit that the profound secrecy that the Government of France has always observed in whatever related to Louisiana was ill calculated to allay those alarms. To this moment, the treaty to which they might have expected to be parties is concealed from them; and while explications are given to another Power upon the destination of the armament, in which the United States were most interested, not the most distant hint is afforded to the Minister of the United States, nor is he informed, except through the medium of

---

[a] There seems to be some mistake either in the date of this letter (March 11) or in that of the preceding letter (March 21) to which this is an answer. The originals have been followed.

another Court, of the present arrangement with respect to that armament.

Under these circumstances, sir, how painful soever it may be to manifest a distrust of a nation to whom they have formerly been indebted, and to whom, in return, they have manifested their gratitude, it would be to discover an ignorance of the change that was about to take place in their situation, and a blamable indifference to their most important interest, if they did not demand those securities to which they are entitled for the performance of engagements that France has assumed by putting herself in the place of Spain. I would earnestly hope, sir, that the information you have received from the legation of France in the United States, was more correct than that which induces me to fear that, seeing in your note a determination to postpone to the latest moment those arrangements which they will conceive need only to have been mentioned to have been taken, they will resort to those precautionary remedies which prudence justifies, and which their situation in the present state of Europe most peculiarly demands.

The United States, sir, have vested me with full powers to receive and make those arrangements; and, in the appointment of Mr. Monroe, jointly with me, as Minister Extraordinary to the First Consul, it was by no means their intention, considering the variety of accidents which may postpone or prevent his arrival, to defer receiving from the Government of France those explicit confirmations of the Treaty of Madrid which must precede every arrangement which it might be thought proper hereafter to enter into.

A treaty, sir, is a work of time; and it can hardly be presumed that an ardent and intelligent people should wait the slow progress of negotiations for the attainment of objects that admit of no dispute, and see with indifference France strengthen herself in their vicinity, while she declines to acknowledge the validity of a treaty which, in their opinion, she has virtually adopted. It is not, sir, to negotiate for this acknowledgment that an additional Minister is sent; for this, as I have before had the honor to inform your Excellency, is not considered in the United States as susceptible of controversy: but it was with a view to such further arrangements as might be rendered necessary, in case (as was generally presumed) the Floridas should be added to the acquisitions of France. It was that he might be the bearer of the strong sentiments of the people upon the late measures of Spain, and show to France the inutility of these acquisitions, and the sentiments of distrust that they would naturally excite between her and the United States.

Having thus, sir, frankly stated the evils that may result to both countries from the indecision of France on a question that admits of no dispute, I can only lament the inefficacy of my representation, and hasten to submit your note to the inspection of my Government. From which, taken in connexion with the general politics of Europe and America, they will naturally draw their own conclusions. And I merely wish that the measures, which it is at their option to adopt, may be such as will tend less to their future harmony with France than to their own security.

The President will receive great pleasure from your assurances of the attachment of the First Consul to the Government and people of the United States; and will felicitate himself upon having fixed upon one so perfectly acceptable to the First Consul in the person of his additional Minister, as to insure him the agreeable reception which you so politely promise him.

I avail myself, sir, of this occasion to renew to you the assurances of my high consideration.

R. R. LIVINGSTON.

Mr. King to the Secretary of State.

LONDON, *April 2, 1803.*

SIR: Nothing further has occurred since the date of my last: no answer has yet been given to the note of the French Ambassador, which declines all discussion respecting Malta. Lord Hawksbury's answer will probably be delivered to-day; it will, without doubt, persist in the determination communicated in his first note, and may disclose new and additional reasons in its support. If, as is said to be the case, the First Consul has lately made an overture to Russia for a partition of the Turkish Empire, the fact may be urged on this occasion, notwithstanding the refusal of Russia to listen to the proposal.

I shall continue to believe the war unavoidable, in which England can have no expectation of a single ally. The system of Russia is pacific, with less attachment, however, to France than to England; Austria is not yet recovered from the blows by which she was driven from the contest; and Prussia will be inclined to adhere to her past policy. Although Denmark and Sweden have been much dissatisfied with England, France, contrary to her usual policy, has done nothing to secure their confidence; while England has been endeavoring to reestablish her ancient friendship with these States. For this purpose, she has given assurances that what is called the two Swedish convoys shall be restored or paid for: the first, which consisted of seventeen vessels, was condemned, and the Envoy of Sweden has given in his claim of compensation, which amounts to sixty thousand pounds sterling; the claim for the second, consisting of twenty-one vessels, and which, I think, is not yet condemned, will be about ninety thousand pounds sterling. By cultivating the friendship of these Powers, England expects, with the good will of Russia, to keep the Baltic open against the efforts that France will again make to close it. Portugal will be compelled to exclude the English trade; and Spain, with all Italy, must obey the orders that shall be given them.

I have sought occasions both with Ministers and other leading men since the discussions with France, to inculcate the disadvantage which England has heretofore brought upon herself by the system of warfare she has been accustomed to pursue, and which has been chiefly directed against the colonies of her enemy, which, after being acquired at the expense of much blood and treasure, in addition to the vexation of the commerce of neutral nations, have been commonly restored, enriched by English capital, at the conclusion of peace. Instead of a warfare liable to these objections, and which has moreover furnished an opportunity to France to appear as the friend and protector of neutral States, a system might be suggested that would not only avoid these disadvantages, but which would materially contribute to the future prosperity of Great Britain. No neutral commerce would be interrupted by it; on the contrary, it would serve to increase and extend it; and, when the object was once attained, no Treaty of Peace would restore things to their former state.

This conversation has been everywhere understood and well received; and it is my firm belief, if the war breaks out, that Great Britain will immediately attempt the emancipation and independence of South America.

In a late conversation with Mr. Addington, he observed to me, if the war happen, it would, perhaps, be one of the first steps to occupy New Orleans. I interrupted him by saying, I hoped the measure would be well weighed before it should be attempted; that, true it was, we could not see with indifference that country in the hands of France; but it was equally true, that it would be contrary to our views, and with much concern, that we should see it in the possession of England; we had no objection to Spain continuing to possess it; they were quiet neighbors, and we looked forward without impatience to events which, in the ordinary course of things, must, at no distant day, annex this country to the United States. Mr. Addington desired me to be assured that England would not accept the country, were all agreed to give it to her; that, were she to occupy it, it would not be to keep it, but to prevent another Power from obtaining it; and, in his opinion, this end would be best effected by its belonging to the United States. I expressed my acquiescence in the last part of his remark, but observed, that, if the country should be occupied by England it would be suspected to be in concert with the United States, and might involve us in misunderstandings with another Power, with which we desired to live in peace. He said, if you can obtain it, well, but if not, we ought to prevent its going into the hands of France; though, you may rest assured, continued Mr. Addington, that nothing shall be done injurious to the interests of the United States. Here the conversation ended.

I have lately received your letter of January 29; and as soon as Lord Hawkesbury shall have named a time to receive me, which I have requested him to do, I will explain to him, in conversation, the President's views relative to the Mississippi.

Considering the critical state of affairs, it is much to be wished that my successor may arrive before my departure. I shall delay taking my leave to the last moment; and should the posture of affairs, in my opinion, require it, I will risk the expense of detaining my vessel even beyond the time in which I have engaged to embark: in any event, I shall not leave London before the last week of the present month.

With perfect respect and esteem, I have the honor to be, sir, your obedient and faithful servant,

RUFUS KING.

Robert R. Livingston to the Hon. James Madison, Secretary of State.

PARIS, *April 11, 1803.*

DEAR SIR: My note will tell you how far I have officially pressed the Government on the subject of Louisiana. I have omitted no means, in conversation, of eradicating their prejudices in its favor; and I informed you that I had reason to think that I had been successful with all, unless it was the First Consul, to whom I addressed myself in the letter and essays that you have seen, and which were attentively read by him, as well as several informal notes to his brother. I had reason to think that he began to waver; but we had nothing to offer but money, and commercial advantages: of the latter, I did not think myself entitled to be liberal; and of the first, I found in them a certain degree of reluctance to treat, as derogatory to the dignity of the Government. The affair of New Orleans gave me two very important strings to touch: I endeavored to convince the Government that the United States would avail themselves of the breach of the treaty to possess themselves of New Orleans and the Floridas; that Britain would never suffer Spain to grant the Floridas to France, even were she so disposed, but would immediately seize upon them as soon as the transfer was made; that without the Floridas, Louisiana would be indefensible, as it possesses not one port even for frigates; and I showed the effect of suffering that important country to fall into the hands of the British, both as it affected our country, and the naval force of all Europe.

These reasons, with the probability of war, have had, I trust, the desired effect. M. Talleyrand asked me this day, when pressing the subject, whether we wished to have the whole of Louisiana. I told him no; that our wishes extended only to New Orleans and the Floridas;

that the policy of France should dictate (as I had shown in an official note) to give us the country above the river Arkansas, in order to place a barrier between them and Canada. He said, that if they gave New Orleans the rest would be of little value; and that he would wish to know "what we would give for the whole." I told him it was a subject I had not thought of; but that I supposed we should not object to twenty millions, provided our citizens were paid. He told me that this was too low an offer; and that he would be glad if I would reflect upon it, and tell him to-morrow. I told him that, as Mr. Monroe would be in town in two days, I would delay my further offer until I had the pleasure of introducing him. He added, that he did not speak from authority, but that the idea had struck him. I have reason, however, to think that this resolution was taken in Council on Saturday. On Friday, I received Mr. Ross's motion: I immediately sent it to M. Talleyrand, with an informal note expressive of my fears that it would be carried into effect; and requesting that General Bernadotte might not go till something effectual was done. I also translated it, and gave it to General Bernadotte, and pressed upon him the necessity of asking express instructions, in case he should find the island in possession of the Americans. He went immediately to Joseph Bonaparte. These, I believe, were exciting causes to the train we are now in, and which I flatter myself we shall be able, on the arrival of Mr. Monroe, to pursue to effect. I think, from every appearance, that war is very near at hand; and, under these circumstances, I have endeavored to impress the Government that not a moment should be lost, lest Britain should anticipate us. I have used every exertion with the Spanish Ambassador and Lord Whitworth, to prevent the transfer of the Floridas; and wrote to Mr. Graham, in Mr. Pinckney's absence, to give every attention to that object, and to avail himself of the coolness which subsisted between the French Ambassador and the Prince of Peace. This has retarded the negotiation; and unless they get Florida I have convinced them Louisiana is worth little. I would rather have confined our views to smaller objects; and I think that, if we succeed, it would be good policy to exchange the west bank of the Mississippi with Spain for the Floridas, reserving New Orleans. Perhaps, however, I am too sanguine in my expectations: we will not, therefore, dispose of the skin till we have killed the bear.

I have written to Mr. King, pressing him to stay until a successor is appointed. The moment is so critical that we can not justify being without a Minister in England, and he is a very useful one.

I believe you may calculate that Britain will not give up Malta, and that France will not leave it in her hands by consent; and, of course, hostilities must commence, or Britain be kept, at immense expense, in her present warlike attitude, while France expends nothing. This she can not submit to, and must, therefore, strike the first stroke, which this country wishes, in order to render the war more popular here. France has marched troops into Holland, and those of Victor are embarking, but, I think will not sail, or, if they do, will be intercepted by England, who will probably think they are designed for the islands, which is very probable.

Mr. Monroe arrived on the 1st at Havre. I expect him here in two days at furthest from this date. His passage was twenty-nine days.

I shall see the Minister again to-morrow, in order to sound him more fully before we offer anything formal on Mr. Monroe's arrival.

I wished and proposed that General Bernadotte should wait until something was done, having formally notified the Minister that Mr. Monroe had arrived, but I could not prevail upon him to make any alteration. He said that Mr. Bernadotte, having received his despatches, was to be considered by him as gone.

You will receive this by Mr. Petrie, his secretary, who waits here until to-morrow.

I am, R. R. LIVINGSTON.

P. S., 12th.—Orders are gone this day to stop the sailing of vessels from the French ports; war is inevitable; my conjecture as to their determination to sell is well founded; Mr. Monroe is just arrived here.

Hon. JAMES MADISON,
  Secretary of State.

Mr. Livingston to Mr. Madison, Secretary of State.

PARIS, *April 13, 1803,* midnight.

DEAR SIR: I have just come from the Minister of the Treasury. Our conversation was so important, that I think it necessary to write it, while the impressions are strong upon my mind; and the rather, as I fear I shall not have time to copy and send this letter, if I defer it till morning.

By my letter of yesterday, you learned that the Minister had asked me whether I would agree to purchase Louisiana, &c. On the 12th, I called upon him to press this matter further. He then thought proper to declare that his proposition was only personal, but still requested me to make an offer; and, upon declining to do so, as I expected Mr. Monroe the next day, he shrugged up his shoulders, and changed the conversation. Not willing, however, to lose sight of it, I told him I had been long endeavoring to bring him to some point; but, unfortunately, without effect: that I wished merely to have the negotiation opened by any proposition on his part; and, with that view, had written him a note which contained that request, grounded upon my apprehension of the consequence of sending General Bernadotte without enabling him to say a treaty was begun. He told me he would answer my note, but that he must do it evasively, because Louisiana was not theirs. I smiled at this assertion, and told him I had seen the treaty recognizing it; that I knew the Consul had appointed officers to govern the country, and that he had himself told me that General Victor was to take possession; that, in a note written by the express order of the First Consul, he had told me that General Bernadotte was to treat relative to it in the United States, &c. He still persisted that they had it in contemplation to obtain it, but had it not. I told him that I was very well pleased to understand this from him, because, if so, we should not commit ourselves with them in taking it from Spain, to whom, by his account, it still belonged; and that, as we had just cause of complaint against her, if Mr. Monroe concurred in opinion with me, we should negotiate no further on the subject, but advise our Government to take possession. He seemed alarmed at the boldness of the measure, and told me he would answer my note, but that it would be evasively. I told him I should receive with pleasure any communication from him, but that we were not disposed to trifle; that the times were critical, and though I did not know what instructions Mr. Monroe might bring, I was perfectly satisfied that they would require a precise and prompt notice; that I was very fearful, from the little progress I had made, that my Government would consider me as a very indolent negotiator. He laughed, and told me that he would give me a certificate that I was the most importunate he had met with.

There was something so extraordinary in all this, that I did not detail it to you till I found some clue to the labyrinth, which I have done, as you will find before I finish this letter; and the rather, as I was almost certain that I could rely upon the intelligence I had received of the resolution to dispose of this country.

This day Mr. Monroe passed with me in examining my papers; and while he and several other gentlemen were at dinner with me, I observed the Minister of the Treasury walking in my garden. I sent out Colonel Livingston to him; he told him he would return when we had dined. While we were taking coffee he came in; and, after being some time in the room, we strolled into the next room, when he told me he heard I had been at his house two days before, when he was at St. Cloud; that he thought I might have something particular to say to him, and had taken the first opportunity to call on me. I saw that this was meant as an opening to one of those free conversations which I had frequently had with him. I accordingly began on the subject of the debt, and related to him the extraordinary conduct of the Minister, &c. He told me that this led to something important, that had been cursorily mentioned to him at St. Cloud; but as my house was full of company, he thought I had better call on him any time before 11 that night. He went away, and, a little after, when Mr.

Monroe took leave, I followed him. He told me that he wished me to repeat what I had said relative to M. Talleyrand's requesting a proposition from me as to the purchase of Louisiana. I did so; and concluded with the extreme absurdity of his evasions of that day, and stated the consequence of any delay on this subject, as it would enable Britain to take possession, who would readily relinquish it to us. He said that this proceeded upon a supposition of her making so successful a war as to be enabled to retain her conquests. I told him that it was probable that the same idea might suggest itself to the United States; in which case, it would be their interest to contribute to render her successful, and I asked whether it was prudent to throw us into her scale? This led to long discussions of no moment to repeat. We returned to the point: he said, that what I had told him led him to think that what the Consul had said to him on Sunday, at St. Cloud, (the day on which, as I told you, the determination had been taken to sell,) had more of earnest than he thought at the time; that the Consul had asked him what news from England? As he knew he read the papers attentively, he told him that he had seen in the London papers the proposition for raising fifty thousand men to take New Orleans. The Consul said he had seen it too, and had also seen that something was said about two millions of dollars being disposed among the people about him, to bribe them, &c.; and then left him. That afterwards, when walking in the garden, the Consul came again to him, and spoke to him about the troubles that were excited in America, and inquired how far I was satisfied with his last note.

Here some civil things were introduced, for which I presume I am more indebted to the Minister's politeness than to his veracity; so let them sleep. He (Marbois) then took occasion to mention his sorrow that any cause of difference should exist between our countries. The Consul told him, in reply, "Well, you have the charge of the treasury; let them give you one hundred millions of francs, and pay their own claims, and take the whole country." Seeing, by my looks, that I was surprised at so extravagant a demand, he added that he considered the demand as exorbitant, and had told the First Consul that the thing was impossible; that we had not the means of raising that. The Consul told him we might borrow it. I now plainly saw the whole business: first, the Consul was disposed to sell; next, he distrusted Talleyrand, on account of the business of the supposed intention to bribe, and meant to put the negotiation into the hands of Marbois, whose character for integrity is established. I told him that the United States were anxious to preserve peace with France; that, for that reason, they wished to remove them to the west side of the Mississippi; that we would be perfectly satisfied with New Orleans and the Floridas, and had no disposition to extend across the river; that, of course, we would not give any great sum for the purchase; that he was right in his idea of the extreme exorbitancy of the demand, which would not fall short of one hundred and twenty-five millions; that, however, we would be ready to purchase, provided the sum was reduced to reasonable limits. He then pressed me to name the sum. I told him that this was not worth while, because, as he only treated the inquiry as a matter of curiosity, any declaration of mine would have no effect. If a negotiation was to be opened, we should (Mr. Monroe and myself) make the offer after mature reflection. This compelled him to declare, that, though he was not authorized expressly to make the inquiry from me, yet, that, if I could mention any sum that came near the mark, that could be accepted, he would communicate it to the First Consul. I told him that we had no sort of authority to go to a sum that bore any proportion to what he mentioned; but that, as he himself considered the demand as too high, he would oblige me by telling me what he thought would be reasonable. He replied that, if we would name sixty millions, and take upon us the American claims, to the amount of twenty more, he would try how far this would be accepted. I told him that it was vain to ask anything that was so greatly beyond our means; that true policy would dictate to the First Consul not to press such a demand; that he must know that it would render the present Government unpopular, and have a tendency, at the next election, to throw the power into the hands of men who were most hostile to a connection with France; and that this would probably happen in the midst of a war. I asked him whether the few millions acquired at this expense would not be too dearly bought?

He frankly confessed that he was of my sentiments; but that he feared the Consul would not relax. I asked him to press this argument upon him, together with the danger of seeing the country pass into the hands of Britain. I told him that he had seen the ardor of the Americans to take it by force, and the difficulty with which they were restrained by the prudence of the President; that he must easily see how much the hands of the war party would be strengthened, when they learned that France was upon the eve of a rupture with England. He admitted the weight of all this: "But," says he, "you know the temper of a youthful conqueror; everything he does is rapid as lightning; we have only to speak to him as an opportunity presents itself, perhaps in a crowd, when he bears no contradiction. When I am alone with him, I can speak more freely, and he attends; but this opportunity seldom happens, and is always accidental. Try, then, if you can not come up to my mark. Consider the extent of the country, the exclusive navigation of the river, and the importance of having no neighbors to dispute you, no war to dread." I told him that I considered all these as important considerations, but there was a point beyond which we could not go, and that fell far short of the sum he mentioned.

I asked him, in case of a purchase, whether they would stipulate that France would never possess the Floridas, and that she would aid us to procure them, and relinquish all right that she might have to them. He told me that she would go thus far. I added, that I would now say nothing on the subject, but that I would converse with Mr. Monroe; and that I was sure to find him disposed to do everything that was reasonable, or could be expected to remove every cause of difference between the two countries. That, however, if any negotiation should go on, I would wish that the First Consul would depute somebody to treat with us, who had more leisure than the Minister for Foreign Affairs.

I said this to see whether my conjectures relative to him were well founded. He told me that as the First Consul knew our personal friendship, he having several times had occasion to speak of me and my family, and the principles that we held, he believed that there would be no difficulty, when this negotiation was somewhat advanced, to have the management of it put into his hands. He earnestly pressed me to make some proposition that was so near the First Consul's as to admit his mentioning it to him. I told him that I would consult Mr. Monroe, but that neither he nor I could accede to his ideas on the subject. Thus, sir, you see a negotiation is fairly opened, and upon grounds which I confess I prefer to all other commercial privileges; and always to some a simple money transaction is infinitely preferable. As to the quantum, I have yet made up no opinion. The field opened to us is infinitely larger than our instructions contemplated; the revenue increasing, and the land more than adequate to sink the capital, should we even go the sum proposed by Marbois; nay, I persuade myself, that the whole sum may be raised by the sale of the territory west of the Mississippi, with the right of sovereignty, to some Power in Europe, whose vicinity we should not fear. I speak now without reflection, and without having seen Mr. Monroe, as it was midnight when I left the Treasury Office, and is now near 3 o'clock. It is so very important that you should be apprized that a negotiation is actually opened, even before Mr. Monroe has been presented, in order to calm the tumult which the news of war will renew, that I have lost no time in communicating it. We shall do all we can to cheapen the purchase; but my present sentiment is that we shall buy. Mr. Monroe will be presented to the Minister to-morrow, when we shall press for as early an audience as possible from the First Consul. I think it will be necessary to put in some proposition to-morrow: the Consul goes in a few days to Brussels, and every moment is precious.

I am, dear sir, with the most respectful consideration, your most obedient, humble servant,

ROBERT R. LIVINGSTON.

Mr. Monroe to Mr. Madison.

PARIS *April 15, 1803.*

DEAR SIR,—It is proper for me to mention to you in confidence some circumstances which I wish not to include in an official letter. I was informed on my arrival here by Mr. Skipwith that Mr. Livingston mortified at my appointment had done everything in his power to turn the occurrences in America, and even my mission to his account, by pressing the Government on every point with a view to show that he had accomplished what was wished without my aid: and perhaps also that my mission had put in hazard what might otherwise have been easily obtained. His official correspondence will show what occurred prior to my arrival & sufficiently proves that he did not abstain even on hearing that I was on my way, from the topics intrusted to us jointly. Col. Mercer who was present says this information was given next morning at the second interview. When I called on him he told me that this government had resolved to sell Louisiana &c but that the resolution had grown out of the state of things in Europe, & the danger of a war with England: that that point would be decided in a fortnight, perhaps immediately on the return of a courrier from Russia who was expected in less time: that he had been with Talleyrand that day, advised him that I was on the way from Havre & pressed him on the subject of my mission, & ultimately on being asked what we would give had actually offered terms. On the next day I dined with Mr. Livingston; while at dinner Mr. Marbois came there, withdrew and returned after we arose from dinner; they had a private conference and it was agreed, there being company with him, that Mr. Livingston should call on him after the company dispersed at his (Mr. Marbois') house to confer relative to the purchase of Louisiana. He told me he was going there & the object, and in a private conference with Mr. Skipwith who dined with him on the same day, after repeating the above, he regretted his misfortune in my arrival, since it took from him the credit of having brought everything to a proper conclusion without my aid. You will perceive the dilemma into which I have been & am still placed by this course of proceeding, since I have not only to negotiate with the French Government, especially its ministers, but my colleagues also. There is a plausible pretext for not presenting me to the Consul till the monthly audience, & in strict propriety I ought to hold no communication or sanction one with this government till I am presented: tho' my colleague considers my reception by the minister, his official notes relative to it, the terms in which he spoke of me on the part of the Consul & the information he gave us that a person would be designated to treat with us, with whom we might hold informal communications in the interim as placing me on the ground of a person recognized. If I held back on the rule of strict etiquette

& permitted no communication at all in case our negotiation failed I exposed myself & our government to the charge of having lost, by the measure taken, a brilliant opportunity of securing all our objects here & myself particularly of sacrificing everything thro' selfish motives. It is well known that the crisis pressed here and still does, that the Consul had resolved to sell, that Marbois was a minister & entitled to credit, that my colleague was one also already recognized & jointly associated with me in the trust. He was also possessed with the views of our government as well as myself, & might speak without my approbation with whom he pleased. I could not withhold confidential communications with him. Under these circumstances I have been driven by necessity, in private communications with him, signing nothing or authorizing it on his part, to permit him to state to Mr. Marbois that I would assent to the purchase of Louisiana at the price we were willing to give for the territory to the left of the river, France relinquishing all pretensions to the Floridas, & engaging to support with her influence our negotiation with Spain for them. By so doing I disarm those who might wish it of charging on me or our government the fault of future events, should they be unpropitious, and am not aware that I substantially hazard anything. All this attention to my colleague &c may be an intrigue tho' on the part of Marbois. I put confidence in the facts he states. It may be wished to inspire jealousy and distrust between my colleague & myself; the minister may suppose he will be less reserved, tho' it is certain till my appointment was known that he often treated him with great neglect & even disrespect. The opinion entertained of the character of the Consul for promptitude & decision, that if he liked the terms he would conclude at once, & if he was disgusted would perhaps not soon return to the subject induced me with the consideration mentioned to assent to the above. My Colleague has now promised me in the most explicit terms to hold no further communication with Mr. Marbois or any other person, till I am recognized, & a person regularly appointed to treat with us. I do not know that any real injury will occur to the object of the mission by what has passed.

Mr. Monroe's Journal or Memoranda.

APRIL 27.

M^r. Marbois came to my lodgings by appointment of M^r. Livingston, at two o'clock and I being indisposed it was agreed that I might repose as it suited me. M^r. Marbois opened the conversation by presenting us with a project of a treaty given him by the gov^t. to be proposed to us, which he admitted he thought hard and unreasonable; he presented at the same time another project which he called his own, which had not been seen by the gov^t., but to which he presumed the first consul would assent, as he had told him he would not insist on the terms contained in the first, and would only ask or propose such as he had drawn in the second; but to which he declared that the first consul had not assented explicitly. M^r. Marbois thought himself however at liberty to propose his own project as the basis of our negotiation. That project claimed one hundred millions & the debts due our citizens estimated at 20. more. His own reduced that demand to 80, including the debt. There were some other differences between them, his going more into detail, in the form of a publick act. M^r. Livingston observed that the debt was a thing to be provided for in an especial manner; that the consul had said to him it should be paid; that we ought to begin from points agreed & proceed to difficulties—that the points agreed were the debts that were due and our right of deposit. M^r. Marbois said that if we made a treaty on the general & great subject of the Louisiana, he would include in it a provision for the debts; that if he did not make a treaty of that kind he would have nothing to do with the debts. M^r. Livingston repeated the promise of the Consul &c. for the payment of them, to which M^r. Marbois replied that he did not mean to impair the force of our claim founded on the treaty & the promise of the gov^t.—what he meant to say was, that if our negotiation succeeded in the object of it, the debts would be comprized in it & provided for, and if it did not succeed he would leave them where he found them; the claim would still be supported by the treaty & any assurance M^r. Livingston may have received from the gov^t. since. M^r. Livingston still pressing the high ground on which the claim to the payment of the debt rested, M^r. Marbois observed that in the promise referred to no time was fixed or sum specified, & intimated that the Consul did not contemplate a greater sum than 3 or 4 millions of livres. I then observed that I thought we were all of the same opinion respecting the debts that the ground on which they stood could not be impaired by the failure of this negotiation; that a provision might be made for the payment of them by it; that we had better go on to the other object & with that view to examine & discuss the project presented by M^r. Marbois. One of the articles contained in M^r. Marbois's project, proposed that the payment to our citizens & the French gov^t. should proceed in equal degree regarding the amount to be paid to each party, by the month, that is that neither should have a priority or preference, to the other as to time or proportion. M^r. Livingston insisted that the payment to our citizens should be prompt & full, which he supposed we might make, without rendering ourselves unable to meet the views of the French gov^t. in any sum we might stipulate to give in point of time: to that M^r. Marbois seemed to have no objection.

APPENDIX I.—I objected to the commerc^l. priviledge, as being calculated to embarrass our revenue system, create irregularities between one part and another, give offense to foreign powers, fix a badge of degradation on the part of the Union, & actually defeat the policy of France in inclining us to Engl^d.—He seemed to think that being the condition of the cession it was not liable to all the objections stated—both my colleague and myself observed that that idea had not been communicated by him to either of us in our former conversations, w^h. he admitted on our word, but observed that it was an omission on his part, his gov^t. having always contemplated it—that it imported the honor of the govt., to furnish a publick motive for the cession distinct from money—I then objected to the perpetuity of the stipulation to which he assented—12 years were proposed to which he agreed.

At the same time that we presented to Mr. Marbois our project we gave him a paper drawn by my colleague on the subject, translated in French, w^h. being long, it was deemed then unnecessary to read it, but proposed by my colleague that Mr. Marbois sho^d. keep & read it himself & shew it to the consul, w^h. he promised. This paper was given me by my colleague some days before, but it being lengthy & I being much engaged in the arrangement of our project had paid but little attention to it—when my colleague called on me on his way to Mr. Marbois he asked me for it; I gave it to him, he asked me to sign it—I told him there were passages I did not like, particularly the admission that the formation of our adm^{ns}. depended on the conduct of foreign powers: that that was not the fact, that that idea was degrading to our country, that the application of the term sovereign to the first consul was improper, that of Ch: Magistrate was the correct one—I also did not like the terms used relative to the debts due by France—tho' I wished & wod secure them in our treaty—he said that the paper contained mere cursory observations,—that the first idea w^h. I objected to wod. have weight here, since this gov^t. did not wish a change of adm^n. in the U. States so that he thought the paper might have use. On the intimation that he considered the paper as containing cursory observations, by which I understood that he meant it as informal, I signed it—I did this on the principle that the negotiation had reached a stage which prevented this paper from doing harm, and to put it out of my colleague's power to say that I prevented his doing good. I never heard of the paper afterwards, tho' my colleague told me next day on leaving the first consul's that Mr. Marbois had informed him that the first consul had approved it—I had conferred with Mr. Marbois just before my colleague did & arranged our meeting that night at his home, in w^h. he said nothing of that paper. I therefore inferred that what he did say was in consequence of the enquiry of my colleague, & on perusing that he felt some interest respecting it.

JOURNAL.—My colleague took M^r. Marbois's project with him & brought one very loosely drawn founded on it, which with our communications together on the subject & the modifications we gave it, will be noted hereafter.

We called on Mr. Marbois the 29th and gave him our project which we read to him & discussed. We proposed to offer 50. millions to France & 20. on acct. of her debt to the citizens of the U States, making 70. in the whole. On reading that article he declared that he would not proceed in the negotiation on a less sum than 80. Millions, since it would be useless as the Consul had been sufficiently explicit on that point; Indeed he assured us that his government had never positively instructed him to take that sum, but that as he had told the Consul it was enough, that he would ask no more, and to which he understood the Consul as giving his assent, he Mr. Marbois had thought himself authorized to accept & propose it to us, but that he could not proceed unless we agreed to give it. On this frank & explicit declaration on his part & after explaining to him the motive which led us to offer that sum we agreed to accede to his idea & give 80. millions. He asked us if we could not advance something immediately, we replied, we did so in discharge of their debt to our citizens; that they had suffered and it was for the interest of France as well as the U States, that they should be promptly paid, or as soon as possible. To the payment in stock he did not object, nor did he say anything respecting the loss to be sustained by it: he asked what effect the protracting the redemption of the stock for 15 years would have on its value; we told him to raise its price.

On the proviso to the commercial stipulation he seemed to entertain a doubt, but on our shewing the abuse of which the article was capable without it, being not simply to give a preference for 12 years to French vessels & manufactures over those of other countries in the ports of the ceded territory, but to enable France to monopolize the carriage of the exports from the Mississippi, and prevent a single article raised there being brought from the other States, such as tobacco, rice, &c. He admitted that such a power was not sought on their part.

He seemed desirous to secure by some strong provision the incorporation of the inhabitants of the ceded country with our union; we told him that we would try to modify the article to meet his ideas as fairly as we could—we left our project with him, in expectation of hearing from him soon the result, as he said he should see the Consul next morning on the subject. He informed me that Mr. Talleyrand had asked him whether I was in health to be presented to the first Consul, & on my answering in the affirmative; advised me to let him know it. My colleague promised as we returned home to inform the minister next day that I had recovered my health. To guard against accidents however I wrote the minister to that effect next morning, and a note to my colleague to request him to call for me as he went to the house of the minister. Just as I was ready to visit the minister my colleague returned from him & informed me that it was arranged that I should be presented next day, that is on the first of May.

(May 1st, 1803, Sunday.)

I accompanied my colleague to the Palace of the Louvre, where I was presented by him to the Consul. While standing in the circle I received a communication by the prefect of the palace, from the minister, stating that he was indisposed, but that I must present the Consul my letter of credence, & that the Consul desired I would dine with him.

When the Consul came round to me, M^r. Livingston presented me to him, on which the Consul observed that he was glad to see me. "Je suis bien aise de le voir." "You have been here 15 days?" I told him I had. "You speak French?" I replied "A little." "You had a good voyage?" Yes. "You came in a frigate?" No in a merchant vessel charged for the purpose. Col. Mercer was presented; says he "He is Secretary of legation?" No but my friend. He then made enquiries of M^r. Livingston & his secretary how their families were, and then turned to M^r. Livingston & myself & observed that our affairs should be settled.

We dined with him. After dinner when we retired into the saloon, the first Consul came up to me and asked whether the federal city grew much. I told him it did. "How many inhabitants has it?" It is just commencing, there are two cities near it, one above, the other below, on the great river Potomack, which two cities if counted with the federal city would make a respectable town, in itself it contains only two or three thousand inhabitants. "Well; M^r. Jefferson, how old is he?" Ab^t. sixty. "Is he married or single?" He is not married. "Then he is a *garcon*." No he is a widower. "Has he children?" Yes two daughters who are married. "Does he reside always at the federal city?" Generally. "Are the publick buildings there commodious, those for the Congress and President especially?" They are. "You the Americans did brilliant things in your war with England, you will do the same again." We shall I am persuaded always behave well when it shall be our lot to be in war. "You may probably be in war with them again." I replied I did not know, that that was an important question to decide when there would be an occasion for it.

At ½ after eight we met M^r. Marbois at his own house, in conformity to an appointment which we made with him at the Consul's, and entered on the subject of our proposed treaty. He objected to the first article as being long & containing superfluities, & shewed us a remark to that effect on it by the department of foreign affairs, as being an act more suited to a private transaction before a notary publick. He objected also to any guarantee against France or Spain, as against France as useless, since the cession was as strong a guarantee against her as she could make, and against Spain as improper & useless since it would be an ungracious act to her from France, & we had nothing to fear from Spain. He had no objection to inserting the art: of the treaty of Il defonso by which France acquired the territory, in our treaty, & would make her good offices with Spain in support of our negotiations for the Floridas. From the 2^d. art: he agreed to strike out whatever restricted the application of publick buildings to the same use hereafter; & to be contented with the security of property to individuals; and also to omit the obligation to transfer the archives &c. to the local authorities. The articles at the close of our project which respected the cession & transfer of the territory, he proposed to put together in the commencement, which we examined & modified somewhat by consent. That which respected the commercial privilege, he said was objected to in the proviso; he admitted however that it was not wished or contemplated to enjoy more than an exemption from foreign duties in favor of French productions, manufactures & tonage in the transportation of the same into the ports of the Mississippi but not to affect the terms on which our produce should be carried from it, since he readily foresaw that such a power might be greatly abused. I proposed an amendment which was in sentiment agreed to. To the payment to be made them in stock, and the mode by which we proposed to ascertain the amount and persons entitled to the debt which they owed our citizens, he said objections were entertained. They wish the payment to be made here of 5. millions of livres the month, which we told him was impossible— He believed it was. He wished the term for which the stock was irredeemable to be omitted & adjusted afterwards between ourselves, intimating that on that point difficulties existed with his gov^t. which proceeded from want of time to examine it, but that we must agree (on) something, indeed seemed to assent explicitly to our ideas on the subject. On our explaining the reasons why some check on the liquidation of the debt due our citizens was necessary, since otherwise the sum destined to them might be absorbed, by liquidations in favor of Americans not entitled, or even not Americans, he admitted the propriety of the check we proposed. He said he would see the Consul next morning, fix the points in question, & come prepared sometime in the course of that day to conclude & sign the treaty as of yesterday, being Saturday.

May 2^d. We actually signed the treaty and convention for the sixty millions of Francs to France in the French language, but our copies in English not being made out we could not sign in our language. They were however prepared and signed two or three days afterwards. The convention respecting American claims took more time

& was not signed till about the 8. or 9th. A more minute view of this business as promised in the third page will be annexed hereafter.

We nominated provisionally Col: John Mercer, J. C. Barnett & W^m. McClure to examine the claims of Americans on the French gov^t. and perform the duties assigned to our board by the convention respecting that subject.

As soon as we had dispatched the treaty &c. by M^r. Hughes, with duplicates & triplicates, I resolved to go to Spain in pursuit of my instructions, which M^r. L. approved of and strongly urged. With that view I wrote a note to the minister of foreign affairs asking the good offices of his gov^t. with Spain as had been promised by M^r. Marbois intimating that I wished to set out in a few days for Madrid. On the Sunday following I dined with the Consul Cambacérès, who arrived late from the council at St. Cloud. The party was not large; I sat next him; he observed "you must not go to Spain at present." I asked his reason. He replied " it is not the time, you had better defer it." I revived the subject repeatedly but he declined going more into it. After dinner when we were in the saloon, he came up to me, and on my telling him that he had given me some concern by what he had said, he replied " it was only his opinion, but you will talk on the subject with the minister of the publick treasury (M^r. Marbois,) which I promised. I went immediately to M^r. Marbois's but he was not at home. Reflecting on the hint from the Consul it occurred it would be proper to call on the ambassador of Spain & confer with him on the subject, as I had always intended before I sate out for Spain. I found him at home with two Spanish gentlemen, one the husband of the daughter of Don Galvez who was also present. I told him that I intended going to Spain to treat for Florida with the ministers of his Catholic Majesty, & asked what he thought of it. He replied with great candor that he wished the affair amicably settled between our gov^{ts}., and that two days before he had written to his Court by an extraordinary courier at the desire of M^r. Livingston to propose to it the question whether it would make the cession to the U States and as I understood to authorize him to treat here for it. As M^r. Livingston had never spoken to me on the subject, as he had pressed my going to Spain, or at least given his decided opinion that I ought to go there, this information surprised me much, especially when I recollected that he not only had no power to treat on the subject, but knew that it was committed to others. I asked when he expected an answer to his letter? He said if it was sent by an extr^y. courier it might be in 12 days, as it required 7 to go and as many to return; & it had been sent 2 already: that if it came by the ordinary post it would take a much longer time as it required 12 days to convey a letter from Paris to Madrid in that mode. I told him that I thought I should go to Madrid & then explained to him something of the nature of the commission which existed for treating with his government, it being thought by *ours* more respectful to *his* to treat at Madrid than here, but without giving cause to infer that I disapproved the measure taken by M^r. Livingston or indeed that I was ignorant of it.

Next day M^r. Livingston and myself called on M^r. Marbois on some question relative to the treaty &c. On our return he asked me when I should set out to Spain? I told him that I had called on the Marquis D'Azara to confer with him on the subject, the night before, and of the step he had taken at his request to draw the subject here; that under those circumstances it would be an idle errand for me to go there, at least till the Marquis got an answer to his letter; that the affair ought not to play between the two countries; He said that what had passed between him and the Marquis had happened casually at the minister of foreign affairs: that the Marquis had sent the Extr^y. courier to announce our treaty, & hearing him say he intended to send one, he had suggested the idea of his proposing to his court to make the cession, but not to obtain the authority to treat here for it. I told him that after the arrangement made by our gov^t. with respect to Spain, the affair ought to have its course in the train in which it was placed by it: that I could not see any benefit to be derived from an application of the Ambassador of Spain to his Court in the manner stated by M^r. Livingston, especially if I was to go there.

Mr. Livingston to Mr. Madison.

PARIS, *April 17, 1803.*

SIR: Mr. Petrie having been detained, I have an opportunity to give you a relation of what has passed since my letter of the 13th. On the 14th I called upon Mr. Monroe, to present him to the Minister, who had, upon my application, fixed 3 o'clock that day for his reception. Before we went we examined our commission, in which there are two circumstances with which I am not quite satisfied; one, indeed, of little moment, because it only respects me personally; and the other very important, as it may, if things should take a turn favorable to France, defeat all that we may do, even at the moment of signing. The first is that I have not the same rank in the commission with Mr. Monroe. It is important that I should be thought to stand as well with our Government as any other person. If so, my age, and the stations I have held entitle me not to have had any other person placed above me in the line I have filled. The second is, that the commission contains power only to treat for lands on the east side of the Mississippi. You will recollect that I have been long preparing this Government to yield us the country above the Arkansas, because I saw the effect of their holding and giving encouragement to settle it would draw off a prodigious population from our side of the river, and from such a connexion between the inhabitants of the Western country and these new settlers, who would be their relations and friends, as would be extremely dangerous. In my private negotiations with Joseph Bonaparte, I had urged every reason that I could think of to induce them to give us the country: and those reasons have had their effect. I am, therefore, surprised that our commission should have entirely lost sight of that object. Mr. Monroe, however, agrees with me that we will proceed as well as we can; and, as we left no copy of the commission, it may possibly escape unnoticed, though it will operate to our prejudice if our negotiation should not please at home. It is absolutely necessary, my dear sir, to repose confidence in Ministers who are placed so far from the seat of Government. You will recollect that I have been absolutely without powers to the present moment; and that though I have hazarded many things upon a presumption that I should have them, none have been received till now, and now they are unfortunately too limited.

But to proceed. On waiting upon the Minister we found M. Marbois there, who told me that he had come to communicate to the Minister what had passed between us, and that he greatly regretted the not being able to bring us to such an offer as he might mention to the First Consul. I told him that it was unnecessary to repeat what would compel us to limit our offers to a much more moderate sum, as I had already detailed them at large;. and he knew they exceeded our means. We were very graciously received by the Minister, whom I pressed to obtain as early a day as possible for the reception of Mr. Monroe, as time pressed, and we were anxious to conclude our business, for reasons arising out of the present disturbed state of America. He told me he would speak to the First Consul that night on the subject; and that he hoped some person would be appointed to treat with us, even before Mr. Monroe was presented. After a little general conversation, he took leave, in expectation that Mr. Monroe would be presented this day, (Sunday,) being a day of reception for the civil officers of the Government. The next day, Mr. Monroe and myself, after spending some time in consultation, determined to offer fifty millions, including our debts; we presumed it would be best only to mention forty in the first instance. This I accordingly did, in a conference I had on the 15th with M. Marbois. He expressed great sorrow that we could not go beyond that sum, because he was sure that it would not be accepted, and that perhaps the whole business would be defeated, which he the more feared, as he had just received a note from the Minister, indicative of the Consul's not being quite pleased that he had so greatly lowered his original proposition. He said that he saw our situation, and he knew that there was a point beyond which we could not go safely to ourselves or the President; but he wished us to advance to that point. He said that he would, if I wished, go that very day to St. Cloud, and let me know the result. I reminded him of the Consul's promise to pay the debt. I placed in the strongest light his personal obligation on this subject; and desired him to urge it as an additional reason to conclude an agreement which would facilitate the means of doing it. The next morning, which was yesterday, I again called to see him. He told me that he had been to St. Cloud; that the Consul received his proposition very coolly; and that I might consider the business as no longer in his hands, since he had given him no further powers; that he had urged the Consul's promise relative to the debt, which he admitted; but said, at the same time, he did not think it had exceeded three millions, though my letter expressly mentioned twenty. He expressed great sorrow upon the occasion; and advised me to press M. Talleyrand to present Mr. Monroe the next day, (that is, this day;) that he hoped that, if the Consul saw me, as he had a very particular esteem for me, he would renew the subject with me himself.

I went to Mr. Monroe, and carried him to the Minister, who had not returned from St. Cloud; and afterwards went again, but could not see him. I dined with the Second Consul yesterday; and in the evening M. Marbois came in. I took him aside, and asked him if anything further had passed: he said not; but, that as he was to go to St. Cloud the next day, it was possible that the Consul might touch upon the subject again; and that, if he did not, I might consider the plan as relinquished; and that, if I had any further proposition to make, it would be well to state it. I then told him that on further conversation with Mr. Monroe, we had resolved to go to the greatest possible length, and that we would give fifty millions. He said he had very little hopes that anything short of his proposition would succeed; but that he would make the best use of the arguments I had furnished him with, if an opportunity was offered; and if nothing was done the next day, I might conclude that the Consul had changed his sentiments; that, having given the Kingdom of Etruria, whose revenues were twenty-five millions, in exchange for this country, it was natural that the First Consul should estimate it beyond its real value.

Thus we stand at present, resolving to rest a few days upon our oars; in the meantime I shall press the payment of the debt as an excitement to forward the other business.

No notice has been given of Mr. Monroe's reception; and I am not without my fears that he will not be received before the usual diplomatic day, which will not be till the 15th, and, before that time, the Consul will probably go upon his tour to Flanders. Mr. Monroe having been compelled, when here, to be well with the party then uppermost, and who are now detested by the present ruler, it will be some time before they know how to estimate his worth; and Talleyrand has, I find, imbibed personal prejudice against him, that will induce him to throw every possible obstruction in his way, that he can do consistently with their own views.

I shall attend to the other subjects of your letter at the first moment of leisure. At present I think it will be improper to touch upon less important matters, which may either divert the attention or irritate.

I am sorry you have not thought it proper to attend to my request as to the Italian Republic. It has, I believe, been acknowledged by all the Powers of Europe except Great Britain. Compliments that cost nothing should, I think, always be paid, where you have points to carry. Be so obliging, in answering my letters, as to notice any project I throw out; because it is not enough to have them passed over in silence, as that leaves me in doubt; whereas the approbation or rejection of them precisely would inform me of your sentiments, and enable me to act accordingly.

I am, dear sir, with much esteem and respect, your most obedient, humble servant.

R. R. LIVINGSTON.

Mr. Madison to Messrs. Livingston and Monroe.

DEPARTMENT OF STATE, *April 18, 1803.*

GENTLEMEN: A month having elapsed since the departure of Mr. Monroe, it may be presumed that, by the time this reaches you, communications will have passed with the French Government, sufficiently explaining its views towards the United States, and preparing the way for the ulterior instructions which the President thinks proper should now be given.

In case a convention and arrangement with France should have resulted from the negotiations with which you are charged; or, in case such should not have been the result—but no doubt should be left that the French Government means to respect duly our rights, and to cultivate sincerely peace and friendship with the United States—it will be expedient for you to make such communications to the British Government, as will assure it that nothing has been done inconsistent with our good faith, and as will prevent a diminution of the good understanding which subsists between the two countries.

If the French Government, instead of friendly arrangements or views, should be found to meditate hostilities, or to have formed projects which will constrain the United States to resort to hostilities, such communications are then to be held with the British Government, as will sound its dispositions, and invite its concurrence in the war. Your own prudence will suggest that the communications be so made as, on the one hand, not to precipitate France into hostile operations;

and, on the other, not to lead Great Britain from the supposition that war depends on the choice of the United States, and that their choice of war will depend on her participation in it. If war is to be the result, it is manifestly desirable that it be delayed until the certainty of this result can be known, and the legislative and other provisions can be made here; and also of great importance, that the certainty should not be known to Great Britain, who might take advantage of the posture of things to press on the United States disagreeable conditions of her entering into the war.

It will probably be most convenient, in exchanging ideas with the British Government, to make use of its public Minister at Paris, as less likely to alarm and stimulate the French Government, and to raise the pretensions of the British Government, than the repairing of either of you to London, which might be viewed by both as a signal of rupture. The latter course, however, may possibly be rendered most eligible by the pressure of the crisis.

Notwithstanding the just repugnance of this country to a coalition of any sort with the belligerent politics of Europe, the advantages to be derived from the cooperation of Great Britain in a war of the United States, at this period, against France and her allies, are too obvious and too important to be renounced. And notwithstanding the apparent disinclination of the British councils to a renewal of hostilities with France, it will probably yield to the various motives which will be felt to have the United States in the scale of Britain against France, and particularly for the immediate purpose of defeating a project of the latter, which has evidently created much solicitude in the British Government.

The price which she may attach to her co-operation can not be foreseen, and, therefore, can not be the subject of full and precise instructions. It may be expected that she will insist at least on a stipulation that neither of the parties shall make peace or truce without the consent of the other; and as such an article can not be deemed unreasonable, and will secure us against the possibility of her being detached, in the course of the war, by seducing overtures from France, it will not be proper to raise difficulties on that account. It may be useful, however, to draw from her a definition, as far as the case will admit, of the objects contemplated by her, that whenever, with ours, they may be attainable by peace, she may be duly pressed to listen to it. Such an explanation will be the more reasonable, as the objects of the United States will be so fair and so well known.

It is equally probable, that a stipulation of commercial advantages in the Mississippi, beyond those secured by existing treaties, will be required. On this point, it may be answered at once, that Great Britain shall enjoy a free trade with all the ports to be acquired by the United States, on the terms allowed to the most favored nations in the ports, generally, of the United States. If made an essential condition, you may admit, that in the ports to be acquired within the Mississippi, the trade of her subjects shall be on the same footing for a term of about ten years with that of our own citizens. But the United States are not to be bound to the exclusion of the trade of any particular nation or nations.

Should a mutual guaranty of the existing possessions, or of the conquests to be made by the parties, be proposed, it must be explicitly rejected, as of no value to the United States, and as entangling them in the frequent wars of that nation with other Powers, and very possibly in disputes with that nation itself.

The anxiety which Great Britain has shown to extend her domain to the Mississippi, the uncertain extent of her claims from North to the South, beyond the Western limits of the United States, and the attention she has paid to the Northwest coast of America, make it probable that she will connect with a war on this occasion, a pretension to the acquisition of the country on the west side of the Mississippi, understood to be ceded by Spain to France, or at least of that portion of it lying between that river and the Missouri. The evils involved in such an extension of her possessions in our neighborhood, and in such a hold on the Mississippi, are obvious. The acquisition is the more objectionable, as it would be extremely displeasing to our Western citizens, and as its evident bearing on South America, might be expected to arouse all the jealousies of France and Spain, and to prolong the war, on which the event would depend. Should this pretension, therefore, be pressed, it must be resisted as altogether repugnant to the sentiments and to the sound policy of the United States. But it may be agreed, in alleviation of any disappointment of Great Britain, that France shall not be allowed to retain or acquire any part of the territory, from which she herself would be precluded.

The moment the prospect of war shall require the precaution, you will not omit to give confidential notice to our public Ministers and Consuls, and to our naval commanders in the Mediterranean, that our commerce and public ships may be as little exposed to danger as possible. It may, under certain circumstances, be proper to notify the danger immediately to the collectors in the principal ports of the United States.

A separate letter to you is enclosed, authorizing you to enter into such communications and conferences with British Ministers as may possibly be required by the conduct of France. The letter is made a separate one, that it may be used with effect, but without the formality, of a commission. It is hoped that sound calculations of interest, as well as a sense of right, in the French Government, will prevent the necessity of using the authority expressed in this letter. In a contrary state of things, the President relies on your own information, to be gained on the spot, and on your best discretion, to open with advantage the communications with the British Government, and to proportion the degree of an understanding with it to the indications of an approaching war with France. Of these indications, also, you will be best able to judge. It will only be observed to you that, if France should avow or evince a determination to deny to the United States the free navigation of the Mississippi, your consultations with Great Britain may be held on the ground that war is inevitable. Should the navigation not be disputed, and the deposit alone be denied, it will be prudent to adapt your consultations to the possibility that Congress may distinguish between the two cases, and make a question how far the latter right may call for an instant resort to arms, or how far a procrastination of that remedy may be suggested and justified by the prospect of a more favorable conjuncture.

These instructions have thus far supposed that Great Britain and France are at peace; and that neither of them intend at present to interrupt it. Should war have actually commenced, or its approach be certain, France will, no doubt, be the more apt to concur in friendly accommodations with us, and Great Britain the more desirous of engaging us on her side. You will, of course, avail yourselves of this posture of things, for avoiding the necessity of recurring to Great Britain, or, if the necessity can not be avoided, for fashioning her disposition to arrangements formed with Great Britain in reference to war, the policy of the United States requires that it be as little entangling as the case will permit.

Our latest authentic information from New Orleans is of the 25th of February. At that date the port had been opened for provisions carried down the Mississippi, subject to a duty of 6 per cent., if consumed in the Province, and an additional duty, if exported; with a restriction, in the latter case, to Spanish bottoms, and to the external ports permitted by Spain to her Colonial trade. A second letter, written by the Spanish Minister here, has been received by the Intendant, but without effect. On the 10th of March his interposition was repeated in a form which you will find, by his translated communication to the Department of State, in one of the enclosed papers, was meant to be absolutely effectual. You will find in the same paper the translation of a letter from the French chargé d'affaires here to the Governor of Louisiana, written with a co-operating view. A provisional letter to any French agents who might have arrived, had been previously written by him, in consequence of a note from this Department, founded on a document published at New Orleans, showing that orders had been given by the Spanish Government for the surrender of the Province to France; and he has of late addressed a third letter on the subject of the Prefect said to have arrived at New Orleans. It does not appear, however, from any accounts received, that Louisiana has yet changed hands.

What the result of the several measures taken for restoring the right of deposit will be, remains to be seen. A representation on the subject was made by Mr. Graham, in the absence of Mr. Pinckney, to the Spanish Government, on the 3d of February. No answer had been received on the 8th, but Mr. Graham was led by circumstances to make no particular inference from the delay. The silence of the French Government to Mr. Livingston's representation, as stated in his letter of the —— day of ——, is a very unfavorable indication. It might have been expected, from the assurances given, of an intention to observe the treaty between Spain and the United States, and to cultivate the friendship of the latter, that the occasion would have been seized for evincing the sincerity of the French Government; and it may still be expected that no interposition that may be required by the actual state of things will be withheld, if peace and friendship with the United States be really the objects of that Government. Of this, the mission of Mr. Monroe, and the steps taken by you on his arrival, will doubtless have impressed the proper convictions.

During this suspense of the rightful commerce of our Western citizens, their conduct has been, and continues to be, highly exemplary. With the just sensibility produced by the wrongs done them, they have united a patient confidence in the measures and views of their Government. The justice of this observation will be confirmed to you by manifestations contained in the Western newspapers, herewith enclosed; and, if duly appreciated, will not lessen the force of prudential as well as other motives, for correcting past, and avoiding future trespasses on American rights.

APRIL 20.

The letter from the Marquis d' Yrujo, of which you will find a translated copy in the enclosed newspaper of this date, was yesterday received. The letters to which it refers, as containing orders for the re-establishment of our deposit at New Orleans, were immediately forwarded. They will arrive in time, we hope, to mitigate considerably the losses from the misconduct of the Spanish Intendant; and they are the more acceptable, as they are an evidence of the respect, in the Government of Spain for our rights and our friendship.

From the allusion in this communication from the Spanish Minister to a future agreement between the two Governments, on the subject of an equivalent deposit, it would seem that the Spanish Government regards the cession to France as either no longer in force, or not soon to be carried into execution. However this may be, it will not be allowed, any more than the result of our remonstrance to Spain on the violation of our rights, to slacken the negotiations for the greater security and the enlargement of these rights. Whether the French or the Spaniards, or both, are to be our neighbors, the considerations which led to the measures, taken with respect to these important objects, still require that they should be pursued into all the success that may be attainable.

With sentiments of great respect, &c.,

JAMES MADISON.

R. R. LIVINGSTON and JAMES MONROE, Esqs.

The Secretary of State to Messrs. Livingston and Monroe.

DEPARTMENT OF STATE, *April 18, 1803.*

GENTLEMEN: The reasonable and friendly views with which you have been instructed by the President to enter into negotiations with the French Government, justify him in expecting from them an issue favorable to the tranquillity and to the useful relations between the two countries. It is not forgotten, however, that these views, instead of being reciprocal, may find, on the part of France, a temper adverse to harmony, and schemes of ambition, requiring, on the part of the United States, as well as of others, the arrangements suggested by a provident regard to events. Among these arrangements, the President conceives that a common interest may recommend a candid understanding, and a closer connexion with Great Britain: and he presumes that the occasion may present itself to the British Government in the same light. He, accordingly, authorizes you, or either of you, in case the prospect of your discussion with the French Government should make it expedient, to open a confidential communication with Ministers of the British Government, and to confer freely and fully on the precautions and provisions best adapted to the crisis, and in which that Government may be disposed to concur; transmitting to your own, without delay, the result of these consultations.

With sentiments of high respect, &c.,

JAMES MADISON.

R. R. LIVINGSTON and JAMES MONROE, Esqs.

[Extract.]

Mr. King to the Secretary of State.

APRIL 19, 1803.

In Lord Whitworth's last despatch, he says: "Two days ago, General Bernadotte left Paris, on his mission to the United States, with assurances of the First Consul's sincere desire to cultivate the friendship of that country; and yesterday Mr. Monroe, the American Envoy, arrived here." The United States, says his Lordship, are likely to reap the first fruits of our disagreement with France; the settlement of their affairs being already so nearly finished that little remains to be done by Mr. Monroe, who is said to be destined to relieve Mr. King at London.

[Extract.]

Mr. King to the Secretary of State.

LONDON, *April 28, 1803.*

"In a conference with Lord Hawkesbury on the 6th instant, I explained to him the object of the extraordinary mission of Mr. Monroe, pursuant to the tenor of your letter of the 29th of January, and I have the pleasure to inform you that his Lordship received the communication in good part, suggested no doubt of our right to pursue separately and alone the objects we aim at, and appeared to be satisfied with the President's views on this important subject."

Mr. Madison to Mr. Monroe.

WASHINGTON, *April 20, 1803.*

DEAR SIR,—You will receive with this all the communications claimed by the actual and eventual posture of our affairs in the hands of yourself and Mr. Livingston. You will find, also, that the Spanish Government has pretty promptly corrected the wrong done by its officer at New Orleans. This event will be a heavy blow to the clamorous for war, and will be very soothing to those immediately interested in the trade of the Mississippi. The temper manifested by our Western Citizens has been throughout the best that can be conceived. The real injury from the suspension of the deposit was, however, much lessened by the previous destruction of the entire crop of wheat in Kentucky, by the number of sea vessels built on the Ohio, and by throngs of vessels from Atlantic ports to the Mississippi, some of which ascended to the Natchez. The permission, also, to supply the market at New Orleans, and to ship the surplus as Spanish property to Spanish ports, was turned to good account. The trial, therefore, has been much alleviated. Certain it is that the hearts and hopes of the Western people are strongly fixed on the Mississippi for the future boundary. Should no improvement of existing rights be gained, the disappointment will be great. Still, respect for principle and character, aversion to poor rates and taxes, the hope of a speedy conjuncture more favorable, and attachment to the present order of things, will be persuasive exhortations to patience. It is even a doubt with some of the best judges whether the deposit alone would not be waived for a while, rather than it should be the immediate ground of war and an alliance with England. This suggested a particular passage in the official letter now sent you and Mr. Livingston. * * *

President Jefferson to Dr. Hugh Williamson.

WASHINGTON, *April 30, 1803.*

DEAR SIR,—I thank you for the information on the subject of navigation of the Herville contained in yours of the 10th. In running the late line between the Choctaws and us, we found the Amite to be about thirty miles from the Mississippi where that line crossed it, which was but a little northward of our southern boundary. For the present we have a respite on that subject, Spain having without delay restored our infracted right, and assured us it is expressly saved by the instrument of her cession of Louisiana to France. Although I do not count with confidence on obtaining New Orleans from France for money, yet I am confident in the policy of putting off the day of contention for it till we have lessened the embarrassment of debt accumulated instead of being discharged by our predecessors, till we obtain more of that strength which is growing on us so rapidly, and especially till we have planted a population on the Mississippi itself sufficient to do its own work without marching men fifteen hundred miles from the Atlantic shores to perish by fatigue and unfriendly climates. This will soon take place. In the meantime we have obtained by a peaceable appeal to justice, in four months, what we should not have obtained under seven years of war, the loss of one hundred thousand lives, an hundred millions of additional debt, many hundred millions worth of produce and property lost for want of market, or in seeking it, and that demoralization which war superinduces on the human mind. To have seized New Orleans, as our federal maniacs wished, would only have changed the character and extent of the blockade of our western commerce. It would have produced a blockade, by superior naval force, of the navigation of the river as well as of the entrance into New Orleans, instead of a paper blockade from New Orleans alone while the river remained open, and I am persuaded that had not the deposit been so quickly rendered we should have found soon that it would be better now to ascend the river to Natchez, in order to be clear of the embarrassments, plunderings, and irritations at New Orleans, and to fatten by the benefits of the depôt a city and citizens of our own, rather than those of a foreign nation.

[Extract.]

Mr. Madison to Mr. Monroe.

WASHINGTON, *May 1, 1803.*

The order from Spain for the restoration of the deposit has had a good effect everywhere. We are told at the same time, in the very words of the Article, that, in the cession of Louisiana, our rights under the Treaty of '95 are saved. On the 1st of April, Laussat, the

Prefect, was at New Orleans, and the late Governor, Casa-Calvo, was expected in a few days from the Havana, to deliver possession to the French. Whether this message will be delayed for the arrival of the Capt. General, or what may result to it from other causes, can be better understood with you than here. Laussat professes to be kindly disposed, and undertakes to affirm that the French Government had nothing to do in the arrest of the deposit by the Spanish officer, and that if he had been there in authority no such thing would have happened. He does not admit that he has any authority to meddle in any way at present, and gives this answer to Pichon's exhortation. The Intendant had declined in like manner to obey the advice of Yrujo. The last more peremptory interpositions of these Ministers had not arrived, and the importance of them was superceded by the orders from Spain. The attention here is much alive to the transfer of the country to France, and it becomes her, if she wishes to be on cordial terms with us, to proceed in every step with strict justice and exemplary frankness.

Extract of a letter from Mr. Cevallos, Minister of His Catholic Majesty, to Charles Pinckney, esq.

ARANJUEZ, *May 4, 1803.*

The system adopted by His Majesty not to dispossess himself of any portion of his States, deprives him of the pleasure of assenting to the cessions which the United States wish to obtain by purchase, as I have intimated for their information to the Marquis of Casa Yrujo.

By the retrocession made to France of Louisiana, this Power regains the said province with the limits it had, and saving the rights acquired by other Powers. The United States can address themselves to the French Government to negotiate the acquisition of territories which may suit their interest.

Mr. King to Messrs. Livingston and Monroe.

LONDON, *May 7, 1803.*

GENTLEMEN: War seems to be quite inevitable, though it is possible that the offer of France to leave Malta in the hands of Russia, Austria, or Prussia, may create some hesitation, and, had it been early made, would perhaps have prevented the present crisis. In case of war, it is the purpose of this Government to send an expedition to occupy New Orleans. If it be ceded to us, would it not be expedient openly or confidentially to communicate the fact here? I have reason to be satisfied that it would prevent the projected expedition. I shall remain here till the 14th, in hopes that I may receive your answer, which might be expedited by a courier, should the communication be deemed prudent.

Mr. Monroe to Mr. Livingston.

MAY 5, 1803.

DEAR SIR,—I have examined with great attention the articles of the project which we presented as agreed & amended between ourselves, to Mr. Marbois & that which he returned to us, & find that neither is drawn with sufficient accuracy to accomplish the object which is intended. A reference to the statement heretofore given to you by the commercial agent here and by you returned to the minister of foreign affairs, cannot be considered, as defining with sufficient accuracy, the claims, that are to be admitted, as it probably comprises many that are excluded, by the latter part of the same article, & may exclude others that ought to be admitted; the time too, at which the interest is to commence does not appear to me to be sufficiently definite, or founded in justice. The irregularity in the condition of the creditors, some of whom are to be paid immediately & others at the end of the 9 months after their claims are liquidated, is also highly objectionable. The absolute submission to the decision of the French bureaus, in cases where the claims of our citizens have, or may be rejected, ought also to be provided against. It is equally proper, that the powers of our board should be enlarged & more clearly defined, especially that it should extend, to the requiring & receiving of evidence, necessary to guide them to a just decision. Some provision is also necessary, in favor of the creditors, whose claims have accrued since the last convention.

If the board is organized, as we propose, it appears to me, to be unnecessary to assign, to our commercial agent, the duty which is proposed in our project; the more so, as if it is not comprised in his duty assigned by the Government, we should incur an useless expense.

I have drawn such a paper as appears to me to be free from those objections, which I beg to submit to your consideration. I have assumed the Debt, reserving to the United States, the sum, which may remain, if any, after paying it, of the 20 millions assigned for the purpose. I will be happy to call on you, or receive you here immediately; after you have examined the enclosed, as may be most convenient to you. Very sincerely &c.

Mr. Monroe to Mr. Livingston.

MAY 6, 1803.

Dear Sir,—

I send you a translation of the project for the debts. The French copy I sent to Mr. Marbois last night at 11. not being able to do it sooner. I informed him that if he wished a meeting this morning we would attend him on a notification to that effect. I find that the 3*d.* Art. does not go as far as it ought to do. It does not give to the board to be established by the U. States a power over the claims to be liquidated, of the same extent as is given to them over those which are, in respect to the character of the debt & of the claimant. The board is also restrained from the cognizance of such claims which are not objected to by our agent, which if proper as to the merit of such claims, can not be so on the principle referred to. The money also should be paid on the certificate of that board & the order of our ministers as in other cases. I send you a note on that subject which I wish you to examine, to be added to the end of that article & incorporated in it, if you approve.

Mr. Monroe's Draft of Convention.

ART. 1. The debts due by France to citizens of the United States which accrued before the 2^d. Vend^{re} 9 year of the French Republic, 30 Sep^t. 1800, shall be paid according to the following principles with interest at six per cent: from the time they respectively became due.

The debts which it is hereby intended to provide for, according to the true intent & meaning of the 5th Art: of the above mentioned convention, are such as are due to American citizens for supplies furnished to the French Republic, for embargoes & other detention of vessels, for captures in which the appeal has been properly lodged within the time specified by the said convention. It being the express intention of the contracting parties to preclude from the benefits of this article, all contracts for covering goods not the sole property of American citizens; all commercial speculations made by American citizens establishing houses of commerce in France, England or other foreign country, in their own names or in conjunction with foreigners, whereby they are to be considered in the commercial transactions of such houses, as domiciliated in the countries where such houses are established, and entitled to the aid of the governments under which they were so established.

It is agreed that the government of France shall by means of its suitable department adjust the whole amount of such of the above claims as have been returned or presented to the several bureaus, within the space of   months from the date of this treaty, & that it will cause all other claims which may hereafter be presented to be adjusted with the least possible delay. As soon as any claim shall be thus adjusted, the department by whom the adjustment is made, shall grant a certificate for the sum due, stating the object or consideration for which it became due, to the person entitled to it, who shall present the same for revision to the board provided for in the following article.

Should any claim be rejected by such department of the French Government, the party thinking himself thereby injured shall be entitled to a statement of his case comprising the motive of the rejection, to be presented in like manner before the said board.

Art. 2. And that suitable & adequate provision may be made for the payment of all just debts due by the French Government to the citizens of the United States, above described & none other, according to the true intent & meaning of the 5th article of the said convention, it is further agreed that the ministers plenipotentiary of the United States shall appoint a board consisting of three persons to act till the same are finally adjusted, or until the President with the advice of the Senate shall appoint others, who or a majority of them shall have full power to revise all such claims thus adjusted or rejected by the said department of the French Government, & to reject or admit the same, in part or in whole, as in their judgment shall appear right & just on the principles above stated. To enable this board fully & completely to execute the duties hereby assigned it, it shall be authorized to require and review such testimony, in all cases as may be necessary to a full & impartial decision & also to examine all authentic pieces & documents in the bureaus of the French Republic, relative to the said claims, & to take copies of the same when necessary.

When any claim is admitted by the above mentioned board, the party entitled to the same shall receive from the said board a certificate for the amount due, in which shall be stated the time at which it became due, & the Ministers Plenipotentiary of the United States in case there be more than one present, shall give orders on the Treasury of the United States for the payment of the same, with interest thereon from the time the debt became due at the rate of six per cent per annum till paid, which orders shall be paid at the Treasury three months after sight, in case the treaty has been previously ratified by both parties, and the ceded territory delivered into the possession of the United States.

It is understood that the rejection of any claim by this board shall produce no other effect than to exempt the United States from the payment of it: The party holding such claim shall have the same right to demand it of the Government of France; as if this treaty had not passed. It is also understood that nothing in this treaty is intended or shall be construed in such manner as to affect the claims of citizens of the United States on the French Government for debts which have been contracted since the 30th of Sept. 1800.

Art. 3. The United States engage to pay the amount of the debt due by the French Republic to their citizens, as above described & whose adjustment is provided for in the preceding articles, which debt is estimated at a sum not exceeding 20 millions of francs.

It is further agreed that should the claims provided for in the preceding articles not amount to the sum of twenty millions of francs, and other claims be hereafter presented to the Government of France, which were they now presented would be entitled to payment under this convention that such surplus shall be applied in discharge of the same.

Messrs. Livingston and Monroe to Mr. King.

PARIS, *May —, 1803.*

SIR: We have the honor to inform you that a treaty (the 30th April) has been signed between the Minister Plenipotentiary of the French Government and ourselves, by which the United States have obtained the full right to and sovereignty in and over New Orleans, and the whole of Louisiana, as Spain possessed the same. If sir, you should find it necessary to make any communication to the British Government on this subject, you may likewise inform them that care has been taken so to frame the treaty as not to infringe upon any of the rights that Great Britain might claim in the navigation of the Mississippi.

Mr. Livingston to the Secretary of State.

PARIS, *May 12, 1803.*

SIR: You have seen in my late letter the direct commencement of the negotiation previous to the arrival of Mr. Monroe, and, in our joint letter, its consummation. It will be matter of curiosity, at least to you, to be more intimately acquainted with the exciting causes which have been long operating, and which I have hinted at in my letters to the President, but which, from their extreme delicacy, I have not thought it proper to detail. As this goes with the treaty by a special and safe messenger, I will send you the papers I referred to in my letters to the President.

On my arrival, I found the credit and character of our nation very low. They were considered as interested speculators, whose god was money. The features of our statesmen, drawn from the caricatures in our newspapers, were viewed as real likenesses; and the democracy of America was believed to be the mad Jacobinism of France. The President was considered as among the most mad, because the head of the party; and it was not doubted that his Minister to France partook of his phrenzy. Some of my former friends were sent artfully to sound me on the subject of the existing Government here. As I had seen and heard enough to be satisfied that nothing short of the change that had taken place could have lessened the calamities of France, I answered them sincerely in such manner as to satisfy them that I meant to have no intrigues with its enemies; I carefully avoided all connexion with them; and, in consequence of this, began to acquire a degree of favor at Court.

As the attention to Great Britain began to diminish, for reasons which it will take me too much time to explain, and was gradually converted into aversion by the freedom with which the election of the First Consul to that dignity for life, and his other great measures, were treated in England, we of course grew more in favor; and if, in any instance, they relaxed from the extreme hauteur with which they treated all the foreign Powers, it was more particularly with us. They answered my notes politely, though not satisfactorily; while they left those of many other Ministers, who had demands upon them, unanswered. Among the most favorite projects of the First Consul, was the colonization of Louisiana. He saw in it a new Egypt; he saw in it a Colony that was to counterbalance the eastern establishment of Britain; he saw in it a provision for his Generals; and, what was more important in the then state of things, he saw in it a pretense for the ostracism of suspected enemies. To render the acquisition still more agreeable to the people, exaggerated accounts of its fertility, &c., were sold in every print shop. My first endeavor was to remove these impressions from the minds of the people most likely to be consulted, in which I was, generally speaking, very successful. But they all told me that it was a favorite project with the First Consul; nor would any of them hear of disposing of it by sale; yet so ignorant were they of the nature of their acquisition, that they never once suspected the Floridas were not included in their treaty, till they were convinced of the contrary by the inquiries they set on foot in consequence of my information. The Floridas, as you know, they endeavored to give in exchange for Parma; and in that negotiation set the price for which they would buy one, or sell the other, at forty millions of francs.

I endeavored, as far as possible, to obstruct that negotiation, and, at the same time, urged the absurdity of attempting to colonize Louisiana without ports in the Gulf. When I found impressions were made by these measures, I wrote the treaties I have sent you, entitled *Memoire sur cette question: Est il avantageux a la France de prendre possession de la Louisiane?* As the first Consul had before read with considerable attention, my notes on the relative naval force and commerce of France and England and the United States, (which I have also sent you,) and paid me some compliments upon it, I got this essay under his eyes through the same channel. It was read with attention; and, though I have reason to think it weakened his belief in the importance of Louisiana, yet, as he does not easily relinquish his plans, he still prosecuted them, though with much less ardor than he had before done. As I knew that his Ministers seldom dared to interpose their opinions, it was necessary to apply directly to him, through the only person who was supposed to have any influence with him; and who that was, you have seen in my private letters to the President. I will not hazard the repetition here. After breaking the subject in a conversation with this gentleman, I sent him the note No. 1. He received it very graciously. Reading it in my presence, he told me that, if I would permit him, he would show it to the First Consul. I made some hesitation on account of the delicacy of the subject. He assured me that he would take care that I should not be committed by it. Some days after, he told me that the First Consul had read it with attention; that so far as it referred to personal objects, he could not listen to it; but that the general and public motives I had mentioned merited particular attention; that he approved my proposition, in part, but not to the extent I had proposed. I am satisfied that from this period they had determined to let us have New Orleans, and the territory above the Arkansas, in exchange for certain commercial advantages; and that, if they could have concluded with Spain, we should also have had West Florida; but that nothing could be done until that business was terminated. This note had the effect of removing, in the fullest degree, every doubt that could possibly have remained relative to my sentiments of the present Government; and certain circumstances in it led to a kind of personal consideration which I have ever since enjoyed here.

Not willing, however, to let the impressions I have made wear off, I wrote the note No. 2, which was also read with attention by the First Consul; and I believe produced a determination to enter upon the subject as soon as matters were arranged with Spain. As I believed, from the First Consul having spoken on this subject to the Minister of Foreign Affairs, that the channel through which I submitted my observations was known to the latter, and of course could not be very pleasing to him; and as this was intimated to me by ———, who, in answer to my note No. 3, requested me to break the subject to the Minister; you will have seen in my several notes, that I did not neglect to do so. But two causes suspended any absolute determination. First, the state of the negotiation with Spain relative to the Floridas; and next, my total want of power or instructions, which reduced me to the necessity of bringing forward nothing more specific; while I endeavored to pave the way for something conclusive when I should, as I had long hoped, receive them. The First Consul, too, had conceived an idea that, by taking possession of the country, he could more advantageously treat with our Government; and Mr. Talleyrand accordingly told me several times, in general terms, that everything would be arranged; but that they must first take possession. After General Bernadotte was appointed, he assured me that he should have powers for this purpose; but as I had then received the newspaper account of the conduct of the Governor of New Orleans, I thought it would be a good ground for pressing something decisive, both with the Minister and through ——— ; with a view then to bring them to make some proposition here, or at least to give such discretionary powers as would facilitate your treaty with General Bernadotte. My notes to the Minister you have. No. 4 is a copy of my letter to ———, which was also submitted to the First Consul, and produced nothing more than a verbal promise that all would be arranged when proper information could be received through General Bernadotte.

I have no doubt that it has long been their intention to make the arrangements I proposed, in exchange for commercial advantages. A sale has always been disrelished, as I was constantly told by Marbois and Talleyrand; and, as is clearly to be inferred, from the Consul's note in answer to my letter. What, however, I believe, principally drove him to this measure, was the promise which the First Consul had hastily made me to pay our debt fully and promptly; and which he found himself in no situation to fulfill, and yet knew not how to elude, as I pressed it at every turn, and spoke of it to Talleyrand and all the Consul's friends, assured them that I had communicated it not only to the Government but to the creditors, with the declaration that they might firmly rely on it, as no one could believe that a man of the Consul's character, a sovereign and a soldier, could break his word. I told the Minister of the Treasury that, as I owed it to myself to justify what I had said, I thought myself bound to publish my letter to the First Consul, with his answer, and the execution of his solemn engagements. I asked what his enemies would say to such a publication? He replied—Or his friends?

The resolutions proposed in Congress, in consequence of the business of New Orleans, coming to hand, I sent a translation of them by General Bernadotte to ———, and also enclosed them to the Minister. They proved we would not be trifled with; and the probability of a rupture with England, and the effects of which upon the country, as you have observed in my notes, have been very strongly stated to them, hastened their determination; and they saw, as Mr. Talleyrand told me, that if they gave what I asked, the rest was not worth keeping. This, and the impossibility of otherwise keeping faith with us, produced a determination to sell; which was communicated to the Council, as I informed you on the 8th of April. There was a moment, even after Talleyrand called on me to set a price, that I thought the whole might drop through. It was then, as I informed you, he pretended he spoke without authority, and that Louisiana was not theirs, &c. But, as I have since written to you, that mystery was cleared the next day.

The subsequent measures you have in my letters and notes, and in those Mr. Monroe and myself have jointly written to you. As I believe that, next to the negotiation that secured our independence, this is the most important the United States have ever entered into,

I thought everything that led to it might interest you and the President. I wished you to be minutely acquainted with every step I had taken; my verbal communications with everybody to whom I had access, whose interest I conceived might be useful, it would be impossible to detail. Nothing, however, was neglected on my part; and I sincerely hope the issue may be acceptable to our country.

Lord Whitworth retired last night, after the arrival of a messenger from Russia. The Emperor undertakes the mediation, but England will certainly decline, as it would be to continue her present ruinous expense, and derange her commerce probably for an unlimited time.

I have yet no time, nor indeed thought it proper, to interpose any business of less importance, while the arrangements relative to, and in consequence of, the treaty were going on. The moment our messengers are despatched I shall give it all my attention.

I have the honor to be, &c.,

R. R. LIVINGSTON.

Messrs. Livingston and Monroe to Mr. Madison.

PARIS, *May 13, 1803.*

SIR: We have the pleasure to transmit to you by M. Dirieux a treaty which we have concluded with the French Republic for the purchase and cession of Louisiana. The negotiation of this important object was committed, on the part of France, to M. Marbois, Minister of the Treasury, whose conduct therein has already received the sanction of his Government, as appears by the ratification of the First Consul, which we have also the pleasure to forward to you.

An acquisition of so great an extent was, we well know, not contemplated by our appointment; but we are persuaded that the circumstances and considerations which induced us to make it will justify us in the measure to our Government and country.

Before the negotiation commenced we were apprized that the First Consul had decided to offer to the United States, by sale, the whole of Louisiana, and not a part of it. We found, in the outset, that this information was correct, so that we had to decide, as a previous question, whether we would treat for the whole, or jeopardize, if not abandon, the hope of acquiring any part. On that point we did not long hesitate, but proceeded to treat for the whole. We were persuaded that, by so doing, it might be possible, if more desirable, to conclude eventually a treaty for a part, since, being thus possessed of the subject, it might be easy, in discussion, at least, to lead from a view of the whole to that of a part, and with some advantages peculiar to a negotiation on so great a scale. By treating for the whole, whereby we should be enabled to ascertain the idea which was entertained by this Government of its value, we should also be able to form some estimate of that which was affixed to the value of its parts. It was, too, probable that a less sum would be asked for the whole, if sold entire to a single purchaser, a friendly Power, who was able to pay for it, and whom it might be disposed to accommodate at the present juncture, than if it should be sold in parcels either to several Powers or companies of individuals; it was equally so, if this Government should be finally prevailed to sell us a part, that some regard would be paid in the price asked for it to that which was demanded for the whole. Lastly, by treating for the whole, whereby the attention of this Government would be drawn to the United States, as the sole purchaser, we might prevent the interference of other Powers, as also that of individuals, who might prove equally injurious in regard to the price asked for it, whether we acquired the whole or any part of the territory. We found, however, as we advanced in the negotiation, that M. Marbois was absolutely restricted to the disposition of the whole; that he would treat for no less portion, and, of course, that it was useless to urge it. On mature consideration, therefore, we finally concluded a treaty on the best terms we could obtain for the whole.

By this measure, we have sought to carry into effect, to the utmost of our power, the wise and benevolent policy of our Government, on the principles laid down in our instructions. The possession of the left bank of the river, had it been attainable alone, would, it is true, have accomplished much in that respect; but it is equally true that it would have left much still to accomplish. By it our people would have had an outlet to the ocean in which no Power would have a right to disturb them; but while the other bank remained in the possession of a foreign Power, circumstances might occur to make the neighborhood of such Power highly injurious to us in many of our most important concerns. A divided jurisdiction over the river might beget jealousies, discontents, and dissensions, which the wisest policy on our part could not prevent or control. With a train of colonial governments established along the western bank, from the entrance of the river far into the interior, under the command of military men, it would be difficult to preserve that state of things which would be necessary to the peace and tranquillity of our country. A single act of a capricious, unfriendly, or unprincipled subaltern might wound our best interests, violate our most unquestionable rights, and involve us in war. But by this acquisition, which comprises within our limits this great river, and all the streams that enter into it, from their sources to the ocean, the apprehensions of these disasters is banished for ages from the United States. We adjust by it the only remaining known cause of variance with this very powerful nation; we anticipate the discontent of the great rival of France, who would probably have been wounded at any stipulation of a permanent nature which favored the latter, and which it would have been difficult to avoid, had she retained the right bank. We cease to have a motive of urgency, at least, for inclining to one Power, to avert the unjust pressure of another. We separate ourselves in a great measure from the European world and its concerns, especially its wars and intrigues. We make, in fine, a great stride to real and substantial independence, the good effect whereof will, we trust, be felt essentially and extensively in all our foreign and domestic relations. Without exciting the apprehension of any Power, we take a more imposing attitude with respect to all. The bond of our Union will be strengthened, and its movements become more harmonious by the increased ity of interests which it will communicate to the several parts which ompose it.

In deliberating on this subject in a financial view, we were strongly impressed with the idea that while we had only right of deposit, or, indeed, while the right bank remained in the possession of a foreign Power, it was always to be expected that we should, at some time or other, be involved in war on questions resulting from that cause. We were well satisfied that any war would cost us more than is hereby stipulated to be given for this territory; that none could produce a more favorable result; while it might, especially in the present disturbed state of the world, prove the ruin of our affairs.

There were other considerations which, though of minor importance, had, nevertheless, their due weight in our decision of this great question. If France, or any other Power holding the right bank of the river, imposed lighter duties than comported with the revenue system of the United States, supposing even that we had acquired the left bank, all the supplies destined for our extensive and populous settlements on the other side would be smuggled in through that channel, and our revenue thereby considerably diminished. Should such Power open offices for the sale of lands on the western bank, our population might be drained to the advantage of such Power, the price of our lands be diminished, and their sale prevented. But, by the possession of both banks, these evils are averted.

The terms on which we have made this acquisition, when compared with the objects attained by it, will, we flatter ourselves, be deemed advantageous to our country. We have stipulated, as you will see by the treaty and convention, that the United States shall pay to the French Government sixty millions of francs, in stock, bearing an interest of six per cent.; and a sum not exceeding twenty more to our citizens, in discharge of the debts due to them by France, under the convention of 1800; and also to exempt the manufactures, productions, and vessels, of France and Spain, in the direct trade from those countries, respectively, in the ports of the ceded territory, from foreign duties for the term of twelve years. The stock is to be created irredeemable for fifteen years, and discharged afterwards in three equal annual installments. The interest on it is to be paid in Europe, and the principal, in case this Government thinks proper to sell it, disposed of in such manner as will be most conducive to the credit of the American funds. The debts due to our citizens are to be discharged by drafts on the Treasury. We omit a more minute view of the stipulations of these instruments, since, as you will possess them, it is unnecessary.

Louisiana was acquired of Spain by France, in exchange for Tuscany, which latter is settled by treaty on the son-in-law of the King of Spain, with the title of King of Etruria, and was estimated in the exchange, in consideration of the revenue, at one hundred millions of francs. The First Consul thought he had made an advantageous bargain in that exchange, as appeared by the high idea which he entertained of its value, as shown on many occasions. Louisiana was the territory which he promised, in his proclamation at the peace, as an asylum to those who had become unfortunate by the Revolution, and which he spoke of as vast and fertile. When he made up his mind to offer the cession of it to the United States, it was contemplated to ask for it one hundred millions, exclusive of the debts they owed to our citizens, which they proposed we should also pay, with a perpetual exemption from foreign duties on the manufactures, productions, and vessels of France and Spain in the ports of the ceded territory. From that demand however (in respect to the sum) he receded, under the deliberations of his own cabinet; for the first proposition which M. Marbois made to us was that we should pay eighty millions—sixty of which in cash, the balance to our citizens, the whole in one year in Paris, with a perpetual exemption from foreign duties as above. The modification in the mode of payment, (that is by stock, for from the quantum he never would depart,) and the limitation of the term of the duties to twelve years, with the proviso annexed to it, which was introduced into the treaty, with every other change from his project, was the effect of negotiation and accommodation, in which we experienced, on his part, and that of his Government, a promptitude and candor which were highly grateful to us.

In estimating the real value of this country to the United States, a variety of considerations occur, all of which merit due attention. Of these, we have already noticed many of a general nature, to which, however, it may be difficult to fix a precise value. Others present themselves of a nature more definite, to which it will be more practicable to fix some standard. By possessing both banks, the whole revenue or duty on imports will accrue to the United States, which must be considerable. The value of exports, we have understood, was last year four millions of dollars. If a portion only of the imports pass through that channel, (as under our Government we presume they will,) the amount of the revenue will be considerable. This will annually increase in proportion as the population and productions in that quarter do. The value of the lands in the province of Louisiana (amounting to some hundred millions of acres, of the best quality, and in the best climate) is perhaps incalculable. From either of these sources, it is not doubted that the sum stipulated may be raised in time to discharge the debt.

We hope to be able to forward you herewith the order of this Government for the delivery of the possession of the ceded territory to the United States, or to communicate its arrangements for that purpose, as also its views relative to the sale of the stock, since it is understood that their intention is to sell it. It has been intimated to us that the house of Baring, in London, connected with that of Hope, in Holland, will take the whole at their risk, at the current price in England, on a commission to be agreed on, paying to France a stipulated sum by the month. Their object is said to be, exclusive of that of making profit by it, to keep up the credit of our stock, they being much interested in it. Considering the great capital of these houses, it is presumable that they would be able to comply with any engagement they might make to that effect. And it can not be doubted that it would be more advantageous to us that the whole should be thus disposed of, than remain in the hands of France, who, under the pressure of difficulties, might have it less in her power to preserve or regard our credit in the disposition of it. We shall communicate with M. Marbois fully on this subject, and apprise you of the result.

We received, some days past, a letter from Mr. King, in which he says, that, in case of war, which he deemed inevitable, the British Government contemplated taking possession of the island of New Orleans. He desired information to be communicated to that Government, whether it had been ceded to the United States, as he presumed a knowledge thereof would prevent the measure. We gave an immediate reply to his letter, in which we informed him that the whole of Louisiana had been ceded to the United States, which he was at liberty to communicate to the British Government. We likewise made the same communication to Lord Whitworth, the British Ambassador here, who expressed himself to be well satisfied with the event.

These countries, France and England, have been on the point of a rupture for some time past. At present, the prospect of an accommodation is more remote, as the English Ambassador left Paris at 10 o'clock last night: still some hope of it is entertained by some persons in power here. This nation is desirous of peace, and it is believed that its Government is similarly disposed.

Permit us to express an earnest wish that the President and Senate may decide with the least possible delay on the treaty and conventions which we have concluded, and have the pleasure to transmit to you. If it is the sense of our Government to ratify them, the sooner that fact is known to this Government the better its effect will be.

The list of the debts due by France to American citizens not being yet prepared, owing to M. Marbois's absence to-day from Paris, and the previous delays of the offices in which the evidences were, can not be sent by this conveyance. In consequence, we retain the original of the convention to which it should be annexed, and send a copy of it: we shall forward in a day or two the original. By the list, it may be inferred that the debts amount to a greater sum than they really do: they will be subject, according to the convention, to the revision of our board, by whom it is expected they will be reduced considerably. We have full confidence that, including the interest, they will not exceed the sum of twenty millions of francs, which is much to be desired, as in that case all our citizens, whose claims are entitled to the support of our Government, will be provided for and paid by it. You will observe that, in the mode adopted, considerable indulgence is given to our treasury. The whole sum is to be paid there, and under delays which will free it from embarrassment.

We have the honor to be, sir, your obedient servants,

R. R. LIVINGSTON.
JAMES MONROE.

P. S.—It was intended to have forwarded this by M. Derieux; but he being forced to leave Paris some days since on his way to Bordeaux, from whence he sails, we commit it to Mr. Hughes, who will embark at Havre. We shall forward to-morrow or next day an exemplification of it by Bordeaux, under the care of M. Derieux.

Mr. King to Lord Hawkesbury.

LONDON, *May 15, 1803.*

MY LORD: In the present critical posture of affairs, I lose no time in communicating to your Lordship, for His Majesty's information, that a treaty was signed at Paris on the 30th April, past, by the Plenipotentiaries of America and France, by which the complete sovereignty of the town and territory of New Orleans, as well as of all Louisiana, as the same was heretofore possessed by Spain, has been acquired by the United States of America.

In drawing up this treaty, care has been taken so to frame the same as not to infringe any right of Great Britain in the navigation of the river Mississippi.

I flatter myself that this communication will be received with satisfaction, and regarded as a new proof of the disposition of the United States to observe towards His Majesty a spirit of amity and confidence, important at all times, and more especially so in present circumstances, to the harmony and mutual prosperity of the two countries.

Lord Hawkesbury to Mr. King.

DOWNING STREET, *May 19, 1803.*

SIR: Having laid before the King your letter of the 15th of this month, in which you inform me that a treaty was signed at Paris on the 30th of last month, by the Plenipotentiaries of America and France, by which the complete sovereignty of the town and territory of New Orleans, as well as of all Louisiana, has been acquired by the United States, I have received His Majesty's commands to express to you the pleasure with which His Majesty has received this intelligence, and to add that His Majesty regards the care which has been taken so to frame this treaty as not to infringe any right of Great Britain in the navigation of the Mississippi as the most satisfactory evidence of the disposition on the part of the Government of the United States (correspondent to that which His Majesty entertains) to promote and improve that harmony and good understanding which so happily subsists between the two countries, and which are so conducive to their mutual benefit. I have it also in command to assure you, sir, that the sentiments which you have expressed, in making this communication, are considered by His Majesty's Government as an additional proof of that cordiality and confidence which you have uniformly manifested in the whole course of your public mission, and which have so justly entitled you to the esteem and regard of His Majesty's Government.

Messrs. Livingston and Monroe to the Secretary of State.

PARIS, *May 16, 1803.*

SIR: We have the honor to enclose the account which should be annexed to the convention transmitted to you. The Bordeaux embargo is in *assignats*, and two-thirds will be deducted. From many of the others, we have reason to think, from a particular account now in our hands, there will be such considerable deductions as will reduce the whole charge to less than twenty millions of livres, including the interest. The Consul has agreed to ratify immediately, and we hope to have the honor of transmitting you the ratified treaty, with an order to deliver the territory, in a few days. Such arrangements will also, we trust, be made relative to the stock as will prevent it coming on the market to any loss, or any part of it from being sold in America.

We have the honor to be, &c.,

R. R. LIVINGSTON.
JAMES MONROE.

Mr. Monroe to Mr. Madison.

PARIS *May 18, 1803.*

SIR,—Since the conclusion of the treaty with France for the purchase of Louisiana, which was forwarded to you on the 13th by Mr.

Hughes, with a joint letter from my colleague and myself, I feel myself much at a loss what part to take respecting the Floridas. There are some considerations in favor of an immediate pursuit of that object with Spain which have great weight on my mind. The cession of Louisiana by France to the U. States must lessen the value of the Floridas to Spain, and she will be apt to feel that effect more sensibly immediately after she hears it than at any other time. France too who has promised her aid in the negotiation with Spain, would probably take more interest in it, at this moment, while the obligation to yield it, is in a manner personal, than she might do hereafter. At this crisis of affairs between France and England which comprises Spain in an equal degree, there is reason to believe that we should derive much aid from a pressure on Spain, from that cause. It is equally presumable that England even in case of war would not interfere with our pursuit, much less break with us for obtaining the Floridas. The exclusion of her manufactures from the Continent of Europe, is a principal cause of her present unquiet and distressed situation. It is her interest to cherish the U. States and Russia, as her best markets; a policy which I believe she understands and pursues with sincerity. To be involved in a war with us at this epoch would prove a great calamity to her. I have no doubt that at this time she is either indifferent respecting our acquisition of Louisiana, and that which we propose to make of the Floridas, or in no situation to oppose it. Indeed it is not improbable that she may wish it, as it weakens these powers, in that quarter and promises to open new markets to her manufactures. Should we not however acquire this territory of Spain at this period, there is danger of its falling into the hands of some other power hereafter; a circumstance which might give us much trouble, as it commands the mouths of several of our rivers, and gives a right to the navigation of the Mississippi. There are also considerations against my pursuing the object at present of great weight. We have already stipulated for a much greater sum than it was contemplated we should give for the object of my mission. To go further might embarrass our treasury. It may be advisable to exchange a portion of Louisiana next Mexico for the Floridas, and I have no power to make such an arrangement. I have weighed these considerations with the attention they merit, and the result is that I am of opinion that it is more in conformity to the spirit of my instructions, and to the interest of my country, that I should proceed immediately to Madrid to endeavour to obtain the Floridas than remain inactive and suffer the favorable occasion which is now presented to be lost. The acquisition of the Floridas is an important object with our government, as is sufficiently shewn by our instructions. The purchase of the whole of Louisiana, tho' not contemplated is nevertheless a measure founded on the principles and justified by the policy of our instructions, provided it be thought a good bargain. The only difference between the acquisition we have made, and that which we were instructed to make in that respect, is, that a favorable occasion presenting itself which indeed was not anticipated by the administration, in the measures which led to that event and laid the foundation for it, we have gone further than we were instructed to do. But the extent of that acquisition does not destroy the motive which existed before of acquiring the Floridas, nor essentially diminish it. In our instructions the idea entertained by the President of the value of that country is defined. It is to be presumed that under existing circumstances it may be had at a cheaper rate, since its importance to Spain is much diminished. And altho' the sum to be paid for Louisiana is considerable, yet the period at which that portion which is applicable to the Government of France is to be paid, is so remote, and such delays are incident to that which will be received by our citizens, that it is to be presumed the payment of what it would be proper to stipulate for the Floridas, would subject our treasury to no embarrassment. I am the more confident in this opinion, from the belief that it would be easy to raise on the land alone, retaining to our government the jurisdiction, a sum which would be sufficient to discharge the greater part of what it is probable Spain would ask for it. The bias of my mind therefore is to pursue this object by repairing immediately to Madrid and endeavoring to obtain by treaty the territory in question thereby extirpating the last remaining source of controversy or indeed jealousy with these powers. If I proceed it will be in a week from this time, within which term every arrangement incident to the treaty and convention we have formed with this republick will probably be compleated, and the little provision necessary for my journey to Spain likewise made. On this subject I shall write you again soon, let the decision which I take be what it may. In case I go I shall leave my family at St. Germain till my return, which I shall expect to do in a few months. I am with great respect & esteem y^r. ob^t. servant.

Mr. Livingston to the Secretary of State.

PARIS, *May 20, 1803.*

DEAR SIR: The subject of this letter is too important to admit of delay, in case the treaties should have been any time in your hands; but, as it has not yet been fully considered by Mr. Monroe, he thinks he can not make it that of a joint letter till we have more fully discussed it, which we propose to do to-morrow or the next day. But as that will be too late for this conveyance, I throw out these hasty thoughts for your consideration. In the meantime you will consider this rather as a private than as a public letter; since it may or may not be made use of to promote such measures as, upon mature deliberation, the President shall think proper to adopt. I do not, however, doubt that Mr. Monroe will concur with me in opinion, after we have discussed the subject; and that we shall, by the next opportunity, write to you officially thereon.

I informed you long since, that, on inquiring whether the Floridas were within the cession of Spain, I was told by M. Marbois he was sure that Mobile was, but could not answer further. I believed his information incorrect, because I understood that Louisiana, as it then was, made the object of the cession; and that since the possession of the Floridas by Britain, they had changed their names. But the moment I saw the words of the Treaty of Madrid I had no doubt but it included all the country that France possessed by the name of Louisiana, previous to their cession to Spain, except what had been conveyed by subsequent treaties. I accordingly insisted, with M. Marbois, at the time we negotiated, that this would be considered as within our purchase. He neither assented nor denied, but said that all they received from Spain was intended to be conveyed to us. That my construction was right, is fairly to be inferred from the words of the treaties, and from a comment upon them contained in the Spanish Minister's letter to Mr. Pinckney, in which he expressly says that France had recovered Louisiana as it formerly belonged to her, saving the rights of other Powers. This leaves no doubt upon the subject of the intention of the contracting parties. Now, it is well known that Louisiana, as possessed by France, was bounded by the river Perdido, and that Mobile was the metropolis. For the facts relative to this I refer you to Reynal and to his maps. I have also seen maps here which put the matter out of dispute.

I called this morning upon M. Marbois for a further explanation on this subject, and to remind him of his having told me that Mobile made a part of the cession. He told me that he had no precise idea on the subject, but that he knew it to be an historical fact, and that on that only he had formed his opinion. I asked him what orders had been given to the prefect, who was to take possession, or what orders had been given by Spain as to the boundary, in ceding it? He assured me that he did not know; but that he would make the inquiry, and let me know. At 4 o'clock I called for Mr. Monroe to take him to the Minister of Foreign Affairs; but he was prevented from accompanying me. I asked the Minister what were the east bounds of the territory ceded to us? He said he did not know; we must take it as they had received it. I asked him how Spain meant to give them possession? He said, according to the words of the treaty. But what did you mean to take? I do not know. Then you mean that we shall construe it our own way? I can give you no direction; you have made a noble bargain for yourselves, and I suppose you will make the most of it.

Now, sir, the sum of this business is, to recommend to you, in the strongest terms, after having obtained the possession, that the French Commissary will give you, to insist upon this as a part of your right; and to take possession, at all events, to the river Perdido. I pledge myself that your right is good; and, after the explanations that have been given here, you need apprehend nothing from a decisive measure. Your Minister here and at Madrid, can support your claim; and the time is peculiarly favorable to enable you to do it without the smallest risk at home. It may also be important to anticipate any designs that Britain may have upon that country. Should she possess herself of it, and the war terminate favorably for her, she will not readily relinquish it. With this in your hand, East Florida will be of little moment, and may be yours whenever you please. At all events, proclaim your rights and take possession.

I am, sir, &c.,

ROBT. R. LIVINGSTON.

Hon. JAMES MADISON.

James Madison, Secretary of State, to Robert R. Livingston, Minister to France.

DEPARTMENT OF STATE, *May 25, 1803.*

SIR: Your several letters of March 3, 11, 18, and 24, with their enclosures, have been duly received, as has been that of March 12, to the President. According to the request in this last, I now acknowledge, also, or perhaps repeat the acknowledgment, of the two papers enclosed, the one in your letter of February 26, the other in that of August 10, 1802.

The assurances given by the Chief Consul, on the subject of our claims, can not but be acceptable, although they amount to less than justice; because no more than justice would have been done if the claims had been satisfied without the delay which has intervened, and according to the example of good faith and punctuality in executing the treaty given by the United States. It is to be hoped that the sincerity of these assurances will be verified by the success of the measures you are taking for a final and favorable settlement in behalf of our citizens, who have never doubted, as far as I know, your solicitude or your exertions to obtain justice for them.

The assurances given, at the same time, by the Chief Consul, of his regard for the United States, and of his personal esteem for their Chief Magistrate, are entitled also to favorable attention, as an indication that a juster value begins to be placed on our friendly relations to the French Republic. Whether this language of the French Government be the effect of the political crisis in which it finds itself, or of a growing conviction of the important destinies and honorable policy of the United States, or, as is probable, of both these considerations, you will, in return, communicate the assurances, with which you are charged by the President, of his disposition to cherish a reciprocity of these sentiments, and that sincere amity between the two nations, which is prescribed to both by such weighty advantages.

The persevering evasion of your demands on the subject of the deposit at New Orleans, and generally of the rights of the United States, as fixed by their treaty with Spain, is not a little astonishing. It is as difficult to be reconciled with the sincerity of the late professions of the French Government, and with the policy which the moment dictates to it, as with any other rational motives. It is the more extraordinary, too, as it appears, by a late communication from the Spanish Government to Mr. Pinckney, (of which, he says, he forwarded a copy to Paris, and of which another is herewith inclosed,) that the treaty of cession expressly saves all rights previously stipulated to other nations. A conduct so inexplicable is little fitted to inspire confidence, or to strengthen friendship; and rendered proper the peremptory declaration contained in your note of the 16th of March. The negotiations succeeding the arrival of Mr. Monroe can not fail to draw out the views of France on this important subject.

You were informed, in my letters of the 18th and 20th of April, that orders had been transmitted by the Spanish Government for restoring the deposit. The answers from New Orleans to the Spanish and French Ministers here show that their successive interpositions, including the peremptory one from the Marquis d'Yrujo, of the 11th of March, were all unavailing. The orders of the King of Spain will, no doubt, be obeyed, if they arrive before possession be given to the French authority; nor is it presumable that, in that event, they would be disregarded. Still it is possible that the French agents may choose to wait for the French construction of the treaty before they relinquish the ground taken by the Intendant; and the more possible, as the orders to the Intendant may contain no disavowal of his construction of it. Under these circumstances, it will be incumbent on the French Government to hasten the orders necessary to guard against a prolongation of the evil, and the very serious consequences incident to it. It can not be too much pressed, that the justice and friendship of France, in relation to our rights and interests on the Mississippi, will be the principal rules by which we shall measure her views respecting the United States, and by which the United States will shape the course of their future policy toward her.

We are still ignorant of the result of the armed negotiations between Great Britain and France. Should it be war, or should the uncertainty of the result be spun out, the crisis may be favorable to our just rights and our just objects; and the President assures himself that the proper use will be made of it. Mr. Monroe's arrival has not yet been mentioned in any accounts which have not been contradicted.

I have the honor to be, &c.

JAMES MADISON.

ROBERT R. LIVINGSTON, Esq.

Mr. Monroe to the Virginia Senators.

PARIS, *May 25, 1803.*

GENTLEMEN,—We have as you will find concluded a treaty & two conventions with this Government for the cession of the whole of Louisiana. I flatter myself that the terms will be thought reasonable when compared with the immense advantages resulting from acquisition. The subject however will be before you, & it belongs to the suitable authorities to decide whether we have acquitted ourselves with propriety in the trust reposed in us. I consider this transaction as resulting from the wise & firm tho' moderate measures of the Executive and Congress during the last session. Without these measures we should not have acquired Louisiana. The pressure of the crisis here, but an approaching rupture with England, assisted in producing the result, but had our country not formed a character, or rather a prominent feature in the transactions of the day, it would not have taken place. Nor could it have succeeded so promptly or advantageously, by taking any other attitude than that which was taken. Had we broken the pacific relations subsisting between these countries & the United States, or indeed had not a respect for this Government, and a desire to preserve peace with it, been clearly marked in our measures I do not think that we should have brought it to the issue we have. It is proper that you should possess a correct knowledge of the facts here which led to this result. I arrived at Havre on the 8th of April, which fact was known here on the 9th. On the 10th this Government resolved to offer us by sale the whole of Louisiana, at a certain price, which was diminished by the negotiation. On the 12. I arrived in town, on the 14th was received by the minister, recognized by him, by order of the First Consul & informed that altho I might not be presented to the Consul till the audience day according to usage, that a person would be appointed to treat with us with whom we might proceed in the interim. This was accordingly done, Mr. Marbois was appointed, the negotiations immediately commenced, & brought to as speedy a conclusion as possible. The decision to offer us the territory by sale was not the effect of any management of mine, for it took place before I reached Paris; nor of my colleague or it would have taken place sooner: Being postponed until my arrival in France or indeed till the mission was known, is a full proof that it was the result of the causes above mentioned & of those only. I enclose you a copy of a letter from Mr. Livingston bearing date on the 10th of April, in answer to one from me of the 8th announcing my arrival, which establishes the above facts. I communicate this letter to you as a measure of precaution, that you may not only know that the above facts exist but the nature of the evidence which supports them. Had the measures of our government, of which my mission was only a subaltern part, failed, whether the failure might be atributed to their impolicy, or to such a delay on my part as suffered the crisis with England to pass, all the responsibility would have been on the government & myself. It is equally just in reference to the result that facts should be correctly known to guard against misrepresentation. Personally I pretend to nothing but zeal & industry after I got here, a merit which is equally due to my colleague. If my mission produced any effect it was owing altogether to the motive which induced the President to nominate me, that is, the pronounced character which I had in reference to the object in question, & the belief that I would bring the affair promptly to an issue. It is to be presumed that the transaction will rest on its true ground in the United States, but as the contrary may be the case & it is impossible to foresee what misrepresentations may be given of it, or the ends that may be intended to subserve, I think it not only justifiable but a duty to make to you this communication. You will consider the letter itself as strictly confidential since altho' it is proper to communicate it to a few from whom it is my custom to withhold nothing, yet it would be otherwise if it should go further, for reasons that will readily occur. It is proper to add that I expect no misrepresentation from my colleague & that I am happy to have it in my power to bear testimony in the most explicit manner in favor of his zealous, sincere & diligent co-operation thro' the whole of this business.

Mr. Madison to Messrs. Livingston and Monroe.

DEPARTMENT OF STATE, *May 28, 1803.*

GENTLEMEN: Since my last, which was of April 18, the tenor of information from France and Great Britain renders a war between these Powers in the highest degree probable. It may be inferred, at the same time, from the information given by Mr. Livingston and Mr. King, that the importance of the United States is rising fast in the estimation both of the French and the British Cabinets; and that Louisiana is as much a subject of solicitude with the latter, as it has been an object of acquisition with the former. The crisis presented by this jealous and hostile attitude of those rival Powers has, doubtless, been seen in its bearings on the arrangements contemplated in your commissions and instructions; and it is hoped, though we have not yet heard, that the arrival of Mr. Monroe will have taken place in time to give full advantage to the means of turning the actual state of things to the just benefit of the United States.

The solicitude of England with respect to Louisiana is sufficiently evinced by her controlling the French expedition from Holland to that country. But her views have been particularly unfolded to Mr. King by Mr. Addington, who frankly told him, that, in case a war should happen, it would, perhaps, be one of their first steps to occupy New Orleans; adding, that it would not be to keep it, for that England would not accept the country were all agreed to give it to her, but to prevent another Power from obtaining it, which, in his opinion, would be best effected by its belonging to the United States; and concluding with assurances that nothing should be done injurious to their interests. If the councils of France should be guided by half the wisdom which is here displayed on the part of her rival, your negotiations will be made very easy, and the result of them very satisfactory.

Although the immediate object of Great Britain in occupying New Orleans may be that of excluding France, and although her prudence may renounce the falacious advantage of retaining it for herself, it is not to be presumed that she will yield it to the United States without endeavoring to make it the ground of some arrangement that will directly or indirectly draw them into her war, or of some important concessions in favor of her commerce, at the expense of our own. This consideration necessarily connects itself with the explanation and friendly assurances of Mr. Addington, and so far leaves in force the inducement to accomplish our object by an immediate bargain with France.

In forming this bargain, however, the prospect held out by the British Minister, with the nature of the crisis itself, authorizes us to expect better terms than your original instructions allow.

The President thinks it will be ineligible, under such circumstances, that any convention whatever on the subject should be entered into, that will not secure to the United States the jurisdiction of a reasonable district on some convenient part of the bank of the Mississippi.

He is made the more anxious, also, by the manner in which the British Government has opened itself to our Minister, as well as by other considerations, that as little concession as possible should be made in the terms with France, on points disagreeable to Great Britain, and particularly that the acknowledgement of the right of France as holding one shore of the Mississippi, to shut it against British vessels, should be avoided, if not essential to the attainment of the great objects we have in view, on terms otherwise highly expedient. It is desirable that such an acknowledgement should not even be admitted into the discussion.

The guaranty of the country beyond the Mississippi is another condition which it will be well to avoid if possible, not only for the reasons you already possess, but because it seems not improbable, from the communications of Mr. King, that Great Britain is meditating plans for the emancipation and independence of the whole of the American continent south of the United States, and consequently, that such a guaranty would not only be disagreeable to her but embarrassing to the United States. Should war, indeed, precede your conventional arrangements with France, the guaranty, if admitted at all, must necessarily be suspended and limited in such a manner as to be applicable only to the state of things which may be fixed by a peace.

The proposed occupancy of New Orleans by Great Britain suggests a further precaution. Should possession be taken by her, and the preliminary sum of two millions, or any part of it, be paid to France, risks and disputes might ensue, which make it advisable to postpone the payment till possession shall be given to the United States, or, if this can not be done, to obtain every possible security against eventual loss.

As the question may arise, how far, in a state of war, one of the parties can, of right, convey territory to a neutral Power, and thereby deprive its enemy of the chance of conquest incident to war, especially when the conquest may have been actually projected, it is thought proper to observe to you, first, That, in the present case, the project of peaceable acquisition by the United States originated prior to the war, and consequently, before a project of conquest could have existed; second, That the right of a neutral to procure for itself, by a *bona fide* transaction, property of any sort, from a belligerent Power, ought not to be frustrated by the chance that a rightful conquest thereof might thereby be precluded. A contrary doctrine would sacrifice the just interests of peace to the unreasonable pretensions of war, and the positive rights of one nation to the possible rights of another. A restraint on the alienation of territory from a nation at war to a nation at peace is imposed only in cases where the proceeding might have a collusive reference to the existence of the war, and might be calculated to save the property from danger, by placing it in a secret trust, to be reconveyed on the return of peace. No objection of this sort can be made to the acquisitions we have in view. The measures on this subject were taken before the existence or the appearance of war, and they will be pursued as they were planned, with the *bona fide* purpose of vesting the acquisition forever in the United States.

With these observations you will be left to do the best you can under all circumstances, for the interest of your country, keeping in mind that the rights we assert are clear; that the objects we pursue are just; and that you will be warranted in providing for both, by taking every fair advantage of emergencies.

For the course of information relating to the deposit at New Orleans, I refer you to my letter of the 25th instant to Mr. Livingston.

I have the honor to be, &c.,

JAMES MADISON.

The Minister of Exterior Relations to Mr. Livingston.

PARIS, *11th Prairial, an 11 (May 30, 1803).*

SIR: The declaration published the 17th of May by the English Government; the embargo laid in the ports of England on the commerce of the French, and of the Batavians, and of other allies of the Republic; the letters of marque distributed to privateers, authorizing them to cruise against the commerce of France; the capture, in fine, of two vessels, made some leagues from Brest, by two English frigates; permit a doubt to exist no longer concerning the intention of the Government of Great Britain.

The First Consul is persuaded that nothing can be wanting to convince all the Governments of Europe of the hostile dispositions of His Britannic Majesty. To manifest his own, it is only this day he publishes the resolution which honor extorts, to repulse an unjust aggression.

In informing your Government of this determination, you will find it, I have no doubt, already apprized of the justice of our claims by the publication, made in France, of the papers which this discussion has elicited.

The history of diplomatic relations has never presented, on the one side, more constant efforts to preserve peace; and, on the other, a more persevering desire, by any means and every pretext, to rekindle the war.

The English Government, even in the publication which has been ordered for the purpose of defending her conduct, has only made her injustice the more apparent. The declaration of war is in palpable contradiction of the official correspondence which follows it. This declaration assigns as a motive for the war, demands of which the French Government has been always ignorant, and complaints of which it was only apprized by the hostilities and Manifesto of England.

I have the honor to transmit to you an exact copy of one of the letters of Lord Whitworth, the original of which has been communicated to your Excellency. This note contains a false allegation, which it has thought proper to expunge from the copy submitted to the British Parliament. By comparing this falsified copy with the original text, your Excellency will be convinced that the British Ministry could find no other means to escape the condemnation of Europe than that of concealing an official untruth under a Parliamentary imposture.

The First Consul flatters himself with the belief that the Governments of Europe will not hesitate to pronounce that France has been uniformly loyal in a just cause; and that amidst the unjust pretensions of England, she has involuntarily imposed upon herself the necessity of adopting measures destitute of propriety, and making declarations in violation of good faith.

Accept, sir, the assurances of my high consideration.

CH. MAU. TALLEYRAND.

Mr. Livingston to the Minister of Exterior Relations.

PARIS, *June 2, 1803.*

SIR: I have received the letter you did me the honor to write on the 11th Prairial, announcing the measures that have unfortunately led to a rupture between France and Britain. I shall transmit the same, together with the papers that accompany it, to the Government of the United States, who will doubtless learn with much pain the circumstances that have rekindled the flame of war in Europe; and while they sincerely regret that the measures pursued by the First Consul for the preservation of the peace which Europe owes to his humanity have failed of success, they will still hope that some expedient may be found for stopping the effusion of blood and restoring that repose to Europe for which she so ardently sighs.

I pray your Excellency to accept the assurances of my high consideration.

R. R. LIVINGSTON.

[Extract.]

Mr. Livingston to Mr. Madison.

PARIS, *June 3, 1803.*

SIR: Mr. Monroe having undertaken to write our joint letter, I shall confine this to objects that do not relate to the treaty. I would only observe to you that, since the ratification, we have had a great deal of trouble with it, an opinion prevailing that we have made too favorable a bargain. My letter to the President and our joint letter will so fully explain this extraordinary business as to make any further observations unnecessary. I must, however, earnestly press you, if you think the object important, to get the ratification as soon as possible, and to do all that on our part remains to be done.

During this transaction, I have thought it improper to press any other business that might excite the smallest irritation.

How happy, my dear sir, are we to have concluded a treaty which will forever exclude us from the politics of this stormy quarter of the globe. I hope that you will not let it totally pass through your hands. My letter to the President will fully explain this. Some commercial arrangements might be advantageously proposed here in the present state of things, had I your instructions thereon and the necessary powers. This, too, is the moment to arrange the affair of extra duty with Batavia; and it might, I believe, be done here advantageously.

General Bernadotte, after waiting for weeks at Rochefort, has returned here, and I think it probable will not go out now, as his services may be required at home. Who will be appointed in his place I know not. Otto is still without office, but does not wish to be sent across the Atlantic.

I am, &c.,
R. R. LIVINGSTON.
Hon. JAMES MADISON.

Messrs. Livingston and Monroe to Mr. Madison.

PARIS, *June 7, 1803.*

SIR: We had the pleasure to forward to you by Mr. Jay, the ratification by the First Consul of the treaty and conventions which we concluded on the 30th of April with this Republic. We have heretofore forwarded to you the original instruments, and two copies by different ways, the original by Havre, under the care of Mr. Hughes, who sailed about two weeks since, expressly charged with that object, and instructed to proceed with the greatest possible despatch after his arrival in the United States, to the City of Washington, to deliver the same in person; the second by the way of England, under the care of Mr. Reed, son of the late President of Pennsylvania, who was instructed to forward it immediately on his arrival in England, by the most prompt and safe opportunity that offered; the third by Mr. Derieux, who sailed from Bordeaux. We flatter ourselves that you will receive those several communications in the course of the present month, and this by Mr. Jay early in July, as it is highly important that our Government should receive and act on the subject of them as soon as possible. The command of the sum stipulated for the cession to be paid to this Government being an object with them, is a motive for despatch, but it is not the only one: a late occurrence, which is suggested by the enclosed letter from M. Marbois, and our reply to it, has excited an anxiety on that point, which it was hoped and believed would not have grown out of the transaction. Several circumstances of late, especially the delay in granting us a passport for Mr. Jay to carry the ratifications to the United States, surprised us. We thought we could discern some symptoms of discontent in the Government with the bargain it had made. The letter from M. Marbois left no doubt on that head. We are convinced that if the transaction was not complete, or was within the reach of the Government, that it would not take place even on terms very different from those stipulated. There is much reason to believe that this letter was not written solely for the purpose of manifesting a sentiment of regret at what had been done, but to create difficulties and embarrass the transaction in the execution of it.

On receiving this letter, we found ourselves placed in a situation of peculiar embarrassment, from personal as well as public considerations, which was much increased by a conference with the Minister of Foreign Affairs. We learned from him that the Consul considered the ratification as under his control till the exchange took place, and that he might annex to it such conditions as appeared to him to be proper; that he claimed every act stipulated on the part of the United States, to be performed strictly within the terms specified, or, on failure, that the parties be restored to the state they were in if the treaties were never made. We asked him what had created any doubt on that point: he said that the clause in the article of the convention respecting the payment of sixty millions of francs to France, which was made dependent on the delivery of possession of the country to our Commissary, might, by accident or other causes, become nugatory; the Spaniards might not surrender it at once, the British might take it, &c. We told him that these things were contemplated by the parties when the treaties were made, and provided for; that we could not add a new article to the treaty, or explain any one in it, since it must be explained by itself only; that delays which proceeded from bad faith were those only for which our Government was responsible; that such as were unavoidable attached to them no blame, and could not affect the treaty: he replied that, after the example of our Government in the last treaty, the Consul might nevertheless annex a condition to the ratification explanatory of his sense of it, which he would do if we did not satisfy him either with respect to the prompt manner in which the treaty would be executed by our Government, or agree to expunge the terms in that convention which respected taking possession of the territory. We did not fail to remark that the treaty must stand as it was to be adopted, rejected, or modified, by the parties having the right to do the same, not by us. Thus the affair was at a stand for a day or two, and it remained for us to decide what course we had better take to put it in motion.

After viewing it in all the lights in which it presented itself to our minds, we thought it best to reply to M. Marbois's letter in the terms of that which is enclosed, which you will perceive, even had we had the power to modify the instruments which were passed and beyond our reach, has in truth not affected them at all: the principles applied or insisted on in M. Marbois's letter are not admitted. We state that the Government is bound to execute the treaty and conventions in the terms specified, which is no more than those instruments state, that our Government is answerable for neglect, and by strong and obvious implications for it only, which is the doctrine of the law of nations; and even in that case, that the right which arises from it of declaring how far the party injured will be bound by the treaty, is reciprocal, since, if our Government is willing to make compensation for the injury resulting from delay, it may equally insist on it. The remaining sentence in the letter states that we confine ourselves to the letter of the treaty, by which it is intended to exclude the construction of either party as the rule of interpretation for the other: this letter was accepted as satisfactory, and will, we presume, remove every difficulty to the execution of the treaty. We expect the order for the surrender of the country to be addressed to M. Pichon, in Washington, to be executed by him or by some person to be appointed by him, will be delivered to us to-morrow, and that Mr. Jay will take it with him with the ratification the day after to-morrow: had we pursued any other course, it is not easy to decide what the effect might have been. The First Consul in the moment of chagrin at what he may consider a bad bargain, (but which we think a good one for him, since he had better have given it away than held it with the expense attending the establishment by troops, which might occasion variance and wars with us,) might have so compromitted himself in opposition to the measure, as to have made the transaction, if not finally defeat the treaties, a cause of future discontent between the two nations, instead of what was contemplated by it, the establishment of perpetual peace, by the removal of every existing cause of variance which could possibly disturb it. The most favorable result that we could have expected was, that the ratification would have been forwarded to M. Pichon, with advice of the dissatisfaction of the First Consul with the treaties, and his desire to extricate himself from them, and with instructions not to exchange the ratifications, if any circumstance on our part, under the most rigid construction, would justify it. It is possible this may be still done: nevertheless, we think it important to put the engagements in a train of execution, without exciting ill-temper, in the belief that every stipulation may be executed in time, and that should the contrary occur by any accident or misfortune, it was the surest mode to prevent discussion and disagreement in the sequel.

It is our earnest wish and advice, if the treaties are approved by the President, that he convene Congress to provide the funds for an immediate compliance with them. It is best to leave nothing to hazard. The surrender of the posts ought to precede the creation of the fund; but as there will be no doubt on that point after taking the necessary measures, we would consider it as done, and act accordingly. If we execute our part strictly within the terms specified, the transaction is at an end; there will be no obstacle from this quarter.

We shall send you a copy of Mr. Baring's contract for the stock with this Government, which will show in what manner the payment is to be made. A third of the whole debt is to be advanced to him in Washington; the remaining two-thirds to be sent here immediately. It was contended lately that these two-thirds must be received here in three months after the exchange of ratifications, but that seems to be given up at present, since the term transfer being technical, and applicable to an act to be performed in our Treasury, and nowhere else, it is admitted that it must have been used by us in that sense only. Still it is much to be wished that the certificates might be sent here within the three months, if possible, and which is presumed may be done if the Congress is immediately convened.

After the funds are created and transferred in our Treasury, it is, by the spirit of the treaty, the duty of the French Minister to forward them here. But it is much to be desired that our Government would undertake that service, and forward them by a public vessel, to guard against accidents which might create delay. Should it happen, unfortunately, that the ratification or creation of the public stock should be protracted beyond the term specified, we think the cause should be made known by a public vessel, with the assurance of the President that every injury resulting from it should be repaired, and ample compensation made for it. We can not too strongly impress an idea, if our conduct is approved, of the most prompt execution of the stipulations to be formed on our part, and of a course of proceeding which leaves nothing to chance, by giving any cause of complaint to this Government.

We are happy to have it in our power to assure you, that, on a thorough examination of the subject, we consider it incontrovertible that West Florida is comprised in the cession of Louisiana. West Florida was a part of Louisiana when it was in the hands of France, and it was not in her hands in any other situation. The transfer of the whole was on the same day, the 3d of November, 1762, that being the day of the secret convention between France and Spain, and of the preliminary articles of the Treaty of the 10th February, 1763, between those Powers and Great Britain. The Treaty of 1783 between Britain and Spain, by which the Floridas were ceded to the latter, put Louisiana in her hands in the same state it was in the hands of France; and the remaining or third member of the article in the Treaty of St. Ildefonso between France and Spain, under which we claim, by referring to that of 1783, (as to that between Spain and the United States of 1795,) and of course in the above character, only tends to confirm this doctrine. We consider ourselves so strongly founded in this conclusion, that we are of opinion the United States should act on it in all the measures relative to Louisiana, in the same manner as if West Florida was comprised within the island of New Orleans; or, lay to the west of the river Iberville, and to the Lakes through which its waters pass to the ocean. Hence the acquisition becomes of proportionably greater value to the United States.

In compliance with the convention, which provides for the payment of the debts due by France to the citizens of the United States, we have organized a board of three Commissioners, whose duty it is to revise the claims that are or may be liquidated by the suitable department of the French Government, according to the principles of that convention. We have appointed to this office Col. John Mercer, Isaac C. Barnet, and William McClure, three of our citizens, who are not interested in any of the claims; and who, for ability, probity, and industry, we think very deserving of the trust. Their appointment is, of course, provisional only, subject to the approbation of the President, whose disposition on the subject you will be pleased to communicate. We shall advance them a sum, by a draft on our bankers in Holland, necessary for defraying their current expenses; leaving it to our Government to fix the rate of compensation.

We consider it important that the stock to be created should not be brought on the American market, nor, indeed, strictly speaking, on the European market; lest it might occasion a decline in the price, to the injury of our credit, and the injury of the holders of it here and there, as well as of France, with whom we have a joint interest in that respect. On that principle we promoted the disposal of it to the company of Baring and Hope, which took place according to a contract which is here enclosed. We consider the arrangement as accomplishing the object referred to, and, in that light, as being advantageous to the United States. We were not competent judges of the price at which the stock ought to have sold, on which account, as well as that that was a question which belonged more peculiarly to the Government of France to attend to, we did not interfere further in the transaction than to communicate to the latter the best information that we possessed. We believe the contract is such as, while it gives to the company an adequate profit, and may prevent sales by compulsion, will prove more beneficial to France than any other disposition she could have made of it. It is a justice due to this house to remark, that the assurances which we received from it through its agent here, of the advances of money on the credit of the United States, in case we should require them in the execution of the trust reposed in us, inspired us with greater confidence than we might otherwise have felt, to make the engagements we have entered into.

We are, with great respect and esteem, your most obedient servants,

R. R. LIVINGSTON.
JAMES MONROE.

P. S.—Since writing the above, this Government has, of its own accord, restored our letter and retaken its own. It has also shown to us the instructions given to M. Pichon, which is substituted for the other measure, and amounts to this: that, on exchanging the ratifications, he is to declare that they are void if the funds, &c., are not created by our Government in the term stipulated. It is possible that this Government is fearful that the British may take the territory, and we, in consequence, delay the payment; though we rather think that the hesitation and procedure arose from some sentiment relative to the contract. It is known that the Consul has said lately, that he thought the territory worth three or four hundred millions of livres. The above change is the effect of further reflection on the subject. It will be well that some of these circumstances be known, and that nothing appear under the sanction of the Government or otherwise, if to be avoided, to excite an unpleasant sensation here: since a belief they stand well with us, which is their political motive in the transaction, will contribute greatly to reconcile the Government and nation to the cession, and promote its harmonious execution.

We have thought it advisable to employ Mr. Jay to bear the ratifications of the First Consul to our Government; to whom we have advanced fifty louis, and undertaken that his expenses shall be borne. The above sum to that object are credited in his account. The ratifications are addressed to M. Pichon, as is the order for the surrender of the territory. The whole, however, is under our ——— to be delivered by Mr. Jay to you, and by you handed over to M. Pichon. The exchange of ratifications in the United States has been very favorable to us.

R. R. LIVINGSTON.
JAMES MONROE.

M. Marbois, Minister of the Public Treasury, to Messrs. Livingston and Monroe.

PARIS, *20th Floreal, 11th year (9th April, 1803.)*

GENTLEMEN: The article of the convention relative to the payment which the United States have to make to France, in three months at most after the ratification of the treaties, and after the taking possession of Louisiana in the name of the United States, determines, in a precise manner, the longest terms agreed upon for the consummation of this affair. They are three months after the ratification and the taking of possession. It is proper to foresee, also, the case in which this business shall not be consummated within the interval above expressed, and as they are precise, it is well understood that every extraordinary delay beyond the terms fixed places the contracting parties in the same situation as if they had never treated. These consequences of the stipulations agreed upon are just and necessary. It has, nevertheless, appeared useful to recall them to view, in consideration of the great distance which separates the parties who contract, and that no doubt may be raised upon this subject. I have, nevertheless, gentlemen, a sure guarantee that delays will be abridged, as far as circumstances will permit, in the good faith which has presided in this negotiation during its whole continuance; and I know by my own and old experience, that it will be consummated by the Government of the United States according to these same principles.

I pray you to accept the assurance of my distinguished consideration.

BARBE MARBOIS.

Messrs. Livingston and Monroe to M. Marbois, Minister of the Public Treasury.

PARIS, *June 2, 1803.*

SIR: We have received the letter with which you have honored us, dated the 20th Floreal. Without entering into the principles it lays down, we are ready to admit, in order to remove, as far as depends on us, all difficulties, that it is the duty of the Government of the United States to carry into effect the provisions of the treaty and conventions in the times therein specified; and that any neglect on their part so to do, puts it in the power of the Government of France to declare how far it will, or will not, be bound thereby, or entitle it to a compensation for the damage it may sustain. We will observe, sir, that in making these concessions, we mean to confine ourselves to the letter of the treaty.

With the highest respect, &c.,

R. R. LIVINGSTON,
JAMES MONROE.

Mr. Monroe to the Secretary of State.

PARIS, *8th of June 1803.*

SIR,—Since my letter of yesterday I have had an interesting communication with the Minister of foreign affairs. Our letter had been restored to M^r. Livingston by M^r. Marbois in a casual interview who also shewed him the order to M^r. Pinchon, which was substituted for it. To see that order and receive one to him for the surrender of the country to the United States, I called yesterday evening by appointment on the Minister, where I found M^r. Marbois also. They had expected M^r. Livingston and myself together, but on my observing that we had not so understood it, he having already seen the paper. The Minister read the order to me and asked how I liked it, I replied that it was not for us to say, it being the act of his government only, but says he, comparatively which do you prefer, this mode or the other? I replied this without doubt. He said it was on the idea it would be more agreeable to us and our government that it was adopted, since suppressing our letter it became, as it ought to be, entirely the act of (the) government and in his opinion strictly a justifiable one, the Consul having a right to annex a condition to the ratification in the spirit of the treaty at any time before the exchange. I told him that having discussed the subject already I had only to repeat that I preferred much this mode to the other. He added that he hoped no difficulty would take place hereafter; that we had sufficient time to perform what we had stipulated, and that he sincerely wished we might do it in due time, as his government had much at heart the future harmony of the two nations. I replied that similar sentiments animated the government of the United States; that I was persuaded the treaty would be ratified; that even before the creation of the stock I was confident that the President far from delaying the payment of what was stipulated, would if (in) his power after the ratification promote aid which might be useful to them in the United States to evince his desire of a prompt execution of the treaty; that on our part and on our own responsibility if it was desired we would prevail on the house of Baring and Hope to advance the first payment, that is six millions of livres, before we heard from our government, in confidence that our conduct would be approved. I told him I thought my colleague would unite in this sentiment. He expressed himself highly gratified with the communication, which he considered as a strong proof of the friendship of the government of the United States for the nation and government of France. (He) declared that as it was made after everything was concluded it was the more honorable to us, and would affect in a greater degree the sensibility of the First Consul, to whom he would make it known, tho' he knew that he would accept nothing but as it became due in strict conformity to the treaty. I should deem it fortunate for the United States if the payment was made as being an act of liberality on our part, and in the degree a prompt execution of the treaty. It would bind this government more completely to the execution of it on its part. I am happy however that the offer was refused, since while it cannot fail to produce a good effect, it avoids all responsibility on our part, or that of the President, tho' indeed in the payment here the responsibility would be entirely on us. It is proper to inform you that the treaty and conventions bear date from the period when (every)thing was agreed on, the thirtieth of April, but as it (was necessary) to reduce them to writing the treaty was signed on the second of May, and the convention concerning the claims of our citizens the ninth or tenth which will explain why they were not sooner despatched from Paris. I am sir with great respect & esteem y^r. ob^t. serv^t.

Mr. Monroe to the Secretary of State.

PARIS *June 19, 1803.*

SIR,—We have rec^d. y^r. communications of the 18. and 20. of April & after due consideration deem it most advisable that I sho^d. proceed immediately to England. The departure of M^r. King from that country at the commencement of a war between it & France, without nominating a *charge des affaires* may expose our commercial concerns to much embarrassment if there is no one there soon to take charge of them. The arrangement however proposed by the President will probably obviate any inconvenience since the place will be occupied in a fortnight from this date. I am happy to have it in my power to add that the state in which our affairs are here admits a complyance with this arrangement without inconvenience to any interest of a publick nature. Since the despatch of the ratifications of the treaty &c, there is nothing to be done here till the question is decided by our government, nor even then in case of ratification, as the instruments will be given by you to the Minister of France to be forwarded to his government here. It is only in case of difficulty from some cause or other, that the commission will have to act again in this affair, & then it will be in your power, if a joint agency is deemed necessary to avail y^rself of it, by suitable instructions to the members who compose it. In regard to Spain it is not likely that any injury can result from the delay which becomes inevitable by this measure. It was never a very clear point that I ought to pursue the object with that power, after what was done here, untill I heard from you. The motive which inclined me to it at first diminished daily by my detention here, so that your late instructions arrived in good time to relieve me from further suspense. My visit to England will not I think be attributed by this gov^t. to an improper motive. It seems to have a just view of the policy of our government in regard to both powers, which is to cultivate their friendship by fair & honorable means while it pays a scrupulous attention & maintains with firmness the respect which is due to our national character rights & interests. My position in England will not prevent my attention in due time to the object with Spain, if the President should be of opinion that it might be useful. I have suggested to this government the probability of my being instructed by him to pursue that object with that power, after the decision on our treaty &c. with France, in which case I informed the Minister that I sho^d., according to the promise made to M^r. Livingston and myself by M^r. Marbois, expect the good offices of his government with its ally, and of which he gave me the most positive & satisfactory assurance. On this subject as on what concerns us more generally I shall write you hereafter more fully. I shall only add at present that in the communications which have passed between this government & myself since my last, to which this incident has in part given the occasion, much has occurred to inspire me with confidence in its friendly disposition towards our gov^t. & country and in a mode that could not otherwise than be peculiarly grateful to me. I am with great respect & esteem y^r. most ob^t. servant.

P. S. I have sent you two copies of the view I have taken of the question whether W. Florida is comprized in the cession of Louisiana, which I think too clear to admit of a doubt. I have many reasons for believing that the gov^t. of Spain entertains the same opinion on that point. I doubt not if it is taken possession of as a part of Louisiana, that the measure will be acquiesced in by that gov^t., or at least that it will not be taken ill by it, or impede an amicable and favorable adjustment relative to the territory of Spain Eastward of the Mississippi.

Mr. Monroe to Mr. Livingston.

(Reply to his of May 23.)

Dear Sir,—I have received your letter of the 23. expressing your idea of the extent of the acquisition we have made by the late treaty with France, which I have read with attention. I thank you for the communication, as it tends to throw light on that interesting topic.

Before however I proceed to make any remark on that subject permit me to observe that I am sorry I cannot agree with you in the last sentiment expressed in your letter, that it is not necessary to probe this business to the bottom nor until future circumstances should render it proper. Had I thought so I should not have asked of you your ideas on paper on the subject. My opinion has been from the moment that our treaty with France was concluded, that it was my first duty to ascertain correctly the extent of that acquisition, by reference to all the authentic documents to which access could be had, & such other sources of information as might illustrate it. There are a variety of considerations which imposed this duty on me; I will however only mention that which grows out of the transaction itself, the propriety of communicating to our government, such information as we possess & such opinion as we have formed of the extent of the acquisition. This consideration is much strengthened by the advice which you propose to give to our government to take possession of W. Florida as a part of Louisiana. We ought not to give such advice till we had probed the question to the bottom, and seen that it was founded in principles of Justice such as could be demonstrated to the impartial world, even to Spain herself. Nor can I agree with you that my motive for asking your ideas on that subject on paper, was because I had not leisure to examine it myself. The fact is I was at the time engaged in the examination of it, as I have been ever since, and with the greatest attention that other duties would permit, as indeed I think I mentioned to you at the time. My object in making the request was that we might examine the question separately, compare our ideas together and after forming our opinions, take the course which in reference to our respective duties might appear to be proper. I have made these observations solely for the purpose of explaining to you the motive which induced me to make the above mentioned request, which I have been sorry to find you had misunderstood.

Having also examined the question with some attention and committed my ideas to paper I shall have the pleasure to communicate them to you at our first interview. I shall only observe at present that we perfectly agree in the opinion that Louisiana, as it was in the hands of France prior to the year 1763, extended to the River Perdigo, & that it was restored to her by Spain, in the treaty of Il Dephonso, precisely in the same extent: that the reservation contained in the last member of the article, which respects the subject, is in favor of the United States only, intended to secure their rights under their treaty with Spain in 1795. I also think with you that the communications of the Spanish Minister at Madrid to Mr. Pinckney tend to confirm this doctrine. But in tracing this subject under the several treaties which respect it, I had a difficulty on a point which appeared to me to be of importance. Did France dismember the country while she was possessed of it? it is not material to how many powers she granted it provided it was at one & the same time, that is that it did not remain her property in a dismembered state. At first I was led to fear that a strong argument might be drawn against us from this source. The secret treaty by which New Orleans & the Western bank of Louisiana was ceded to Spain bears date on the 3rd Nov. 1762; the order of the King to his governor for the surrender of it on the 21 April 1764 and the actual surrender did not take place till some years afterwards, according to one of the papers which I have seen, not till 18 Augt 1769. The treaty between France, Great Britain, Spain &c by which the part since called W. Florida was ceded to Great Britain bears date on the 10th Feby 1763. I presume that the cession of a country takes its date from the treaty making the cession, not from the surrender: but in the present case whether we date the cession referred to, under the secret treaty of '62, to Spain from the one or the other epoch, the effect would be the same. If these were the only facts in the case, it might be said that there was a dismemberment of Louisiana in the hands of France. Happily these are not the only facts existing; by a note in one of the books I have obtained, it appears that the preliminary articles of the treaty of 1763 were actually signed on the same day with the secret convention above mentioned, & of course that the transfer or cession of the whole country by France was made on the same day. I presume that this note may be relied on, & verified by reference to authentic documents, to which access may be had. I communicate its contents with pleasure, because it seems to place beyond all controversy our right to West Florida under the treaty we have lately formed with France.

[Extract.]

Mr. Livingston to Mr. Madison.

PARIS, *June 25, 1803.*

SIR: I have received your letter of the —— with the commissions, &c. Before this reaches you, you will have learned that they were unnecessary, as they respected our negotiations. You will find, by looking back to my letters, that I had long anticipated something of this kind, and I was greatly surprised when Mr. Monroe came without it. I, however, in all my conversations, held out the idea very strongly and you will see it hinted at in my notes and in my letters to J. B.; so that it doubtless has had a considerable operation in bringing this Government to the resolution they took, before the arrival of Mr. Monroe, to part with Louisiana. You will remember that in one of my letters I request you to set on foot a negotiation with Britain for ascertaining your Northwestern boundary, but not to come to a conclusion. Indeed, as I was at that time endeavoring to excite an alarm here that should put us in possession of the country above the Arkansas, I own I have felt very much distressed that I never found any of these suggestions noticed or encouraged by our Government. But presuming always that they ultimately would be, I have carefully concealed my want of powers, and acted as decidedly as if I had possessed them; and to this, as well as to the firm attitude that our Government took, you may attribute the success of our negotiations. I hope that nothing will prevent your immediate ratification, without altering a syllable of the terms. If you wish anything changed, ratify unconditionally and set on foot a new negotiation. Be persuaded that France is sick of the bargain; that Spain is much dissatisfied; and that the slightest pretense will lose you the treaty. Nothing has raised the reputation of our country in Europe so high as the conduct of our Government upon this occasion, both at home and abroad. In pursuance of the wish expressed in your letter, Mr. Monroe proceeds, in a few days, as your resident Minister Plenipotentiary to England; for though it was doubtful whether this was or was not intended to depend upon the contingency mentioned therein, yet, as you were unrepresented there, and the war rendered some representation necessary, we thought it most conformable to the President's intentions that he should go.

I am, &c.,

R. R. LIVINGSTON.

Hon. JAMES MADISON,
    Secretary of State.

President Jefferson to General Gates.

WASHINGTON, *July 11, 1803.*

DEAR GENERAL,—I accept with pleasure, and with pleasure reciprocate your congratulations on the acquisition of Louisiana; for it is a subject of mutual congratulations, as it interests every man of the nation. The territory acquired, as it includes all the waters of the Missouri and Mississippi, has more than doubled the area of the United States, and the new parts is not inferior to the old in soil, climate, productions and important communications. If our Legislature dispose of it with the wisdom we have a right to expect, they may make it the means of tempting all our Indians on the east side of the Mississippi to remove to the west, and of condensing instead of scattering our population. I find our opposition is very willing to pluck feathers from Monroe, although not fond of sticking them into Livingston's coat. The truth is, both have a just portion of merit; and were it necessary or proper, it would be shown that each has rendered peculiar services, and of important value. These grumblers, too, are very uneasy lest the administration should share some little credit for the acquisition, the whole of which they ascribe to the accident of war. They would be cruelly mortified could they see our files from May, 1801, the first organization of the administration, but more especially from April, 1802. They would see, that though we could not say when war would arise, yet we said with energy what would take place when it should arise. We did not, by our intrigues, produce the war; but we availed ourselves of it when it happened. The other party saw the case now existing, on which our representations were predicated, and the wisdom of timely sacrifice. But when these people make the war give us everything, they authorize us to ask what the war gave us in their day? They had a war; what did they make it bring us? Instead of making our neutrality the ground of gain to their country, they were for plunging into the war. And if they were now in place, they would now be at war against the atheists and disorganizers of France. They were for making their country an appendage to England. We are friendly, cordially and conscientiously friendly with England. We are not hostile to France. We will be rigorously just and sincerely friendly to both. I do not believe we shall have as much to swallow from them as our predecessors had.

Mr. Madison to Mr. Livingston.

DEPARTMENT OF STATE, *July 29, 1803.*

SIR: Since the date of my last, which was May 24, I have received your several letters of April 11, 13, 17, and May 12th. As they relate almost wholly to the subject which was happily terminated on the 30th of April, a particular answer is rendered unnecessary by that event, and by the answer which goes by this conveyance to the joint letter from yourself and Mr. Monroe of the 13th of May. It will only be observed, first, that the difference in the diplomatic titles given to Mr. Monroe from that given to you, and which you understood to have ranked him above you, was the result merely of an error in the clerk, who copied the document, and which escaped attention when they were signed. It was not the intention of the President that any distinction of grade should be made between you. Indeed, according to the authority of Vattel, the characters of Minister Plenipotentiary and Envoy Extraordinary are precisely of the same grade; although it is said that the usage in France, particularly, does not correspond with this idea. Secondly, that the relation of the First Consul to the Italian Republic received the compliment deemed sufficient in the answer to a note of M. Pichon, communicating the flag of that nation. A copy of the communication and of the answer are now enclosed.

The boundaries of Louisiana seem to be so imperfectly understood, and are of so much importance, that the President wishes them to be investigated whenever information is likely to be obtained. You will be pleased to attend particularly to this object, as it relates to the Spanish possessions both on the west and on the east side of the Mississippi. The proofs countenancing our claim to a part of West Florida may be of immediate use in the negotiations which are to take place at Madrid. Should Mr. Monroe proceed thither, as is probable, and any such proofs should, after his departure, have come to your knowledge, you will of course have transmitted them to him.

You will find by our gazettes that your memorial, drawn up about a year ago on the subject of Louisiana, has found its way into public circulation. The passages in it which strike at Great Britain have undergone some comment; and will probably be conveyed to the attention of that Government. The document appears to have been sent from Paris, where you will be able, no doubt, to trace the indiscretion to its author.

No answer has yet been received either from you or Mr. Monroe to the diplomatic arrangement for London and Paris. The importance of shortening the interval at the former, and preventing one at the latter, makes us anxious on this point. As your late letters have not repeated your intention of returning home this fall, it is hoped that the interesting scenes which have since supervened may reconcile you to a longer stay in Europe.

I have the honor to be, &c.,

JAMES MADISON.

The Secretary of State to Messrs. Livingston and Monroe.

DEPARTMENT OF STATE, *July 29, 1803.*

GENTLEMEN: Your dispatches, including the treaty and two conventions signed with a French Plenipotentiary, on the 30th of April, were safely delivered on the 14th instant by Mr. Hughes, to whose care you had committed them.

In concurring with the disposition of the French Government to treat for the whole of Louisiana, although the western part of it was not embraced by your powers, you were justified by the solid reasons which you give for it; and I am charged by the President to express to you his entire approbation for so doing.

This approbation is in no respect precluded by the silence of your commission and instructions. When these were made out, the object of the most sanguine was limited to the establishment of the Mississippi as our boundary. It was not presumed, that more could be sought by the United States, either with a chance of success, or perhaps without being suspected of greedy ambition, than the island of New Orleans and the two Floridas; it being little doubted that the latter was, or would be comprehended in the cession from Spain to France. To the acquisition of New Orleans and the Floridas, the provision was, therefore, accommodated. Nor was it to be supposed that in case the French Government should be willing to part with more than the territory on our side of the Mississippi, an arrangement with Spain for restoring to her the territory on the other side, would not be preferred to a sale of it to the United States. It might be added, that the ample views of the subject carried with him by Mr. Monroe, and the confidence felt that your judicious management would make the most favorable occurrences, lessened the necessity of multiplying provisions for every turn which your negotiations might possibly take.

The effect of such considerations was diminished by no information, or just presumptions whatever. The note of Mr. Livingston, in particular, stating to the French Government the idea of ceding the Western country above the Arkansas, and communicated to this Department in his letter of the 29th January, was not received here till April 5, more than a month after the commission and instructions had been forwarded. And, besides, that this project not only left with France the possession and jurisdiction of one bank of the Mississippi from its mouth to the Arkansas, but a part of West Florida, the whole of East Florida, and the harbors for ships of war in the Gulf of Mexico. The letter enclosing the note, intimated that it had been treated by the French Government with decided neglect. In truth, the communications in general between Mr. Livingston and the French Government, both of prior and subsequent date, manifested a repugnance to our views of purchase, which left no expectation of any arrangement with France, by which an extensive acquisition was to be made, unless in a favorable crisis, of which advantage should be taken. Such was thought to be the crisis which gave birth to the extraordinary commission in which you are joined. It consisted of the state of things produced by the breach of our deposit at New Orleans; the situation of the French islands, particularly the important island of St. Domingo; the distress of the French finances; the unsettled posture of Europe; the increasing jealousy between Great Britain and France; and the known aversion of the former to see the mouth of the Mississippi in the hands of the latter. These considerations, it was hoped, might so far open the eyes of France to her real interest, and her ears to the monitory truths which were conveyed to her through different channels, as to reconcile her to the establishment of the Mississippi as a natural boundary to the United States; or, at least, to some concessions which would justify our patiently waiting for a fuller accomplishment of our wishes, under auspicious events. The crisis relied on has derived peculiar force from the rapidity with which the complaints and questions between France and Great Britain ripened towards a rupture; and it is just ground for mutual and general felicitation that it has issued under your zealous exertions in the extensive acquisitions beyond the Mississippi.

With respect to the terms on which the acquisition is made, there can be no doubt that the bargain will be regarded as on the whole highly advantageous. The pecuniary stipulations would have been more satisfactory if they had departed less from the plan prescribed; and particularly if the two millions of dollars in cash, intended to reduce the price to hasten the delivery of possession, had been so applied, and the assumed payments to American claimants placed on a footing specified in the instructions. The unexpected weight of the draft now to be made on the Treasury will be sensibly felt by it, and may possibly be inconvenient in relation to other important objects.

The President has issued his proclamation convening Congress on the 17th of October, in order that the exchange of the ratifications may be made within the time limited. It is obvious that the exchange, to be within the time, must be made here, and not at Paris; and we infer from your letter of —— that the ratifications of the Chief Consul are to be transmitted hither with that view.

I only add the wish of the President to know from you the understanding which prevailed in the negotiation with respect to the boundaries of Louisiana; and particularly the pretensions and proofs for carrying it to the river Perdido, or for including any lesser portion of West Florida.

With high respect and consideration, &c.,

JAMES MADISON.

[Extract.]

Mr. Livingston to Mr. Madison.

PARIS, *July 30, 1803.*

SIR: The house of Hope and Baring will to-morrow lodge with me the amount in bills of the stock they have purchased from the French Government, to be delivered by me according to the terms of their contract. If the treaty is ratified, I believe that this meets with no delay. Be assured that were the business to do again it never would be done. They think we have obtained an immense advantage over them. Though the appearance of war had some influence, it had much less than is ascribed to it. Whenever I mentioned its falling into the hands of England, they admitted the possibility, but insisted that, as it must abide the event of the war, they had no doubt of ultimate success; they would get it back with the British improvements. Mr. Skipwith still thinks that the American debt will fall much within the twenty millions for which we have engaged, and all the fair creditors be fully satisfied; the supposed debt being extremely exaggerated in America. Other nations, creditors of France, have, at present, no prospect of being paid.

I this day got a sight of a letter from the Minister to M. Laussat, containing directions for giving up the country, and assigning the reasons for the cession. I was much flattered to find their reasons wholly drawn from the memoir I had presented; and that the order for the cession was full, and contained no other description of the country than that which had been designated in the Treaty of St. Ildefonso: so that I hope you have not failed to insist on West Florida.

I have also this day been favored with a duplicate of yours of the 26th (25th) of May. You observe that the promise I had obtained for payment was still short of justice. This may be true; but, sir, were you here, or, indeed, in any Court in Europe, you would admit that obtaining of anything that approaches to justice, required some skill and much good fortune. At present, I believe, you may purchase millions of just debt of Denmark, Sweden, &c., here at fifty-seven in the pound, and purchase it dear enough; and I think that I may, without vanity, ascribe my obtaining the promise to what are here considered as very delicate measures; and to that promise, a ruling influence in procuring a treaty that I trust will be considered in America (as in Europe) among the most important and advantageous the United States ever made.

I have the honor, &c.,

R. R. LIVINGSTON.

Mr. Madison to Mr. Monroe.

WASHINGTON, *July 30, 1803.*

DEAR SIR,—I received your favor of —— by Mr. Hughes, the bearer of the public despatches from you and Mr. Livingston. The purchase of Louisiana in its full extent, tho' not contemplated, is received with warm, and, in a manner, universal approbation. The uses to which it may be turned render it a truly noble acquisition. Under pendent management it may be made to do much good, as well as to prevent much evil. By lessening the military establishment otherwise requisite or countenanced, it will answer the double purpose of saving expence and favoring liberty. This is a point of view in which the Treaty will be particularly grateful to a most respectable description of our Citizens. It will be of great importance, also, to take the regulation and settlement of that Territory out of other hands into those of the U. S., who will be able to manage both for the general interest and conveniency. By securing, also, the exclusive jurisdiction of the Mississippi to the mouth, a source of much perplexity and collision is effectually cut off. The communications of your colleague hither have fully betrayed the feelings excited by your message, and that he was precipitating the business soon after your arrival, without respect to the measure of the government, to yourself, or to the advantage to be expected from the presence and co-operation of the more immediate depository of the objects and sensibilities of his Country. It is highly probable that if the appeal to the French Government had been less hackneyed by the ordinary minister, and been made under the solemnity of a joint and extraordinary embassy, the impression would have been greater and the gain better.

What course will be taken by his friends here remains to be seen. You will find in the Gazettes a letter from Paris, understood to be from Swan, indorsing a copy of his memorial, representing it as the primary cause of the cession, praising the patriotism which undertook so great a service without authority, and throwing your agency out of any real merit, while, by good fortune, it snatched the ostensible merit. This letter, with the memorial, has been published in all our papers; some of them making comments favorable to Mr. Livingston, others doing justice to you, others ascribing the result wholly to the impending rupture. Another letter from Paris has been published, which makes him Magnus Apollo. The publication of the memorial is so improper, and in reference to the writer invites such strictures, that from him is not to be presumed. The passages against England have not escaped the lash. It would not be very wonderful if they were to be noticed formally or informally by the British legation here.

My public letter will show the light in which the purchase of all Louisiana is viewed, and the manner in which it was thought proper to touch the policy of Mr. Livingston, in complaining that the communication did not authorize the measure, notwithstanding the information given that he was negociating for more than the East side of the Mississippi. The pecuniary arrangements are much disrelished, particularly by Mr. Gallatin. The irredeemability of the stock, which gives it value above par, the preference of the conditions to the true object in the cash payment, and the barring of a priority among them, are errors most regarded. The claims of the different creditors rest on principles as different.

Mr. Monroe to the Secretary of State.

LONDON, *July 20 1803.*

SIR,— I am too recently on this theatre to give you any information of the state of public affairs which you will not obtain of the gazettes which I shall therefore not repeat.

It will be more useful to go back to the transactions in which I have been lately engaged, and to communicate some incidents which occurred in them with which you are not yet acquainted. The pressure of business at the time, the necessity of hastening here as soon as that measure was decided on, and the hope that I should enjoy more leisure here than I had done in France, induced me to reserve them for the present communication.

You saw by my letters after the conclusion of our treaties with France that I had in a great measure decided to proceed to Spain, on the idea that by so doing I should best fulfil the ulterior object of my instructions. You saw likewise by the joint letter of M\`. Livingston and myself of June 7th that I had been prevented pursuing that object, by an obstacle, the circumstances attending which were fully detailed in it. There occurred however another difficulty which you are yet to be apprized of.

At the time when my judgment inclined in favor of that measure, I applied to M\`. Talleyrand for the support of his Gov\`. in the negotiation according to the promise made us by M\`. Marbois, with which you are acquainted. This application was made on the 19 of May immediately before the discussion mentioned in the letter of the 7 June above referred to. On the Sunday following, three or four days afterwards, I dined with the Consul Cambaceres who had been with the First Consul in council at S\` Cloud whence he returned late to dinner. He said to me soon after entering the room "you must not go to Spain at present." I asked his reason. He replied "it is not the time; you had better defer it." I revived the subject repeatedly but he declined going farther into it. After dinner when we were in the Salon, he came up to me, and on my informing him that he had given me much concern by what he had said, he replied "that it was only his opinion; but you will talk on the subject with the Minister of the public treasury," which I assured him that I would not fail to do. I went immediately to M\`. Marbois, but had not the good fortune to find him at home.

On the Tuesday following I saw the Consul le Brun, who suggested to me precisely the same idea which I had received from the Consul Cambaceres, and who I was persuaded had imbibed it at the same time in the Council at S\` Cloud. I proposed to him the same question that I had done to his Colleague, and received nearly the same answer. He told me that we should obtain our object, but that this was not the time for it. About this time the incident mentioned in the letter of June 7th occurred, which increased and continued my suspense till we rec'd. yours of the 18 & 20 of April which directed my route here.

As soon as my course was marked I called on the Minister of foreign Affairs, and reminded him of my application to him for the aid of his gov't. in our negotiation with Spain, which as he well recollected had been promised. I then told him, without waiting for an answer, that my route was changed; that I had just received the order of the President to proceed to England in case our affairs were amicably adjusted with France; that the motive for it was, a knowledge that M'. King was about to return home; the probability of a rupture between France & Britain and the consequent exposure of our commerce; and the propriety of our being represented there in case of that event: that the urgency was increased by the circumstance under which I received the order, M'. King having sailed without having nominated any one to take charge of our affairs till his successor arrived. I adverted in the commencement to the affair with Spain, to fix in his mind, by evidence not to be resisted, an important fact, the date at which the late order was received, that he might see that it grew out of recent circumstances, those mentioned, and was not part of a system of menace adopted at the time of my appointment. I had seen the advantage of inculcating this truth on more than one occasion, or thought I had, & wished to have it in full force on the present one. The Minister acknowledged in explicit terms the frankness of the communication, which he considered as a strong proof of the fair dealing of our Government in its conduct towards his, and of its sincere desire to preserve peace and friendship between the two nations. Then taking a cursory review of what had passed in the late negotiation, he declared that nothing short of the course which had been taken by our Government would have produced the result which had attended it. He asked me when I proposed setting out on the proposed mission? I answered very soon, as there was nothing to detain me longer there. I requested him to communicate the above to the First Consul, and to express my wish to be favored with a private audience, for the purpose of taking my leave of him before my departure. This he readily undertook, but observed that as the first Consul was to set out in a few days for the Belgic and his time was preengaged by appointments for the whole of the interval, he doubted whether it would be in his power to grant me an audience, tho' he was persuaded he would if he could. Having asked an audience I resolved to wait an answer till his departure, and the more so as I knew it would not detain me long. As soon as I had made the above communication to the minister, I made a like one to M'. Marbois, whose candid and upright deportment through the whole of our negotiation, had inspired me with a very high respect for his character. I asked and obtained about the same time & for the same purpose, a private audience of the Consuls Cambaceres & le Brun, by whom I had been received with kindness, and treated with attention during my mission in France, & who I had reason to believe had promoted the object of it. It was not strictly in course to make to these characters such a communication, but I felt that I owed it to the part they had taken in the late important transactions with our country, and am persuaded that it was received in the spirit in which it was made. I called on Joseph Bonaparte the elder brother of the first Consul with the same view, but as he had left town I had not the pleasure to see him.

The day before the Consul commenced his tour I received a note from the Minister of foreign affairs requesting me to meet him the next day at 1 o'clock at St Cloud to be presented by him to the first Consul, which was accordingly done. The audience was of some length.

I made a communication similar in substance to what I had already done to the Minister, to which I added that it was the wish of the President that I should assure him before my departure of his high respect & esteem for him personally & for the French Nation, and of his earnest desire to preserve peace & friendship with it. The first Consul reciprocated the sentiment toward the President and the U. S. in strong terms. He said that he considered the President as a virtuous and enlightened man, who understood and pursued the interest of his country, as a friend of liberty and equality: That no one wished more than himself the preservation of a good understanding between the two Republics: that he had been prompted to make the late Cession to the U. States not so much on account of the sum given for the territory as from views of policy: that France had been their first friend and he wished to preserve that relation between the two countries for ever: he had perceived that we entertained a jealousy of their possession of Louisiana which was likely to drive us into measures & connexions that would prove not only hurtful to France, but as he presumed to ourselves also: He therefore wished to remove the cause by an act which would free us from all apprehension on that head and leave us at liberty to pursue our course according to our interest and inclination. I told him in reply that I had considered the cession of Louisiana as having been prompted by the motives which he stated, as being an act of great and enlightened policy rather than an affair of commerce, and was persuaded that our government would view it in the same light: that the cession would place us on the ground he mentioned of real independence: that we had however been willing to give what was deemed an equivalent for it. He observed that there was no rivalship between us, our relation to France being chiefly commercial; but that we must be on our guard, not to give the protection of our flag to the British. I told him that the latter was a question which merited all his deliberation and candor, since the principle that free ships made free goods, if sustained by him as I understood it to be, precluded any discussion on that point. He admitted that there were difficulties in the case which he should examine with care. He then observed, without my leading to the subject tho' I had intended doing it, with respect to Florida that this was not the time to pursue that object: that the Spaniards had complained much of the cession they had made to us of Louisiana. I told him that we were neighbors of Spain and wished to be on friendly terms with her, which the possession would promote: that it was a little piece of land comprized within our present limits which we ought to have. He replied that it was because we were their neighbors that they were jealous of our possessing that territory which by its ports commanded the gulph of Mexico. I told him it would be better for Spain that we held it than the British, which might take place if we did not. Still he urged that this was not the time to negotiate for it. I ceased therefore to press the subject further, preferring to let it be understood that the negotiation was postponed for the present, to be revived at a more suitable season, when we should expect his good offices in it, to which he seemed to assent.

It is to be presumed that the natural weight and respectability of the United States will enable their government to obtain this object of Spain, without the aid of any other power: It cannot be doubted however that France, has the means of essentially promoting or embarrassing it. It was on that principle that we sought to avail ourselves of her aid in the late negotiation & that I applied for it when I was about to go to Spain. To have gone after the promise made us, without this communication, might have produced an ill effect; to have gone after my application for it in opposition to her advice would most probably have had the same tendency, which it seemed peculiarly proper to avoid especially while our treaties with her were depending. The Consul set out on his tour the evening of the day on which I had the above audience, which was on the (24th) of June. On the Monday following I requested my passport of Mr. d'Hermand the chief in the department of foreign relations charged with that business who I found had not the power to grant one. I immediately wrote to the Minister of foreign relations, who had left Paris about the same time with the Consul to apprize him of this fact & request that he would be pleased to send me a passport immediately as I was ready for my journey and only waited one.

* * * * * * *

[Extract.]

Mr. Monroe to the Secretary of State.

LONDON *26 July 1803*

Our government ought to know to the minutest detail the motives which induced the government of France to adopt this measure, to enable it to do justice to those motives & bring the affair itself to a happy conclusion. The extrication of ourselves from a dangerous, perhaps a disastrous, war, by the acquisition of an important territory which gives such vast relief and comfort to so many of our people, is an event which if the causes which produced it are well understood, may se've as a monitory lesson to influence if not prescribe the course to be pursued in our future controversies with the European powers, if any should occur. America certainly bears a very distinct relation to Europe, from what the several powers of the latter bear to each other, which it is equally important for her to understand & to have understood by the latter. Of this truth the event referred to is a striking example as it is a very satisfactory illustration. I should weary you if I pursued this subject. I have touched it to remark that for these and other obvious reasons I have considered it my duty to communicate to you every fact belonging to this transaction with which I was acquainted that it might be seen by the President in its true light. To these I shall at present take the liberty to add a few observations.

You saw by M^r. Livingstons and my joint letter which bore date a day or two before I left Paris about the 11th ulto^{mo} that the English government had no agency in this affair: that it never had made a question of Louisiana in its discussions with the government of France, at any period since the French possessed it. This information was obtained of Lord Whitworth on the application of M^r. Livingston on his & my part at a time when we deemed it important to know what interest that power had taken in the affair if any. Lord Whitworth's answer was as I understand frank and explicit to that effect. It therefore proves fully that the Cession of Louisiana did not proceed from any interference of G. Britain respecting it.

The proof is in other respects positive and conclusive that it was produced by the measures of our Government and that the decision to make the cession was intended to meet them in the spirit in which they were taken. It is a well established fact that before those measures were well known in France the First Consul had manifested no inclination to make the Cession. For some time after they were known his disposition to retain the territory remained unshaken, tho' it was evident he had become more conciliatory in his deportment towards our country. As late as the 10. of March he announced his resolution not even to discuss the subject in any light until after he had sent a Minister to the U. S. and received from him such information as he deemed necessary for the purpose. On the 22^d. of March he manifested his desire to retain the country to be as strong as ever, intimated that he had always considered the possession of it as furnishing him with the means of giving new proofs of his friendship for the U. States, by which he meant, as is presumed, the opening of the river to our Citizens, on more favorable terms than had yet been enjoyed by them, he absolutely refused to treat at that time, tho' he acknowledged his sensibility to the conduct of the President in the conjuncture which had produced an extraordinary mission, and declared that he would receive the Envoy with pleasure & hoped that his mission would terminate to the satisfaction of both powers. The decision to make the cession was taken on the 10th of April after the arrival of that Envoy at Havre (which was on the 8th) was known at Paris, and with a view to lay the foundation for the negotiation which was so soon to commence. For the proof of these facts I refer you to the official notes of Mr. Talleyrand to Mr. Livingston of the 10th and 22nd of March, which I presume are in your possession, and to such other information as you have heretofore received of the latter. The demonstration which they furnish of what I have above stated, is too strong to be resisted by any one whose mind is not sealed by prejudice against the clearest result. Had the disposition of the first Consul to make the cession been produced by any but the measures of our government and country taken together, but more especially by the firm & dignified yet conciliatory conduct of the President, he would not have postponed the discussion of the subject till he was apprized of those measures, nor would he, after he knew of them, have delayed the avowal of his disposition to the period that he did, or assigned the motive which he gave in the letter of March 22d. for the delay.

It was impossible, had we possessed the requisite power, after our negotiation commenced to have opened any communication with this government without great hazard to our interest & credit, while it was impossible to derive any advantage from it. A proposition to Britain for her agency in the affair, could not have been expected to succeed without our paying some equivalent for it, which must have been by making common cause with her in her own controversy and perhaps also by giving her some portion of the territory or rights in the navigation of the river. Had we stipulated either of these considerations we should most probably have been carried into the war with her, the result of which is very uncertain. By making any stipulation in favor of G. Britain we should have tied up our hands in the degree from doing anything for ourselves, while we bound ourselves to her fortunes. Had we made any overture for any such an arrangement we hazarded its being made known, with a view to her own interest, to the government of France, with whom it could not fail to have produced an ill effect in regard to ours. Perfect freedom to take such part as our interest required was the happiest situation, in which we could be placed in the negotiation, & it equally comported with honor & policy not only to remain so in reality, but to preserve also the appearance of it, while there was a prospect of success. Had we erred in the present case our folly and disposition for intrigue must have been extreme, since from the commencement there was great probability of success, which continued to increase till the object was accomplished.

It cannot be doubted that there were a variety of causes, which contributed to produce a change in the mind of the first Consul relative to Louisiana, & to facilitate the cession which I flatter myself our government has been fortunate in obtaining. Among these may be calculated the failure of the Expedition to S^t. Domingo, the pressure of the crisis in Europe &c. There are occasions which it is fair and honorable for every government to take advantage of & which none fail to do, when those at their head have discernment enough to see them. They are such as our distance from Europe, & fortunate situation in other respects, will I hope always furnish us, when they may be necessary. I affirm, however, with perfect confidence in the opinion, that notwithstanding these favorable circumstances, we should not have succeeded had the amiable relations between America & France been broken, or had the President have taken an attitude of menace towards that power, or any other than precisely that which he did take.

Extract of a letter from James Monroe, esq., Minister Plenipotentiary, London, to the Secretary of State.

AUGUST 15, 1803.

The enclosed, which I received last night from Paris by an American gentleman, containing important information, is, therefore, transmitted to you.

[Extract of a letter from Mr. Fenwick to Mr. Monroe.]

PARIS, *August 5, 1803.*

Since you left this city nothing very material has transpired. I know, however, from a faithful source, that the Spanish Government has made the most serious remonstrances against the cession of Louisiana, and their instructions here are to prevent its being carried into execution, if yet possible: and if pecuniary arguments could succeed, the hands of their Ministers are not tied on that score. This might be a useful hint, if our Senate should not disregard federal examples in modifying treaties, as it is now well understood, that, if any conditional clause of ratification should be introduced by the United States, this Government would profit of the circumstance to annul the whole work.

President Jefferson to Mr. Breckenridge.

MONTICELLO, *August 12, 1803.*

DEAR SIR,—The enclosed letter, though directed to you, was intended to me also, and was left open with a request, that when forwarded, I would forward it to you. It gives me occasion to write a word to you on the subject of Louisiana, which being a new one, an interchange of sentiments may produce correct ideas before we are to act on them.

Our information as to the country is very incomplete; we have taken measures to obtain it full as to the settled part, which I hope to receive in time for Congress. The boundaries, which I deem not admitting question, are the high lands on the western side of the Mississippi enclosing all its waters, the Missouri of course, and terminating in the line drawn from the northwestern point of the Lake of the Woods to the nearest source of the Mississippi, as lately settled between Great Britain and the United States. We have some claims, to extend on the seacoast westwardly to the Rio Norte or Bravo, and better, to go eastwardly to the Rio Perdido, between Mobile and Pensacola, the ancient boundary of Louisiana. These claims will be a subject of negotiation with Spain, and if, as soon as she is at war, we push them strongly with one hand, holding out a price in the other, we shall certainly obtain the Floridas, and all in good time. In the meanwhile, without waiting for permission, we shall enter into the exercise of the natural right we have always insisted on with Spain, to-wit, that of a nation holding the upper part of streams, having a right of innocent passage through them to the ocean. We shall prepare her to see us practice on this, and she will not oppose it by force.

Objections are raising to the eastward against the vast extent of our boundaries, and propositions are made to exchange Louisiana, or a part of it, for the Floridas. But, as I have said, we shall get the Floridas without, and I would not give one inch of the waters of the Mississippi to any nation, because I see in a light very important to our peace the exclusive right to its navigation, and the admission of no nation into it, but as into the Potomac or Delaware, with our consent and under our police. These federalists see in this acquisition the formation of a new confederacy, embracing all the waters of the Mississippi, on both sides of it, and a separation of its eastern waters from us. These combinations depend on so many circumstances which we can not foresee, that I place little reliance on them. We have seldom seen neighborhood produce affection among nations. The reverse is almost the universal truth. Besides, if it should become the great interest of those nations to separate from this, if their happiness should depend on it so strongly as to induce them to go through that convulsion, why should the Atlantic States dread it? But especially why should we, their present inhabitants, take side in such a question? When I view the Atlantic States, procuring for those on the eastern waters of the Mississippi friendly instead of hostile neighbors on its western waters, I do not view it as an Englishman would the procuring future blessings for the French nation, with whom he has no relations of blood or affection. The future inhabitants of the Atlantic and Mississippi States will be our sons. We leave them in distinct but bordering establishments. We think we see their happiness in their union, and we wish it. Events may prove it otherwise; and if they see their interest in separation, why should we take side with our Atlantic rather than our Mississippi descendants? It is the elder and the younger son differing. God bless them both, and keep them in union, if it be for their good, but separate them, if it be better. The inhabited part of Louisiana, from Point Coupée to the sea, will of course be immediately a territorial government, and soon a State. But above that, the best use we can make of the country for some time, will be to give establishments in it to the Indians on the east side of the Mississippi, in exchange for their present country, and open land offices in the last, and thus make this acquisition the means of filling up the eastern side, instead of drawing off its population. When we shall be full on this side, we may lay off a range of States on the western bank from the head to the mouth, and so, range after range, advancing compactly as we multiply.

This treaty must of course be laid before both Houses, because both have important functions to exercise respecting it. They, I presume, will see their duty to their country in ratifying and paying for it, so as to secure a good which would otherwise probably be never again in their power. But I suppose they must then appeal to *the nation* for an additional article to the Constitution, approving and confirming an act which the nation had not previously authorized. The Constitution has made no provision for our holding foreign territory, still less for incorporating foreign nations into our Union. The executive in seizing the fugitive occurrence which so much advances the good of their country, have done an act beyond the Constitution. The Legislature in casting behind them metaphysical subtleties, and risking themselves like faithful servants, must ratify and pay for it, and throw themselves on their country for doing for them unauthorized, what we know they would have done for themselves had they been in a situation to do it. It is the case of a guardian investing the money of his ward in purchasing an important adjacent territory; and saying to him when of age, I did this for your good; I pretend to no right to bind you: you may disavow me, and I must get out of the scrape as I can: I thought it my duty to risk myself for you. But we shall not be disavowed by the nation, and their act of indemnity will confirm and not weaken the Constitution, by more strongly marking out its lines.

[Extract.]

President Jefferson to Mr. Madison.

MONTICELLO, *August 25, 1803.*

I suppose Monroe will touch on the limits of Louisiana only incidentally, inasmuch as its extension to Perdido curtails Florida, and renders it of less worth. I have used my spare moments to investigate, by the help of my books here, the subject of the limits of Louisiana. I am satisfied our right to the Perdido is substantial, and can be opposed by a quibble on form only; and our right westwardly to the Bay of St. Bernard, may be strongly maintained. I will use the first leisure to make a statement of the facts and principles on which this depends. Further reflection on the amendment to the Constitution necessary in the case of Louisiana, satisfies me it will be better to give general powers, with specified exceptions, somewhat in the way stated below. * * *

P. S.—Louisiana, as ceded by France to the United States, is made a part of the United States. Its white inhabitants shall be citizens, and stand, as to their rights and obligations, on the same footing with other citizens of the United States in analogous situations.

Save only that as to the portion thereof lying north of the latitude of the mouth of the Oreansa river, no new State shall be established, nor any grants of land made therein, other than to Indians, in exchange for equivalent portions of land occupied by them, until amendment to the Constitution shall be made for these purposes.

Florida also, whensoever it may be rightfully obtained, shall become a part of the United States. Its white inhabitants shall thereupon be citizens, and shall stand, as to their rights and obligations, on the same footing with other citizens of the United States in analogous circumstances.

President Jefferson to Wilson C. Nicholas.

MONTICELLO, *September 7, 1803.*

DEAR SIR,—Your favor of the 3d was delivered me at court; but we were much disappointed at not seeing you here, Mr. Madison and the Governor being here at the time. I enclose you a letter from Mr. Monroe on the subject of the late treaty. You will observe a hint in it, to do without delay what we are bound to do. There is reason, in the opinion of our ministers, to believe, that if the thing were to do over again, it could not be obtained, and that if we give the least opening, they will declare the treaty void. A warning amounting to that has been given to them, and an unusual kind of letter written by their minister to our Secretary of State, direct. Whatever Congress shall think it necessary to do, should be done with as little debate as possible, and particularly so far as respects the constitutional difficulty. I am aware of the force of the observations you make on the power given by the Constitution to Congress, to admit new States into the Union, without restraining the subject to the territory then constituting the United States. But when I consider that the limits of the United States are precisely fixed by the treaty of 1783, that the Constitution expressly declares itself to be made for the United States, I cannot help believing the intention was not to permit Congress to admit into the Union new States, which should be formed out of the territory for which, and under whose authority alone, they were then acting. I do not believe it was meant that they might receive England, Ireland, Holland, &c., into it, which would be the case on your construction. When an instrument admits two constructions, the one safe, the other dangerous, the one precise, the other indefinite, I prefer that which is safe and precise. I had rather ask an enlargement of power from the nation, where it is found necessary, than to assume it by a construction which would make our powers boundless. Our peculiar security is in the possession of a written Constitution. Let us not make it a blank paper by construction. I say the same as to the opinion of those who consider the grant of the treaty-making power as boundless. If it is, then we have no Constitution. If it has bounds, they can be no others than the definitions of the powers which that instrument gives. It specifies and delineates the operations permitted to the federal government, and gives all the powers necessary to carry these into execution. Whatever of these enumerated objects is proper for a law, Congress may make the law; whatever is proper to be executed by way of a treaty, the President and Senate may enter into the treaty; whatever is to be done by a judicial sentence, the judges may pass the sentence. Nothing is more likely than that their enumeration of powers is defective. This is the ordinary case of all human works. Let us go on then perfecting it, by adding, by way of amendment to the Constitution, those powers which time and trial show are still wanting. But it has been taken too much for granted, that by this rigorous construction the treaty power would be reduced to nothing. I had occasion once to examine its effect on the French treaty, made by the old Congress, and found that out of thirty odd articles which that contained, there were one, two, or three only which could not now be stipulated under our present Constitution. I confess, then, I think it important, in the present case, to set an example against broad construction, by appealing for new power to the people. If, however, our friends shall think differently, certainly I shall acquiesce with satisfaction; confiding, that the good sense of our country will correct the evil of construction when it shall produce ill effects. * * *

Mr. Madison to Mr. Livingston.

DEPARTMENT OF STATE, *October 6, 1803.*

SIR: My last was of July 29, written a few days before my departure from Virginia, whence I returned, as did the President, ten or twelve days ago. Your letters received since that date are of May 20, June 3 and 25, and July 11, 12, and 30th.

In the reply to the communication made by the French Government on the subject of the war, you are charged by the President to express the deep regret felt by the United States at an event so afflicting to humanity. Deploring all the calamities with which it is pregnant, they devoutly wish that the benevolent considerations which pleaded in vain for a continuance of peace, may have a due effect in speedily restoring its blessings. Until this happy change shall take place, the French Government may be assured that the United States will forget none of the obligations which the laws of neutrality impose on them. Faithful to their character, they will pay to every belligerent right the respect which is due to it; but this duty will be performed in the confidence that the rights of the United States will be equally respected. The French Government will do justice to the frankness of this declaration, which is rendered the more proper by the irregularities of which too many examples have been heretofore experienced. The President does not permit himself to doubt that the French Government, consulting equally its own honor and the true interests of France, will guard, by effectual regulations, against every abuse under color of its authority, whether on the high seas or within French or foreign jurisdiction, which might disturb the commerce, or endanger the friendly relations so happily subsisting, and which the United States are so much disposed to cherish, between the two nations.

Your interposition against the arret of the 1st Messidor, an 11, was due to the just interests of your fellow-citizens. It is to be hoped, that the strong views which you have presented of the subject, will lead the French Government to retract, or remodify, a measure not less unjust to foreigners than injurious to the interests of France: regulations which, by their suddenness, ensnare those who could not possibly know them, and who meant to observe those naturally supposed to be in force, are, to all intents, retrospective—having the same effect, and violating the same privileges, as laws enacted subsequent to the cases to which they are applied. The necessity of leaving between the date and the operation of commercial regulations an interval sufficient to prevent surprise on distant adventurers, is, in general, too little regarded, and so far there may be room for common complaint; but when great and sudden changes are made, and above all, when legal forfeitures, as well as mercantile losses, are sustained, redress may fairly be claimed by the innocent sufferers. Admitting the public safety, which rarely happens, to require regulations of this sort, and the right of every Government to judge for itself of the occasions, it is still more reasonable that the losses should be repaired than that they should fall on the individuals innocently ensnared.

Your suggestion as to commercial arrangements of a general nature with France, at the present juncture, has received the attention of the President, but he has not decided that any instructions should be given you to institute negotiations for that purpose; especially as it is not known on what particular points, sufficiently advantageous to the United States, the French Government would be likely to enter into stipulations. Some obscurity still hangs on the extra duty exacted by the Batavian Government. The state of our information leaves it doubtful, whether the interests of the United States would be promoted by the change authorized by our treaty with that Republic.

Mr. Pinckney will doubtless have communicated to you his conversation with Mr. Cevallos, in which the latter denied the right of France to alienate Louisiana to the United States, alleging a secret stipulation by France not to alienate. Two notes on the same subject have lately been presented here by the Marquis d'Yrujo. In the first, dated September 4, he enters a caveat against the right of France to alienate Louisiana, founding it on a declaration of the French Ambassador at Madrid, in July, 1802, that France would never part with that territory; and affirming that on no other condition Spain would have ceded it to France. In the second note, dated September 27, it is urged, as an additional objection to the treaty between the United States and France, that the French Government had never completed the title of France, having failed to procure the stipulated recognition of the King of Etruria from Russia and Great Britain, which was a condition on which Spain agreed to cede the country to France. Copies of these notes of the Minister here, with my answer, as also extracts from Mr. Pinckney's letter to me, and from a note of the Spanish Minister at Madrid to him, are also enclosed.

From this proceeding on the part of Spain, as well as by accounts from Paris, it is not doubted, that whatever her views may be, in opposing our acquisition of Louisiana, she is soliciting the concurrence of the French Government. The interest alone which France manifestly has in giving effect to her engagement with the United States, seems to forbid apprehensions that she will listen to any entreaties or temptations which Spain may employ. As to Spain, it can hardly be conceived that she will, unsupported by France, persist in her remonstrances, much less that she will resist the cession to the United States by force.

The objections to the cession advanced by Spain, are in fact too futile to weigh either with others or with herself. The promise made by the French Ambassador, that no alienation should be made, formed no part of the treaty of retrocession to France; and, if it had, could have no effect on the purchase by the United States, which was made in good faith, without notice from Spain of any such condition, and even with sufficient evidence that no such condition existed. The objection drawn from the failure of the French Government to procure from other Powers an acknowledgment of the King of Etruria, is equally groundless. This stipulation was never communicated either to the public or to the United States, and could, therefore, be no bar to the contract made by them. It might be added, that, as the acknowledgment stipulated was, according to the words of the article, to precede possession by the King of Etruria, the overt possession by him was notice to the world that the conditions on which it depended had been either fulfilled or had been waived. Finally, no particular Powers whose acknowledgment was to be procured are named in the article, and the existence of war between Great Britain and France at the time of the stipulation, is a proof that the British acknowledgment, the want of which is now alleged as a breach of the treaty, could never have been in its contemplation.

But the conduct of the Spanish Government, both toward the United States and France, is a complete answer to every possible objection to the treaty between them. That Government well knew the wish of the United States to acquire certain territories which it had ceded to France, and that they were in negotiation with France on the subject; yet the slightest hint was never given that France had no right to alienate, or even that an alienation to the United States would be disagreeable to Spain. On the contrary, the Minister of His Catholic Majesty, in an official note, bearing date May 4 last, gave information to the Minister of the United States at Madrid, that "the entire province of Louisiana, with the limits it had when held by France, was retroceded to that Power, and that the United States might address themselves to the French Government in order to negotiate the acquisition of the territories which would suit their interest." Here is at once a formal and irrevocable recognition of the right as well of France to convey, as of the United States to receive, the territory which is the subject of the treaty between them. More than this can not be required to silence, forever, the cavils of Spain at the titles of France, now vested in the United States: yet, for more than this, she may be referred to her own measures at New Orleans, preparatory to the delivery of possession to France; to the promulgation, under Spanish authority at that place, that Louisiana was retroceded, and to be delivered to France; and to the orders signed by His Catholic Majesty's own hand, now ready to be presented to the Government of Louisiana, for the delivery of the province to the person duly authorized by France to receive it.

In a word, the Spanish Government has interposed two objections only to the title conveyed to the United States by France. It is said, first, that the title in the United States is not good, because France was bound not to alienate. To this it is answered, that the Spanish Government itself referred the United States to France, as the Power capable, and the only Power capable, of conveying the territory in question. It is said, next, that the title in France herself was not good. To this, if the same answer is less decisive, the orders of the King of Spain for putting France into possession are an answer which admits of no reply.

The President has thought proper that this view of the subject should be transmitted to you; not doubting that you will make the proper use of it with the French Government, nor that that Government will feel the full force of its stipulated obligations to remove whatever difficulties Spain may interpose towards embarrassing a transaction, the complete fulfillment of which is as essential to the honor of France as it is important to the interests of both nations. In the meantime, we shall proceed in the arrangements for taking possession of the country ceded, as soon as possession shall be authorized; and it may be presumed, that the provisions depending on Congress will be sufficient to meet the discontents of Spain, in whatever form they may assume.

The United States have obtained, by just and honorable means, a clear title to a territory too valuable, in itself, and too important to their tranquillity and security, not to be effectually maintained. And they count on every positive concurrence, on the part of the French Government, which the occasion may demand from their friendship and their good faith.

The rightful limits of Louisiana are under investigation. It seems undeniable, from the present state of the evidence, that it extends eastwardly as far, at least, as the river Perdido; and there is little doubt that we shall make good both a western and northern extent highly satisfactory to us.

The considerations which led Mr. Monroe to decline his trip to Madrid, having the same weight with the President, the mission is suspended until other instructions shall be given, or until circumstances shall strongly invite negotiations at Madrid for completing the acquisition desired by the United States.

With great respect,

JAMES MADISON.

ROBERT R. LIVINGSTON, &c.

P. S., October 14.—Since the above was written, I have received a third note from the Marquis d'Yrujo in reply to my answer to his two preceding. A copy of it is herewith added. It requires no comment beyond what may be applicable in the above observations on his two first notes; being probably intended for little more than a proof of fidelity to his trust and of a zeal recommending him to the favor of his Sovereign.

It having been thought proper to communicate to M. Pichon, the French Chargé d'Affaires here, the tenor of the notes from the Marquis d'Yrujo, he has presented, in a note just received, a vindication of his Government, and its treaty with the United States, against the objections proceeding from the Spanish Government. A copy of this note is herewith inclosed.

The Marquis d'Yrujo to the Secretary of State.

PHILADELPHIA, *September 4, 1803.*

Through the medium of the Ambassador of the King my master, in Paris, it has come to His Royal knowledge that that Government has sold to that of the United States the Province of Louisiana, which His Majesty has retroceded to the French Republic. This information has occasioned to the King my master no small surprise, seeing that the French Government had contracted with His Majesty the most solemn engagements never to alienate the said province. In order to convince the Government of the United States of the nature of these engagements, I take the liberty here to insert a paragraph of a note presented on the 22d July, 1802, by M. de St. Cyr, Ambassador of the French Republic, at Madrid, to the Secretary of State of His Majesty, as follows:

"His Catholic Majesty has appeared to wish that France should engage not to sell nor alienate, in any manner, the property and the enjoyment of Louisiana. Its wish in this respect is perfectly conformable with the intentions of the Spanish Government; and its sole motive for entering therein was because it respected a possession which had constituted a part of the French territory. I am authorized to declare to you in the name of the First Consul that France will never alienate it."

The mere reading of the paragraph which precedes will convince you, as well as the President of the United States, that the sale of Louisiana, which France has lately made, is a manifest violation of the obligations contracted by her with His Catholic Majesty, and that France wants the powers to alienate the said province without the approbation of Spain, as is seen incontestably in the above-recited note of the Ambassador St. Cyr, authorized by his Government.

The King my master charges me to inform this Government as soon as possible of this important circumstance; and, in compliance with His Royal will, I hasten to acquaint you therewith, in order that it may as soon as possible come to the knowledge of the President of the United States. God preserve you many years.

M. DE CASA YRUJO.

JAMES MADISON, Esq.

From Marquis d'Yrujo to Mr. Madison.

VICINITY OF PHILADELPHIA. *September 27, 1803.*

SIR: On the 4th current I had the honor to intimate to you the extraordinary surprise with which the King my master had heard of the sale of Louisiana, made to the United States, in contravention of the most solemn assurances given in writing to His Majesty by the Ambassador of the French Republic near his person, and with the consent and approbation of the First Consul. The King my master charges me again to remind the American Government that the said French Ambassador entered, in the name of his Republic, into the positive engagement that France never would alienate Louisiana, and to observe to it that the sale of this province to the United States is founded in the violation of a promise so absolute that it ought to be respected; a promise, without which the King my master would, in no manner, have dispossessed himself of Louisiana. His Catholic Majesty entertains too good an opinion of the character of probity and good faith which the Government of the United States has known how to obtain so justly for itself, not to hope that it will suspend the ratification and effect of a treaty which rests on such a basis. There are other reasons no less powerful which come to the support of the decorum and respect which nations mutually owe each other. France acquired from the King my master the retrocession of Louisiana under obligations, whose entire fulfillment was absolutely necessary to give her the complete right over the said province; such was that of causing the King of Tuscany to be acknowledged by the Powers of Europe; but, until now, the French Government has not procured this acknowledgment promised and stipulated, either from the Court of London or from that of St. Petersburg. Under such circumstances it is evident that the treaty of sale entered into between France and the United States does not give to the latter any right to acquire and claim Louisiana, and that the principles of justice as well as sound policy ought to recommend it to their Government not to meddle with engagements as contrary in reality to her true interests as they would be to good faith, and to their good correspondence with Spain.

Such are the sentiments which the King my master has ordered me to communicate to the President of the United States; and, having done it through you, I conclude, assuring you of my respect and consideration towards your person, and of my wishes that our Lord may preserve your life, &c.

M. DE CASA YRUJO.

JAMES MADISON, Esq.

From Mr. Madison to the Marquis d'Yrujo.

OCTOBER 4, 1803.

SIR: I have duly received your two letters of the 4th and 27th ultimo, and have laid them before the President.

The repugnance manifested in these communications, on the part of His Catholic Majesty, to the cession of Louisiana lately made by the French Republic to the United States, was as little expected as the objections to the transaction can avail against its solidity.

The United States have given unquestionable proofs to the Spanish Government and nation of their justice, their friendship, and their desire to maintain the best neighborhood; and the President confides too much in the reciprocity of these sentiments, so repeatedly and so recently declared on the part of His Catholic Majesty, to have supposed that he would see with dissatisfaction a convenient acquisition by the United States of territories which were no longer to remain with Spain. With respect to the transaction itself, by which the United States have acquired Louisiana, it would be superfluous to say more in justification of its perfect validity than to refer to the official communication made by Mr. Cevallos to the Minister Plenipotentiary of the United States at Madrid, in a note dated on the 4th of May last. His words are: "*Por la retrocesion hecha a la Francia de la Luisiana, recobro esta Potencia dicha provincia con los limites con que lon tubo, y salvos los derechos adquiridos por otras Potencias. La de los Estados Unidos podra dirigirse al Gobierno Frances para negociar la adquisicion de territorios que convengan a su interes.*"*a* Here is an explicit and positive recognition of the right of the United States and France to enter into the transaction which has taken place.

To these observations, which I have been charged by the President to make to you, I have only to add, sir, that his high respect for His Catholic Majesty, and his desire to cherish and strengthen the friendly sentiments happily subsisting between the two nations, will induce him to cause such explanations and representations to be made through the Minister Plenipotentiary of the United States at Madrid as can not fail to reconcile His Catholic Majesty to an event so essentially connected with the respect which the United States owe to their character and their interest.

Be pleased, sir, to accept assurances of the high respect and consideration with which I have the honor to be, your most obedient, humble servant,

JAMES MADISON.

---

a Translation: "By the retrocession made to France of Louisiana, this Power has recovered the said province with the limits which it had, and saving the rights acquired by other Powers. The United States can address themselves to the French Government to negotiate the acquisition of territories which may suit their interest."

Mr. Madison to Mr. Monroe.

WASHINGTON, *Oct. 10, 1803.*

DEAR SIR,— Finding that Mr. Purveyance is within reach of a few lines, I add them to what he is already charged with, to observe that Yrujo has written another remonstrance against our acquisition of Louisiana, alleging as a further objection, that France, by not obtaining the stipulated acknowledgements of the King of Etruria from the Courts of Petersburg and London, had a defective title herself to the Cession. Nothing can be more absurd than these cavils on the part of Spain, unless it should be her using in support of them force against our taking possession. This she will scarlely attempt, if not backed by France, which we hope is impossible. I am writing on this subject to Livingston and Pinckney. I have already done so to Yrujo, giving him to understand that we shall not withhold any means that may be rendered necessary to secure our object. Pichon is perfectly well disposed, is offended with the Spanish Minister, and, if left under the orders he now has, will co-operate zealously, with an honest view to the honor and obligations of his own Country. On our part, I trust every thing that the crisis demands will be done, and that we shall speedily be in possession of the valuable object which the Treaty with France has gained for us. Baring is here, but having not yet called on me I have had no opportunity of paying him civilities, or obtaining explanations from him.   * * *

Marquis d'Yrujo to the Secretary of State.

BALTIMORE, *October 12, 1803.*

SIR: I have received your letter of the 4th current in reply to those which I had the honor to write to you on the 4th and 27th of last month; and as, without entering into the examination of the powerful reasons which, in the name of the King my master, I unfolded therein, against the sale of Louisiana, you refer generally to the explanations which, as you inform me, the Minister of the United States near His Majesty is to make at Madrid. I shall at present confine my observations to that which you are pleased to make to me, founded upon certain expressions which you cite to me from an official letter of the Secretary of State, of the King my master, to the above-mentioned American Minister in Spain. The expressions are the following:

"By the retrocession made to France of Louisiana, this Power has recovered the said province, with the limits which it had, and saving the rights acquired by other Powers. The United Stated can address themselves to the French Government to negotiate the acquisition of territory which may suit their interests."

These expressions, which you consider as an explicit and positive acknowledgment of the right of the United States and France to enter into the engagements which they afterwards did, do not, in my opinion, weaken in any manner the foundation and the force of the representations which I had the honor to make to you against the sale of Louisiana.

There is an expression, among those you cite, which will suffice to refute the inference which you draw from them, and it is that of saving the rights acquired by other Powers. Although the general form of this expression gives, in other respects, much latitude to its true meaning, it is indubitable that Spain having made the retrocession of Louisiana, to France, under certain conditions and modifications, Spain has the indubitable right to claim their execution. Of this nature was the stipulation, that France should not sell or alienate Louisiana in any manner whatever, and likewise the solemn and positive accession and declaration of the French Government adhering to the wishes of Spain; consequently this expression destroys the possibility that, according to existing circumstances, the French Government should possess the right of selling the said province, or that of the United States of buying it.

There is another consideration still stronger, and which is not at all subject to the interpretation of equivocal expressions. It is evident that the engagement entered into by France with Spain not to alienate Louisiana in any manner, is much older in date than the official letter of Mr. Cevallos, whose expressions you are pleased to cite to me. In that letter those which you have scored, *that the United States can address themselves to the French Government to negotiate the acquisition of the territory which may suit their interests*, neither signify nor can signify anything but a deference towards France, whose Government alone is now concerned to give a decisive answer to the requests of the United States, an answer analogous and conformable to the nature of the previous engagements which had been entered into with Spain. The repugnance of the Spanish Government may likewise be recognized to give to that of the United States a necessary negative at a time when it found itself united with them by bands of the most sincere friendship.

Other interpretations of equal force may be derived from the obvious meaning of the expressions of the official letter of the Secretary of State of His Majesty mentioned by you; but as those which I have just made are, in my opinion, conclusive, I abstain from entering upon others in detail, and I take the liberty to call to them the attention, as well of yourself as of the President of the United States, in order that you may be more and more convinced of the reason and justice with which the King my master objects to the ratification of a treaty founded upon a manifest violation of the most solemn engagements entered into by France. I avail myself, with pleasure, of this occasion to reiterate to you my wishes to serve you and that our Lord would preserve your life, &c.

M. DE CASA YRUJO.

JAMES MADISON, Esq.

James Madison, Secretary of State, to Charles Pinckney, Minister to Spain.

DEPARTMENT OF STATE, *October 12, 1803.*

Since my last of July 29th, I have received your several letters of April 12th and 20th, May 2d and 4th, June 12th, and July 18th.

Mr. Monroe has already informed you of his having proceeded to London, and of his intention not to repair to Madrid for the present. He will have since received instructions, given on a contrary supposition; but it is probable he will wait where he is for the determination of the President, on the reasons which kept him from proceeding to Madrid. I have just informed him that the President approves the course he has taken, so that he is not to be expected to join you at Madrid, until he shall be so instructed, or until a change of circumstances shall, in his view, clearly invite him to do so. My last letter to you, having provided for the case of Mr. Monroe's postponing this trip, I need not repeat the instructions and observations then made to you. I shall only add that it is more proper now than ever that you should not be in haste, without the concurrence of your colleague, to revive the negotiation jointly committed to you.

Among the reasons which weighed with the President, as well as with Mr. Monroe, against attempting, at present, to procure from the Spanish Government the residuum of territory desired by the United States, is the ill-humor shown by that Government at the acquisition already made by them from France; and of which the language held to you by Mr. Cevallos, as communicated in your letter of ——, is a sufficient proof. A still fuller proof of the same fact is contained in three letters lately received from the Spanish Minister here; copies of which, with the answer to my two first, are herewith enclosed. I enclose also a copy of a letter written on the occasion to Mr. Livingston, which was rendered more proper by the probability, as well as by information from Paris, that efforts would be used by Spain to draw the French Government into her views of frustrating the cession of Louisiana to the United States.

In these documents you will find the remarks by which the objections made by the Spanish Government to the Treaty of Cession between the United States and France are to be combatted. The President thinks it proper, that they should, without delay, be conveyed to the Spanish Government, either by note from you or in conversation, as you may deem most expedient; and in a form and style best uniting the advantages of making that Government sensible of the absolute determination of the United States to maintain their right with the propriety of avoiding undignified menace and unnecessary irritation.

The conduct of Spain, on this occasion, is such as was, in several views, little to be expected, and as is not readily explained. If her object be to extort Louisiana from France, as well as to prevent its transfer to the United States, it would seem that she must be emboldened by an understanding with some other very powerful quarter of Europe. If she hopes to prevail on France to break her engagement with the United States, and voluntarily restore Louisiana to herself, why has she so absurdly blended with the project the offensive communication of the perfidy which she charges on the First Consul? If it be her aim to prevent the execution of the treaty between the United States and France, in order to have for her neighbor the latter instead of the United States, it is not difficult to show that she mistakes the lesser for the greater danger against which she wishes to provide. Admitting, as she may possibly suppose, that Louisiana, as a French Colony, would be less able, as well as less disposed, than the United States, to encroach on her southern possessions, and that it would be too much occupied with its own safety against the United States to turn its force on the other side against her possessions, still it is obvious, in the first place, that in proportion to the want of power in the French the colony would be safe for Spain; compared with the power of the United States, the colony would be insufficient as a barrier against the United States; and, in the next place, that the very security which she provides would itself be a source of the greatest of all the dangers she has to apprehend.

The collisions between the United States and the French would lead to a contest, in which Great Britain would naturally join the former, and in which Spain would, of course, be on the side of the latter; and what becomes of Louisiana and the Spanish possessions beyond it, in a contest between the Powers so marshaled? An easy and certain victim to the fleets of Great Britain and the land armies of this country. A combination of these forces was always, and justly, dreaded by both Spain and France. It was the danger which led both into our Revolutionary war, and much inconsistency and weakness is chargeable on the projects of either which tend to reunite, for the purposes of war, the power which has been divided. France, returning to her original policy, has wisely, by her late treaty with the United States, obviated a danger which could not have been very remote. Spain will be equally wise in following the example; and, by acquiescing in an arrangement which guards against an early danger of controversy between the United States, first with France, and then with herself, and removes to a distant day the approximation of the American and Spanish settlements, provides in the best possible manner for the security of the latter, and for a lasting harmony with the United States. What is it that Spain dreads? She dreads, it is presumed, the growing power of this country, and the direction of it against her possessions within its reach. Can she annihilate this power? No. Can she sensibly retard its growth? No. Does not common prudence then, advise her to conciliate, by every proof of friendship and confidence, the good will of a nation whose power is formidable to her; instead of yielding to the impulses of jealousy and adopting obnoxious precautions which can have no other effect than to bring on, prematurely, the whole weight of the calamity which she fears? Reflections such as these may, perhaps, enter with some advantage into your communications with the Spanish Government; and, as far as they may be invited by favorable occasions, you will make that use of them.

Perhaps, after all this interposition of Spain, it may be intended merely to embarrass a measure which she does not hope to defeat, in order to obtain from France, or the United States, or both, concessions of some sort or other as the price of her acquiescence. As yet no indication is given that a resistance, by force, to the execution of the treaty is prepared or meditated. And if it should, the provisions depending on Congress, whose session will commence in two days, will, it may be presumed, be effectually adapted to such an event.

With sentiments, &c.,   JAMES MADISON.
CHARLES PINCKNEY, Esq.

Mr. Pichon to the Secretary of State.

GEORGETOWN, *21 Vendemiaire, 12th year (October 14, 1803).*

The undersigned, to whom the Secretary of State has been pleased to communicate the proceedings of the Minister of His Catholic Majesty to the United States, in relation to the treaty by which the French Republic has ceded Louisiana to the United States, thinks that he owes it to his own Government as well as to the American Government, to present to Mr. Madison the observations of which those proceedings, as far as they attack the rights and even the dignity of the French Government, have appeared to him susceptible.

The Court of Madrid, according to the notes of its Minister, considers the cession made by France to the United States as irregular and invalid: 1st. Because France had renounced the right of alienating the territories in question: 2d. Because the Treaty of St. Ildefonso, by which Spain retroceded those territories to France, has not been fully executed with respect to the acknowledgment of the King of Etruria, an acknowledgment which was one of the conditions of the retrocession to be fulfilled by France.

On the first point, the undersigned will observe that the Treaty of

St. Ildefonso retrocedes Louisiana in full sovereignty, and without any limitation as to the future domain of France. To operate a limitation so essential as is that to which the Court of Madrid appeals, nothing less would have been necessary, according to the nature of contracts in general and of treaties in particular, than a stipulation to this effect inserted in the treaty itself. A promise made fifteen months after the signature of this pact, and which might, on one side, have been yielded to the solicitations of one of the contracting parties, and, on the other, dictated by dispositions which might then exist in the other party, but which ulterior circumstances might have changed; such a promise can not create in favor of Spain a right sufficient to enable her to charge with invalidity the transactions which have contravened it. The contrary pretension would certainly confound all the principles relative to the nature of obligations, and would destroy the solemnity of treaties. These general reasonings would receive a new force from the circumstances which are peculiar to different nations in relation to the subject of pacts; but the undersigned will not enter into the examination of these circumstances, under the persuasion that general principles sufficiently repel the pretensions of the Court of Madrid.

On the second point, the objections of that Court do not appear to the undersigned to be better founded. It is known that the King of Etruria was placed on the throne since the Treaty of St. Ildefonso. We have a right to suppose that His Catholic Majesty was satisfied from that period with the measures and efforts employed by France, to cause the title of this Prince to be acknowledged by the other nations. It is at least what might be concluded from facts within the knowledge of all the world. In the Treaty of Amiens, concluded on the 27th of March, 1802, Great Britain did not acknowledge the King of Etruria. Notwithstanding the silence of the Court of London, on so solemn an occasion, that of Madrid ordered, in the month of October following, the delivery of the Colony to France, as is proved by the Royal cedula, which the undersigned has received and exhibited to Mr. Madison; a cedula, which, as all the world knows, was long ago forwarded to the Captain-General of Louisiana, who sent the Marquis of Casa Calvo to New Orleans to superintend its execution.

To these conclusive observations, the undersigned will add, that the Court of Madrid might have been informed in the course of the month of February last, by its Minister to the United States, that the American Government was sending to Paris a Minister Extraordinary, in order to negotiate with the French Government the acquisition of New Orleans. If the Court of Madrid had seen, in the object of this mission, an injury offered to its rights, what prevented it, after being thus early apprized, from informing thereof the Minister of the United States at Paris, and the French Government, and from interposing, before the conclusion of the treaty, its intervention in a form adapted to suspend it? It does not appear that that Court has taken, at Paris, any steps of this nature. To suppose it, would be inconsistent with the instructions which the undersigned has received from his Government, to accelerate as much as is in his power the execution of the treaty concluded on the 30th of April last, between the French Republic and the United States.

The undersigned therefore hopes, that the American Government will not see in the proceedings of the Court of Madrid, in order to obstruct the execution of this treaty, anything but specious reasonings, and will proceed to its execution with the same earnestness which the French Government has employed on its part. The undersigned has received the necessary orders to exchange the ratifications, and to effect the taking of possession of Louisiana by France, and its transfer to the United States. He does not presume that the Court of Madrid would wish to oppose the execution of the first orders. This supposition would be as contrary to its loyalty as to the dignity of the French Government. In any event, as soon as the ratifications are exchanged, the undersigned will proceed without delay, in concert with the Commissary appointed for that purpose by the First Consul, to the delivery of the colony to the persons whom the President of the United States shall appoint to take possession of it.

The undersigned has the honor to request Mr. Madison to submit to the President of the United States the contents of this note, which is intended to prevent the imputations cast by the Minister of Spain against the French Government, from remaining without reply. The undersigned prays, at the same time, Mr. Madison to receive the assurance of his respect and of his high consideration.

L. A. PICHON.

Message from the President of the United States, October 17, 1803.

To the Senate and House of Representatives of the United States:

In calling you together, fellow-citizens, at an earlier day than was contemplated by the act of the last session of Congress, I have not been insensible to the personal inconveniences necessarily resulting from an unexpected change in your arrangements. But matters of great public concernment have rendered this call necessary, and the interest you feel in these will supersede in your minds all private considerations.

Congress witnessed, at their last session, the extraordinary agitation produced in the public mind by the suspension of our right of deposit at the port of New Orleans, no assignment of another place having been made according to treaty. They were sensible that the continuance of that privation would be more injurious to our nation than any consequences that could flow from any mode of redress; but, reposing just confidence in the good faith of the Government whose officer had committed the wrong, friendly and reasonable representations were resorted to, and the right of deposit was restored.

Previous, however, to this period we had not been unaware of the danger to which our peace would be perpetually exposed whilst so important a key to the commerce of the Western country remained under a foreign power. Difficulties too were presenting themselves as to the navigation of other streams, which arising in our territories, pass through those adjacent. Propositions had therefore been authorized for obtaining on fair conditions the sovereignty of New Orleans, and of other possessions in that quarter, interesting to our quiet, to such extent as was deemed practicable; and the provisional appropriation of two million dollars, to be applied and accounted for by the President of the United States, intended as part of the price, was considered as conveying the sanction of Congress to the acquisition proposed. The enlightened Government of France saw, with just discernment, the importance to both nations of such liberal arrangements as might best and permanently promote the peace, interests and friendship of both; and the property and sovereignty of all Louisiana, which had been restored to them, has, on certain conditions, been transferred to the United States, by instruments bearing date the 30th of April last. When these shall have received the constitutional sanction of the Senate, they will, without delay, be communicated to the Representatives for the exercise of their functions, as to those conditions which are within the powers vested by the Constitution in Congress. Whilst the property and sovereignty of the Mississippi and its waters secure an independent outlet for the produce of the Western States, and an uncontrolled navigation through their whole course, free from collision with other Powers, and the dangers to our peace from that source, the fertility of the country, its climate and extent, promise, in due season, important aids to our Treasury, an ample provision for our posterity, and a wide spread for the blessings of freedom and equal laws.

With the wisdom of Congress it will rest to take those ulterior measures which may be necessary for the immediate occupation and temporary government of the country; for its incorporation into our union; for rendering the change of government a blessing to our newly adopted brethren; for securing to them the rights of conscience and of property; for confirming to the Indian inhabitants their occupancy and self-government, establish friendly and commercial relations with them, and for ascertaining the geography of the country acquired. Such materials for your information relative to its affairs in general, as the short space of time has permitted me to collect, will be laid before you when the subject shall be in a state for your consideration.

* * * * * * *

OCTOBER 17, 1803.
TH. JEFFERSON.

Treaty between the United States of America and the French Republic.

The President of the United States of America, and the First Consul of the French Republic, in the name of the French people, desiring to remove all source of misunderstanding, relative to objects of discussion mentioned in the second and fifth articles of the Convention of (the 8th Vendemiaire, an 9,) September 30, 1800, relative to the rights claimed by the United States, in virtue of the treaty concluded at Madrid, the 27th October, 1795, between His Catholic Majesty and the said United States, and willing to strengthen the union and friendship, which at the time of the said Convention was happily reestablished between the two nations, have respectively named their Plenipotentiaries, to-wit: The President of the United States of America, by and with the advice and consent of the Senate of the said States, Robert R. Livingston, Minister Plenipotentiary of the United States, and James Monroe, Minister Plenipotentiary and Envoy Extraordinary of the said States, near the Government of the French Republic; and the First Consul, in the name of the French people, the French citizen Barbe Marbois, Minister of the Public Treasury, who, after having respectively exchanged their full powers, have agreed to the following articles:

ART. 1. Whereas, by the article the third of the Treaty concluded at St. Ildefonso, (the 9th Vendemiaire, an 9,) October 1, 1800, between the First Consul of the French Republic and His Catholic Majesty, it was agreed as follows: His Catholic Majesty promises and engages on his part to cede to the French Republic, six months after the full and entire execution of the conditions and stipulations herein, relative to His Royal Highness the Duke of Parma, the Colony or Province of Louisiana, with the same extent that it now has in the hands of Spain, and that it had when France possessed it; and such as it should be after the treaties subsequently entered into between Spain and other States: And whereas, in pursuance of the Treaty, particularly of the third article, the French Republic has an incontestible title to the domain and to the possession of the said territory, the First Consul of the French Republic, desiring to give to the United States a strong proof of friendship, doth hereby cede to the said United States, in the name of the French Republic, for ever and in full sovereignty, the said territory, with all its rights and appurtenances, as fully and in the same manner as they might have been acquired by the French Republic, in value of the above mentioned treaty, concluded with His Catholic Majesty.

ART. 2. In the cession made by the preceding article, are included the adjacent islands belonging to Louisiana, all public lots and squares, vacant lands, and all public buildings, fortifications, barracks, and other edifices, which are not private property. The archives, papers, and documents, relative to the domain and sovereignty of Louisana and its dependencies, will be left in the possession of the Commissaries of the United States, and copies will be afterwards given in due form to the magistrates and municipal officers, of such of the said papers and documents as may be necessary to them.

ART. 3. The inhabitants of the ceded territory shall be incorporated in the Union of the United States, and admitted as soon as possible, according to the principles of the Federal Constitution, to the enjoyment of all the rights, advantages, and immunities, of citizens of the United States; and, in the meantime, they shall be maintained and protected in the free enjoyment of their liberty, property, and the religion which they profess.*

ART. 4. There shall be sent by the Government of France a Commissary to Louisana, to the end that he do every act necessary, as well to receive from the officers of His Catholic Majesty the said country and its dependencies in the name of the French Republic, if it has not been already done, as to transmit it, in the name of the French Republic, to the Commissary or agent of the United States.

ART. 5. Immediately after the ratification of the present treaty by the President of the United States, and in case that of the First Consul shall have been previously obtained, the Commissary of the French Republic shall remit all the military posts of New Orleans, and other parts of the ceded territory, to the Commissary or Commissaries named by the President to take possession; the troops, whether of France or Spain, who may be there, shall cease to occupy any military post from the time of taking possession, and shall be embarked as soon as possible in the course of three months after the ratification of this treaty.

ART. 6. The United States promise to execute such treaties and articles as may have been agreed between Spain and the tribes and nations of Indians, until, by mutual consent of the United States and the said tribes or nations, other suitable articles shall have been agreed upon.

ART. 7. As it is reciprocally advantageous to the commerce of

---

* Said to have been drawn by Napoleon himself.

France and the United States, to encourage the communication of both nations, for a limited time, in the country ceded by the present treaty, until general arrangements relative to the commerce of both nations may be agreed on, it has been agreed between the contracting parties, that the French ships coming directly from France or any of her Colonies, loaded only with the produce or manufactures of France or her said Colonies, and the ships of Spain coming directly from Spain or any of her Colonies, loaded only with the produce or manufactures of Spain or her Colonies, shall be admitted during the space of twelve years in the port of New Orleans, and in all other legal ports of entry within the ceded territory, in the same manner as the ships of the United States coming directly from France or Spain, or any of their Colonies, without being subject to any other or greater duty on the merchandise, or other or greater tonnage than those paid by the citizens of the United States.

During the space of time above mentioned, no other nation shall have a right to the same privileges in the ports of the ceded territory. The twelve years shall commence three months after the exchange of ratifications, if it shall take place in France, or three months after it shall have been notified at Paris to the French Government, if it shall take place in the United States; it is, however, well understood, that the object of the above article is to favor the manufactures, commerce, freight, and navigation of France and Spain, so far as relates to the importations that the French and Spanish shall make into the said ports of the United States, without in any sort affecting the regulations that the United States may make concerning the exportation of the produce and merchandise of the United States, or any right they may have to make such regulations.

ART. 8. In future and forever, after the expiration of the twelve years, the ships of France shall be treated upon the footing of the most favored nations in the ports above-mentioned.

ART. 9. The particular convention signed this day by the respective Ministers, having for its object to provide the payment of debts due to the citizens of the United States by the French Republic, prior to the 30th of September, 1800, (8th Vendemiaire, an 9,) is approved, and to have its execution in the same manner as if it had been inserted in the present treaty; and it shall be ratified in the same form and in the same time, so that the one shall not be ratified distinct from the other. Another particular convention, signed at the same date as the present treaty, relative to a definitive rule between the contracting parties is, in the like manner, approved, and will be ratified in the same form and in the same time, and jointly.

ART. 10. The present treaty shall be ratified in good and due form, and the ratification shall be exchanged in the space of six months after the date of the signature by the Ministers Plenipotentiary, or sooner if possible.

In faith whereof, the respective Plenipotentiaries have signed these articles in the French and English languages, declaring, nevertheless, that the present treaty was originally agreed to in the French language, and have thereunto put their seals.

Done at Paris, the 10th day of Floreal, in the 11th year of the French Republic, and the 30th April, 1803.

R. R. LIVINGSTON,
JAMES MONROE,
BARBE MARBOIS.

A Convention between the United States of America and the French Republic.

The President of the United States of America, and the First Consul of the French Republic, in the name of the French people, in consequence of the Treaty of Cession of Louisiana, which has been signed this day, wishing to regulate definitively everything which has relation to the said cession, have authorized, to this effect, the Plenipotentiaries, that is to say: the President of the United States has, by and with the advice and consent of the Senate of the said States, nominated for their Plenipotentiaries, Robert R. Livingston, Minister Plenipotentiary of the United States, and James Monroe, Minister Plenipotentiary and Envoy Extraordinary of the said United States, near the Government of the French Republic; and the First Consul of the French Republic, in the name of the French people, has named, as Plenipotentiary of the said Republic, the French citizen Barbe Marbois, who, in virtue of their full powers, which have been exchanged this day, have agreed to the following articles.

ART. 1. The Government of the United States engages to pay to the French Government, in the manner specified in the following articles, the sum of sixty millions of francs, independent of the sum which shall be fixed by any other convention for the payment of the debts due by France to citizens of the United States.

ART. 2. For the payment of the sum of sixty millions of francs, mentioned in the preceding article, the United States shall create a stock of eleven million two hundred and fifty thousand dollars, bearing an interest of six per cent. per annum, payable, half yearly, in London, Amsterdam, or Paris, amounting, by the half year to three hundred and thirty-seven thousand five hundred dollars, according to the proportions which shall be determined by the French Government, to be paid at either place: the principal of the said stock to be reimbursed at the

Treasury of the United States, in annual payments of not less than three millions of dollars each; of which the first payment shall commence fifteen years after the date of the exchange of ratifications: this stock shall be transferred to the Government of France, or to such person or persons as shall be authorized to receive it, in three months, at most, after the exchange of the ratifications of this treaty, and after Louisiana shall be taken possession of in the name of the Government of the United States.

It is further agreed that, if the French Government should be desirous of disposing of the said stock, to receive the capital in Europe at shorter terms, that its measures, for that purpose, shall be taken so as to favor, in the greatest degree possible, the credit of the United States, and to raise to the highest price the said stock.

ART. 3. It is agreed that the dollar of the United States, specified in the present convention, shall be fixed at five francs 3333–10000ths or five livres eight sous tournois.

The present convention shall be ratified in good and true form, and the ratifications shall be exchanged in the space of six months, to date from this day, or sooner if possible.

In faith of which, the respective Plenipotentiaries have signed the above articles, both in the French and English languages, declaring, nevertheless, that the present treaty has been originally agreed on and written in the French language, to which they have hereunto affixed their seals.

Done at Paris, the 10th day of Floreal, eleventh year of the French Republic, (30th April, 1803.)

ROBERT R. LIVINGSTON.
JAMES MONROE,
BARBE MABBOIS.

Convention between the French Republic and the United States.

The President of the United States of America, and the First Consul of the French Republic, in the name of the French people, having, by a treaty of this date, terminated all difficulties relative to Louisiana, and established on a solid foundation the friendship which unites the two nations, and being desirous, in compliance with the second and fifth articles of the convention of the 8th Vendemiaire, 9th year of the French Republic, (30th Sept. 1800,) to secure the payment of the sum due by France to the citizens of the United States, have respectively, nominated as Plenipotentiaries, that is to say: the President of the United States of America, by and with the advice and consent of their Senate, Robert R. Livingston, Minister Plenipotentiary, and James

Monroe, Minister Plenipotentiary and Envoy Extraordinary of the said States, near the Government of the French Republic, and the First Consul, in the name of the French people, the French citizen Barbe Marbois, Minister of the Public Treasury, who, after having exchanged their full powers, have agreed to the following articles:

ART. 1. The debts due by France to citizens of the United States, contracted before the 8th of Vendemiaire, 9th year of the French Republic, (30th September, 1800,) shall be paid according to the following regulations, with interest at six per cent., to commence from the periods when the accounts and vouchers were presented to the French Government.

ART. 2. The debts provided for by the preceding article are those whose result is comprised in the conjectural note annexed to the present convention, and which, with interest, cannot exceed the sum of twenty millions of francs. The claims comprised in the said note, which fall within the exceptions of the following articles, shall not be admitted to the benefit of this provision.

ART. 3. The principal and interest of the said debts shall be discharged by the United States by orders drawn by their Ministers Plenipotentiary on their Treasury; these orders shall be payable sixty days after the exchange of ratifications of the treaty and the conventions signed this day, and after possession shall be given of Louisiana by the Commissaries of France to those of the United States.

ART. 4. It is expressly agreed that the preceding articles shall comprehend no debts but such as are due to citizens of the United States who have been, and are yet, creditors of France for supplies, for embargoes, and prizes made at sea, in which the appeal has been properly lodged, within the time mentioned in the said convention of the 8th Vendemiaire, 9th year, (30th September, 1800.)

ART. 5. The preceding articles shall apply only, first, to capture of which the council of prizes shall have ordered restitution, it being well understood that the claimant cannot have recourse to the United States, otherwise than he might have had to the Government of the French Republic, and only in case of the insufficiency of the captors; secondly, the debts mentioned in the said fifth article of the convention contracted before the 8th Vendemiaire, an 9, (30th September, 1800,) the payment of which has been heretofore claimed of the actual Government of France, and for which the creditors have a right to the protection of the United States. The said fifth article does not comprehend prizes whose condemnation has been or shall be confirmed. It is the express intention of the contracting parties not to extend the benefit of the present convention to reclamations of American citizens, who shall have established houses of commerce in France, England, or other countries than the United States, in partnership with foreigners, and who, by that reason, and the nature of their commerce, ought to be regarded as domiciliated in the places where such houses exist. All agreements and bargains concerning merchandise, which shall not be the property of American citizens, are equally excepted from the benefit of the said convention; saving, however, to such persons their claims in like manner as if this treaty had not been made.

ART. 6. And that the different questions which may arise under the preceding articles may be fairly investigated, the Ministers Plenipotentiary of the United States shall name three persons, who shall act from the present, and provisionally, and who shall have full power to examine, without removing the documents, all the accounts of the different claims already liquidated by the bureau established for this purpose by the French Republic, and to ascertain whether they belong to the classes designated by the present convention, and the principles established in it; or if they are not in one of its exceptions, and on their certificate declaring that the debt is due to an American citizen, or his representative, and that it existed before the 8th Vendemiaire, ninth year, (30th September, 1800,) the debtor shall be entitled to an order on the Treasury of the United States, in the manner prescribed by the third article.

ART. 7. The same agents shall likewise have power, without removing the documents, to examine the claims which are prepared for verification, and to certify those which ought to be admitted by uniting the necessary qualifications, and not being comprised in the exceptions contained in the present convention.

ART. 8. The same agents shall likewise examine the claims which are not prepared for liquidation, and certify in writing those which, in their judgments, ought to be admitted to liquidation.

ART. 9. In proportion as the debts mentioned in these articles shall be admitted, they shall be discharged with interest at six per cent. by the Treasury of the United States.

ART. 10. And that no debt, which shall not have the qualifications above-mentioned, and that no unjust or exorbitant demand may be admitted, the commercial agent of the United States at Paris, or such other agent as the Minister Plenipotentiary of the United States shall think proper to nominate, shall assist at the operations of the bureau, and co-operate in the examination of the claims; and if this agent shall be of opinion that any debt is not completely proved, or if he shall judge that it is not comprised in the principles of the fifth article above-mentioned, and if, notwithstanding his opinion, the bureau established by the French Government should think that it ought to be liquidated, he shall transmit his observations to the board established by the United States, who, without removing documents, shall make a complete examination of the debt, and vouchers which support it, and report the result to the Minister of the United States. The Minister of the United States shall transmit his observations, in all such cases, to the Minister of the Treasury of the French Republic, on whose report the French Government shall decide definitively in every case.

The rejection of any claim shall have no other effect than to exempt the United States from the payment of it; the French Government reserving to itself the right to decide definitely on such claims, so far as it concerns itself.

ART. 11. Every necessary decision shall be made in the course of a year, to commence from the exchange of ratifications, and no reclamation shall be admitted afterwards.

ART. 12. In case of claims for debts contracted by the Government of France with citizens of the United States since the 8th Vendemiaire, 9th year, (September 30, 1800,) not being comprised in this convention, may be pursued, and the payment demanded in the same manner as if it had not been made.

ART. 13. The present convention shall be ratified in good and due form, and the ratifications shall be exchanged in six months from the date of the signature of the Ministers Plenipotentiary, or sooner, if possible.

In faith of which, the respective Ministers Plenipotentiary have signed the above articles, both in the French and English languages, declaring, nevertheless, that the present treaty has been originally agreed on and written in the French language, to which they have hereunto affixed their seals.

Done at Paris, the 10th day of Floreal, the 11th year of the French Republic, (30th of April, 1803.)

ROBT. R. LIVINGSTON,
JAMES MONROE,
BARBE MARBOIS.

[Extract.]

Mr. Madison to Mr. Monroe.

DEPARTMENT OF STATE, *October 24, 1803.*

SIR: I have received from you letters of the following dates, written after your arrival in London, viz: the 19th, 20th, and 26th of July, and the 11th and 15th of August.

I have the pleasure to inform you that the treaty for Louisiana has been ratified in form, and is now before both Houses for the legislative provisions necessary with respect to the stock, to taking possession, and to governing the country. There is no doubt that they will be made by very large majorities.

It will be agreeable to you to know that the ratifications were exchanged by M. Pichon and myself, unshackled by any condition or modification whatever. The note from me to him, with his reply, of which copies are enclosed, will show the turn and issue of our consultations on that point.

The information from Paris, enclosed in your letter of the 15th of August, had been previously received here from the same source, and was followed by full proof of the discontent of Spain at the transfer of Louisiana to the United States, in a formal protest against it from the Spanish Minister here, in pursuance of orders from his Government. You will find herewith copies of his correspondence with this Department, and of my letters to Mr. Livingston and Mr. Pinckney, and of M. Pichon's to me on this subject; all of which were included in the communications to the Senate. These documents will put you in possession of all that has passed, as well as of the present posture of the business. It remains to be seen how far Spain will persist in her remonstrances, and how far she will add to them resistance by force. Should the latter course be taken, it can lead to nothing but a substitution of a forcible for a peaceable possession. Having now a clear and honest title, acquired in a mode pointed out by Spain herself, it will, without doubt, be maintained with a decision becoming our national character, and required by the importance of the object.

I have the honor, &c.,

JAMES MADISON.

JAMES MONROE, Esq.

President Jefferson to M. Dupont De Nemours.

WASHINGTON, *November 1, 1803.*

MY DEAR SIR,—Your favors of April the 6th, and June the 27th, were duly received, and with the welcome which everything brings from you. The treaty which has so happily sealed the friendship of our two countries, has been received here with general acclamation. Some inflexible federalists have still ventured to brave the public opinion. It will fix their character with the world and with posterity, who, not descending to the other points of difference between us, will judge them by this fact, so palpable as to speak for itself in all times and places. For myself and my country, I thank you for the aids you have given in it; and I congratulate you on having lived to give those aids in a transaction replete with blessings to unborn millions of men, and which will mark the face of a portion on the globe so extensive as that which now composes the United States of America. It is true that at this moment a little cloud hovers in the horizon. The government of Spain has protested against the right of France to transfer;

and it is possible she may refuse possession, and that this may bring on acts of force. But against such neighbors as France there, and the United States here, what she can expect from so gross a compound of folly and false faith, is not to be sought in the book of wisdom. She is afraid of her enemies in Mexico; but not more than we are. Our policy will be, to form New Orleans, and the country on both sides of it on the Gulf of Mexico, into a State; and, as to all above that, to transplant our Indians into it, constituting them a Marechaussee to prevent emigrants crossing the river, until we shall have filled up all the vacant country on this side. This will secure both Spain and us as to the mines of Mexico, for half a century, and we may safely trust the provisions for that time to the men who shall live in it. *   *   *

President Jefferson to Mr. Livingston.

WASHINGTON, *November 4, 1803.*

DEAR SIR,—A report reaches us this day from Baltimore, (on probable, but not certain grounds,) that Mr. Jerome Bonaparte, brother of the First Consul, was yesterday married to Miss Patterson, of that city. The effect of this measure on the mind of the First Consul, is not for me to suppose; but as it might occur to him *prima facie*, that the Executive of the United States ought to have prevented it, I have thought it advisable to mention the subject to you, that, if necessary, you may by explanations set that idea to rights. You know that by our laws, all persons are free to enter into marriage, if of twenty-one years of age, no one having a power to restrain it, not even their parents; and that under that age, no one can prevent it but the parent or guardian. The lady is under age, and the parents, placed between her affections, which were strongly fixed, and the considerations opposing the measure, yielded with pain and anxiety to the former. Mr. Patterson is the President of the Bank of Baltimore, the wealthiest man in Maryland, perhaps in the United States, except Mr. Carroll; a man of great virtue and respectability; the mother is the sister of the lady of General Samuel Smith; and, consequently, the station of the family in society is with the first in the United States. These circumstances fix rank in a country where there are no hereditary titles.

Your treaty has obtained nearly a general approbation. The federalists spoke and voted against it, but they are now so reduced in their numbers as to be nothing. The question on its ratification in the Senate was decided by twenty-four against seven, which were ten more than enough. The vote in the House of Representatives for making provision for its execution was carried by eighty-nine against twenty-three, which was a majority of sixty-six, and the necessary bills are going through the Houses by greater majorities. Mr. Pichon, according to instructions from his government, proposed to have added to the ratification a protestation against any failure in time or other circumstances of execution, on our part. He was told, that in that case we should annex a counter protestation, which would leave the thing exactly where it was. That this transaction had been conducted, from the commencement of the negociation to this stage of it, with a frankness and sincerity honorable to both nations, and comfortable to the heart of an honest man to review; that to annex to this last chapter of the transaction such an evidence of mutual distrust, was to change its aspect dishonorably for us both, and contrary to truth as to us; for that we had not the smallest doubt that France would punctually execute its part; and I assured Mr. Pichon that I had more confidence in the word of the First Consul than in all the parchment we could sign. He saw that we had ratified the treaty; that both branches had passed, by great majorities, one of the bills for execution, and would soon pass the other two; that no circumstances remained that could leave a doubt of our punctual performance; and like an able and an honest minister, (which he is the highest degree,) he undertook to do what he knew his employers would do themselves, were they here spectators of all the existing circumstances, and exchanged the ratifications purely and simply: so that this instrument goes to the world as an evidence of the candor and confidence of the nations in each other, which will have the best effects. This was the more justifiable, as Mr. Pichon knew that Spain had entered with us a protestation against our ratification of the treaty, grounded, first, on the assertion that the First Consul had not executed the conditions of the treaties of cession; and, secondly, that he had broken a solemn promise not to alienate the country to any nation. We answered, that these were private questions between France and Spain, which they must settle together; that we derived our title from the First Consul, and did not doubt his guarantee of it; and we, four days ago, sent off orders to the Governor of the Mississippi territory and General Wilkinson to move down with the troops at hand to New Orleans, to receive the possession from Mr. Laussat. If he is heartily disposed to carry the order of the Consul into execution, he can probably command a volunteer force at New Orleans, and will have the aid of ours also, if he desires it, to take the possession, and deliver it to us. If he is not so disposed, we shall take the possession, and it will rest with the government of France, by adopting the act as their own, and obtaining the confirmation of Spain, to supply the non-execution of their stipulation to deliver, and to entitle themselves to the complete execution of our part of the agreements. In the meantime, the Legislature is passing the bills, and we are preparing everything to be done on our part towards execution; and we shall not avail ourselves of the three months' delay after possession of the province, allowed by the treaty for the delivery of the stock, but shall deliver it the moment that possession is known here, which will be on the eighteenth day after it has taken place. * * *

Mr. Madison to Mr. Marbois.

DEP^T OF STATE, *Novr 4, 1803.*

Sir,—I received your favor of the 21 prairial, with a pleasure which is redoubled by the consideration that I am able, in acknowledging it, to inform you of the formal approbation of the late Treaty, and   by every branch of our Government. The event establishes, I hope forever, perfect harmony between the two Countries. It is the more likely to do so, as it is founded in a policy, coeval with their political relations, of removing as much as possible all sources of jealousy and collision. The frankness and uprightness which marked the progress of this transaction are truly honorable to all concerned in it; and it is an agreeable circumstance that, in the exchange of ratifications, it was closed in the same spirit of mutual confidence, Mr. Pichon inferring, doubtless with the truest reason, that an unqualified exchange, under actual circumstances, would best accord with the real views of his Government.

It remains now to compleat the work by an honest execution of the mutual stipulations. On our part, the sequel will certainly correspond with the good faith and prompt arrangements thus far pursued; and full reliance is placed on the reciprocal disposition of your Government, of which so many proofs have been seen.

The interposition of Spain is an incident not more unexpected than it is unreasonable. It is to be wished that it may terminate without any serious consequences, even to herself. Whatever turn it may take, the honor of the French Government guaranties the object at which our measures are pointed; and the interest of France will equally lie in making the fruits of these measures hers, as well as ours.

Mr. Madison to Mr. Livingston.

DEPARTMENT OF STATE, *November 9, 1803.*

SIR: In my letter of the 22d ultimo, I mentioned to you that the exchange of the ratifications of the treaty and conventions with France, had taken place here, unclogged with any conditions or reserve. Congress has since passed an act to enable the President to take possession of the ceded territory, and to establish a temporary Government therein. Other acts have been passed for complying with the pecuniary stipulations of those instruments. The newspapers enclosed will inform you of these proceedings.

By the post which left this city for Natchez on Monday last, a joint and several commission was forwarded to Governor Claiborne and General Wilkinson, authorizing them to receive possession of and occupy those territories, and a separate commission to the former as temporary Governor. The possibility suggested, by recent circumstances, that delivery may be refused at New Orleans on the part of Spain, required that provision should be made as well for taking as receiving possession. Should force be necessary, Governor Claiborne and General Wilkinson will have to decide on the practicability of a *coup de main* without waiting for the reinforcements, which will require time on our part, and admit of preparations on the other. The force provided for this object is to consist of the regular troops near at hand, as many of the militia as may be requisite, and can be drawn from the Mississippi Territory, and as many volunteers from any quarter as can be picked up. To them will be added 500 mounted militia from Tennessee, who, it is expected, will proceed to Natchez with the least possible delay.

M. Pichon has, in the strongest manner, pressed on M. Laussat, the French Commissary appointed to deliver possession, the necessity of co-operating in these measures of compulsion, should they prove necessary by the refusal of the Spanish officers to comply without them. On the 8th of October it was not known, and no indications have been exhibited at New Orleans, of a design, on the part of Spain, to refuse or oppose the surrender of the province to France, and thereby to us. With high respect and consideration, &c.

JAMES MADISON.

ROBERT R. LIVINGSTON, Esq.

P. S.—The President approves of the individuals appointed as commissioners to liquidate the claims payable under the convention of the 30th of April last. But as it now appears that difficulties have arisen, and are likely to increase, respecting the true construction of that instrument, and especially as it seems more than possible that the twenty millions allotted for the payments to be made under it, may be insufficient to cover all which, in equity, and by a sound interpretation, ought to be included, it is the desire of the President you apply to the French Government for its consent to suspend the issuing of any drafts upon the awards which may be given, until it is ascertained whether the twenty millions be sufficient or not, and with a view to give time for such mutual explanations and arrangements as may tend to effectuate the true spirit and object of the convention. In taking this step, you will refer yourself to the further communications you are to expect from your Government upon the subject; the application you may make upon it to that of France being intended only as a preliminary to a further development.

Mr. Livingston to Mr. Madison.

PARIS, *November 15, 1803.*

SIR: I have only within these few days been honored by your letter to me of the 29th July, by way of Hamburg, together with one of the same date to Mr. Monroe, which I have sent to him by Mr. ——, an American gentleman, by the way of Holland, none more direct offering here, as the intercourse is very strictly forbidden. I shall make the communication you direct, of Mr. Pichon's note, and your reply, relative to the flag of the Italian Republic. It appears to me, however, that this notice rather recommends than supersedes the propriety of a direct recognition of the First Consul, and the compliment of a commission, upon the principle I have mentioned; but of this, the President is the best judge. The letters you have received since the date of yours, you will find have anticipated your direction relative to information on the subject of West Florida, since they refer to documents and historic facts that it will be easy to adduce. As I presume you will have no trouble on this ground, I do not think it necessary to put you to the expense of procuring original papers. Should it happen otherwise, I shall obey your orders; and if any negotiation is necessary at Madrid, I shall transmit to Mr. Pinckney all the proofs I can collect; and I think they will be too numerous to admit of doubt, especially taken in connexion with the letter of the Spanish Minister to Mr. Pinckney, of which a copy has been transmitted to you. The moment is so favorable for taking possession of that country, that I hope it has not been neglected even though a little force should be necessary to effect it. Your Minister must find the means to justify it.

I have seen, as you mention, a publication of my memoir on the subject of Louisiana. But, as it is not an official paper, as it is not signed or delivered in my public character, I do not see that it can ever be noticed on this side of the water as such; besides that, there is nothing in it relative to Britain that has not been told them officially by our Government and by almost every maritime Power in Europe, on the subject of their vexations at sea. Nor can they blame any endeavor of mine to effect the objects of my country, by such arguments as I thought would have weight here. It could hardly be expected that this paper could be secret; since, as I informed you at the time, I had delivered printed copies of it, not only to the First and other Consuls, and to the French Ministers, but to most of those persons who I believed would be consulted upon the occasion. A few were also sent to America, with injunctions, however, not to publish them. I am very sorry a bad translation of it has found its way into the papers, though it may serve, in some measure, to justify the President's appointment of me, by showing that I had not been inattentive to the great interests of my country. The zeal of our friends often carries them too far. Some of them, finding that Mr. Monroe was appointed (through circumstances which you have done me the honor to explain, but which they could not know) with a higher grade than myself; seeing him only mentioned in the newspapers, as the acting Minister; and finding some endeavor here to impress a belief that he was the principal agent in treating with France; it was natural that they should feel some mortification, and endeavor to do me the justice they know I was entitled to. This may apologize for, I mean not by it to justify, their imprudence. There is another, on the part of Mr. Monroe's friends, which I should not mention, but that it carries with it a circumstance for which I may be under the necessity of apologizing to the President, should my private letter to Mr. Monroe have reached the United States; since it argues a difference of sentiment upon an important point, which I fear will be laid hold of by our common enemies. I have, in my former letter, informed you of M. Talleyrand's calling upon me previous to the arrival of Mr. Monroe, for a proposition for the whole of Louisiana; of his afterwards trifling with me, and telling me that what he had said was unauthorized. This circumstance, for which I have accounted to you in one of my letters, led me to think, though it afterwards appeared without reason, that some change had taken place in the determination which I knew the Consul had before taken to sell. I had just then received a line from Mr. Monroe, informing me of his arrival.

I wrote to him a hasty answer, under the influence of ideas, excited by these prevarications of the Minister, expressing the hope that he had brought information that New Orleans was in our possession; that I hoped our negotiation might be successful; but that, while I feared nothing but war would avail us anything, I had paved the way for him. This letter is very imprudently shown and spoken of by Mr. Monroe's particular friends, as a proof that he had been the principal agent in the negotiation. So far, indeed, as it may tend to this object, it is of little moment; because facts and dates are too well known to be contradicted. For instance, it is known to everybody here that the Consul had taken his resolution to sell previous to Mr. Monroe's arrival. It is a fact well known that M. Marbois was authorized, informally, by the First Consul, to treat with me before Mr. Monroe reached Paris; that he actually made me the very proposition we ultimately agreed to, before Mr. Monroe had seen a Minister, except M. Marbois, for a moment, at my house, where he came to make the proposition: Mr. Monroe not having been presented to M. Talleyrand, to whom I introduced him the afternoon of the next day. All, then, that remained to negotiate, after his arrival, was a diminution of the price; and in this our joint mission was unfortunate; for we came up, as soon as Mr. Monroe's illness would suffer him to do business, after a few days' delay, to the Minister's offers. There is no doubt that

Mr. Monroe's talents and address would have enabled him, had he been placed in my circumstances, to have effected what I have done. But he unfortunately came too late to do more than assent to the propositions that were made to us, and to aid in reducing them to form. I think he has too much candor not to be displeased that his friends should publicly endeavor to depreciate me by speaking of a private letter, hastily written, under circumstances of irritation, with which Mr. Monroe is fully acquainted; a letter, too, which may contribute in two ways to advance the views of the enemies of the Administration. It is in this light only that it gives me pain. First, it shows that it was my sentiment, founded upon the knowledge I must have been supposed to possess of the temper of this Court, and the state of things here, that we should have availed ourselves of the circumstance of the denial of the right of depot to possess New Orleans. That this was my sentiment, I confess; and you have found, by my notes, that I labored to impress this Government with a belief that it would be done. And I have every reason to think that the treaty would have been concluded in March, had not M. Pichon's letter, at the moment, contradicted my suggestion on this subject.

As the President's views have been happily more correct than mine; as he has effected, without this harsh measure, his great object; it certainly is not advisable to publish that we differed in sentiment; and introduce discussions on the comparative advantages that might be derived from the one or the other mode of proceeding. The next point in which the letter may do harm, is in authorizing an opinion, which the enemies of the Administration are most zealous in promoting, viz: that no credit is due either to the President or his Ministers, since the war only produced the measure. The war, doubtless, had its effect upon the First Consul; but it is equally true that every person he consulted had long before been convinced, and even the Consul's opinion shaken, and I will venture to say by my means, of the little advantage France would derive from the possession of that country; and he had even, as I have before informed you, through Joseph Bonaparte, given me assurances that such arrangements should be made as we should approve. The not selling was a sort of personal point of honor, particularly as he was bound by the express stipulation of his treaty with Spain not to do so. Nor, until he found himself hampered by another personal consideration, to wit, his promise to pay the American claims, which I had purposely published, could he bring himself to take the step which the prospect of war and the spirited measures of our Government, among which I number the special mission of Mr. Monroe, gave him the strongest apology for doing; particularly as, in case of war, he had no other means of keeping his word with us. Thus, sir, you see that it is very difficult for the most prudent man to restrain the ill-judged zeal of his friends; and

I dare say that Mr. Monroe will as sincerely lament that of his friends, who, indeed, ought not to have seen a mere private letter, as I do that of the gentleman that I suspect to have occasioned the publication which you so justly blame.

Having had the goodness, sir, to correct one of the errors of the clerk that gave me some cause of complaint, I must notice another which added to my doubts of success at the moment I wrote to Mr. Monroe. In the copy of our joint instructions which you had forwarded to me, the ultimatum that we were limited to was thirty millions, out of which the American claims were to be paid. Now, I was satisfied that, if Mr. Monroe, on his arrival, should adhere to this, our prospect of success was not very great; since ten millions in cash to the Government was an object of but little moment. More might have been got from Spain by a transfer. On looking over, however, the original instructions, of which Mr. Monroe was the bearer, I found that we were authorized to give fifty millions for New Orleans and the Floridas; so that we could, without, too, an extraordinary assumption of powers, go to the price they expected for Louisiana.

I have applied to M. Talleyrand on the subject of East Florida, thinking the moment favorable for making the acquisition. I have endeavored to alarm him and Spain about the danger that will result to Spain and France if England takes possession of the ports on the Gulf; and I have obtained from him a positive promise that this Government shall aid any negotiation that may be set on foot for its purchase. I have written on this subject to Mr. Pinckney, and advised him to open his negotiation by reiterating this argument, and by making some offer of payment in American stocks. I shall inform Mr. Monroe of these circumstances, and will forward for him any instructions he may choose to send to Mr. Pinckney.

I am, &c.,

ROBERT R. LIVINGSTON.

Hon. JAMES MADISON,
Secretary of State.

[Extract.]

Mr. Madison to Mr. Livingston.

DEPARTMENT OF STATE, *January 31, 1804.*

SIR: The two last letters received from you bear date on the — and 30th September; so that we have been now four months without hearing from you. The last from me to you was dated on the 16th day of January, giving you information of the transfer of Louisiana, on the 20th December, by the French Commissioner, M. Laussat, to Governor Claiborne and General Wilkinson, the Commissioners appointed on the part of the United States to receive it. The letters subsequent to that date from Governor Claiborne, who is charged with the present administration of the ceded territory, show that the occupancy by our troops of the military posts on the island of New Orleans, and on the western side of the Mississippi, was in progression; and that the state of things, in other respects, was such as was to be expected from the predisposition of the bulk of the inhabitants, and the manifest advantages to which they have become entitled as citizens of the United States. A bill providing for the government of the territory has been some time under the deliberation of the Senate, but has not yet passed to the other branch of the Legislature. The enclosed copy shows the form in which it was introduced. Some alterations have already been made, and others may be presumed. The precise form in which it will pass can not, therefore, be foreknown; and the less so as the peculiarities and difficulties of the case give rise to more than the ordinary differences of opinion. It is pretty certain that the provisions generally contemplated will leave the people of that district, for a while, without the organization of power dictated by the republican theory; but it is evident that a sudden transition to a condition so much in contrast with that in which their ideas and habits have been formed, would be as unacceptable and as little beneficial to them as it would be difficult for the Government of the United States. It may fairly be expected that every blessing of liberty will be extended to them as fast as they shall be prepared and disposed to receive it. In the meantime, the mild spirit in which the powers derived from the Government of the United States will, under its superintendence, be administered, the parental interest which it takes in the happiness of those adopted into the general family, and a scrupulous regard to the tenor and spirit of the treaty of cession, promise a continuance of that satisfaction among the people of Louisiana which has thus far shown itself. These observations are made that you may be the better enabled to give to the French Government the explanations and assurances due to its solicitude in behalf of a people whose destiny it has committed to the justice, the honor, and the policy of the United States.

It does not appear that, in the delivery of the Province by the Spanish authorities to M. Laussat, anything passed denoting its limits, either to the east, the west, or the north; nor was any step taken by M. Laussat, either whilst the Province was in his hands, or at the time of his transferring it to ours, calculated to dispossess Spain of any part of the territory east of the Mississippi. On the contrary, in a private conference, he stated positively that no part of the Floridas was included in the eastern boundary; France having strenuously insisted to have it extended to the Mobile, which was peremptorily rufused by Spain.

We learn, from Mr. Pinckney, that the Spanish Government holds the same language to him. To the declaration of M. Laussat, however, we can oppose that of the French Minister, made to you, that Louisiana extended to the river Perdido: and to the Spanish Government, as well as to that of France, we can oppose the treaty of St. Ildefonso, and of September 30, 1803, interpreted by facts and fair inferences. The question with Spain will enter into the proceedings of Mr. Monroe, on his arrival at Madrid, whither he will be instructed to repair as soon as he shall have executed at London the instructions lately transmitted to him in relation to the impressment of seamen from American vessels, and several other points which call for just and stipulated arrangements between the two countries. As the question relates to the French Government, the President relies on your prudence and attention for availing yourself of the admission, by M. Marbois, that Louisiana extended to the river Perdido, and for keeping the weight of that Government in our scale against that of Spain. With respect to the western extent of Louisiana, M. Laussat held a language more satisfactory. He considered the Rio Bravo or Del Norte, as far as the thirtieth degree of north latitude, as its true boundary on that side. The northern boundary, we have reason to believe, was settled between France and Great Britain by Commissioners appointed under the Treaty of Utrecht, who separated the British and French territories west of the Lake of the Woods by the forty-ninth degree of latitude. In support of our just claims in all these cases, it is proper that no time should be lost in collecting the best proofs which can be obtained. This important object has already been recommended generally to your attention. It is particularly desirable that you should procure an authenticated copy of the commercial charter granted by Louis XIV. to Crozat, in 1712, which gives an outline to Louisiana favorable to our claims, at the same time that it is an evidence of the highest and most unexceptionable authority. A copy of this charter is annexed to the English translation of Joutel's Journal of La Salle's voyage, the French original not containing it.

A record of the charter doubtless exists in the archives of the French Government; and it may be expected that an attested copy will not be refused to you. It is not improbable that the charter, or other documents relating to the Mississippi project, a few years after, may afford some light, and be attainable from the same source. The proceedings of the Commissioners under the Treaty of Utrecht will merit particular research, as they promise not only a favorable northern boundary, but as they will decide an important question involved in a convention of limits now depending between the United States and Great Britain. To these may be added whatever other documents may occur to your recollection or research, including maps, &c. If the secret treaty of Paris, in 1762–'3, between France and Spain, and an entire copy of that of St. Ildefonso, in 1800, can be obtained, they may also be useful.

An authentication of the precise date, at least, of the former is very important. You will be sensible of the propriety of putting Mr. Monroe in possession of all the proofs and information which you may obtain. Should he take Paris in his way to Madrid, you will have the best of opportunities for the purpose.

In my letter of the 9th of November last I communicated the ideas entertained by the President, with respect to the pecuniary provision in the last convention with France in behalf of our citizens. It is presumed that you will have found no difficulty in obaining the concurrence of the French Government in suspending drafts in favor of any until the claims of all shall have been ascertained. Should the sum of three million seven hundred and fifty thousand dollars be insufficient for the payment of all, as becomes daily more probable, the least that ought to be attempted will be an apportionment of it among them. Perhaps more than this may now be attended with great difficulty; although it is clear that the patronage of the Government of the United States is due, on prior considerations, more to some classes of the claimants than to others; to those, for example, whose property was wrongfully taken on the high seas by force, than to those who, by voluntary contracts, placed a confidence in the French Government, which was disappointed. It seems requisite, nevertheless, that some effort should be made in behalf of those whose claims were embraced by the convention of September 30th, 1800, and not provided for by that of April 30th, 1803.

With this view, the President thinks it proper that you should adjust with the French Government a provision for comprehending in the convention of 1803 the claims still remaining under the convention of 1800; and for apportioning the money payable at the Treasury of the United States among the claimants under both; as the object next to be pursued, a provision for apportioning among the whole, the money so payable, and also the balance chargeable on France, according to the tenor of the last convention. Or, as the object next in order, a provision for apportioning, among the whole, the money payable at the Treasury of the United States, leaving to the claimants under the last convention the balance from France to which it entitles them; or, lastly, a provision for apportioning among the claimants under the last convention the money so payable, instead of paying it in the order of settlement, or according to any other rule of preference.

The first arrangement takes for granted that France considers herself bound, notwithstanding the last convention, to satisfy all the claims provided for by the first convention, permitted by the last. The supposition is founded on several expressions and implications of its text, as the head of the fifth article, "all agreements," &c., and particularly in the closing words of article tenth; and with respect to debts, the provision is express in article twelve. This construction is the more reasonable also, inasmuch as the reciprocal stipulation of the convention of 1800, in this particular, were carried into immediate and full effect on the part of the United States; and as a contrary construction would imply the relinquishment, without equivalent, of vested rights never formally contested by France.

Should France, however, be unlikely to admit her responsibility for the pretermitted claims, and there be danger that, by urging her responsibility at this time, an equitable modification of any sort may be rendered more difficult, it will be best to pass over the question for the present, taking care that no waiver be made which may either still further weaken the claims against France, or give color for turning them over against the United States.

Neither of the succeeding alternatives will increase the balance payable by France, nor is it contemplated that in these or any other modifications whatever, the Treasury of the United States is to be made chargeable with more than three million seven hundred and fifty thousand dollars; or rather, with more than so much of that sum as would satisfy the debts to which it is subjected by the last convention.

The object of each of the proposed modifications is to distribute whatever is to be paid by the United States and by France among all the claimants, as well those omitted as those included in the last convention; and in such a manner that every claimant of both descriptions shall receive a fair proportion from the Treasury of the United States, as well of the balance to be paid by France.

The claimants who were provided for in the last convention can not justly complain of any arrangement that will replace on the same footing with themselves their fellow-claimants left by the last, under the first convention, as being a retrospective measure working a disadvantage to them. The retrospective proceeding will be found to lie in the last convention, so far as it is advantageous in its operation, to those claiming under the first only. An act superseding a retrospective act is not itself retrospective. The effect of it is to restore and enforce the original rule of justice.

Should the French Government refuse to concur in any proposition that will restore the latitude given to claims as defined by the first convention, and which is narrowed and obscured by the text of the last, it will be proper to settle with the Government, if it can be done, such a construction of this text as will be most favorable to all just claims, particularly those for freights, indemnities, property put in requisition, and the separate property of individuals who are concerned in the disqualifying partnerships mentioned in the convention, which are said to be threatened with rejection by the board at Paris. It is to be kept in view, however, that in case the whole sum of three million seven hundred and fifty thousand dollars should not be ab̲ ̲ ̲b̲c̲ ̲.

by the construction of the board, the construction settled with the French Government is not to enlarge the sum to be paid by the Treasury of the United States beyond that to which the Treasury would be made liable by the construction of the board.

It will occur to you that, in case the field of claims should be enlarged, the time for presenting and settling them ought to be lengthened. You can yourself best decide how far a prolongation of the time necessary for the claims now admissible before the board may be necessary, and ought to be attempted.

There is reason to believe that not a few of this description are yet to be forwarded from this side the Atlantic.

I have the honor to be, &c.,

JAMES MADISON.

ROBERT R. LIVINGSTON, Esq.

[Extract.]

President Jefferson to Dr. Priestley.

WASHINGTON, *January 29, 1804.*

I very early saw that Louisiana was indeed a speck in our horizon which was to burst in a tornado; and the public are unapprized how near this catastrophe was. Nothing but a frank and friendly development of causes and effects on our part, and good sense enough in Bonaparte to see that the train was unavoidable, and would change the face of the world, saved us from the storm. I did not expect he would yield till a war took place between France and England, and my hope was to palliate and endure, if Messrs. Ross, Morris, &c. did not force a premature rupture, until that event. I believed the event not very distant, but acknowledge it came on sooner than I had expected. Whether, however, the good sense of Bonaparte might not see the course predicted to be necessary and unavoidable, even before a war should be imminent, was a chance which we thought it our duty to try; but the immediate prospect of rupture brought the case to immediate decision. The *denoument* has been happy; and I confess I look to this duplication of area for the extending a government so free and economical as ours, as a great achievement to the mass of happiness which is to ensue. Whether we remain in one confederacy, or form into Atlantic and Mississippi confederacies, I believe not very important to the happiness of either part. Those of the western confederacy will be as much our children and descendants as those of the eastern, and I feel myself as much identified with that country, in future time, as with this; and did I now foresee a separation at some future day, yet I should feel the duty and the desire to promote the western interests as ... 'ously as the eastern, doing all the good for both portions of our future family which should fall within my power.

[Extract.]
President Jefferson to Wm. Dunbar.

WASHINGTON, *March 13, 1804.*

In the first visit, after receiving the treaty, which I paid to Monticello, which was in August, I availed myself of what I have there, to investigate the limits. While I was in Europe, I had purchased everything I could lay my hands on which related to any part of America, and particularly had a pretty full collection of the English, French and Spanish authors, on the subject of Louisiana. The information I got from these was entirely satisfactory, and I threw it into a shape which would easily take the form of a memorial. I now enclose you a copy of it. One single fact in it was taken from a publication in a newspaper, supposed to be written by Judge Bay, who had lived in West Florida. This asserted that the country from the Iberville to the Perdido was to this day called Louisiana, and a part of the government of Louisiana. I wrote to you to ascertain that fact, and received the information you were so kind as to send me; on the receipt of which, I changed the form of the assertion, so as to adapt it to what I suppose to be the fact, and to reconcile the testimony I have received, to-wit, that though the name and division of West Florida have been retained; and in strictness, that country is still called by that name; yet it is also called Louisiana in common parlance, and even in some authentic public documents.

Mr. Madison to Mr. Livingston.

DEPARTMENT OF STATE, *March 31, 1804.*

SIR: Since my acknowledgment of yours of October 20 and 31, I have received those of 2d, 15th, and 23d, November, and 11th December.

In mine of January 31, I informed you that Louisiana had been transferred by the French Commissioner to our Commissioners on the 20th of December; that nothing had officially passed on the occasion concerning the boundaries of the ceded territory; but that M. Laussat had confidentially signified that it did not comprehend any part of West Florida; adding, at the same time, that it extended westwardly to the Rio Bravo, otherwise called Rio del Norte. Orders were accordingly obtained from the Spanish authority for the delivery of all the posts on the west side of the Mississippi, as well as on the island of New Orleans. With respect to the posts in West Florida, orders for the delivery were neither offered to, nor demanded by, our Commissioners. No instructions have, in fact, been ever given them to make the demand. This silence on the part of the Executive was deemed eligible; first, because it was foreseen that the demand would not only be rejected by the Spanish authority at New Orleans, which had, in an official publication, limited the cession westwardly by the Mississippi and the island of New Orleans, but it was apprehended, as has turned out, that the French Commissioner might not be ready to support the demand, and might even be disposed to second the Spanish opposition to it; secondly, because, in the latter of these cases, a serious check would be given to our title; and, in either of them, a premature dilemma would result between an overt submission to the refusal, and a resort to force; thirdly, because mere silence would be no bar to a plea at any time that a delivery of a part, particularly of the seat of Government, was a virtual delivery of the whole; whilst, in the meantime, we could ascertain the views, and claim the interposition of the French Government, and avail ourselves of that and any other favorable circumstances for effecting an amicable adjustment of the question with the Government of Spain. In this state of things, it was deemed proper by Congress, in making the regulations necessary for the collection of revenue in the ceded territory, and guarding against the new danger of smuggling into the United States, through the channels opened by it, to include a provision for the case of West Florida, by vesting in the President a power which his discretion might accommodate to events.

This provision is contained in the eleventh, taken in connexion with the fourth, section of the act herewith inclosed. The act had been many weeks depending in Congress with these sections, word for word, in it; the bill had been printed as soon as reported by the committee, for the use of the members, and as two copies are, by a usage of politeness, always allotted for each foreign Minister here, it must in all probability have been known to the Marquis d'Yrujo in an early stage of its progress. If it was not, it marks much less of that zealous vigilance over the concerns of his Sovereign than he now makes the plea for his intemperate conduct. For some days even after the act was published in the gazette of this city, he was silent. At length, however, he called at the Office of State, with the gazette in his hand, and entered into a very angry comment on the eleventh section, which was answered by remarks (some of which it would seem from his written allusion to them were not well understood) calculated to assuage his dissatisfaction with the law, as far as was consistant with a candid declaration to him that we considered all of West Florida, westward of the Perdido, as clearly ours by the treaty of April 30, 1803, and that of St. Ildefonso. The conversation ended, as might be inferred from his letters which followed it on the 7th and 17th instant, of which copies are herewith enclosed, as are also copies of my answer of —, and of his reply of —. You will see by this correspondence the footing on which a rudeness, which no Government can tolerate, has placed him with this Government, and the view of it which must be unavoidably conveyed to our Minister at Madrid. It may be of some importance, also, that it be not misconceived where you are. But the correspondence is chiefly of importance as it suggests the earnestness with which Spain is likely to contest our construction of the treaties of cession, and the Spanish reasoning which will be employed against it; and, consequently, as it urges the expediency of cultivating the disposition of the French Government to take our side of the question. To this she is bound no less by sound policy than by regard to right.

She is bound by the former, because the interest she has in our friendship interests her in the friendship between us and Spain, which can not be maintained with full effect, if at all, without removing the sources of collision lurking under a neighborhood marked by such circumstances; and which, considering the relation between France and Spain, can not be interrupted without endangering the friendly relations between the United States and France. A transfer from Spain to the United States of the territory claimed by the latter, or rather of the whole of both the Floridas, on reasonable conditions, is, in fact, nothing more than a sequel and completion of the policy which led France into her own treaty of cession; and her discernment and her consistency are both pledges that she will view the subject in this light. Another pledge lies in the manifest interest which France has in the peaceable transfer of these Spanish possessions to the United States, as the only effectual security against their falling into the hands of Great Britain. Such an event would be certain in case of a rupture between Great Britain and Spain, and would be particularly disagreeable to France, whether Great Britian should retain the acquisition for the sake of the important harbors and other advantages belonging to it, or should make it the basis of some transaction with the United States, which, notwithstanding the good faith and fairness toward France, (which would doubtless be observed on our part,) might involve conditions too desirable to her enemy not to be disagreeable to herself. It even deserves consideration that the use which Great Britain could make of the territory in question, and the facility in seizing it, may become a casting motive with her to force Spain into war, contrary to the wishes and the policy of France.

The territory ceded to the United States is described in the words following: "The colony or province of Louisiana, with the same extent that it now has in the hands of Spain, that it had when France possessed it, and such as it ought to be, according to the treaties subsequently passed between Spain and other States."

In expounding this three-fold description the different forms used must be so understood as to give a meaning to each description, and to make the meaning of each coincide with the others.

The first form of description is a reference to the extent which Louisiana now has in the hands of Spain. What is that extent, as determined by its eastern limits? It is not denied that the Perdido was once the eastern limit of Louisiana. It is not denied that the territory now possessed by Spain extends to the river Perdido. The river Perdido, we say, then, is the limit to the eastern extent of Louisiana ceded to the United States.

This construction gives an obvious and pertinent meaning to the term "now," and to the expression "in the hands of Spain," which can be found in no other construction. For a considerable time previous to the Treaty of Peace in 1783, between Great Britain and Spain, Louisiana, as in the hands of Spain, was limited eastwardly by the Mississippi, the Iberville, &c. The term "now" fixes the extent, as enlarged by that treaty, in contradistinction to the more limited extent in which Spain held it prior to that treaty. Again: the expression "in the hands or in the possession of Spain," fixes the same extent; because, the expression can not relate to the extent which Spain, by her internal regulations, may have given to a particular district under the name of Louisiana, but evidently to the extent in which it was known to other nations, particularly to the nation in treaty with her, and in which it was relatively to other nations in her hands, and not in the hands of any other nation. It would be absurd to consider the expression "in the hands of Spain," as relating not to others, but to herself and her own regulations; for the territory of Louisiana in her hands must be equally so, and be the same, whether formed into one or twenty districts, or by whatever name or names it may be called by herself.

What may now be the extent of a provincial district under the name of Louisiana, according to the municipal arrangements of the Spanish Government, is not perfectly known. It is at least questionable, even whether these arrangements have not incorporated the portion of Louisiana acquired from Great Britain with the western portion before belonging to Spain, under the same provincial Government. But, whether such be the fact or not, the construction of the treaty will be the same.

The next form of description refers to the extent which Louisiana had when possessed by France. What is this extent? It will be admitted, that for the whole period prior to the division of Louisiana between Spain and Great Britain in 1762-3, or at least from the adjustment of boundary between France and Spain in 1719, to that event, Louisiana extended, in the possession of France, to the river Perdido. Had the meaning, then, of the first description been less determinate, and had France been in possession of Louisiana at any time with less extent than to the Perdido, a reference to this primitive and long-continued extent would be more natural and probable than to any other. But it happens that France never possessed Louisiana with less extent than to the Perdido; because, on the same day that she ceded a part to Spain, the residue was ceded to Great Britain; and, consequently, as long as she possessed Louisiana at all, she possessed it entire, that is, in its extent to the Perdido. It is true, that after the cession of Western Louisiana to Spain in the year 1762–3, the actual delivery of the territory by France was delayed for several years: but it can never be supposed, that a reference could be intended to this short period of delay, during which France held that portion in the right of Spain only, not in her own right, when, in other words, she held it as the trustee of Spain; and, that a reference to such a possession for such a period should be intended, rather than a reference to the long possession of the whole territory in her own acknowledged right, prior to that period.

In the order of the French King in 1764, to Monsieur d'Abbadie, for the delivery of Western Louisiana to Spain, it is stated that the cession by France was on the 3d of November, and the acceptance by Spain, on the 13th of that month, leaving an interval of ten days. An anxiety to find a period, during which Louisiana, as limited by the Mississippi and the Iberville, as held by France in her own right, may possibly lead the Spanish Government to seize the pretext into which this momentary interval may be converted. But it will be a mere pretext. In the first place, it is probable that the treaty of cession to Spain, which is dated on the same day with that to Great Britain, was, like the latter, a preliminary treaty, consummated and confirmed by a definitive treaty bearing the same date with the definitive treaty, including the cession to Great Britain; in which case, the time and effect of each cession would be the same, whether recurrence be had to the date of the preliminary or definitive treaties.

In the next place, the cession by France to Spain was essentially made on the 3d of November, 1762, on which day, the same with that of the cession to Great Britain, the right passed away from France. The acceptance by Spain, ten days after, if necessary at all to perfect the deed, had relation to the date of the cession by France, and must have the same effect, and no other, as if Spain had signed the deed on the same day with France. This explanation, which rests on the soundest principles, nullifies the interval of ten days, so as to make the cession to Great Britain and Spain simultaneous, on the supposition that recurrence be had to the preliminary treaty, and not to the definitive treaty; and, consequently, establishes the fact that France, at no time, possessed Louisiana with less extent than to the Perdido; the alienation and partition of the territory admitting no distinction of time. In the last place, conceding even that during an interval of ten days the right of Spain was incomplete, and was in transitu only from France; or in another form of expression, that the right remained in France, subject to the eventual acceptance of Spain, is it possible to believe that a description, which must be presumed to aim at clearness and certainty, should refer for its purposes to so fugitive and equivocal state of things, in preference to a state of things where the right and the possession of France were of long continuance, and susceptible of neither doubt nor controversy? It is impossible. And, consequently, the only possible construction which can be put on the second form of description coincides with the only rational construction that can be put on the first: making Louisiana of the same extent, that is to the river Perdido, both "as in the hands of Spain" and "as France possessed it."

The third and last description of Louisiana is in these words: "Such as it ought to be, according to the treaties subsequently passed between Spain and other States."

This description may be considered as auxiliary to the two others, and is conclusive as an argument for comprehending within the cession of Spain territory eastward of the Mississippi and the Iberville, and for extending the cession to the river Perdido.

The only treaties between Spain and other nations that affect the extent of Louisiana, as being subsequent to the possession of it by France, are, first, the treaty of 1783 between Spain and Great Britain; and, secondly, the treaty of 1795 between Spain and the United States.

The last of these treaties affects the extent of Louisiana, as in the hands of Spain, by defining the northern boundary of that part of it which lies east of the Mississippi and the Iberville; and the first affects the extent of Louisiana, by including in the cession from Great Britain to Spain the territory between that river and the Perdido; and by giving to Louisiana, in consequence of that reunion of the eastern and western part, the same extent eastwardly in the hands of Spain as it had when France possessed it. Louisiana, then, as it ought to be, according to treaties of Spain subsequently to the possession by France, is limited by the line of demarcation settled with the United States, and forming a northern boundary, and is extended to the river Perdido as its eastern boundary.

This is not only the plain and necessary construction of the words, but is the only construction that can give a meaning to them. For they are without meaning, on the supposition that Louisiana, as in the hands of Spain, is limited by the Mississippi and the Iberville, since neither the one nor the other of those treaties have any relation to Louisiana that can affect its extent, but through their relation to the limits of that part of it which lies eastward of the Mississippi and the Iberville. Including this part, therefore, as we contend, within the extent of Louisiana, and a meaning is given to both as pertinent as it is important. Exclude this part, as Spain contends, from Louisiana, and no treaties exist to which the reference is applicable.

This deduction can not be evaded by pretending that the reference to subsequent treaties of Spain was meant to save the right of deposit, and other rights stipulated to the commerce of the United States by the treaty of 1795; first, because, although that may be an incidental object of the reference to that treaty, as was signified by His Catholic Majesty to the Government of the United States, yet the principal object of the reference is evidently the territorial *extent* of Louisiana; secondly, because the reference is to more than one treaty—to the treaty of 1783, as well as to that of 1795; and the treaty 1783 can have no modifying effect whatever, rendering it applicable, but on the supposition that Louisiana was considered as extending eastward of the Mississippi and the Iberville, into the territory ceded by that treaty to Spain.

In fine, the construction which we maintain gives to every part of the description of the territory ceded to the United States a meaning clear in itself, and in harmony with every other part, and is no less conformable to facts than it is founded on the ordinary use and analogy of the expressions. The construction urged by Spain gives, on the contrary, a meaning to the first description which is inconsistent with the very terms of it; it prefers, in the second, a meaning that is impossible or absurd; and it takes from the last all meaning whatever.

In confirmation of the meaning which extends Louisiana to the river Perdido, it may be regarded as most consistent with the object of the First Consul in the cession obtained by him from Spain. Every appearance, and every circumstance, pronounces this to have been to give lustre to his Administration, and to gratify a natural pride in his nation, by re-annexing to its domain possessions which had, without any sufficient consideration, been severed from it; and which, being in the hands of Spain, it was in the power of Spain to restore. Spain, on the other side, might be the less reluctant against the cession in this extent, as she would be only replaced by it within the original limits of her possessions; the territory east of the Perdido having been regained by her from Great Britain in the peace of 1783, and not included in the late cession.

It only remains to take notice of the argument derived from a criticism on the term "retrocede," by which the cession from Spain to France is expressed. The literal meaning of this term is said to be that Spain gives back to France what she received from France; and that as she received from France no more than the Territory west of the Mississippi and the Iberville, that, and no more, could be given back by Spain.

Without denying that such a meaning, if uncontrolled by other terms, would have been properly expressed by the term "retrocede," it is sufficient, and more than sufficient, to observe, first, that with respect to France, the literal meaning is satisfied; France receiving back what she had before alienated; secondly, that with respect to Spain, not only the greater part of Louisiana had been confessedly received by her from France, and, consequently, was literally ceded back by Spain, as well as ceded back to France; but, with respect to the part in question, Spain might not unfairly be considered as ceding back to France what France had ceded to her, inasmuch as the cession of it to Great Britain was made for the benefit of Spain, to whom, on that account, Cuba was restored. The effect was precisely the same as if France had, in form, made the cession to Spain, and Spain had assigned it over to Great Britain; and the cession may the more aptly be considered as passing through Spain, as Spain herself was a party to the treaty by which it was conveyed to Great Britain. In this point of view, not only France received back what she had ceded, but Spain ceded back what she had received, and the etymology even of the term "retrocede" is satisfied. This view of the case is the more substantially just, as the territory in question passed from France to Great Britain, for the account of Spain, but passed from Great Britain into the hands of Spain in 1783, in consequence of a war to which Spain had contributed but little compared with France, and in terminating which so favorably in this article for Spain, France had doubtless a preponderating influence. Thirdly, that if a course of proceeding might have existed to which the term "retrocede" would be more literally applicable, it may be equally said that there is no other particular term which would be more applicable to the whole proceeding, as it did exist. Fourthly. Lastly, that if this were not the case, a nice criticism on the etymology of a single term can be allowed no weight against a conclusion drawn from the clear meaning of every other term, and from the whole context.

In aid of these observations, I enclose herewith two papers, which have been drawn up with a view to trace and support our title to Louisiana in its extent to the Perdido. You will find in them, also, the grounds on which its western extent is maintainable against Spain, and its northern in relation to Great Britain.

On the whole, we reckon with much confidence on the obligations and dispositions of the French Government, to favor our object with Spain, and on your prudent exertions to strengthen our hold on both; not only in reference to the true construction of the treaty, but to our acquisition of the Spanish territory eastward of the Perdido on convenient and equitable conditions.

You will find herewith enclosed copies of another correspondence, sufficiently explaining itself, with the Marquis d'Yrujo, on the commerce from our ports to St. Domingo; to which is added a letter on that subject from M. Pichon. The ideas of the President, as well to the part which the true interest of France recommends to her, as to the part prescribed both to her and to the United States by the law of nations, were communicated in my letter of the 31st of January last. It is much to be desired that the French Government may enter into proper views on this subject.

With respect to the trade in articles not for war, there can not be a doubt that the interest of France concurs with that of the United States. With respect to articles for war, it is, probably, the interest of all nations that they should be kept out of hands likely to make so bad a use of them. It is clear, at the same time, that the United States are bound by the law of nations to nothing further than to leave their offending citizens to the consequences of an illicit trade; and it deserves serious consideration, how far their undertaking, at the instance of one Power, to enforce the law of nations, by prohibitory regulations to which they are bound, may become an embarrassing precedent, and stimulate pretensions and complaints of other Powers. The French Government must be sensible, also, that prohibitions by one nation would have little effect, if others, including Great Britain, should not follow the example. It may be added, that the most which the United States could do in the case, short of prohibiting the export of contraband articles altogether, a measure doubtless beyond the expectations of France, would be to annex to the shipment of these articles a condition, that they should be delivered elsewhere than in St. Domingo, and that a regulation of this kind would readily be frustrated by a reshipment of the article after delivery elsewhere, in the same or other vessels, in order to accomplish the forbidden destination. If, indeed, the prohibitory regulations, on the part of the United States, were the result of a stipulation, and recommended by an equivalent concession, the objection to it as an inconvenient precedent would be avoided. If, for example, France would agree to permit the trade with Santo Domingo in all other articles, on condition that we would agree to prohibit contraband articles, no objection of that sort would lie against the arrangement; and the arrangement would, in itself, be so reasonable, on both sides, and so favorable, even to the people of Santo Domingo, that the President authorizes you not only to make it, if you find it not improper, the subject of a frank conference with the French Government, but to put it into the form of a conventional regulation; or, should this be objectionable, the object may be attained, perhaps, by a tacit understanding between the two Governments which may lead to the regulations on each side respectively necessary. Although a legal regulation, on our part, can not be absolutely promised, otherwise than by a positive and mutual stipulation, yet, with a candid explanation of this constitutional circumstance, there can be little risk in inspiring the requisite confidence that the legislative authority here would interpose its sanction.

It is the more important that something should be done in the case, and done soon, as the pretext, founded upon the supposed illegality of any trade whatever with the negroes in St. Domingo, is multiplying depredations on our commerce, not only with that island, but with the West Indies generally, to a degree highly irritating, and which is laying the foundations for the extensive claims and complaints on our part. You will not fail to state this fact to the French Government in its just importance; as an agreement for some such arrangement as is above suggested, or if that be disliked, as requiring such other interposition of that Government as will put an end to the evil.

It is represented that a part of the depredations are committed by French armed vessels without commissions, or with commissions from incompetent authorities. It appears, also, that these lawless proceedings are connected with Spanish ports and subjects, probably Spanish officers, also, in the West Indies, particularly in the island of Cuba. So far as the responsibility of Spain may be involved, we shall not lose sight of it. An appeal, at the same time, to that of France, is as pressing as it is just; and you will please to make it in the manner best calculated to make it effectual.

In one of your letters you apprehended that the interest accruing from the delay of the Commissioners at Paris may be disallowed by the French Government, and wish for instructions on the subject. I am glad to find, by later communications from Mr. Skipwith, that the apparent discontent at the delay had subsided. But whatever solicitude that Government might feel for despatch in liquidating the claims, it would be a palpable wrong to make a disappointment in that particular a pretext for refusing any stipulated part of the claims. In a legal point of view, the treaty could not be in force until mutually ratified; and every preparatory step taken for carrying it into effect, however apposite or useful, must be connected with legal questions arising under the treaty.

In other parts of your correspondence, you seem to have inferred from some passage in mine, that I thought the ten millions of livres in cash, over which a discretion was given, ought to have been paid rather to France than to our creditor citizens. If the inference be just, my expressions must have been the more unfortunate as they so little accord with the original plan, communicated in the instructions to yourself and Mr. Monroe; the more unfortunate still, as they not only decide a question wrong, but a question which could never occur. The cash fund of ten millions was provided on the supposition, that, in a critical moment, and in a balance of considerations, the immediate payment of that sum, as a part of the bargain, might either tempt the French Government to enter into it, or to reduce the terms of it. If wanted for either of these purposes, it was to be paid to the French Government; if not wanted for either, it was made applicable to no other. The provision contemplated for the creditors had no reference to the fund of ten millions of livres; nor was it even contemplated that any other cash fund would be made applicable to their claims. It was supposed not unreasonable, that the ease of our Treasury and the chance and means of purchasing the territory remaining to Spain eastward of the Mississippi, might be so far justly consulted as to put the indemnification of the claims against France on a like footing with that on which the indemnification of like claims against Great Britain had been put. And it was inferred, that such a modification of the payments would not only have fully satisfied the expectations of the creditors, but would have encountered no objections on the part of the French Government, who had no interest in the question, and who were precluded by all that had passed from urging objections of any other sort.

Congress adjourned on Tuesday, the 27th of March, to the first Monday in November next. Copies of their laws will be forwarded to you as soon as they issue from the press. For the present, I enclose herewith a list of all their acts, and copies of a few of them, particularly of the acts providing for the government of Louisiana, and for the war in the Mediterranean. The former, it is hoped, will satisfy the French Government of the prudent and faithful regard of the Government of the United States to the interest and happiness of the people transferred into the American family.

I have the honor to be, &c.,

JAMES MADISON.

ROBERT R. LIVINGSTON, Esq.

President's Message.

To the Senate and House of Representatives of the United States:

In execution of the act of the present session of Congress for taking possession of Louisiana, as ceded to us by France, and for the temporary government thereof, Governor Claiborne of the Mississippi Territory, and General Wilkinson, were appointed Commissioners to receive possession. They proceeded, with such regular troops as had been assembled at Fort Adams from the nearest posts, and with some militia of the Mississippi Territory, to New Orleans. To be prepared for anything unexpected which might arise out of the transaction, a respectable body of militia was ordered to be in readiness in the States of Ohio, Kentucky, and Tennessee, and a part of those of Tennessee was moved on to the Natchez. No occasion, however, arose for their services. Our Commissioners, on their arrival at New Orleans, found the Province already delivered by the Commissaries of Spain to that of France, who delivered it over to them on the 20th day of December, as appears by their declaratory act accompanying this. Governor Claiborne, being duly invested with the powers heretofore exercised by the Governor and Intendant of Louisiana, assumed the government on the same day, and, for the maintenance of law and order, immediately issued the proclamation and address now communicated.

On this important acquisition, so favorable to the immediate interests of our Western citizens, so auspicious to the peace and security of the nation in general, which adds to our country territories so extensive and fertile, and to our citizens new brethren to partake of the blessings of freedom and self-government, I offer to Congress and our country my sincere congratulations.

JANUARY 16, 1804. TH. JEFFERSON.

Articles of Exchange of Possession.

CITY OF NEW ORLEANS, *December 20, 1803.*

SIR: We have the satisfaction to announce to you that the Province of Louisiana was this day surrendered to the United States by the Commissioner of France; and to add, that the flag of our country was raised in this city amidst the acclamations of the inhabitants.

The enclosed is a copy of an instrument of writing, which was signed and exchanged by the Commissioners of the two Governments, and is designed as a record of this interesting transaction.

Accept assurances of our respectful consideration.

WM. C. C. CLAIBORNE.
JAMES WILKINSON.

JAMES MADISON,
Secretary of State.

The undersigned, William C. C. Claiborne and James Wilkinson, commissioners or agents of the United States, agreeably to the full powers they have received from Thomas Jefferson, President of the United States, under date of the 31st October, 1803, and twenty-eighth year of the independence of the United States of America, (8th Brumaire, 12th year of the French Republic,) countersigned by the Secretary of State, James Madison, and citizen Peter Clement Laussat, Colonial Prefect and Commissioner of the French Government, for the delivery, in the name of the French Republic, of the country, territories, and dependencies of Louisiana, to the commissioners or agents of the United States, conformably to the powers, commission, and special mandate which he has received, in the name of the French people, from citizen Bonaparte, First Consul, under date of the 6th June, 1803, (17th Prairial, eleventh year of the French Republic,) countersigned by the Secretary of State, Hugues Maret, and by his Excellency the Minister of Marine and Colonies, Decres, do certify by these presents, that on this day, Tuesday, the 20th December, 1803, of the Christian era, (28th Frimaire, twelfth year of the French Republic,) being convened in the hall of the Hotel de Ville of Orleans, accompanied on both sides by the Chiefs and Officers of the Army and Navy, by the municipality and divers respectable citizens of their respective

Republics, the said William C. C. Claiborne and James Wilkinson, delivered to the said citizen Laussat their aforesaid full powers, by which it evidently appears that full power and authority has been given them jointly and severally to take possession of, and to occupy the territories ceded by France to the United States by the treaty concluded at Paris on the 30th day of April last past, (10th Floreal,) and for that purpose to repair to the said Territory, and there to execute and perform all such acts and things, touching the premises, as may be necessary for fulfiling their appointment conformably to the said treaty and the laws of the United States; and thereupon the said citizen Laussat declared that, in virtue of, and in the terms of the powers, commission, and special mandate dated at St. Cloud, 6th June, 1803, of the Christian era, (17th Prairial, 11th year of the French Republic,) he put from that moment the said Commissioners of the United States in possession of the country, territories, and dependencies of Louisiana, conformably to the first, second, fourth, and fifth articles of the treaty and two conventions, concluded and signed the 30th April, 1803, (10th Floreal, 11th year of the French Republic,) between the French Republic and the United States of America, by citizen Barbe Marbois, Minister of the Public Treasury, and Messrs. Robert R. Livingston and James Monroe, Ministers Plenipotentiary of the United States, all three furnished with full powers, of which treaty and two conventions the ratifications, made by the First Consul of the French Republic on the one part, and by the President of the United States, by and with the advice and consent of the Senate, on the other part, have been exchanged and mutually received at the City of Washington, the 21st October, 1803, (28th Vendemiaire, 12th year of the French Republic,) by citizen Louis André Pichon, chargé des affaires of the French Republic near the United States, on the part of France, and by James Madison, Secretary of State of the United States, on the part of the United States, according to the *procès verbal* drawn up on the same day; and the present delivery of the country is made to them, to the end that, in conformity with the object of the said treaty, the sovereignty and property of the colony or province of Louisiana may pass to the said United States, under the same clauses and conditions as it had been ceded by Spain to France, in virtue of the treaty concluded at St. Ildefonso, on the 1st October, 1800, (9th Vendemiaire, 9th year,) between these two last Powers, which has since received its execution by the actual re-entrance of the French Republic into possession of the said colony or province.

And the said citizen Laussat in consequence, at this present time, delivered to the said Commissioners of the United States, in this public sitting, the keys of the City of New Orleans, declaring that he discharges from their oaths of fidelity towards the French Republic, the citizens and inhabitants of Louisiana, who shall chose to remain under the dominion of the United States.

And that it may forever appear, the undersigned have signed the *procès verbal* of this important and solemn act, in the French and English languages, and have sealed it with their seals, and have caused it to be countersigned by the secretaries of commission, the day, month, and year above written.

        WM. C. C. CLAIBORNE. [L. S.]
        JAMES WILKINSON. [L. S.]
        LAUSSAT.   [L. S.]

Proclamation by His Excellency, William C. C. Claiborne, Governor of the Mississippi Territory, exercising the powers of Governor-general and Intendant of the Province of Louisiana.

Whereas, by stipulations between the Governments of France and Spain, the latter ceded to the former the colony and province of Louisiana, with the same extent which it had at the date of the above-mentioned treaty in the hands of Spain, and that it had when France possessed it, and such as it ought to be after the treaties subsequently entered into between Spain and other States; and whereas the Government of France has ceded the same to the United States by a treaty duly ratified, and bearing date the 30th of April in the present year, and the possession of said colony and province is now in the United States, according to the tenor of the last-mentioned treaty; and whereas the Congress of the United States on the 31st day of October in the present year, did enact that, until the expiration of the session of Congress then sitting, (unless provisions for the temporary government of the said territories be made by Congress,) all the military, civil, and judicial powers exercised by the then existing government of the same, shall be vested in such person or persons, and shall be exercised in such manner as the President of the United States shall direct, for the maintaining and protecting the inhabitants of Louisiana in the free enjoyment of their liberty, property, and religion; and the President of the United States has, by his commission, bearing date the same 31st day of October, invested me with all the powers, and charged me with the several duties heretofore held and exercised by the Governor-General and Intendant of the Province.

I have, therefore, thought fit to issue this, my proclamation, making known the premises, and to declare, that the government heretofore exercised over the said Province of Louisiana, as well under the authority of Spain as the French Republic has ceased, and that of the United States of America is established over the same; that the inhabitants thereof will be incorporated in the Union of the United States, and admitted as soon as possible, according to the principles of the Federal Constitution, to the enjoyment of all the rights, advantages, and immunities of citizens of the United States; that, in the meantime, they shall be maintained and protected in the free enjoyment of their liberty, property, and the religion which they profess; that all laws and municipal regulations which were in existence at the cessation of the late government, remain in full force; and all civil officers charged with their execution, except those whose powers have been specially vested in me, and except, also, such officers as have been intrusted with the collection of the revenue, are continued in their functions, during the pleasure of the Governor for the time being, or until provision shall otherwise be made.

And I do hereby exhort and enjoin all the inhabitants, and other persons within the said province, to be faithful and true in their allegiance to the United States, and obedient to the laws and authorities of the same, under full assurance that their just rights will be under the guardianship of the United States, and will be maintained from all force or violence from without or within.

In testimony whereof I have hereunto set my hand.

Given at the city of New Orleans, the 20th day of December, 1803, and of the independence of the United States of America, the twenty-eighth.

WM. C. C. CLAIBORNE.

The Governor's Address to the Citizens of Louisiana.

NEW ORLEANS, *September 20, 1803.*

FELLOW-CITIZENS OF LOUISIANA: On the great and interesting event now finally consummated—an event so advantageous to yourselves and so glorious to United America—I can not forbear offering you my warmest congratulations. The wise policy of the Consul of France has, by the cession of Louisiana to the United States, secured to you a connexion beyond the reach of change, and to your posterity the sure inheritance of freedom. The American people receive you as brothers, and will hasten to extend to you a participation in those inestimable rights which have formed the basis of their own unexampled prosperity. Under the auspices of the American Government, you may confidently rely upon the security of your liberty, your property, and the religion of your choice. You may with equal certainty rest assured that your commerce will be promoted and your agriculture cherished—in a word, that your true interests will be among the primary objects of our National Legislature. In return for these benefits, the United States will be amply remunerated if your growing attachment to the Constitution of our country, and your veneration for the principles on which it is founded, be duly proportioned to the blessings which they will confer. Among your first duties, therefore, you should cultivate with assiduity among yourselves the advancement of political information. You should guide the rising generation in the paths of republican economy and virtue. You should encourage literature; for without the advantages of education, your descendants will be unable to appreciate the intrinsic worth of the Government transmitted to them.

As for myself, fellow-citizens, accept a sincere assurance, that during my continuance in the situation in which the President of the United States has been pleased to place me, every exertion will be made on my part to foster your internal happiness, and forward your general welfare; for it is only by such means that I can secure to myself the approbation of those great and just men who preside in the councils of our nation.

WM. C. C. CLAIBORNE.

[Extract.]

Mr. Cevallos to Mr. Pinckney.

PARDO, *February 10, 1804.*

At the same time the Minister of His Majesty in the United States is charged to inform the American Government respecting the falsity of the rumor referred to, he has likewise orders to declare to it that His Majesty has thought fit to renounce his opposition to the alienation of Louisiana made by France, notwithstanding the solid reasons on which it is founded; thereby giving a new proof of his benevolence and friendship toward the United States.

Mr. Yrujo to Mr. Madison.

PHILADELPHIA, *May 14, 1804.*

SIR: The explanations which the Government of France has given to His Catholic Majesty concerning the sale of Louisiana to the United States, and the amicable dispositions on the part of the King my master toward these States, have determined him to abandon the opposition which, at a prior period, and with the most substantial motives, he had manifested against that transaction. In consequence, and by special order of His Majesty, I have the pleasure to communicate to you his royal intentions on an affair so important; well persuaded that the American Government will see, in this conduct of the King my master, a new proof of his consideration for the United States, and they will correspond, with a true reciprocity, with the sincere friendship of the King, of which he has given so many proofs.

God preserve you many years.

M. CASA YRUJO.

JAMES MADISON, Esq.

Remarks on Signing the Treaty.

Mr. Marbois said: As soon as they had signed they rose, shook hands, and Livingston, expressing the satisfaction of all, said: "The treaty we have signed has not been brought about by pressure nor dictated by force. Equally advantageous to both the contracting parties, it will change vast solitudes into a flourishing country. To-day the United States take their place among the Powers of the first rank. Moreover, if wars are inevitable, France will have in the new world a friend increasing year by year in power, which cannot fail to become puissant and respected on all the seas of the earth. These treaties will become a guarantee of peace and good will between commercial States. The instrument we have signed will cause no tears to flow. It will prepare centuries of happiness for innumerable generations of the human race. The Mississippi and the Missouri will see them prosper and increase in the midst of equality, under just laws, freed from the errors of superstition, from the scourges of bad government, and truly worthy of the regard and care of Providence."

[Extract.]

Mr. Madison to Dr. J. W. Francis.

MONTPELIER, Nov. 7, 1831.

The friendly relations in which I stood to both Chancellor Livingston and Mr. Monroe would make me a reluctant witness, if I had happened to possess any knowledge of facts favoring either at the expense of the other in the negotiations which preceded the transfer of Louisiana to the United States. But my recollections throw no light on the subject beyond what may be derived from official papers in print, or on the files of the Department of State, and especially in the work on Louisiana by Mr. Marbois, the French negotiator. I have no doubt that each of the envoys did everything, according to his opportunities, that could evince official zeal and anxious patriotism; at the same time that the disclosures of Mr. Marbois sufficiently shew that the real cause of success is to be found in the sudden policy suggested to Napoleon by the foreseen rupture of the peace of Amiens, and, as a consequence, the seizure of Louisiana by Great Britain, who would not only deprive France of her acquisition, but turn it, politically and commercially, against her, in relation to the United States or Spanish America.

INDEX.

A.

Address by Governor Claiborne, 289.
Alliance with England, Jefferson suggests, 16.
Alliance with France or England, which, 52.
American boats forbidden to trade, 57.
American claims classified, 133.
    Livingston remonstrates, 88, 116.
    Talleyrand guarantees, 142.
American territory, France renounced right to acquire, 26.
Arkansas River suggested as boundary, 83, 90, 100, 158.
Articles of exchange of possession, 286.

B.

Bernadotte will treat on Livingston basis, 100, 143.
Boundaries all unsettled, 32.
  of Louisiana, 234, 271.
  of west Florida, 86.
Britain would have seized New Orleans, 205.
British alliance, Livingston threatens, 150.
British Government notified of cession, 196.

C.

Canada and Mexico threatened, 21.
Causes that led to cession to United States, 187, 189, 203, 221, 225, 231, 268, 291.
  Same—Reasons taken from Livingston Memoirs, 225.
Cede, right of France to alienate, 244.
  Spain denies right of France to, 233, 239, 242, 245.
Cession to France, disapproved by French statesmen, 13.
    denied by French minister, 9.
    confirmed by Livingston, 11.
    England's objection, 4.
    England's views sounded, 25.
    Livingston's discussion of, 89.
    opposed by Frenchmen, 28.
    reasons France wanted Louisiana, 12.
    reasons for, by Madison, 5.
    rumors of, 3, 5, 8.
    threatens peace with United States, 25.
Cession to United States, Livingston proposes, 121.
    what induced it, 187, 189, 221, 225, 229, 231, 268, 291.
Claims commission named, 171, 213.

294 INDEX.

Claims, classified, 133.
    Livingston binds First Consul to payment, 190.
    Monroe's draft of convention, 185.
    payments to be prorated, 272.
    Talleyrand guarantees payment, 142.
Colonial commerce discussed, 36.
    officers, abuses of, 64, 136, 139.
Colonies, are they useful to France, 39.
Congress appropriates two millions, 84.
    committee report, 84.
Constitutional amendment necessary, 235.
    limitations, by Jefferson, 237.
Convention of purchase, 256.
    on claims, 257.

D.

Deposit, importance of right, 85.
    Jefferson on restoring, 182.
    Livingston presses First Consul, 119, 148.
    Madison on waiving right, 181.
    right of, denied by Spanish officer, 53.
    Intendant's proclamation suspending, 54.
    right restored, 179.
    right of United States irrevocable, 149.
    right of, by treaty, 31.
    suspension, governor of Louisiana disowns, 67.
        Governor Claiborne's letter, 55.
        Livingston remonstrates, 89.
        Madison protests, 63.
        proclamation of Intendant, 54.
        protests pour into Washington, 67.
        Western indignation, 64.
Discontent with treaty in France, 209, 225.
Duplicity of French minister, 11.

E.

England and Spain, policy to alarm, 20.
    favors acquisition by United States, 156.
England's interest in Louisiana, 21.
England opposes cession to France, 25, 27, 102.
    to occupy New Orleans in case of war, 156.
England's opposition to cession incited, 10.
Expedition for Louisiana, 23, 29, 61, 81, 146.

F.

First Consul acknowledges memoir, 142.
    autocracy of, 51, 81.
    colloquy with British minister, 145.
    friendly disposition of, 62, 143.
    Livingston communicates with, 59, 71, 99, 115.
    makes proposition to sell, 161.
    receives Monroe, 169.

Floridas, acquisition of, the first desire of United States, 126.
    first mention of, 9.
Florida, West, Livingston advises seizure, 201.
    Madison discusses, 275.
    more valuable than New Orleans, 35.
    Monroe discusses, 198.
    negotiation with France for, 24.
        Spain for, 171.
    Spain declines to sell, 183.
    was it included in Louisiana? 23, 29, 33, 50, 60, 200, 212, 218, 236, 275.
    why not demanded of Spain, 275.
Florida rivers, right to navigate, 126.
Floridas, First Consul advises postponement, 230.
Foreign colonies, value of, Livingston, 36.
    territory, United States can not acquire, 235.
    trade, France and England compared, 37.
France renounced acquisition in America, 26.
French emigrants, Louisiana intended for, 3, 11.
    minister gives assurances, 62.
        to go to Washington to treat, 143.
        reasons for selling, copied from Livingston, 225.

G.

Governor Claiborne's address, 289.
    letter, 55.
    proclamation, 288.
    protest, 56.
Governor of Kentucky protests, 57.
Government of United States, its nature, 87.

H.

House of Representatives, resolutions of, 67.

I.

Impotency of French ministers, 64.
Independent Western State, 124, 141, 234, 274.
Indians, attachment of to France, 20.
Instructions, joint, 122.
    Livingston asks for, 23, 29, 35, 61, 101.
    Monroe bears them, 70.
    acquire Florida, first purpose of United States, 7.
    to Livingston, 16, 17, 112.
    to make the Mississippi the boundary, 28, 70, 122.
    to minister to Spain, 98.
    later, 175, 205.
    limited, Madison explains, 223.
Intendant's order without authority, 67, 113.
    proclamation suspending deposit, 54.

J.

Jefferson's cautious instructions to Livingston, 52.
Jefferson describes alarming conditions, 68.
    on restoring deposit, 182.

Jefferson on the pending crisis, 94.
    on independent Western States, 234, 274.
    remonstrates against cession to France, 16
    seeks to interest Nemours, 18.
    value of purchase, 221, 261, 274.
Joseph Bonaparte favors Livingston's propositions, 100.
    Livingston's medium with First Consul, 59, 82.

L.

Livingston anticipates instructions, 220.
    and Monroe's joint report, 191.
    asks instructions, 23, 29, 35, 61, 65, 101.
    advises defensive measures, 62.
    advises negotiation with Britain as blind, 66.
    announces events ready for Monroe, 158.
    account of negotiation, 162, 173.
    advises seizure of Floridas, 201.
    begins making propositions, 51.
    bewails lack of instructions, 97.
    communicates with First Consul direct, 65, 99, 115.
    convinces Frenchmen, 50, 157.
    discusses right of deposit, 91.
    explains activity pending Monroe's arrival, 147.
    explains letter to Monroe, 267.
    first memoir, 36.
    gets ear of First Consul, 65.
    incites English opposition, 10.
    makes many converts, 50, 65.
    his medium is Joseph Bonaparte, 59.
    makes converts of entire court, 115, 157.
    midnight letter, 159.
    outwits French minister, 160.
    persistency with First Consul, 140.
    presents another memoir, 66, 71, 82, 103, 108.
    remarks at signing treaty, 291.
    error in his commission, 221.
    replies to strictures on memoir, 266.
    recites the moving causes, 187–189.
    seeks to alarm England, 21.
    severe expostulations of, 149.
    suggests Natchez as depot, 20.
    suggests trans-Mississippi expansion, 83.
    to Joseph Bonaparte, 82.
    to Talleyrand, 153.
Louisiana, cession of whole not anticipated at Washington, 199.
    first proposition by Talleyrand, 157.
    First Consul prepares to take possession, 50.
    reasons why France should not possess, 16.
    Talleyrand offers the whole, 159.
    would not be profitable to France, 39

M.

Madison approves purchase, 223.
    criticises Livingston, 226.
    observations on proposed treaty, 129.

INDEX.

Madison discusses Spain's opposition, 247.
        West Florida, 275.
    explains why instructions were limited, 223.
    on causes, twenty-eight years later, 291.
    outlines treaty, 127.
    protests to Spanish Government, 63.
    replies to Spanish minister, 244.
    Marbois deputed to treat, 163.
Maritime powers compared, 72.
Memoirs of Livingston, 36, 71, 103, 108.
Merchant marine, French interest in, 37.
Monroe's appointment a disadvantage, 115.
Monroe and Livingston's joint report, 191.
    arrives in London, 227.
        at Havre, 159.
    complains of Livingston, 164.
    differs with Livingston, 218.
    interview with First Consul, 229.
    journal of the negotiation, 165.
    letter to Virginia Senators, 203.
    mission to Spain suspended, 241.
    nomination of, Livingston informed, 69.
        reasons for, 68, 96, 114.
    predicts long delay in negotiations, 138.
    proceeds to London, 217.
    and Livingston equal in rank, 222.
    recites incidents of negotiation, 227, 231.
    his participation limited, 267.
    to Jefferson, on situation, 136.
Motive of First Consul for selling, 187, 203, 225, 231, 268, 291.

N.

Natchez suggested as substitute for New Orleans, 20, 23.
Navigation of Florida rivers sought, 22.
    Mississippi, a treaty right, 27, 30.
        guaranteed, 26.
        indefeasible right to, 125.
        its importance, 84.
        treaty obligations of Spain, 31.
Negotiations for the Floridas postponed, 247.
    with France, Livingston's account of, 172.
        on before Monroe is presented, 163.
    with Britain authorized, 180.
Nemour's interest sought by Jefferson, 18.
New Orleans, cession to United States suggested by Jefferson, 17.
    and Floridas, why United States must possess, 87.
        alone desired, 28, 34, 52, 70, 81, 84.
    Livingston advises United State to seize, 101.
        suggests independent State, 141.
    why it should be a free port, 44.
New States, Jefferson on admission, 236.
    out of new territory inadmissible, 236.
Noninterference in Europe, policy of United States, 19.

H. Doc. 431——20

P.

Penal colony, Louisiana suggested for, 13, 15.
Politics of Europe, Livingston on, 58.
Possession, articles of exchange of, 286.
        of Louisiana by United States ordered, 265.
Powers of United States ministers insufficient, 172.
President's message to extra session, 251.
        on taking possession, 285.
Price, eighty millions agreed on, 168.
    First Consul asks one hundred millions, 161.
    Jefferson discusses, 95.
        places limit on, 133.
    Marbois names eighty millions, 162, 166.
Proclamation of Governor Claiborne, 288.
Protection to American commerce, 12.
Purchase not authorized by Constitution, 235.
        of whole not anticipated by Administration, 199.
        why made, 191.

R.

Ratification by Congress, 260.
        vote on, 262.
        French government notified, 264.
        Livingston urges haste, 208, 211.
Reticence of French Government, 35, 61.
Rivers of Florida, navigation of, 86.

S.

Sale determined before Monroe's arrival, 267.
    of territory beneath dignity of France, 103.
    when determination was taken, 232, 267.
Secrecy and duplicity of French minister, 11.
        remonstrance of Livingston, 14.
Separate government for Western people, 124, 141, 234, 274.
Slave labor indispensable, 38, 43.
Spain's guaranty of United States right to deposit, 34.
Spanish Government opposes cession to United States, 233, 239, 242–243, 245.
        opposition, French minister replies, 249.
        withdrawn, 290.

T.

Talleyrand guarantees payment of claims, 142.
        offers Louisiana, 159.
Talleyrand's hostility, attempt to placate, 19.
        profession of friendliness, 152.
        promise of satisfaction, 151.
Territorial extension disavowed, 59.
The garden episode, 160.
Trade with Americans forbidden, 57.
    on Mississippi, value of, 64.
Treaties forwarded to Washington, 209.

Treaty, difficulties after signing, 210.
    of purchase, full text, 253.
    of 1778 cited, 26.
    outlined by Livingston, 90.
        by Madison, 127.
    rights of United States in Mississippi, 30.
Trans-Mississippi territory not desired by United States. 28, 34, 52, 59.
Troops ordered to New Orleans, 263–265.

U.

United States, destiny in balance, 69, 97.
    will maintain her rights, Jefferson, 95.

V.

Value of Louisiana, by Jefferson, 221, 274.
    by First Consul, 214.
    prevalent French ideas, 20.
    to United States, 194.

W.

War between France and England imminent, 146.
    cloud appears, 51.
    declared by France, 207.
    with United States, possession of Louisiana can alone avert, 97.
    with France, United States will be ready for, 88.
    will result from French occupation of Louisiana, 18.
Western commerce affected by, 126.
Western people, predilections of, 124.
Western independent state, 124, 141, 234, 274.

www.ingramcontent.com/pod-product-compliance
Lightning Source LLC
Chambersburg PA
CBHW020639230426
43665CB00008B/241